MW01073184

AUG - 4 2010

D. R. Toi
PO Box 1698
Newport News, VA 23601

8-4-2010 — 8-9-2010

ALIEN ENERGY

UFOs, Ritual Landscapes And the Human Mind

Andrew Collins

Memphis, Tennessee
Eagle Wing Books, Inc.

ALIEN ENERGY
UFOs, Ritual Landscapes And the Human Mind
Copyright © 1994 by Andrew Collins
www.andrewcollins.net

All rights reserved.

No part of this book may be reproduced or transmitted in any form or by any means, electronic or mechanical, including photocopy, recording, or any other information storage and retrieval system now known or to be invented, without permission, in writing, from the author, except by a reviewer who wishes to quote brief passages in conjunction with a review written for inclusion in a newspaper, magazine, internet book review site, or broadcast.

Published in America by
Eagle Wing Books, Inc.
P.O. Box 9972
Memphis, TN 38190

www.eaglewingbooks.com

ISBN: 0-940829-37-1
Retail Price: $21.95
First U.S.A. Edition: April 2003

Table of Contents

Andrew Collins

Andrew was born in Bedford, England, in 1957, and for the past 16 years has lived in the Essex Thameside town of Leigh-on-Sea. As a young UFO researcher, he investigated Britain's first ever record account of an alien abduction experience at Aveley in Essex, before going on to join the magazine STRANGE PHENEMONA, writing on subjects such as the occult, the paranormal, UFOs, Atlantis, and past live experiences. He became particularly interested in the inter-relationship between mind, landscape and strange light phenomena, and in 1978 proposed that those who underwent genuine UFO experiences were very often psychic in nature. This led to his life-long passion for psychic questing — the use of intuitively inspired information to uncover hidden artefacts, historical enigmas and landscape mysteries.

Andrew has since gone on to write several internationally acclaimed books, such as FROM THE ASHES OF ANGELS (1996), which explores the origins of the Watchers and Nephilim of Biblical tradition; GODS OF EDEN (1998), which investigates the origins of Egyptian civilisation; GATEWAY TO ATLANTIS (2000), which explores Plato's Atlantis and identifies Cuba as its flagship, and TUTANKHAMUN: THE EXODUS CONSPIRACY (co-authored with Chris Ogilvie Herald), which uncovers the scandal surrounding secret papyri found in the tomb of the boy king. He is also the organiser of the Questing Conference, Britain's foremost gathering on forbidden archaeology, alternative history and psychic questing, which annually attracts around 450 delegates. For further information on the world of Andrew Collins visit www.andrewcollins.net.

Acknowledgements

I would like to acknowledge the love and devotion of my wife Sue, and the support she gives me in my life. Additionally, I would like to thank those who helped bring together this book, including Rodney Hale, for all the effort he put into Orgone 93/94/95 and for the part he continues to play in my strange world; Tim and Polly Carson, for their hospitality and for allowing us to use the wonderful Woodborough Hill; Lisa Adams, Kerry Bar, Tony Beddoe, Debbie Benstead, Karl Dawkins, Jason Digby, Paul Hailey, John Horrigan, Johnny Merron, Oliver and Daniella Stummer, Roger Wilkins and Judi Smith, Richard Ward, and the many more who took part in this pioneering project; Brian Froud, for the use of his fairy illustrations; Graham Hancock, for his enthusiasm in our orgone research, and for taking part in one of the experiments; Esther James, for the original cover image; the Mary Evans Picture Library, for the use of their pictures, and Graham Phillips, for the use of the Brinklow picture.

Other names which must be mentioned include Stephen Alexander, Nel Bat, Tom and Kerry Blower, Gary Bond, Simon Burton, David Carson, Terry Cox, David and Kim Crow of Avebury's The Henge Shop, Rod Dickinson, Chris Hitchen, Rob Irving, John the Circlemaker, Montague Keen, Jurgen Kronig, Chris Mansell, John and Rachel Martineau, John Michell, Reg Presley, Pam Price, Jenny Randles, Nick Riley, Geoff Roberts, Ed Sherwood, Rob Stphenson, Dr Roger Taylor, Tom Trubidge, Paul Vigay, Steve Wade, John and Julie Wakefield, Julie Whitear, Caroline Wise and George Wingfield.

Lastly, I would like to thank Greg and Lora Little, for taking up the publication of this book in the USA, and for the friendship shown to Sue and I when in their country.

Preface

by Gregory L. Little, Ed.D.

My first contact with Andrew Collins was through his 1996 book *From The Ashes of Angels.* Few books have grabbed my attention so thoroughly. I read the book lying in bed over a week's time and listened to music from the "Fields of the Nephilim" since they were prominently mentioned in the text. I was immediately convinced that Andrew was onto something really important. He was meticulous and careful and was an author who was willing to do fieldwork—something that is rare in today's world of authors.

When his next book, *Gateway to Atlantis,* was published I was just as transfixed and became convinced that his work needed wider exposure in America. Through contacts at the Virginia Beach-based Association for Research and Enlightenment (A.R.E.; the official Edgar Cayce organization) I managed to have him invited to speak at the 2002 Ancient Civilizations Conference. While Andrew and his wife were at the conference we became friends and I discovered, to my pleasant surprise, that we both started investigating the UFO mystery long ago. Even more surprising was the fact that our interests and ideas about the UFO phenomenon and related enigmas such as crop circles were nearly identical.

Both of us realized quite early in our investigations that modern UFO reports appeared to be an updated, evolving version of an energy manifestation that made its presence known by periodically emerging at specific locations over thousands of years. I have come to term these locations sacred sites where mounds and ritualistic earthworks were constructed in ancient times. In *Alien Energy* Andrew refers to these locations as ritual landscapes. That term better describes the interaction of the energy emerging at particular locations with the human observers.

My first UFO book, *The Archetype Experience* (1984), delved into Jung's concept of archetypes and how these intelligent energy forms interact with human consciousness. *Alien Energy* also delves into Jung's archetypes. But few people seem to really grasp what Jung actually said about archetypes and how the process worked: "In his writings Jung repeatedly stressed that archetypes are independent, autonomous factors. Jung stated that archetypes consist of pure nature as *psychoid* factors existing invisibly on the ultraviolet end of the unconscious spectrum. Psychoid is a Jungian term that means a process that is able to bridge the gap between psychological reality and objective reality. Archetypes, as pure nature, are pure energy remaining primarily invisible but occasionally manifest themselves. That is, they occasionally become a physical reality in an objective sense." Indeed, this is a bold statement, but it's one that *Alien Energy* explores in a hands-on way.

By 1990 I began to understand that these archetypal manifestations tended to occur periodically in the same places and that many sacred sites had been built at these locations. In America these sites were usually at mounds and ancient earthworks. In England, as *Alien Energy* shows, it appears that the same occurs. By 1994 I was convinced that the energy manifestations at sacred sites interacted with human brain chemistry to produce profound experiences. I outlined these conclusions in *People of the Web* (1990) and *Grand Illusions* (1994). Scientific understanding of exactly how these electromagnetic forces interact with brain processes has progressed somewhat and promises to produce a revolution in our thinking.

During the 1990s I wrote a series of articles on UFOs and related energy manifestation in *Alternate Perceptions Journal* and in Ronald Story's *UFO Encyclopedia* calling the revised theory the "Geomagnetic Energy Theory of UFO Phenomena." The theory has ten primary propositions, most of which are also found in some form in *Alien Energy*. A few of the most important propositions are: 1) That UFO manifestations are an intrusion of intelligent energy forms from the unseen portions of the electromagnetic (EM) energy spectrum; 2) That these forms have always been present; 3) That an observer can interact with them; 4) That specific rituals can tap the energy of these forms; 5) That brain levels of the mineral magnetite determine the degree to which a particular individual can interact with these energy forms; and 6) That natural earth energies focusing on specific surface locations are the primary source of UFO abductions and other bizarre experiences.

Beginning with the ill-fated experiments of Dr. Wilhelm Reich, *Alien Energy* reaches essentially the same conclusions as those above. But *Alien Energy* is the result of genuine field research that is so important that it begs to be studied and repeated. Ufologists who seek to study the phenomenon first-hand would do well to carefully study how Collins' many experiments produced results. Collins tested many of Reich's orgone theories in the field and shows how the enigmatic crop circles are related to energy manifestations. In addition, Collins shows how various energies applied at ritual landscapes appear to produce profound mental effects and paranormal experiences. *Alien Energy* holds an amazing amount of information gathered by hands-on experiments that are fully repeatable in America's vast ufological landscape. The net cast by Andrew's *Alien Energy* encompasses just about every unnatural and otherworldly experience imaginable. It is a "must-read" for serious UFO researchers and is another nail in the casket of the "nuts-and-bolts" ufologists who have too long dominated the American UFO scene.

The Tale of Eugenio de la Terra

Eugenio de la Terra is a native of the Philippines. He lives with his wife beside the road fork to Irosin, near the scenic Lake Bulusan, a great steep-walled crater filled with water and engulfed by a sea of trees and flowers.

Often Eugenio climbs the slopes of Bulusan Peak or ascends the banks of Agingai Lake, another volcanic crater formed long ago by one single eruption.

Eugenio knows the terrain well, and often acts as a guide to foreign volcanologists visiting the island. Yet in his youth he was witness to something strange. Something that both amazed and frightened him - an illuminated sphere of the sort known to so many Philippinos as St Elmo's Fire, after the martyred Roman saint whose burning body was carried through the air by angels.(1)

On that fateful day Eugenio was close to the village of San Roque when he had been surprised to see a globe of deep-red to purple light resting silently on the ground, some five metres in front of him. In height it would easily have reached his chest, so he estimated it must have been at least one metre in diameter.

Confronted by this puzzling sight, unlike anything he had ever seen before, Eugenio decided that he needed a cigarette. Removing one from the packet, he discovered that he had no matches. So, being the happy-go-lucky fool that he was, he walked up to the funny thing sitting on the ground and stuck his cigarette into its curved surface.

To his bafflement, the cigarette did not light. So, summoning all his courage, Eugenio reached out with his hand and touched the gently glowing orb. It felt cold to the touch, not hot like one might expect of a fireball.

Fear then overtook Eugenio, and without further thought he quickly turned around and ran away from the devilish ball.

Eugenio de la Terra told the story of his encounter with the spherical lightform to Californian geologist Egon Bach, author of *UFOs from the Volcanoes*, who in 1993 spent four whole months collecting first hand accounts of the so-called St Elmo lights being seen on the Philippine Islands of South East Asia. In just four months he amassed literally dozens of extraordinary cases from remote farming, fishing or wood-cutting communities who had lived with stories of such strange phenomena all their lives - communities completely isolated from the Western concept of UFOs as space vehicles of extra-terrestrial origin.

To many Philippinos the extraordinary glowing spheres that appear in many different forms, both on land and on water, are interpreted either as angels, devils, ghosts, rainbow fairies, female divinities clothed in white light or as the souls of drowned sailors and fishermen.(2)

To Egon Bach and his geologist colleagues the strange light spheres, which can appear as small as a coin or as large as a football field, are nothing more than electrically-charged 'fluid minerals' produced by the earth - balls of energy with specific features and characteristics. For instance, they are said to ooze from places known to be above fault lines and underground volcanic upheavals. They can expand and contract, split apart and come back together, rest or slide on water, change colour in accordance with the visible spectrum, emit spotlight-like rays of light and blink on and off in rhythmic cycles.

So convinced is Egon Bach of the reality of this hitherto unknown phenomena, that he has announced plans to create the first ever power station to convert this unlimited source of free energy into electricity.(3) These plans include ingenious ways of attracting the light spheres using infrared lights and then catching them as they rise into the air.

But is it that simple? Although there are huge flaws in the extra-terrestrial solution to the UFO enigma, these gossamer-like energy forms of pure light have certain abilities and characteristics that beg explanation and lead us to conclude that they are far more than just untapped sources of natural energy - attributes which, if correct, will require us to re-define the nature of the unseen world recognised and understood through mystic processes and shamanic practices since the dawn of time.

Whether UFOs exist or not is no longer under debate. More important today is *what* they are. If a happy-go-lucky Philippino can light a cigarette from one of these objects, while a westerner in a similar position would probably have been abducted by space beings, then I feel a few sensible answers are needed before alien contact becomes the next world religion.

Introduction

'The trouble with those supporting the orgone theory is that they think they can explain everything - aliens, crop circles, earth energies, psychic abilities, UFOs - you name it, they can give you an answer.' Reservations such as this are the grumble of many within the different insular communities championing one or other area of the world's greatest mysteries.

Why a universal theory should not be put forward to suitably explain a diversity of different paranormal phenomena is simply beyond me, especially as the readily available evidence points towards a clear overlap between such matters as mystical experiences, psychic phenomena, shamanic practices and UFO sightings. These in turn seem reliant on place and time, and in doing so appear to pass beyond the realms of pure chance. Such patterns should not be ignored.

In 1978 I was a young and somewhat naive UFO investigator, interviewing witnesses, visiting the locations concerned and preparing detailed case reports for one or other of the national organisations. From the outset it became clear that nine out of 10 reported UFO sightings could be easily explained as misinterpretations of known natural or man-made phenomena. Of the remaining 10 per cent an above average proportion of witnesses appeared to possess a history of psychic experiences, such as ghostly encounters, out-of-the-body experiences, poltergeist activity, precognitive dreams and the sensing of presences and atmospheres at certain locations.

I wrote about the apparent psychic overtones of the UFO phenomenon, but sadly my words fell on deaf ears.(1) The sceptics argued that if UFOs were alien hardware, why should psychics be more prone to witnessing them? It did not make sense. In my defence I suggested that some UFOs might exist on electromagnetic frequency ranges invisible to the human eye, yet somehow psychic individuals were able to witness them on a subjective, clairvoyant level. Maybe these people were susceptible to an assortment of unknown phenomena simply because they were more psychically-sensitive than the next person.

Still no one was interested - most of the UFO community believed that UFOs were 'nuts and bolts' spaceships travelling to Earth and, as a consequence, all forms of investigation and research were unquestionably biased towards this simplistic conclusion.

In 1978 a London student named Graham Phillips was investigating alleged outbreaks of poltergeist activity in the county of Essex as part of a post-graduate BA course in communications studies. He had become perplexed by the high number of principal witnesses who also claimed to have observed some form of unknown aerial or ground-based light phenomena, either just before or during spates of poltergeist activity in their homes. What possible connection could there have been between UFOs and psychokinetic capabilities of the human mind if poltergeists were simply the unwanted actions of restless spirits? It did not add up and, what's more, no one from respected scientific bodies such as the Society of Psychical Research seemed even remotely interested in misplaced comments from someone who had been involved in the subject for only five minutes.

Phillips continued his case study of poltergeist witnesses and eventually came to the conclusion that telekinetic abilities were merely one minor facet of a much greater jewel. Like myself, he realised it was not the phenomenon itself that was the key to solving this mystery, but the witness or witnesses involved - their sensitivity allowing them to more easily perceive or trigger into manifestation all kinds of psychic activity, including, it seemed, the appearance of UFOs and ghost lights. Phillips and I worked together on this problem, and our findings concerning the genetic similarities of hereditary psychics were published under the title *Psygenics* in 1979.(2)

Of equal importance to our early research was the placement of paranormal events and UFO sightings. Certain areas or locations tended to crop up again and again in respect to paranormal activity, suggesting some kind of special quality or inherent power acting as a catalyst to produce such phenomena on a repeatable basis. In the ufological community these locations were, and still are, known as 'window areas', a term coined by American UFO pioneer John Keel. The most well-known British example of a 'window area' is the chalk downland surrounding the Wiltshire town of Warminster where, from 1964 through till the end of the 1970s, unidentified light phenomena were reported with an uncanny frequency (indeed, it is the only place I have personally witnessed inexplicable light phenomena(3)).

During 1979 Graham Phillips and I made an intensive study of the Loch Ness mystery, focusing initially on the reported sightings of unknown aquatic beasts in this deep Scottish loch. A week of intensive on-site investigations, which included talking to dozens of local people and scouring library and newspaper archives, revealed something quite unexpected - not only was the area around Loch Ness the focus of recurring monster sightings, but it also appeared to play host to extraordinary UFO encounters, modern-day visitations of the fairy folk, sightings of phantom big cats, various accounts of poltergeist activity and alleged time-slip occurrences.(4) In one instance we learned of a little-known folk story of a couple who in the 18th century had disappeared whilst travelling in a horse and trap near Loch End on the southern side of the loch. They were thought either to have been abducted or thrown into the loch after being set on by thieves. In the mid-19th century, over 100 years later, two strangers walked into a local almshouse seeking refuge from a freak storm. According to the priest who took them in, they were dressed in clothes of the previous century. They could offer no explanation as to their origin and passed the next two days in a highly confused state, after which they simply walked out into the open and were never seen again!(5)

Loch Ness might be described as a ufological 'window area', but its spatial potency goes far beyond this description - it is a gateway, a doorway, into the totally unbelievable, but truly possible. Phillips and I examined the evidence and came to the conclusion that the only explanation for its paranormal properties was geological in origin and appeared to be linked with the presence of the Great Glen fault which follows the entire axis of the loch. Indeed, brightly glowing UFOs had occasionally been seen traversing the length of the loch as if following the very line of the fault. Somehow the stresses and strains of the earth were, we felt, acting as a catalyst to produce an enormous variety of inexplicable phenomena never before linked together as the product of one cause.

Phillips and I also realised that on a more localised level there appeared to be an intrinsic link between the proximity of prehistoric or historic sites and reports of psychic experiences and UFO sightings. Such locations included the stone and earthen monuments constructed by the Neolithic, Bronze Age and Iron Age communities of Britain, as well as the early chapels, churches and holy wells, so often built by early Christian communities on much earlier sites of a ceremonial or ritual importance. For instance, in the valley of Glenmoriston, which adjoins Loch Ness, a secluded housing estate was found to be the focus of pronounced poltergeist activity and the reported appearance, among sane and sober folk, of impish elemental spirits that would appear to the residents and, on one occasion, even left behind tiny hand prints on a window sill! At the centre of the activity was a prehistoric burial mound named Torshee, Gaelic for the 'fairy hill', a coincidence that could not be overlooked.(6)

It became clear that it was not just the presence of 'window areas' that played some role in catalysing paranormal events, but also the nature of the location. So why should prehistoric monuments and sacred places be so important to our understanding of the supernatural? Was it simply the local geology? Or did our ancestors have some now lost knowledge concerning the paranormal potency of the environment?

During the autumn of 1979 Graham and I announced plans to conduct a series of controlled experiments in an attempt to test the various different theories we had proposed concerning the relationship between geological features, parapsychology, ritual monuments and the UFO enigma.(7) A number of proven, psychically-sensitive individuals were invited to take part in co-ordinated meditations at a soon to be constructed stone circle on Dartmoor in Devon in the hope that this would produce recordable paranormal effects and other aerial anomalies. Although our aims were true, our circumstances soon changed and the experiments were eventually abandoned in favour of other more immediate pursuits.

The matter was forgotten until the summer of 1991 when, fired by the mystery of the crop circles that had been appearing in the fields of southern England since the late 1970s, I found myself re-assessing these much earlier findings in the hope of establishing a workable solution to this most recent mystery of our times. The result was a book entitled *The Circlemakers*, published during the summer of 1992. It proposed that exiled Austrian scientist Wilhelm Reich may have stumbled upon the key to unravelling the mysteries surrounding crop circles, places of ancient power and the UFO enigma with his discovery, during the 1930s, of a previously undefined universal force he christened orgone energy. Following calls to support the various theories this book proposed, I launched the Orgone 93 project to once again test the apparent relationship between UFOs, ritual landscapes and the human mind. This took place in July 1993 and was followed in 1994 with a further research programme entitled Orgone 94.

The results drawn from these extensive, scientifically-based projects are presented here for the first time. Their findings, though still tentative, will, I'm sure, go some way to dispelling people's fears about accepting *one* workable solution to explain a multitude of hidden mysteries that have eluded the nets of science for far too long.

1

Reich's Legacy

Wilhelm Reich - an outspoken Freudian analyst born in Austria during 1897 - may well have held the key to understanding the elusive energy force thought to be behind the manifestation of what we know today as UFOs as early as the 1930s. At a time when national socialism and severe poverty was escalating in neighbouring Germany, Reich became convinced that some form of unknown dynamic force lay behind the process of the sexual orgasm, something Sigmund Freud had previously identified as a psychological process known as the 'libido'.

Fuelled by these early ideas, Reich became engrossed in his own brand of biophysics, searching for this unknown energy behind the creation of life. In 1933 this work was interrupted when Reich was forced to leave his native land, owing to the rising threat posed both to democracy and his own life by Hitler and the Nazi regime. He settled first in Oslo, and here, using a sophisticated microscope, Reich began an intensive series of experiments into the micro-biology of plant life.

In 1936 Reich first noted that under extreme magnifications, pulsating vesicles could be seen discharging from plant tissue immersed in a sterile solution of water. These tiny vesicles Reich saw as a form of 'biological ether' matching the discoveries of an eminent 19th-century French chemist named H. Charlton Bastian, who in a book entitled *The Beginnings of Life* had outlined his apparent discovery in human tissue of a tiny biological particle he named the 'bion'.

Bion Research

Excited by his discovery of these energy vesicles, Reich tried to establish their true nature and exact biological function, and after much time in the laboratory he concluded they were in fact tiny lifeforms in themselves. Furthermore, they appeared to be present not only in decaying matter, but in all foodstuffs as well as in other substances such as sand and coal, and, like Bastian, Reich came to believe they played some role in fighting disease and regenerating body tissue.

Reich also noted certain quite disturbing side-effects in his microscopic study of bions - first his eyes began to hurt badly and then he developed a violent form of conjunctivitis. In addition to these quite physical effects, he found that the skin on one side of his face - the side facing the microscope eyepiece - had become noticeably tanned. More curious still, in the dark, metal-lined basement used for these experiments Reich repeatedly saw streaks and spots of blue or blue-violet light rippling across the walls or surrounding certain objects.(1)

As a consequence of his observations, Reich attempted to contain and isolate the discharging bions, and for this he constructed a metal-lined box in which he placed the bion cultures. Unfortunately, this only intensified the influence of the bions and also produced baffling side effects, including a notable temperature rise inside the layered casing. The secondary study of these new effects soon led to the construction of the first so-called Orgone Energy Accumulator, consisting of a rectangular metal box insulated with alternating layers of a metallic substance (usually steel wool) and an 'organic' substance (generally either glass wool, rock wool or upson board). This time, even without the introduction of the bion cultures, a clear, unaccountable temperature rise was recorded both above and inside the device, suggesting that the alternating layers were acting as an efficient means of caging, intensifying or even producing this energy force.

In 1939 Reich was forced to move again - this time across the Atlantic to Forest Hills, New York, where he quickly established a thriving psycho-therapy clinic. Here he began to construct a laboratory where he could re-commence his ground-breaking work into the nature of bioenergy or SAPA radiation, as he initially referred to it.

Orgone Energy

Reich eventually came to realise that his observation of bions in both living and decaying tissue was simply bringing into focus a much more primary process involving the presence of some kind of unknown energy force. What's more, it was the prolonged periods of exposure to its presence - and not to the bions themselves - that had caused the conjunctivitis and tanning effect. Reich concluded that he had identified a form of organic radiation, one which was present in both living and decaying matter and could be observed as tiny discharging energy globules or bions.

Reich also came to believe that this life force - which in 1940 he began referring to as Orgone Energy or Orgone Radiation (OR) - was produced by the sun and was either absorbed through the skin or taken in by breathing. Orgone was also thought to be present in the atmosphere, in the environment and universally in space - in which form he referred to it as either Cosmic Orgone Energy or the 'Cosmic Energy Ocean'. It also collected in what he saw as an 'orgone envelope', which he conceived as some kind of etheric energy belt present in the upper atmosphere.

To detect this unclassified energy Reich developed a simple device known as an 'orgonoscope', which apparently detected orgone in the environment, as well as an 'orgone field meter' which registered the subtle energy fields surrounding living organisms. He was also able to repeatedly illuminate orgone inside a vacuum, or 'vacor' tube, and in time Reich decided that atmospheric orgone was directly associated with the generation of meteorological occurrences such as the formation of clouds, hurricanes, tornadoes, even the Northern and Southern Lights.

In later years Reich tried to apply his discovery of orgone energy to current-day physics and put forward the view that the 'Cosmic Energy Ocean' acted as a medium by which other dynamic forces, such as electromagnetism and gravitation, could be brought into focus.(2) He also concluded that orgone acted as a vehicle to allow the manifestation of light.(3)

Orgone Energy Accumulators

With the knowledge that the level of bodily orgone appeared to affect or even counteract the presence of harmful bacteria, Reich wondered what would happen if he exposed volunteers to concentrated amounts of this energy. Would it stimulate bodily regeneration? Would it cause other, more profound healing effects? Or would it do nothing? Even at this stage in his career, Reich saw the potential of orgone as a possible cure for the cancer menace which by the 1940s had been identified as a major cause of mortality in the United States.

At the secluded, 280-acre estate he purchased at Rangeley, Maine, in 1942, Reich constructed much larger versions of the Orgone Energy Accumulator (ORAC for short) using the same layering process as the smaller box-like containers. In these a person could sit in relative or total darkness for controlled durations - usually no more than 20 minutes at a time. During such sessions the subject would generally experience a distinct rise in body warmth as well as a prickling sensation on the skin.(4) Others would feel a sense of well-being or light-headedness, while still others would experience a host of adverse physiological effects prompting Reich to introduce basic guidelines on how best to use an accumulator.(5)

Often a mild form of reddening or tanning would also occur, an effect Reich likened to the original physiological problems he had suffered when microscopically studying bions. Most curious of all were the reports both by Reich and others of blue or blue-green luminosities seen to emerge from the sides of an accumulator and spin rapidly through the air before disappearing without trace. On other occasions 'yellowish-white, lightninglike streaks of light ("Strichstrahlen")' were apparently seen rippling across its metal-lined walls.(6)

In just a few short years Reich developed a complete understanding of his orgone energy and was able to control it to such a degree that in 1948 he developed an orgone engine, supplemented with an electrical current, which could increase speed when a hand was brought near it or reverse its thrust suddenly and without any apparent inertia effects. This curious 'free energy' device was eventually stolen under mysterious circumstances, despite this misfortune there are still people alive today who recall it in operation. There is also a cine film showing this engine at the Wilhelm Reich Museum at Rangeley, Maine.

In 1950 Reich decided he would attempt to explore the relationship between orgone energy (OR) and nuclear energy (NE) and, although this dangerous exercise almost destroyed everything he had ever worked for, it also introduced him to what is for us the most important element of Reich's work - his direct confrontation with the UFO enigma.

The ORANUR Experiment

On 5 January 1951 technicians working at Orgonon - the name given to the Reich Institute at Rangeley - took one milligram of radium, sheathed in a sealed lead container, and placed it in a specially prepared, 20-layer energy accumulator, situated within a laboratory lined with iron plate to even further enhance the concentration of orgone. It was then left in position for five hours and the experiment was repeated for one whole week, ending with just 30 minutes on the final day. The extraordinary and rather disturbing results of these actions were published in a document entitled *The Oranur experiment: First Report 1947-51*.

In theory, such a tiny amount of a radioactive isotope, sheathed completely in lead, could never have affected the immediate environment. However, immediately the substance was placed inside the accumulator an interior Geiger counter recorded a steady rise in the background count before finally jamming completely. Laboratory mice used in body-cell healing experiments with orgone keeled over and died. A 'peculiar, sickening, acrid' odour started to hang heavily in the air and one by one the Institute's laboratory technicians began to fall ill.(7) Despite these disturbing effects, apparently induced by the bringing together of nuclear radiation and orgone energy, Reich decided to continue the ORANUR experiment.

In the days, then weeks that followed, oppressive black clouds gathered overhead Rangeley and would not disperse. It was said that at night both the Institute's buildings and the surrounding environment would 'glow' with an eerie purple hue. Some five members of the Institute's staff were admitted to hospital with symptoms of radiation sickness, and it was said that Reich became quite seriously ill and was unable to sleep for days on end; the situation may even have catalysed a heart attack he suffered during this same period. Even more curious, Reich noted that white birch trees and bushes in the vicinity of the Institute were abnormally blackening and withering without any obvious cause.(8)

Reich and his colleagues also began to notice a thick black powder-like substance gathering on rock surfaces close to the Institute. It was given the name Melanor, although other distinguishable variations were also noted, and these he named Brownite and Orite. It was even filmed forming on rocks.

Melanor was found to attack and destroy rocks and could either crystallise into rock-like particles, looking like coal clinker, or form into a dark sticky substance. Unfortunately, its presence seemed to cause only further ill-effects among the Institute's staff, including cyanosis (a blueness of the skin), nausea, intense thirst and miscellaneous pains. Trying to collect samples only made matters worse.

Through the ORANUR experiment Reich came to realise that the combination of nuclear energy and orgone energy (OR for short) appeared to accelerate an energetic process that seriously disturbed the fundamental equilibrium of both the immediate environment and the atmosphere above Rangeley. In doing so it had catalysed the production of some kind of antithesis - a malignant or stagnant form of OR henceforth referred to as DOR (Deadly Orgone or Deadly Orgone Radiation), pronounced 'door'. In simple terms, DOR appeared to have been seen by Reich as a highly concentrated, over-excited variation of OR - its creation accelerated by man-made factors such as excessive radiation in the air and electromagnetic emissions.

Whereas OR appeared to act as a life-giving process with regenerative qualities, DOR was its reverse - a death-inducing power source of unknown capability that could cause deserts, droughts, flat stale environments and mass ill-health. Reich concluded that the radioactive substances used in ORANUR had greatly accelerated the production of OR to such an extent that it had created a pocket of DOR above Rangeley. Worse still, the chain reaction apparently started by ORANUR was, Reich decided, absorbing the healthy levels of orgone not only from the environment, but also from their own bodies. It was this energy effect, and not the initial introduction of the radio-active substance into the accumulator, that was repeatedly producing the ill-effects among his staff, as well as the oppressive meteorological conditions, the wilting of local flora and the appearance of the powder-like Melanor.

An eye-witness to this strange scenario was biologist Robert A. McCullough, Research Associate at the Institute at the time of the ORANUR experiments. He was greatly disturbed by what was going on as the following account written at the time clearly shows:

> The whole area was infected with a very material DOR, cloying to everything, and it made things absolutely unlivable. You had to get out of it periodically by driving west, or up to some high spot, or just drive fast to keep it from dragging you down to its level. Everything was purple or purplish mauve. The white birch trees were bending over like rubber hoses, as though laden with invisible snow. The condition was all around Orgonon and down toward Farmington.
>
> There was a tremendous sense of something impending - of waiting for something dreadful to happen. This anticipatory waitfulness was oppressive. Something was coming and it wouldn't be good. There were periods of gremlins, also. Small objects disappeared and reappeared where no one had placed them. Pins in maps were moved or just pulled out. Unmarked aircraft repeatedly overflew Orgonon. There was a sense of harassment - of being pursued - that it is hard to fully understand.(9)

Despite the controversial nature of the ORANUR experiment, it was but a prelude to the infinitely more mystifying problem that began to plague those at Orgonon from 1952 onwards. In the night skies above Rangeley, first the laboratory technicians, then visitors, and then finally Reich himself, began witnessing unaccountable moving lights - initially described as 'stars'.(10) These varied in colour and could easily be distinguished from military aircraft or passenger planes which, of course, were far less frequent in those days.

Perhaps not unnaturally, Reich considered the appearance of these mysterious aerial luminosities to be visible signs of alien spacecraft - 'flying saucers' - come to spy on the Institute because of the acute environmental problems created in the wake of ORANUR. The mechanics of the orgone engine helped convince him that if he could develop orgonomic technology, then alien cultures, or CORE men (Cosmic ORgone Engineering men) as he called them, could also develop highly advanced propulsion systems in a similar manner. It is known that Reich absorbed 'flying saucer' literature as early as 1950, three years after the much-publicised sighting of nine shimmering objects seen crossing the Cascade Mountains of Washington State by pilot Kenneth Arnold on 24 June 1947. This included the work of Major Donald E. Keyhoe who had shot to fame in 1953 with a much-acclaimed book entitled *Flying Saucers from Outer Space*.

Reich soon came to believe there was a direct relationship between the quality of orgone in the atmosphere and the appearance of UFOs in the night sky. However, he explained this connection by suggesting that the alien propulsion systems emitted a form of exhaust that contributed to the rise of DOR in the upper atmosphere and, consequently, the advancement of desert terrains and the presence of droughts.(11)

In his book *Contact with Space: ORANUR Second Report 1951-1956,* Reich describes his views on the UFO phenomenon and its relationship to DOR-infested environments. In this extraordinary work, years ahead of its time, he refers to UFOs as Ea - the E standing for 'energy' and the 'a' representing alpha, or primordial, while Ea was also seen as an abbreviation of 'enigma'.(12) Although Reich clearly saw UFOs as mechanical spaceships made by alien cultures, the great many mysterious lights he and his colleagues so commonly observed in the skies above Rangeley were seemingly viewed more as individual lifeforms enveloped in 'cosmic' orgone energy than as actual 'nuts and bolts' hardware.

Between the years 1953 and 1956, Reich dedicated much time and effort to the study of the Ea problem,(13) as he referred to it, recording its characteristics and discerning its relationship to the subject of orgone engineering. He was most concerned that the US Air Force should be continually updated on any developments in this area and on 17 March 1954 he presented a document entitled 'Survey on Ea' to the Air Force Intelligence consisting of a four-page precis, with accompanying equations, expounding the links between UFOs and orgonomy (the study of orgone). He even compared the reported 'bluish shimmering lights' of the 'flying saucers' with the 'blue illumination' created in 'pressure vacuum tubes' during his early experiments with orgone energy.(14)

Around this same time Reich despatched a completed USAF sighting report form covering just one example of the type of aerial phenomenon seen regularly by him and his staff at Rangeley. The observation in question was made by Reich and his partner Ilse Ollendorff between 22.00 and 22.15 on 28 January 1954.(15)

At the time Reich was watching the clear night sky when he apparently noticed an elliptical mass of yellow-white light move down from the west and descend slowly in front of 'Spotted Mountain' - a distance of just one mile from Orgonon. The object was seen through binoculars to illuminate the valley bottom, before changing its colour to orange and passing behind a distant tree-line as it moved silently over the ground. It was finally lost from view in the vicinity of a location called 'Round Pond' near the Badger's Camp ridge. Minutes later another similar luminosity appeared among the same trees, and this time Ilse also saw it. Reich highlighted this case in favour of any other example simply because the objects seen on 28 January 1954 were 'distinguished by mountain background', making it impossible for them to have been either stars or high-flying aircraft.(16)

Reich was at pains to demonstrate to both the USAF and the world as a whole that UFOs not only existed, but that they were also a growing menace that needed to be dealt with immediately, and it was *how* he dealt with them that took him firmly into the realms of science fiction.

Development of the Cloudbuster

In the aftermath of ORANUR, Reich developed the now famous orgone engineering device known as a cloudbuster. Initially, it consisted of a series of long steel tubes mounted together on a pivoting device. From these came thick, flexible cables attached to a huge multi-layered accumulator seated on a swivelling turntable. Hollow cables then earthed the accumulator into a fast-moving, underground water source, usually a deep well or natural spring. The intention of this curious, and rather cumbersome, contraption was to draw away excess DOR from the atmosphere using the cloudbuster as a directional energy beacon.

Reich believed that among the properties of orgone was its apparent contradiction of the law of entropy, for instead of flowing from higher to lower potentials, as in the case of electricity and heat, orgone appeared to flow from lower to higher concentrations. With this understanding, Reich came to believe that substances of a high orgone, or 'orgonomic', potential, whether biological, geophysical or mechanistic, appeared to attract further energy from sources of a lower potential. So by employing this so-called reverse entropy theory, he could use the cloudbuster's tubes to focus on a certain area of sky and force a drawing process to occur. In this way he believed he could remove 'pockets' of DOR to restore a natural equilibrium to the atmosphere above Rangeley.

Inexplicably, Reich's cloudbuster appeared to work to his and his staff's satisfaction, and gradually the orgone potential in the local environment began to increase in quality and, to Reich's astonishment, the thick, black DOR clouds that were said to have prevailed for over a year now began to fade away.

As a strange side effect to this drawing process, Reich quickly discovered that by directing the cloudbuster skyward in a prescribed manner, he could disperse clouds - hence its name - and, more importantly, he found he could create new rain clouds which could then be forced to release their load. The validity of this controversial process need not detain us here, for what is more important to our own debate is the apparent effect the cloudbusters had on the mysterious lights that continued to plague the skies above Rangeley during the first half of 1954.

Still concerned by the ever present Ea problem, Reich decided to direct a cloudbuster at a bright, anomalous 'star' hanging in the night sky during the evening of 12 May 1954. To his utter astonishment this anomalous light source appeared to respond by fading out of view. The exercise was then repeated a second time and the same result was achieved. In all, this was repeated four times, and on each occasion the object disappeared from view, the final time for good.(17) After due thought, Reich concluded that he had forced the Ea to withdraw rapidly since the cloudbuster was drawing away its 'cosmic energy'. So shocked was he by these initial results that Reich decided against any further experiments of this nature, lest he risk precipitating 'an interplanetary war'!(18)

During the summer of 1954 Reich decided to dig up the radio-active material he had buried in an uninhabited area near Rangeley, following the disastrous ORANUR experiment over two and a half years beforehand. The total of three milligrams of radium and a few micrograms of radioactive cobalt were then returned to Orgonon and tested with a Geiger counter. Among the many findings he made in respect to these nuclear substances, which he codenamed ORUR, was that their half-life had been considerably reduced by their intense exposure to concentrated amounts of orgone during ORANUR; some had even been rendered harmless by this process.(19) Even stranger, one lead container containing radium was found to be 'almost full' of what appeared to be water, even though it had remained hermetically sealed when in the ground.(20) He also found that when ORUR was brought into contact with the tubes of an operational cloudbuster the atmospheric drawing process was quickened dramatically. Excited by this bizarre discovery, Reich, McCullough and the other technical staff at the Institute planned to take this new combination of ORUR and cloudbuster to the deserts of Tucson, Arizona, where Reich believed that a DOR-infested environment, accelerated by the Ea problem, had resulted in the region's current drought leaving it deprived of rainfall for over five years.(21)

From 5 October to 9 October 1954, Reich and his staff apparently saw UFOs hanging low in the skies above Orgonon during weather engineering operations with the ORUR-equipped cloudbuster, or 'spacegun', as they liked to call it.(22) Having deliberately refrained from attempting to 'draw' the energy off any Ea since May that year, they refrained from intervening during these sightings. However, around 19.00 on 10 October they were again using the cloudbuster when they noticed a large red object in the western sky above Bald Mountain. Unable to resist the temptation, the cloudbuster was pointed directly at the Ea and to their amazement the object noticeably 'jumped' upwards - a purposeful response as if to evade the drawing process.(23) It also diminished in size and Eva Reich, Reich's daughter and the cloudbuster operator at the time, then watched as the object sank below the horizon.

At 19.30 a second, yellow object appeared in the western sky, and this was made to fade out after a two-minute direct draw. It briefly returned on two occasions before fading out completely. Reich later described its demise by saying it '... disappeared weakening, waning and blinking.'(24) The same, or a similar object, came into view shortly afterwards and was quickly joined by three other objects. These hung motionless in the sky until something quite extraordinary occurred. At 20.08, with the cloudbuster trained in their direction, all four objects simply vanished from view at the same moment as if by 'common command'.(25)

What happened on 10 October 1954 led Reich to conclude that he was at 'war' with the Ea. But the space 'battle' had also taken its toll on those involved. Reich experienced nausea for some days afterwards, his daughter Eva felt continually dizzy and ate little, while Reich's dog Troll fell sick and would not eat, leaving them to assume that the DOR drawn away from the UFOs had been partially absorbed into their bodies.(26) Similar illnesses almost invariably accompanied these Ea operations, with the most vulnerable being Eva Reich who would frequently become nauseous or suffer stomach pains when operating a cloudbuster.

Several other examples of what happened when the 'spacegun' was trained on these aerial luminosities can be found not only in *Contact with Space*, but also in the moving account of Reich's final years as seen through the eyes of his 10-year-old son Peter in his essential masterpiece entitled *A Book of Dreams*.

In spite of various tragic drawbacks, Reich's use of the cloudbuster finally resulted in defeat for the DOR in Tucson, Arizona, where Reich set up a temporary base named 'Little Orgonon'. The summer of 1955 was apparently Tucson's wettest in 20 years, with several inches of rainfall being recorded - according, at least, to the mostly anecdotal evidence accumulated by Reich at the time. Greenery flourished in this less-than fertile desert region, and Reich came to believe that his desert-and-drought weather engineering operations were clearly responsible for this acute climatic change.(27)

Furthermore, in the midst of their daily use of one or more of the ORUR-equipped cloudbusters, an extraordinary number of UFO sightings were studiously recorded by Reich and his team. For instance, in just one month between 21 December 1954 and 20 January 1955, they catalogued no less that 20 confirmed Ea observations, mostly pulsating lights seen hanging in the barren desert skies.(28) How many of these alleged sightings were misidentified natural or man-made phenomena will never be known. Yet if they really *were* genuine aerial luminosities, then might the drawing operations have catalysed their manifestation?

Among the extraordinary conclusions drawn by Reich following his Tucson expedition of 1954-5 was that DOR was a major drought-causing and desert-supporting factor linked also with the formation of water, *i.e.* water changes into DOR and *vice versa*. He also concluded that DOR dissolves rain clouds, prevents cloud formation and creates the unhealthy environment necessary for the manifestation of Ea. In contrast, he believed that healthy OR environments appeared to drastically reduce the chances of UFO manifestations.(29)

Such ideas were revolutionary. Yet were any of Reich's pseudo-scientific beliefs actually correct? Had Reich really discovered the key to unlocking the mysteries of not only the primordial energy continuum, his 'Cosmic Energy Ocean', but also the UFO enigma as well? Did these mysterious lights really have an integral link with the formation of clouds, rain and other meteorological conditions? Or was Reich simply a paranoid dreamer careering into oblivion, as some orgonomists later came to believe? Hopefully this current work will help to answer at least some of these vital questions.

The Final Curtain

By the spring of 1954 Reich was experiencing other, more immediate problems in his life. On 19 March that year the US Food and Drug Administration had issued a court injunction directing him to cease research into orgone energy and discontinue the publication of his Institute papers.(30) These writs were the culmination of seven years' harassment from the FDA who seemed hell-bent on curtailing Reich's work and ruining his reputation. They had decided that the sale, rent or hire of orgone accumulators across state borders contravened interstate export laws. Since there was no such thing as orgone energy, the devices were therefore mislabelled or 'misbranded'.

In a pitiful scenario that smacks of suppression and conspiracy, the FDA deemed that the shipment of orgone accumulators should be halted and those existing be destroyed by Reich and his staff. Not content at leaving it there, the FDA decided to ban Reich's books from publication and to burn any remaining stocks. The inevitable legal drama that resulted from the FDA's court ruling led to Reich being charged with contempt. He was sent to a federal penitentiary, where he sadly died on 3 November 1957, two days before a parole hearing. Reich was never found guilty of any charge brought against him in connection with his work. In spite of this, the inevitable media attention that accompanied the trials effectively sullied his name in the eyes of orthodox science, and the public at large, right through to the present day.

Yet despite his untimely death, Reich's legacy lived on and was continued not just by freethinking psycho-therapists and off-beat biophysicists, but also by other more controversial figures in the UFO world who pushed his theories on to dangerous new heights that were to infuriate even the most liberal students of orgonomy.

2

The Constable Controversy

Following Wilhelm Reich's tragic death in 1957, the association between orgone energy and 'nuts and bolts' flying saucers was all but forgotten. Few references to Reich's extraordinary work can be found in any standard textbook chronicling the history of the UFO phenomenon from its inception in 1947. Worse still, although modern-day orgonomists continue to support Reich's findings in respect to psychotherapy, orgone energy and weather engineering, they view his incursions into ufology with some embarrassment. Indeed, it is generally considered that Reich was not in his right mind during this difficult stage in his life, so his commentaries on the nature of the UFO phenomenon and its relationship to orgone energy should be treated with some caution.

This may be so, but most orgonomists tend to overlook the overwhelming evidence of those who bore witness to this remarkable interaction with anomalous light phenomena at both Rangeley, Maine, and at Tucson, Arizona. These included Dr Elsworth Baker, Robert A. McCullough, Eva Reich and Peter Reich - all of whom have publicly voiced their opinions regarding Reich's ORANUR experiment and his work with UFOs.

Fortunately, there *were* those who did take up the gauntlet and continued Reich's study into the apparent relationship between orgone energy and the UFO phenomenon. One such person was New Zealand-born aviation writer Trevor James Constable. He settled in the United Sates in 1952 having completed his service as a naval radio operator. Through his interest in the flying saucer mystery, Constable was soon introduced to colourful individuals such as George Van Tassel who, like his more famous contemporary George Adamski, claimed to have flown inside an alien spaceship.

George Van Tassel

Van Tassel gave regular meetings in a hewn-out chamber beneath Giant Rock in the South Californian desert. During these seance-like communications with the space brothers some 60 to 70 people would join with him in singing, chanting and saying prayers. The idea was that together they could form an emotional beacon in the hope that, as biological receivers or channels, the aliens would hear their call.

These lively gatherings were usually rewarded, for out of the darkness a deep, resonating voice would boom from Van Tassel's entranced body. He would then speak of the aliens' mission to earth and of various otherworldly matters. Sometimes these communications would include instructions concerning the appearance of UFOs. On one occasion the Space People said they would appear at a specific time in a nearby desert and, sure enough, at the appointed hour mysterious lights came into view and remained visible until a military aircraft appeared to intercept them.(1)

Constable attended these spiritual gatherings and was clearly impressed by Van Tassel's open sincerity and conviction in his otherworldly beliefs. He was especially interested in Van Tassel's apparent ability to contact his Space People through the use of biological processes. He also became intrigued by the concept, inspired by Van Tassel's communications, that the upper atmosphere may in fact harbour invisible lifeforms that are *not* inter-planetary spacecraft. Space, so Constable came to believe, could conceivably play host to etheric energies existing beyond the normal range of scientific detection, and yet are intelligent and responsive in their behaviour. He believed these amoeba-like entities could deliberately evade human detection, and yet on occasions could penetrate the known ranges of the electromagnetic spectrum, take on a quasi-solid form and register their presence as radar blips, photographic anomalies or as actual sightings as they penetrated the visible light spectrum. During such rare visual occurrences these etheric forms would appear by night as iridescent glowing objects, able to change colour at will, and by day as shimmering objects giving the impression of metallic discs reflecting sunlight.

Trevor James Constable found a greater understanding of the etheric sciences in the teachings of Rudolf Steiner, the founder of the Anthroposophical Society, and during this same period he became acquainted with the work of Wilhelm Reich as well as with the energy healing formulated by Dr Albert Abrams and developed by Dr Ruth Beynar Drown under the title radionics; this also brought him into contact with Reich's daughter Eva who was also an avid supporter of Drown's teachings. Gradually, Constable was able to align his own views of UFOs as ether ships with Reich's concept of orgone energy, particularly its association with both the ORANUR experiment of 1951-2 and the flying saucer mystery. This convinced him even further of the existence of invisible lifeforms living in the upper atmosphere - so-called 'critters' or 'sky creatures' as he decided to christen them.

During the summer of 1957, the year of Reich's tragic death, Constable teamed up with a colleague named Jim X. Woods for the purposes of trying to obtain photographic evidence of his 'critters'. Having chosen a suitable location in the Californian desert between Yucca Valley and Old Woman Springs, the two men set up their camera equipment loaded with infrared-sensitive black and white film. The agreed plan was for Constable to stand on a slight eminence and conduct a meditational practice known as the Star Exercise. This was believed to align his body with the earth's magnetic field, while setting himself up as a 'bioenergetic beacon' in the hope that it would attract inquisitive 'critters' into the recordable ranges of the IR (infrared) spectrum.

At the same time Woods would take up position a little way away and photograph the empty sky against background features, generally with Constable in the lower part of the frame. The experiments would normally take place in the pre-dawn desert air - the time they decided most conducive for this kind of psychic experiment.

By mid 1958 the results of the two men's photographic sessions were clear to see. In just one year they had captured over 100 anomalous images on film. Some showed dark objects, others showed extraordinary ellipses looking like living cells, while still others resembled more classic UFOs. All appeared to be of considerable size and were framed by physical features such as desert landscapes, hills and people.

The potency of what Constable and Woods had achieved can be judged by the remarkable series of images recorded on an IR motion film in the Mojave Desert on an unspecified date. The sequence, shot at 24 frames per second and reproduced in his 1976 book *The Cosmic Pulse of Life*, shows six consecutive pictures in which Constable stands some distance away with his hands raised in the air. Descending into frame is a clear amoeba-like anomaly that, in a mere quarter second of exposure, divides in two, joins back together, before finally ascending out of frame.

Constable came to believe that his photographs showed 'aerial fauna' - conscious 'bioforms' of etheric energy of the sort believed in by followers of Rudolf Steiner and studied scientifically by Wilhelm Reich. In the years that followed Constable constructed a cloudbuster and used it not just for weather control operations, but also to draw alleged 'bioforms' into manifestation (in contrast to Reich who used the device to make them *fade* from appearance). By employing this process, Constable and Woods were able to obtain many more photographic anomalies to support their case. To Constable it eventually became clear that whether he used the Star Exercise or a cloudbuster they *both appeared to produce exactly the same results.*

By far the most intriguing of the photographic anomalies recorded by Constable were the dark elliptical shapes captured on IR-sensitive, black and white film, often set against a suitable backdrop such as a distant horizon, a hill summit, or, on occasions, the upright tubes of the cloudbuster. These amorphous images were believed to represent invisible bioforms encroaching the very fringes of the IR frequency range, hence their appearance only on IR-sensitive film. Constable noted that Reich had achieved almost identical black 'dots' when attempting to photograph microscopic bion cultures. Although minute, these black and white photographs taken in 1944 showed sharply defined circles, with a less sharp periphery or 'field'.(2) They often varied in size and some even displayed an inexplicable white corona. Reich believed they appeared as black shadow-like forms because 'high concentrations' of orgone energy tended to desensitize or nullify film emulsion and so were reproduced on photographs as reversed imagery, *i.e.* as dark, absorptive holes or 'dots'.(3)

Whatever it was that Constable caught on film during 1957-8, Reich had achieved as early as 1944. So what were these photographic anomalies? If not artefacts of some sort, *i.e.* film or developing faults, then they were tentative evidence linking the bions observed by Reich under the microscope with the invisible aerial anomalies believed by Constable to be accessible to IR photography.

Despite retaining his firm belief in inter-planetary spacecraft of the sort supposedly ridden in by the likes of George Adamski and George Van Tassel, Constable went on to champion the idea of the upper atmosphere being inhabited by cellular-like lifeforms. These living entities were, he concluded, present in a semi-plasmatic or 'fourth matter' state and utilised orgone energy as part of their functional process. They were a 'living heat-substance' existing outside our laws of physics, yet containing chemical substances such as calcium and fluids. Constable envisaged their normal habitat as being the stratosphere and beyond, and estimated their size to be anything up to half a mile in length. They could 'bioenergetically' propel themselves great distances in an instant of time and as such might be seen as meteors streaking across the sky. Constable's summary of their nature was even more curious:

> As living organisms, critters appear to be an elemental branch of evolution probably older than most life on earth, dating from the time when the planet was more gaseous and plasmatic than solid. They are part of what occultists term "elementals." They live invisibly like fish in the ocean of atmosphere. Like fish, I estimate them to be of low intelligence. They will probably one day be better classified as belonging to the general field of macrobiology or even macrobacteria inhabiting the aerial ocean we call the sky.(4)

Constable found confirmation of his bioform theory in the works of other contemporaries. These included exobiologists such as Ivan T. Sanderson, who saw a biological solution to the UFO phenomenon, and proponents of etherian physics such as W. Gordon Allen, John M. Cage, Carl F. Krafft, Countess Zoe Wassilko-Serecki and Mead Layne - the founder of the influential Borderland Sciences Research Foundation in San Diego, through whom Constable met Reich's former research assistant, Robert A. McCullough.

Constable's Published Works

The response to Constable's suggestion that a percentage of the UFOs seen in our skies were not in fact alien spacecraft but intelligent masses of primary energy went down like a lead balloon among the various ufological communities. I recall the British release of his *magnum opus* entitled *The Cosmic Pulse of Life* in 1977 and was subsequently able to purchase a 1978 abridged edition entitled *Sky Creatures*. Nobody in the circles I moved took the book seriously, other than to accept that it did paint a rather unique picture of the UFO phenomenon. Most ufologists were simply not interested in a biological solution to the flying saucer mystery.

Worse still, *The Cosmic Pulse of Life* was to attract the wrath of contemporary orgonomists who abhorred its misrepresentation of Reich's scientific research. In a review written by the late Jerome Eden - himself a student of Dr Elsworth Baker, Reich's direct successor - and published in *The Journal of Orgonomy*, he opens with the following words: 'I intend to demonstrate that Trevor James Constable has rendered a grave disservice to orgonomy by publishing a book...(that) thoroughly distorts Reich's work in a miasma of occult mystification.'(5)

Eden went on to assert that Constable: 'Evades and distorts the serious realities of ufology (the study of UFOs) in a mystical maze of occult confusion...' and, in doing so, 'has performed a shameful disservice to the work of Wilhelm Reich.'(6)

Eden - whose own book *Scavengers in Space* continued the link between UFOs, DOR and orgone energy - was unduly hard on Constable's revolutionary new ideas. He was, however, reflecting the general view of the orgonomists who for over 20 years had been trying desperately to disassociate Reich's name from both flying saucers and the modern-day metaphysics preached by the likes of Rudolf Steiner.

Disowned by both the mainstream ufologists and the conventional orgonomists, Constable's controversial findings outlined in *The Cosmic Pulse of Life* were destined to be neglected and overlooked for the next 15 years. As a consequence, Constable immersed himself in commercially-funded, off-shore weather engineering operations which employed the use of both conventional cloudbusters as well as other more recent inventions. Even today he still writes regularly for the journal published by the Borderland Science Research Foundation, who champion his work and currently hold the copyright on many of Constable's 'critter' pictures (which I have been unable to obtain for the purposes of this present work - please see the examples used in *The Circlemakers*).

As a legacy for future researchers of the UFO phenomenon, Constable has left some poignant statements concerning this controversial debate, the most pertinent being his suggestion that: 'By the year 2000 - if there is one for our species - hosts of young investigators in exobiology will be in full pursuit of the critters of our atmosphere. They will undoubtedly marvel at our stupidity in not tumbling to such presences far earlier.'(7) But he also warns that '... nobody on this earth will understand UFOs in a technical sense unless they first master Reich's discovery of the orgone energy. Lacking knowledge of the energy itself and the functional mode of thought that comes from its understanding, human beings can only stumble and grope as they try and penetrate the mystery with the old mechanistic knowledge. The manifold and multiform UFO phenomena are essentially *orgonotic* [TJC's italics] and therefore beyond mechanistic reach.'(8)

Anomaly Photography

Since the publication of *The Cosmic Pulse of Life* in 1976, others have attempted to achieve photographic anomalies akin to those captured by Constable. Of these, the most well-known is the late Luciano Boccone, an Italian ufologist with a deep interest in Reich. In 1980 he wrote a book entitled *UFO - La Realta Nascosta* ('UFOs - The Hidden Reality') which contains a selection of plates showing various photographic anomalies.

In the English county of Cornwall, ufologist Terry Cox has also been able to produce very similar photographic imagery using both IR-sensitive black and white film and visible light colour film. Some of his more intriguing photographs were taken at the command of his wife Pam, who is today sadly almost blind. In the past she has been able to 'sense' unseen aerial presences in an otherwise clear sky - an ability that has resulted in a number of photographic anomalies on development of the exposed film.

By far the bulk of the curious pictures taken by both Luciano Boccone and Terry Cox show dark, even black, elliptical or circular forms. So, if these images are representative of a genuine unknown phenomenon, then what is their relationship to the UFO enigma? Do they show invisible masses of intelligent primary energy, the so-called 'bioforms' or 'critters' of Trevor James Constable? If so, can they really be linked to the orgone energy discovered in 1940 by Wilhelm Reich?

Earth Lights

Aside from my own forays into a terrestrial solution to the UFO enigma with Graham Phillips in 1979 (see Introduction), very few researchers took the matter seriously until some years after the publication of Constable's *The Cosmic Pulse of Life*. Probably the most important researcher and writer working in this field in Britain is Paul Devereux, editor of *The Ley Hunter* magazine, who, like the Californian geologist Egon Bach mentioned in the Preface, has actively pursued the idea that UFOs are created under certain geological and atmospheric conditions by the earth itself. A brief resume of Devereux's work is essential before we can go any further.

Between 1972 and 1976 Devereux and his colleague Andrew York collected literally hundreds of unexplained incidents originating from the English county of Leicestershire. In similar with Bach, their findings indicated an unquestionable link between geological faulting, geomagnetic fields, geophysical anomalies, ancient or sacred sites and what we know today as the UFO phenomenon. The two researchers also acknowledged the French ufologist Ferdinand Lagarde for having first examined the apparent relationship between UFOs and geological faulting, following his own extensive study of the legendary wave of French sightings during 1954. Concluding his findings, Lagarde had stated: 'UFOs occur by preference on geological faults.'(9) He went on to point out that faults were not simply 'the external aspect of an irregularity in the earth's crust, but are also the scenes of delicate phenomena - piezo-electrical, or electrical, or magnetic, and at times perhaps of gravimetric variation or discontinuity'. Earth mysteries writer and visionary John Michell also acknowledged Lagarde's perceptive observations in his 1969 classic *The View Over Atlantis* adding that: 'There is no doubt that such phantom lights are manifestations of electromagnetic energy most commonly encountered in the neighbourhood of geological faults, during episodes of magnetic disturbance.'(10)

The results of Devereux's extensive research into a terrestrial solution to the UFO phenomenon were finally published in his 1982 book *Earth Lights*, co-written with geologist Paul McCartney. This was followed in 1989 with *Earth Light Revelations*. Both titles adequately demonstrate that tectonic tensions and stresses, in association with an assortment of possible atmospheric conditions, produce inexplicable light manifestations, a conclusion also drawn by Egon Bach and his geologist colleagues in respect to the balls of light known as St Elmo's Fire seen so frequently in connection with earthquakes, faulting and volcanic activity in the Philippine Islands of South East Asia.(11) These energy masses, or 'earth lights' as Devereux calls them, are seen as belonging to the same family as mountaintop discharges, earthquake lights, ghost lights, spooklights, even the marsh-related Will-o'-the-Wisps of folklore tradition.

Working with McCartney and anomaly researcher Johnny Merron, Devereux has also been able to repeat earlier experiments conducted by Dr Brian Brady of the US Bureau of Mines in Denver, Colorado, in which tiny globes of light have been photographed leaving a cylindrical granite core moments before its controlled disintegration inside a rock crusher.(12, 13)

Despite his extensive work in this field, Devereux is reluctant to place a definitive tag on the actual nature of his earth lights, preferring to describe them only as 'exotic energy'. He is not, however, unaware of Constable's own work in this field. In *Earth Lights* he briefly discusses the orgone specialist's concept of UFOs as 'living creatures', but dismisses the majority of Constable's photographic evidence as simply the result of 'refractive effects', 'poor processing and chemical damage', yet admits that: 'Constable may well have captured some cases of an extraordinary atmospheric phenomenon which may one day lead us to an extended understanding of UFOs as natural phenomena of a currently unknown kind.'(14)

Space-time Transients

Other researchers, such as Dr Michael Persinger, a Canadian psychologist studying brain chemistry, and his partner, Gyslaine Lafreniere, have come to similar conclusions concerning the nature of UFOs, as may be seen from the series of papers they have published since 1977.(15) The two men's main area of study has been the relationship between paranormal events and electrical fields in respect to their effects on the human brain. They have proposed that a spinning column of ionised air, or plasma, described by them as a 'space-time transient', can be produced by tectonic stress below ground level and then released into the open air. Through atmospheric ionisation it can attain luminescent form, and should observers come into the proximity of this light manifestation, they will probably experience varying physiological effects depending on the distance involved (see Chapter 35).

Ball Lightning and Plasma Lights

Other researchers have put forward different ideas concerning the nature of the UFO phenomenon. Some believe it can be explained in terms of the little understood scientific phenomenon called ball lightning, or thunderballs - spherical, spinning masses of electrical energy that achieve luminescence through ionisation. The exact nature of ball lightning is still highly debatable, although it is thought to be associated with the so-called plasma lights produced by temperature inversions in the atmosphere. These are caused when warmer air currents pass over much colder fronts, or *vice versa*. This effect creates variations in the air potential which in turn supplies enough energy to produce what are referred to as plasma lights.

The inversion theory also bears similarities to the meteorological solution put forward in 1989 to explain the crop circle enigma by Dr Terence Meaden, an academic physicist and meteorologist from Bradford-on-Avon, Wiltshire. After years of exhaustive research into this blighted phenomenon, Dr Meaden concluded that the formation of a true circle 'involves the descent of an energetic vortex from the atmosphere, a vortex of air which is ionised to the point at which it is better regarded as a species of low-density cool plasma producing a high-energy electromagnetic field.'(16) This electrification of the

FIG 1. Ball lightning appears in a French barn during the eighteenth century. Could a similar phenomenon have been responsible for Jeems Meppom's fatal encounter with alleged Pharisees, the name given to Sussex fairies, during the same century?

air is believed to produce a quasi-solid 'plasma' with a defined shell and a powerful electromagnetic field. Such a hypothesis, so Dr Meaden has suggested, might also account for a great many UFO sightings, including their alleged electromagnetic effects, such as audible sounds, ghost images on radar, magnetic anomalies, radio effects and vehicle interference. This idea was adopted and revised by Jenny Randles and Paul Fuller in their 1989 book *Crop Circles - A Mystery Solved.*

Dr Meaden's work is backed by Dr Yoshi-Hiko Ohtsuki, a Professor of Physics at the Waseda University, Tokyo, who was the first person to recreate spinning vortices of ball lightning under laboratory conditions using microwave energy inside a specially-built container. He has also found that if a tray of aluminium powder is placed in the apparatus, circular marks will be left in the dust after the production of ball lightning; so for dust circles read crop circles.

Ball lightning and plasma lights do hold certain clues to our understanding of the UFO phenomenon. However, such theories cannot, I feel, account for the majority of unidentified atmospheric and terrestrial lightforms reported year after year across the world. Bach's St Elmo lights, Constable's bioforms, Devereux's earth lights and Persinger and Lafreniere's space-time transients come closer to our overall knowledge of this unique natural phenomenon, although even these theories may simply be expressions describing the visible manifestation of more primary energy forms existing beyond the boundaries of normal space-time. Changing atmospheric and geophysical conditions almost certainly contribute to this complex process which - despite all the modern theories - is little understood in scientific terms.

3

The Bioform Connection

My first real introduction to the relationship between photographic anomalies and the UFO phenomenon came quite unexpectedly in October 1979, whilst investigating the case of an eight-year-old girl who claimed to have witnessed an unidentified object above the rooftops of the houses opposite her family home in Prestatyn, North Wales. For the interview I was accompanied by UFO investigator Martin Keatman, along with a friend of ours from nearby Flint named Marion Sunderland and her 12-year-old daughter Gaynor, who had also experienced some quite remarkable UFO events.(1)

During the course of conversation the party stepped out onto the front doorstep to allow the young witness to point out the exact position her UFO had appeared. I took several black and white, visible light photographs on a Zenit-E SLR camera using Ilford 100 ASA HP5 film, and on Tuesday, 9 October these were developed in the dark room of the Wolverhampton flat I shared with my colleague Graham Phillips. The resulting negatives perplexed us, for on two frames showing the very area of sky in which the young girl had seen her UFO, there was a distinct photographic anomaly. When transferred to positive, the first of the two frames showed a sharply-defined, black circular mass with a slight corona penetrating into the surrounding greyness. At its base were two tiny white spots giving the subjective visual impression of headlights. The second frame showed a more diffuse-edged elliptical or doughnut-shaped mass bearing a striking resemblance to a classic UFO.

We shook our heads. Phillips and I had been developing our own black and white negatives for many months and had never before suffered from photographic artefacts. Having already confirmed there were no obvious chemical blemishes on the emulsion surface, and knowing that the two anomalies were positioned in an area of sky coincident to where the young girl had reported seeing her UFO, we contacted Marion Sunderland. Without mentioning the photographic anomalies, Marion asked Gaynor if she had 'felt' anything whilst standing on the front doorstep of the girl's home. In response, she said she had 'sensed' the presence of something 'watching' us from a position above the rooftops. This 'something' she related at the time to the alien intelligence she believed to have been behind her own UFO contactee experiences.

The Prestatyn pictures were subsequently used in various books on both the paranormal and the UFO phenomenon, and there the matter had rested until my interest in Constable's work was rekindled in 1991. Similar dark anomalies had, I realised, been turning up on photographs taken in or around the enigmatic configurations of crop circles and crop formations that had been appearing with growing frequency in the fields of southern England since the beginning of the 1980s.

Of these, two of the most interesting anomalies are to be seen in a colour picture of a crop circle found at Chilcomb Head, near Winchester in Hampshire, during the summer of 1987. It was taken using a ground pole extension by aerial photographer Fred 'Busty' Taylor of Andover in Hampshire and shows about a quarter of the flattened circle with a curved wall of standing crop in the background. Almost off camera to the left-hand side is a bare-chested youth examining the fallen stems. Of more interest, however, are the two clumps of black lines rising upwards - one set originating from the floor of the flattened circle and the other rising from the heads of the standing crop just beyond the circle.(2)

The only possible explanation for these strange marks seems to be either dirt or fluff clinging to the emulsion during development of the negatives. However, since Taylor is an experienced photographer, this solution appeared inadequate to fully explain the clear visual effects produced in the picture. Furthermore, some exponents of the crop

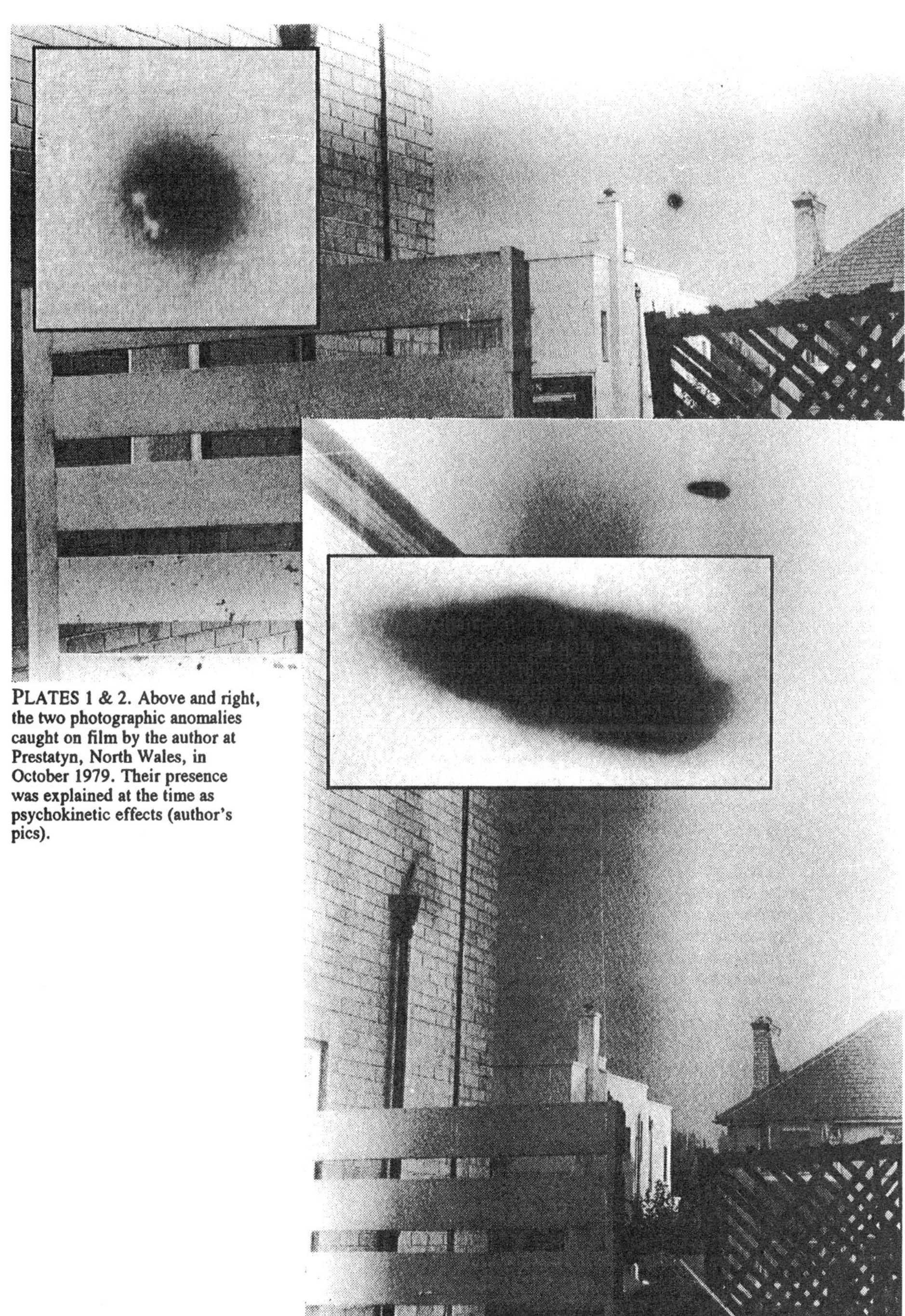

PLATES 1 & 2. Above and right, the two photographic anomalies caught on film by the author at Prestatyn, North Wales, in October 1979. Their presence was explained at the time as psychokinetic effects (author's pics).

PLATE 3. Photograph showing the two dart-like anomalies caught on camera by photographer Busty Taylor at a crop circle discovered at Chilcomb Head, near Winchester, Hampshire, in 1987. Nothing was seen at the time (photo: Busty Taylor).

circle enigma had seen fit to link these shadow-like marks with the presence of some kind of energy force believed to be behind the construction of supernaturally-produced crop circles (this particular example is now believed to have been constructed by Southampton circle-making sexagenarians Doug Bower and Dave Chorley - see Chapter 4).

Another prime example of an apparent photographic anomaly produced in association with a crop circle location is the black cylindrical form caught on camera by circles researcher George Wingfield directly above the 'pendulum' formation that appeared in East Field, near the village of Alton Barnes in Wiltshire, on Tuesday, 2 July 1991. Wingfield had taken the photograph just hours after the discovery of this crop 'pictogram' and could offer no logical solution for the clear photographic anomaly.

Another curious picture taken by an art photographer named Michael shows the view of a ploughed field at Ickleton, Cambridgeshire. Here, in August 1991, a cerealogical representation of the Mandelbrot computer fractal had been discovered hidden among the standing crop. Although taken seven months after both the wheat and the crop formation had been harvested, something very odd is to be seen in the picture. Superimposed on the broken flints and brown earth is a large anomalous blob with a dark centre and a fuzzy corona, similar in style to the examples I captured on film at Prestatyn, North Wales, in October 1979.

At first I thought Michael's picture could show a piece of fluff or a large insect in front of the camera lens, but this was quickly dismissed by the amateur photographer who emphasised that he had never before experienced photographic artefacts of this kind.

Other similar photographic anomalies also came to my attention, particularly in association with the area around Alton Barnes and the Pewsey Vale Downs of Wiltshire, where by far the greatest concentration of crop circles have appeared since the summer of 1990.(3) These include an elliptical blob caught on camera above Knap Hill, north of East Field, Alton Barnes, by crop circle surveyor John Langrish in July 1991. The original photograph is in colour and when computer enhanced the diffuse image displays multiple layers of yellow, orange, red and black (see Chapter 7).

Another similar photographic anomaly was caught on film that same summer by Warminster man Chris Trubridge above the Adam's Grave Neolithic long barrow, just north of Alton Barnes. Once again, after computer enhancement the circular image reveals concentric rings of colour graduating from white through to yellow, orange, red and ending finally in black.(4) Both John Langrish and Chris Trubridge assure me they have checked the negatives to make sure these images are not artefacts caused by emulsion blemishes (see Chapter 8).

Saucer Nests

Whether these colour anomalies had the same root cause as their black and white counterparts was difficult to determine, but their similarity to Constable's work of the 1950s is difficult to ignore. The crop circle connection also intrigued me for in his 1976 book *The Cosmic Pulse of Life*, Trevor James Constable had suggested that scorched or flattened circles of vegetation, the so-called 'saucer nests' occasionally reported in association with apparent UFO sightings, were the result of orgone-related aeroforms coming into contact with the ground. Since he also believed that unseen UFOs could

PLATE 4. A dark tube-like anomaly appears in a photograph taken by cerealogist George Wingfield of the 'pendulum' crop formation soon after its discovery at Alton Barnes, in July 1991. Nothing was seen at the time (pic: George Wingfield).

PLATE 5. A large, silhouetted blob superimposes itself on the ploughed earth of a field at Ickleton, Cambridgeshire, in a picture taken during the spring of 1992. Nothing was seen at the time. The previous summer this location had played host to a cerealogical version of the Mandelbrot set computer fractal (pic: Michael).

appear as dark photographic anomalies, then a connection between his concept of atmospheric bioforms and modern-day crop circles seemed a tantalising possibility.

Constable's opinions on 'saucer nests' had been fuelled by the growing reports of swirled circles of flattened reeds appearing in the swamps at Euramo, near the town of Tully in Queensland, Australia, from January 1966 onwards.(5) My own findings have led me to conclude that the Tully phenomenon is of such importance to this debate that it should be discussed in some detail.

The Tully Phenomenon

The town of Tully lies at the foot of two huge mountains engulfed in tropical rain forests - Mount Tyson to the west and Mount Mackay to the east. The whole region is dominated by mountain ranges and vast plains on which white settlers established banana and cane plantations in the first quarter of the twentieth century. In more recent years, Tully's scenic beauty has made it a major tourist resort, attracting visitors from across Australia. Euramo, where the circles were first found, lies on lower ground some 12 km south of Tully. Vast swamps dominate the area, and it was in one of these that the incident in question occurred around nine o'clock on the morning of 19 January 1966.

It began with Euramo banana grower George Pedley driving his tractor through a neighbouring cane farm. He had reached within 25 m of a swamp known as Horse-shoe Lagoon when, above the constant drone of the tractor engine, he distinctly heard a loud hissing noise, compared later to the sound of air rapidly escaping from a tyre. It was then that Pedley caught sight of a spinning, 'vapour-like saucer' (his own words) about 10 m above the reeds.(6) Open mouthed, he watched as it rose to a height of around 20 m, before making a shallow dive and vanishing in a south-westerly direction. Owing to his assumed preconceptions about flying saucers, Pedley later reported that the object he saw possessed 'no portholes', 'no aerials' and displayed 'no sign of life'. Pedley did, however, report a lingering smell likened to 'sulphur' which he said permeated the air for some moments after the event. He also reported that the tractor engine had begun missing before stopping completely during his sighting of the 'saucer', a statement which might imply some kind of electrical stoppage induced by the presence of the aerial object.

On moving into the reeds Mr Pedley had been astonished to find a 10 m circular area of flattened plants in an otherwise dense reed growth. As in the modern-day crop circles of southern England, the swirled stems were radially distributed in a noticeable clockwise rotation.(7)

George Pedley was so excited by the incident that he immediately reported his observations to Albert Pennisi, the owner of the cane farm. Pennisi was intrigued by Pedley's claims, as around 05.30 that morning his dog had gone uncontrollably 'mad' before bounding off in the direction of the lagoon. The two men decided to return to the site of the flattened circle of reeds and, on arrival, Pennisi promptly stripped off and waded out to the 'saucer nest'. He found it consisted of a 22 cm layer of reeds torn away from the muddy bed of the lagoon, with untouched green reeds up to 75 cm tall around the outside of the circle. Colour photographs taken at five o'clock that afternoon showed that the upper surfaces of the floating reeds had already turned brown, whereas the plant surfaces still underwater remained green. What this meant, the two men were unsure. Subsequent searches beneath the nest apparently revealed three unusual holes thought to be connected with the 'saucer' incident.

In the weeks that followed six additional 'nests' were discovered in the thick swamp grass that covered Horse-shoe Lagoon, amid further reports of unidentified aerial lights seen hanging in the skies above Tully and its surrounds. Furthermore, at least five new circles were discovered on the same property 21 years later, on 20 February 1987. These were between three and five metres in diameter and were said to have been positioned in a perfect arc.(8)

PLATE 6. The first documented reeds circle that appeared at Euramo, near Tully in Queensland, Australia, on 19 January 1966 following the dramatic appearance of a 'vapour-like' saucer at the same spot (pic: Claire Noble).

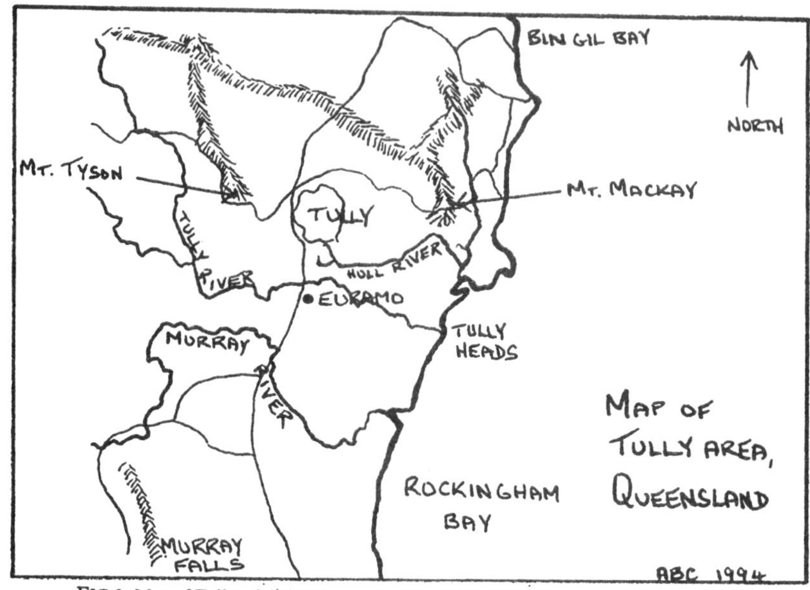

FIG 2. Map of Tully, showing the position of the first reeds circle found at nearby Euramo.

The initial Tully incident had, it later emerged, been preceded by a spate of UFO sightings which had begun several months earlier. According to local sources there is some evidence to suggest that the Euramo reeds circle was not the first to occur in the area. Yet despite the overwhelming fact that an event of some kind did take place on 19 January 1966, some critics dismissed the reeds circles as the result of hoaxers. This theory can, however, be more or less ruled out as Horse-shoe Lagoon is the habitat of poisonous snakes, making the idea of deliberate hoaxing much less appealing than it is, say, in the crop fields of southern England!

Chic-ah-Bunnah

Today Tully is dominated by its thriving tourist industry and by the remaining white plantation growers who have drained many of the swamps and lowlands for agricultural purposes. Yet long before the European settlers came to the area it was populated by the Old People, the indigenous aborigines who wandered the region and made their homes in the river valleys. There were the Mullenbuttas, who hunted to the south of the Tully River, and the Koorkunbuttas, who inhabited the area around Murray River, further to the south; their separate hunting regions being divided by a sacred boundary stone known as Edinge-eebah, or the Horse Fly.

There are a large number of aboriginal sacred places around Tully and many of these are marked by prominent rocks and stones that preserve some kind of ancestral folk memory. A number of these legends were recorded during the 1960s by a Tully resident named Gladys Henry in her book *Girroo Gurrll: the First Surveyor and Other Aboriginal Legends* - a copy of which was kindly sent to me by Claire Noble, another local resident, with whom I have corresponded on matters relating to the Tully UFO phenomenon. Claire has spoken much of the belief, even to this day, among the local aborigines of mysterious luminosities seen generally in the night sky and referred to in English as the 'moving lights'. *Girroo Gurrll* strongly supports this assertion with its aboriginal account of the legendary Chic-ah-Bunnah lights that have haunted the region since time immemorial, for the book records:

> The CHIC-AH-BUNNAH was a spirit in the shape of a man, and was always sighted rushing through the air. He emitted a strange blue light and was blinding to look upon. When he took off from the earth there was a frightful bang and a roaring rushing noise. He ate glowing red coals and only came to earth at certain places. The three known places in the area were Goondarlah Hill on the Murray River, the large rock at the back or western side of the crest of Mt. Tyson (Mt. Bulleroo) and another rock away up the Davidson Valley. The creature was frightful to behold and had a long, hideous nose. Kitty Chilburrah was said to have seen one personally while on Palm Island, and the local witness, a little girl named Jaa-Jin-oo (the little eel), claims to have seen one in the last few years. There is no evidence of the chic-ah-bunnah having done anyone harm. He merely instilled a great fear in the hearts of the beholders.(9)

Accompanying the above story is a picture of Mount Tyson with an arrow pointing to the summit bearing the words 'landing place of chick [sic] a bunnah'.

It is evident to anyone who has studied folklore accounts of phantom lightforms, that the Chic-ah-Bunnah appears to be a generic title describing a form of unidentified light phenomenon. Descriptive attributes such as 'rushing through the air', emitting a 'strange blue light' that was 'blinding to look upon', 'frightful to behold', and eating 'glowing red coals', all clearly affirm this view. Statements such as 'it only came to earth at certain places' seem also to suggest that this light phenomenon was attached to specific locations, hinting strongly at a geological component to this mystery. Of the sites mentioned, two are cited as being rocks while the third is placed upon the summit of

PLATE 7. Illustration of Mount Tyson from Gladys Henry's book on aboriginal folk tales entitled *Girroo Gurrll: The First Surveyor*, showing the 'landing place' of Chic-ah-Bunnah, the name given to the mysterious aerial lights seen locally (pic: Gladys Henry).

Mount Tyson, a mountain sacred in the minds of the aborigines due to its links with Chic-ah-bunnah. In recent years ample evidence has been put forward to show the integral relationship between UFOs, mountain-top discharges and other forms of terrestrially-created lightforms.(10)

Claire Noble, who is now quite elderly, informs me that unidentified aerial lights have been a regular occurrence in and around Tully for as long as she can remember. They continue to be seen, and on many occasions these apparent UFOs have been observed by aborigines and white settlers alike to emerge from behind the summit of Mount Tyson before moving down into the plains. Interestingly enough, what the Old People see in terms of a restless ancestral spirit, white Australians generally express in terms of alien hardware visiting the earth.

Unexplained Ground Markings

Aside from the continued presence of UFOs in the Tully area, Claire has also catalogued many unexplained ground markings that have appeared locally since George Pedley's discovery of the Euramo reeds circle back in January 1966. She cites a figure of 86 known markings in and around the lagoons and cane plantations of the region. Some appear in grass, some are only three to five feet across, while others are said to have been elliptical in appearance or to have possessed concentric rings around the main flattened circle.

The Tully phenomenon is a prime example of the apparent relationship between unidentified aerial luminosities, indigenous beliefs and folklore, and the recurring proximity of swirled circles of flattened vegetation. The appearance of mysterious lights in this one region also appears to confirm that certain places or zones appear to act as catalysts to allow the manifestation of such curious phenomena.

Aside from the Tully phenomenon, there are a great many more examples from around the world that show a clear-cut relationship between the appearance of unexplained ground markings (UGMs) and the proximity of unidentified aerial lightforms. In my book *The Circlemakers* I cited several cases of scorched circles appearing under curious circumstances on North Island, New Zealand, between August and October 1969 amid a wave of UFO sightings locally. I also outlined similar cases from Van Horne, Iowa, in 1969 and from Speed, Victoria, Australia, in 1989. Not that this necessarily means that they were *made* by UFOs, only that the two appear to have an integral relationship of some kind.

Jenny Randles and Paul Fuller - who suspected hoaxing to be the main cause of 99% of modern-day crop circles as long ago as 1986 - detail many more examples of UFO-linked UGMs in their 1990 book *Crop Circles A Mystery Solved*. They also cite various eye-witness accounts of crop circles seen forming during daylight hours. Moreover, as editor of *The Crop Watcher* journal, Fuller has published details of some 120 cases of crop circles or UGMs that have appeared in Britain alone between the years 1909 to 1975.(11) Very few of these cases are likely to have been hoaxes.

Australian UFO researcher Keith Basterfield has uncovered evidence of over 100 cases of UGMs that have appeared in his own continent (and this excludes the bulk of the Tully material),(12) while Chris Rutkowski of Ufology Research of Manitoba has recorded a total of 407 examples found in his native North America since the 1920s. This listing includes cases of calcined or missing vegetation, the yellowing of grass, stunted plant growth, burned and flattened circles, ground depressions, strange geometrically-placed holes and swirled circles of flattened crop.(13)

Most of these historical cases occurred before the dramatic rise of interest in the much-maligned phenomenon we refer to today as the crop circle enigma, so a careful look at the apparent relationship between UFOs, unexplained ground markings and the modern-day concept of crop circles is essential before we can venture any further down this road.

4

Curse of the Fairies

Despite the cherished hopes of many, there is ample evidence to show that the greater majority of all modern-day crop circles are of human manufacture. Clandestine activities of this nature probably began in the fields around Warminster, Wiltshire, during the late 1960s, early 1970s, although it was not until Southampton sexagenarians Doug Bower and Dave Chorley started to make crop circles in their home county of Hampshire during the late 1970s that the subject was truly born.

Having learnt of the furore that had surrounded the discovery of the Tully reeds circles of 1966 (they themselves were UFO enthusiasts), Bower and Chorley hoped simply to fool the gullible into believing that their nocturnal handiwork was the result of flying saucers leaving nest-like impressions in the ripened barley or wheat. It was a joke, a whim, something to do after the pubs closed on a Friday night.

The two men's bizarre nocturnal pursuits took place infrequently at first, but once the subject had reached the attention of the regional, and then the national and international media, they extended their activities to include other nights as well. Over a period of 15 years they created literally hundreds of simple circles before moving on to construct more complex crop formations, or crop 'pictograms', as they became known. This, in turn, induced other groups and individuals to mimic and evolve the two men's artistic talents, using the ripened crop fields of Hampshire and Wiltshire as a giant canvas.

Bower and Chorley say they invented the crop circle enigma, claiming it was they who, during the summer of 1980, constructed the three simple circles at Westbury, Wiltshire, that first drew both the public's and the media's, attention to this subject. They also believe - as do most of the general public - that *all* crop circles, if not manufactured by themselves, are the product of copy-cat hoaxers, whether they be in Hampshire, Wiltshire, or anywhere else in Britain or abroad.

Such bold statements are easy to make, but in my opinion there is overwhelming evidence to support the belief that some crop circles are not of human construction. Even if Bower and Chorley did initiate the modern-day revival of interest in crop circles in 1980, their claims cannot account for the hundreds of instances of unexplained ground markings - and this includes crop circles - recorded by UFO researchers world-wide before this time. Even the Tully reeds circles, the inspiration for the two men's own nocturnal pursuits, still defy logical explanation.

Cotswolds Fairy Rings

My own research into this contentious area of study has also uncovered indisputable evidence to show that crop circles were appearing in Britain long before the birth of the flying saucer mystery in 1947. For instance, circles of depressed barley and wheat are known to have appeared in the fields of Oxfordshire each summer between the years 1939 and 1946. This information comes from a woman named Gwen Horrigan, who is a figure of high standing in her home town of Leigh-on-Sea in Essex and is also known to me personally. During the Second World War she was evacuated as a girl of six from her home in London to the sleepy Cotswold village of Kingham, close to the Oxfordshire/Gloucestershire border. Here she quickly found herself leading a new lifestyle among a rural farming community who adhered to many ancient customs and superstitious practices completely alien to children living in London.

Gwen said that throughout this period the fields were constantly planted with cereal crops to cater for war demands, and on several occasions she and her young friends came across huge flattened circles of fallen corn. Like the modern-day examples, each had sharp cut-off edges and radial swirl patterns - always clockwise, or so she recalls. Some were up to 16.5 m across, while others were a little smaller. They appeared most frequently on sloping ground belonging to Slade Farm, situated to the south of an east-west track running between Kingham Hill School and Daylesford Hill Farm (SP260262), close to the woods of Whitequarry Hill. They were always considered a genuine mystery by local farmers, and villagers referred to them as 'fairy rings', despite their use of the same term to describe the circular discolourations of grass caused by fungi. A certain amount of superstition was attached to their presence, for the children would never step into them, just glean crops from their edges before moving on.

The association with the fairy folk is important here, as mysterious luminosities, known locally as 'fairy lights', were often seen in and around the woods at Whitequarry Hill. Gwen said it was also common knowledge that these same woods were used at night by a local witch coven who saw this location as 'special' in some way.

Gwen also wishes to point out that the Cotswold villagers would speak of an ancient power the land held, especially at local prehistoric sites. These included the Rollright Stones, or 'Kingsmen', a megalithic stone circle three miles to the north-east of Kingham Hill, as well as various barrows, scattered tumuli and a circular Iron Age earthwork named Chastleton Barrow Camp (SP259283). This can be found on the top of a ridge, a mile and a half north of where both the crop circles and the lights appeared.

Sceptics might doubt the research value of an account over 45 years old, remembered by a woman from her childhood. However, I scanned the records for any possible confirmation of her words and discovered that one of the few documented cases of a circular indentation appearing in Britain prior to 1980 stems from the village of Evenlode, Gloucestershire, *less than 5 km* from Whitequarry Hill, and just 3 km west of Chastleton Barrow Camp.

The Evesham Journal carried a news-story in its edition of 8 June 1960, concerning two perfectly formed concentric rings of flattened crop, one 7.6 m across, the other 5.3, which appeared one inside the other. They were found during the early morning of 3 June in a meadow halfway between Evenlode and Chastleton by Bill Edwards of Poplars Farm, who at the time was out tending his sheep. In an interview with the author on Sunday, 16 February 1992, the now retired farmer admitted he had never seen anything quite like it before or since that time. The rings were so perfectly round, he said, it was as if a giant stamp had come down and left a deep imprint. The long grass had been so pressed flat that it looked like a heavy waggon had made precise 15 cm wide bands without marking anywhere else, and yet their remoteness ruled out the possibility of a mundane explanation. A local reporter also witnessed the rings first hand and later said it was as if they had been drawn with a giant pair of compasses.(1)

The area of the Cotswolds that incorporates the Rollright Stones complex of megalithic sites is known to be a region of intense paranormal activity, particularly inexplicable light phenomenon. For instance, in his book *Earth Lights Revelation,* Paul Devereux cites the tradition of a light phenomenon, often blood-red in colour, seen in the area between Chipping Norton and Burford since at least the turn of the century and known locally, simply, as 'the Light'. It is said to haunt a stretch of road above Shipton-under-Wychwood, some five miles south of Whitequarry Hill.(2)

Superstitious Beliefs

Among the many pre-1980 crop circle cases that have come to my attention are some with recurring folklore concerning not only their believed supernatural origin, but also the fear of stepping inside them. Parapsychologist and author Ralph Noyes received a personal communication from a woman whose husband had regularly come across circles whilst farming in Hampshire during the 1940s. She claimed that when they did appear, the superstitious country folk would not hand reap them, fearing they were 'uncanny and of devilish origin.'(3)

I have uncovered a similar example of this curious rural superstition. Mrs Irene Bridge, a resident of Doncaster, South Yorkshire, is now 69 years old, but in 1932 she was a girl of seven living with her family in the county of Kent. She vividly recalls large flattened circles of wheat appearing during the 'hot summer months' in the fields at the base of the downs near the village of Aylesham. She says they were slightly rougher than the modern-day examples she has seen when visiting friends in Alton Barnes, but more importantly, she clearly recalls that no one dared enter them as their manufacture was attributed to the devil himself. This extraordinary superstitious belief appears to echo

FIG 3. Victorian engraving of a devil on the edge of a bare circle of crop. Infernal spirits, such as lesser devils, were accredited with the construction of crop circles in the English counties of Kent and Hampshire as late as the 1930s. Does this diabolic association have any connection with the strange illnesses experienced by visitors to modern-day circle sites?

Gwen Horrigan's account of the circles of flattened wheat found on the Oxfordshire-Gloucestershire border during the very same period, the only difference being that in the Cotswolds their construction was accredited to the fairies and not the devil.

From these early accounts of crop circle appearances in rural England, it seems clear that until comparatively recent times farming communities treated their presence with the utmost caution and saw their formation not as acts of God, but as the work of infernal spirits. This brings us to the relevance, or not, of the so-called 'mowing devil' story cited in an obscure Hertfordshire pamphlet dated 1678, which could record our earliest account of crop circle formation. The publication's full title is an adequate description of its contents:-

> THE MOWING DEVIL: OR, STRANGE NEWS OUT OF HARTFORDSHIRE Being a True Relation of a Farmer, who Bargaining with a Poor Mower, about the Cutting down Three Half Acres of Oats: upon the Mower's asking too much, the Farmer swore That the Devil should Mow it rather than He. And so it fell out, that very Night, the Crop of Oat shew'd as if it had been all of a Flame: but the next Morning appear'd so neatly mow'd by the Devil or some Infernal Spirit, that no Mortal Man was able to do the like.
>
> Also, How the said Oats ly now in the field, and the Owner has not Power to fetch them away.
>
> Licensed, August 22nd 1678.

The text elaborates in a prosaic manner the statements of the front cover, speaking of the farmer refusing to pay the price asked by a neighbour to reap his crop, and how that very night a strange fire is seen to illuminate his field of oats. On approaching the area in question the farmer discovers circular areas of perfectly 'mowed' crop, flattened in a manner similar to the general description of crop circles today.

The woodcut accompanying the pamphlet shows a small impish figure using a scythe to meticulously mow flat a circle of oats in concentric bands. Beyond the fallen

FIG 4. The cover illustration from a pamphlet first published in 1678 that describes the plight of a poor farmer who seems to have been striken with illness after entering flattened circles left by the so-called 'mowing devil'. Is this the oldest known account of crop circle construction?

crop are tongues of flame representing the infernal fire seen in the field while the mowing devil is at work.

Certain conclusions can be drawn from the existence of this single pamphlet. Firstly, if such an incident did take place, then it implies that more than one circle appeared in a Hertfordshire field one night in August 1678. More importantly, the farmer was drawn to their presence by a mysterious luminosity in the crop, leading him to accredit their formation to an infernal spirit referred to as the 'mowing devil'. He looked upon the circles' presence as a misfortune brought about by his failure to pay the neighbour.

A name like 'mowing devil' would indicate that a mischievous spirit of this title existed in folklore beforehand, and was an accepted phenomenon known to cause farmers grief by visiting their fields at night and striking down standing crops. Until quite recently the trolls of Norway were likewise made scapegoats for all manner of mischief occurring in remote farming districts. The mowing devil story suggests that crop circles of this kind were known in Hertfordshire prior to 1678, and that, like those in Hampshire during the 1940s, they were seen as ill-omens.(4)

I can go further on this topic, for the apparent tendency to blame the mysterious appearance of crop circles and strange lights on infernal spirits, such as the mowing devil or the fairy folk, opens up new doorways to archive material not previously brought into this debate.

Gwen Horrigan is quite certain that the crop circles she saw at Kingham Hill were known locally as 'fairy rings', and that the dancing luminosities purported to have been seen in the same vicinity were referred to as 'fairy lights' - an archaic interpretation of such unknown phenomena which until comparatively recent times were seen in many European countries as the lanterns of mischievous spirits such as elves, fairies and hobgoblins. If so, then just how many accounts in folklore mask bastardised versions of mysterious light displays associated with crop circle formation? Let me give you an example taken from the annals of the 17th-century antiquarian John Aubrey, who was one of the first people to bring the marvels and mysteries of Avebury and Silbury Hill to the public's attention.

The story concerns a Mr Hart, Aubrey's schoolmaster, who lived in a small village

FIG 5. Old English woodcut of fairies dancing in a circle next to a fairy mound. Although grass fungal rings were once seen as fairy rings, evidence now suggests that historical crop circles were also known by this same name.

named Yatton Keynell, just outside Chippenham in Wiltshire. Mr Hart was said to have become convinced of the reality of the fairy folk after an extraordinary encounter upon 'the downs' beyond Chippenham in either 1633 or 1634. He told his pupils that crossing the hills at twilight one evening he chanced upon a 'fairy ring' in which a number of fairies were going round and round, singing 'and making all maner of small odd noyses'. Upon his approach they were said to have pinched him all over 'and made a quick humming noyse all the time.'(5)

Enthused by his schoolmaster's remarkable account, Aubrey and his 'bedfellow Stump' walked across the downs some nights later hoping for a repeat performance from the fairy folk, but unfortunately they were to come away disappointed. The antiquarian reported that 'we saw none of the elves or fairies. But indeede it is saide they seldom appeare to any persons who go to seeke for them.' And these were his last words on the matter.

Despite Aubrey and Stump's disappointment, it is clear that Mr Hart encountered something very unusual whilst out on the downs beyond Chippenham. Was the 'fairy ring' a forming crop circle, the fairies themselves some sort of accompanying light phenomenon, and the 'small odd noyses' and 'quick humming noyse' upon his approach, some kind of related sound effect? Mr Hart being 'pinched all over' seems a classic example of the prickling or tingling sensation so often reported during UFO close encounters as well as by those seated inside an orgone accumulator. It is also worth remembering that the downs beyond Chippenham, spoken of in this account, are likely to have been the North Downs between Calne and Cherhill, territory that has become the focus of modern-day crop circle events.

It is not the time or the place to enter into a lengthy debate as to the authenticity of individual crop circles or crop formations (this I have discussed at length in *The Circlemakers*). All that can be said with any certainty is that unexplained ground markings, including crop circles, have been around in one form or another for a long time indeed. In Britain they have been seen as the product of infernal spirits such as the devil (Hertfordshire, 17th century; Kent, 1930s and Hampshire, 1940s) and the fairy folk (Gloucestershire/Oxfordshire, 1940s).

Furthermore, such recurring folklore and taboos concerning entry into these swirled circles of crop cannot, I feel, be simply ignored as misguided memories. Some kind of strong belief must have built up over successive generations to instil such superstitious fear in the minds of agricultural communities in different parts of England. What might this have been? Could it have had anything to do with the statement in the title to the mowing devil story about the oats lying in the field untouched, while the farmer 'has not Power to fetch them away'? Does this imply that the farmer was struck down by some kind of illness after entering the circles?

I feel the answer lies in the fact that in European folklore encounters with infernal spirits, such as the fairy folk, were generally believed to bring only bad luck, ill-health and even death to those unfortunate enough to bear witness to their mischievous activities.

A Fairy's Revenge

One prime example of a particularly horrific confrontation with fairies, that may well relate to the mowing devil account of 1678, is be found in E. V. Lucas' classic *The Highways and Byways of Sussex*, first published in 1904. The story in question originally appeared in an 1845 work entitled *Contributions to Literature* by Mark Anthony Lower, who learnt it from the lips of a South Downs man named Master Fowington.(6)

Under the sub-title 'a fairy's Revenge', Fowington relates how one night long ago, a brother of his wife's great grandmother, named Jeems Meppom, staked himself out inside a hay barn in an attempt to catch those responsible for mysteriously threshing his corn at night. After patiently waiting for some while Jeems was about to give up when he heard strange sounds emanating from outside the remotely-placed farm building.

Suddenly, Jeems noticed amidst the bales of hay two tiny Pharisees, the old Sussex name for fairies, who began merrily threshing the corn with little 'frails'.

FIG 6. Early nineteenth-century illustration of ball lightning descending the chimney of a house in England, much to the horror of the residents. Both ball lightning and UFOs exhibit traits suggestive of independent intelligence.

FIG 7. A 1976 illustration by Brian Froud of a fairy ring being surveyed by an elvish creatures not unlike the alien entities associated by some people today with the construction of crop circles. Have our current views simply been updated to suit the times? (Pic: B. Froud).

The sight so amused him that he burst into laughter. In that instant the tiny Pharisees sped pass the farmer, and in their rush to reach the open air, Jeems Meppom received 'a queer pain in de head as if somebody had gi'en him such a lamentable hard thump wud a hammer.'

The force of the Pharisees 'knocked him down as flat as a flounder' and here he lay unconscious until first light when he was finally able to 'doddle' back to the house. On arrival home 'he looked so tedious bad,' that his wife sent for a doctor. With some amusement, he listened to the farmer's account of his encounter with the Pharisees before deciding that he had suffered a fit and would be well soon. Master Meppom knew otherwise, for in his mind 'de cuss [curse] of de Pharisees is uppan me,' and he was right, for one year later ole' Jeems was dead.

Quite obviously this is a country tale that was passed down from generation to generation until it bore little resemblance to any original incident; and yet the gist of the story is that the farmer encountered some form of light phenomenon (probably ball lightning) in his hay barn and as a consequence suffered first a headache, then unconsciousness, then delirium and then, finally, death. It was probably these rudimentary components that allowed it to be preserved for so long. Whatever the truth behind this tale, comparisons can be made with other similar encounters with the infernal spirits of folklore and legend, including, I feel, the mowing devil story. What's more, in the original Jeems Meppom story, as given by Master Fowington, one Pharisee addresses the other as 'Puck', a name given to both the devil and mysterious moving lights in folklore and deriving from the Old English *puca*, or the Welsh *pwca*, meaning an *infernal spirit*.

The link here between devilish entities, strange illnesses and UGMs is further strengthened by the fact that the Pharisees of Sussex were, like the fairies in other parts of Britain, accredited with the manufacture of the rings of discoloured grass caused by fungi. According to Master Fowington, his own grandfather, 'who was a very truthful woman,' had herself witnessed the Pharisees on the South Downs, for he says: 'They were liddle folks not more than a foot high, and used to be uncommon fond of dancing. They jound hands and formed a circle, and danced upon it till the grass came three times as green there as it was anywhere else. That's how these here rings come upon the hills.'(7)

We have seen how in the Cotswolds crop circles were clearly referred to as 'fairy rings' as late as the 1940s, so it seems reasonable to suggest that whatever was seen as responsible for crop circles would also have been seen as responsible for fungal rings of grass, and *visa versa*.

If the afflictions of the farmer in the mowing devil story are to be linked with the bad luck, ill-health and even death that might be expected as a consequence of encounters with the fairy folk, then what could have caused the belief in such adverse physiological effects? Furthermore, what relevance does any of this have to Reich's theories of orgone energy and UFOs, and Constable's bioform solution to unexplained ground markings?

5

The Plughole Effect

Ever since the advent of the ill-named 'saucer nests' during the 1960s, those who have visited either UGM or crop circle locations have often reported an array of inexplicable physiological, psychological and environmental effects that beg explanation. These have included the appearance of blue-white (or even black) flashes of light and small globular lights akin to ball-lightning, the experiencing of inexplicable time-slips or time-distortion occurrences, repeated accounts of peculiar animal reactions and, as we have already seen, baffling photographic evidence matching that obtained by Reich, Constable and others.

On a more mechanical level, there have been accounts of radiation anomalies and magnetic variations, as well as electrical malfunctions reported in connection with mobile telephones, still cameras, video recording equipment and LCD watches. On a more subjective level, incidents at modern-day crop circles have included accounts of spontaneous altered states or visionary experiences, the hearing of strange sounds, the sensing of presences and occasional stories of miraculous healing or unaccountable bouts of artistic creativity. There have also been accounts of people experiencing a sense of warmth and well-being on entering certain circles, while others have experienced vertigo or giddiness.

Yet by far the most disturbing factor of this enigma is the repeated accounts of visitors becoming ill after stepping inside a crop circle. The symptoms can vary, but generally they include acute nausea, dizziness, dry or sore throats, dehydration, flu symptoms, headaches, a prickling or tingling on the skin, 'sea sickness', throat constrictions, vomiting and, most curious of all, a metallic or sour taste in the mouth.

Symptoms

The sheer volume of cases on the files of crop circle researchers suggests these ill-effects are unlikely to be the result of a severe reaction to crop pesticides or psycho-somatic effects induced through some kind of euphoric belief in the supernatural origin of crop circles. As you will see in Chapter 8, some reports of ill-effects are made by local residents who have little interest in the crop circle enigma. What's more, certain critics of the subject have confided to me personal accounts of acute ill-effects they themselves have experienced after entering one crop circle or another.

In 1991 Lucy Pringle and Diana Clift began a survey on behalf of the Centre for Crop Circle Studies (CCCS) in which they have been cataloguing the physiological and psychological effects experienced by visitors to crop circles. To their amazement they have discovered that out of the 187 people consulted between 1991 and 1993 no less than 71% had experienced 'unpleasant reactions' whilst inside circles. Of these, 21% suffered nausea, 18% experienced headaches, 15% suffered tiredness, while a further 21% had experienced actual physical pain; this is against a total of 48% who reported experiencing pleasant or neutral effects inside the circles.(1) Furthermore, no less than 31% of those consulted experienced adverse physiological effects lasting more than 24 hours.

Lucy Pringle openly accepts that no rigid conclusions should be drawn from these figures. She also recognises that negative effects are more easily observed and recalled than positive ones; however, these statistics are certainly food for thought and bear out the many more anecdotal stories that have circulated among the crop circle community in recent years.

My own introduction to this baffling aspect of the crop circle enigma was when my partner Debbie Benstead became quite ill after visiting the huge triangular pictogram that appeared below the Iron Age camp of Barbury Castle, some 6.5 km south of Swindon, Wiltshire, during the early hours of Wednesday, 17 July 1991. On entering the formation

PLATE 8. The majestic crop pictogram that appeared below Barbury Castle, near Swindon, Wiltshire, in July 1991. Although determined to be man-made by meteorologist Terence Meaden, strange illnesses and electrical malfunctions were still reported by several visitors. No one has as yet come forward to claim responsibility for its construction (pic: Calyx Photo Agency).

around midday on Saturday, 20 July she had begun to feel dizzy and started complaining of distinct flu symptoms. An hour later she felt drained of all vitality and was experiencing aching limbs, a sore throat and a sour, metallic taste in the mouth. It was the first crop circle she had ever seen, and neither she nor I were then aware that similar ill-effects had been reported by other people at such locations. The severity of what happened that day, along with Debbie's intuitive interpretation of what she believed was going on, led to my active involvement in the crop circle debate.

Much later I found that others had also experienced similar problems when visiting the mammoth Barbury Castle formation of 1991. These included crop circle sceptic Adrian Dexter, who suffered acute flu symptoms, and Austrian crop circle researcher Oliver Stummer, who had entered the formation with his girlfriend Daniela Schroter an hour or so before Debbie had fallen ill at the same location. This was despite the fact that Stummer believed the landscape design to be of human manufacture.

Almost immediately on entering the tractor tram-lines, Stummer had experienced a 'sinking feeling' above his knees. This was rapidly followed by optical distortions, the sensation of blood rushing to his ears, sudden dizziness, a pressure in his neck glands and general mental numbness.

Stummer said nothing to Daniela, knowing that similar effects had already accompanied his visits to two previous formations. Instead he walked forward and entered the huge crop pictogram. Soon afterwards he began experiencing heart palpitations, so he quickly decided to exit the field. Yet having concluded that the strange effects were probably the result of induced hysteria, Stummer turned around and returned to the central circle with the intention of taking some photos. Picking up his camera, he was about to take a picture when he again realised that 'something was brewing' inside him, so instead opted to return to his car, having sensibly decided to give this formation a miss. Yet before he had a chance to say anything to his girlfriend, a 'blow', likened to an electric shock, hit him from behind. For a while he then suffered 'light spots before his eyes...' I will leave Stummer to explain what happened next:

From that moment on the situation was escalating. My organism was incessantly pouring out adrenalin, my heart accelerated incredibly beating up to my throat. The extremities were prickling all over and seemed to be bloodless; it was an absolute dreadful state - somehow I had the feeling as if I was flowing out of my body. I could not help uttering a scream and then I ran like mad - leaving the formation along the tramline. The painful 'attacks' causing fear of losing my consciousness did not let me stop until the field was far behind me; then I sank to [the] ground.

My body trembled and I felt exhausted, even the rest of the day I was afflicted with an aching solar-plexus as if I had been punched against the pit of my stomach... I think it is needless to point out that this event gave birth to new questions and of course - theories.

The above information was extracted from the detailed report Stummer sent to Diana Clift and Lucy Pringle of the CCCS. Compare these ill-effects with those independently experienced by my partner Debbie just one hour later. She blamed her worsening condition on the 'energies' present in the formation and, like Oliver Stummer, was unable to visit any other formation for the rest of the day.

Interestingly enough, the Barbury Castle formation was also the scene of some quite extraordinary electrical malfunctions, as the following example demonstrates. In July that year Professional photographer Richard Ansett was commissioned by *The Mail on Sunday*'s *You* magazine to take some human interest shots of the pictogram for a forthcoming feature. From the outset his expensive equipment was dogged with unique problems he had never before experienced. A radio-linked flash gun held by his assistant failed to respond to the camera's trigger mechanism, so had to be operated manually. Even then it would only flash intermittently, prompting him to bring out a reserve flash gun. But this too failed to work properly, and to add final insult to injury, the camera shutter decided to jam.

The photographer is very sceptical about the paranormal, and yet these inexplicable happenings led him to half-heartedly conclude that the crop formation must have been jinxed. Reports such as this are commonplace and cannot, I believe, simply be dismissed as the product of people's imaginations. Furthermore, many of these experiences befall visitors in the full knowledge that the formation concerned is of *man-made* construction. For instance, during the summer of 1993 a group of 20 Germans visited a crop formation that appeared on Waden Hill, just outside the Avebury megalithic complex in Wiltshire. Half of them accepted that crop circles were of human manufacture, while the rest were open-minded on the subject - they had no fixed views one way or another. In spite of these opinions, no less than 18 members of the party experienced strong physiological and psychological effects after entering the crop formation. German journalist Jurgen Kronig, who lives in nearby Calne, learnt of this incident and individually questioned those involved. He established that 60% had suffered adverse effects such as dizziness, headaches, nausea, stomach cramps, while 40% experienced beneficial effects, such as the cessation of headaches and other ailments. Moreover, nearly all of those affected accepted that the strange effects had been induced by their visit to the formation.(2)

Could similar adverse physiological effects have struck down the farmer featured in the Mowing Devil story? If so, then could the superstitious taboo surrounding historical crop circles have stemmed from the knowledge that illness often befell those who strayed inside them? Such a belief would also account for why they were thought to have been manufactured by infernal spirits, like the mowing devil, who would presumably have cursed or jinxed the circles before departing from the spot after their night of revelry. Such ill-luck can be compared with 'de cuss' of the Pharisees that struck down Jeems Meppom. It was the Pharisees, of course, that were also accredited with the manufacture of the rings of darkened grass seen on the hills of the South Downs.

Ancient Sites

Even more curious, and almost certainly of relevance to this debate, are the striking parallels between the anomalous effects reported by people visiting prehistoric monuments and those already cited in connection with crop circles. The occurrence of mysterious lights, photographic anomalies, time-slips or time distortions, visionary experiences, senses of well-being, unusual animal reactions, involuntary altered states, electromagnetic and geomagnetic effects and radiation anomalies have all been reported in association with Neolithic, Bronze Age and Iron Age monuments such as earthworks, holy wells, long barrows, stone circles and subterranean chambers, including the fogous of Cornwall and the souterrains of Ireland. Furthermore, there are also accounts of visitors to prehistoric monuments suffering acute physiological and psychological effects.

The following case from 1981 adequately demonstrates the clear similarities between experiences reported at crop circles and those that occur at prehistoric monuments. It concerns an Essex man named Bernard, whom I have known as a friend since 1984. He is what might be described as a psychically-sensitive individual, although in 1981 he was actively engaged in scientific monitoring work for the so-called Dragon Project (see Chapter 6) at the Kit's Coty House megalithic dolmen in the county of Kent. Although Bernard was able to take an extraordinary infrared photograph of fog-like energies above the dolmen, he experienced no adverse psychic effects here. It was quite another matter, however, when he visited a tree-covered tumulus named Wormwood Hill, close to Wandlebury Camp upon the Gog Magog Hills in Cambridgeshire, with fellow UFO investigator Bill Eden on 5 April, 1981.

On approaching the earthen mound he could clearly see it engulfed by swirling bands of light, unseen by his colleague. Ignoring this, he stepped on to the mound, amid the vibrant coloured light, and instantly sustained a powerful headache, a bitter metallic taste, acute nausea and sudden dizziness. With this came the rising sound of a deep tonal note that emanated from the ground and rose in pitch the higher he climbed. Even more curious (and, in common with Oliver Stummer) was the disconcerting sensation that he was about to leave his physical body through the process known as astral projection. He also glimpsed priestly figures in saffron-coloured robes approaching the site in a ceremonial fashion.

The moment he was helped away from the mound, the physical and quite bizarre psychic effects ceased completely. Yet on tempting fate and approaching the site once more the whole process restarted, beginning with the swirling lights and then moving on to the more physical problems, the rising tonal sound, the out-of-the-body experience and the clairvoyant vision of the saffron-clad priests. It all ended as abruptly as it had begun, when he was again helped away from the ancient monument.

The pair left convinced that some sort of inherent power within the tumulus had caused Bernard's ill-effects, owing to his acute psychic sensitivity. The experience made him very wary of visiting ancient sites in case any further incidents of this nature occurred.

I included this account in *The Circlemakers* and was amazed to receive anecdotes from people who had also experienced physiological effects when visiting prehistoric monuments. Since we know that virtually all modern-day crop circles and crop formations are man-made, then the catalogue of effects noted in connection with their appearance and presence begs explanation. Quite obviously, if these picturesque designs are simply a form of clandestine land art then they should be unable to induce physiological effects, not only among visitors, but also in the environment in which they are placed. So how is it that such innocuous locations can apparently induce such dramatic ill-effects?

Nocturnal Crop Artists

To achieve some semblance of an answer we must turn to a most unlikely source indeed - the human circlemakers or crop artists who illegally make crop circles and crop formations under the cover of darkness. For it seems that they themselves have become the target of various inexplicable incidents as they carve out their works of art in virgin fields of barley and wheat during the dark, early hours of the morning.

Our first case concerns a male circlemaker who was out constructing a formation at Shaw Farm, near Lockeridge in Wiltshire, one night in July 1992. With his female accomplice some distance from him, he was using a plastic garden roller to lay flat standing crop when he was suddenly stunned by a burst of light that emanated from a position directly beside him. Believing he had just been photographed, he span around only to find no one there and no logical solution to explain what had occurred. So strong was the flash that the light source registered in his eyes for some moments before gradually fading away. His partner saw nothing at all.

The couple left the newly-created formation around 01.30, and around 03.00 that same morning a woman parked nearby in a dormobile apparently saw a bright glow emanating from the field in question. She later realised that this etheric light had appeared at exactly the same position as the newly-created crop formation. The circlemaker responsible for the Shaw Farm formation of 1992 has also told me that during the summer of 1993 he and three other co-conspirators witnessed a ball of light at close quarters as they constructed another major crop formation in Wiltshire.

Also during the summer of 1992 a young Northampton crop artist named Julian Richardson (aka 'Bill Bailey') was constructing a large pictogram at Cranford St Andrew, near Kettering in Northants, when he suddenly became aware of a presence burning into his back. Turning around he was startled to see a small globe of orange-red light hanging motionless above the adjoining field, some 50 m off the ground and at a distance of no more than 100 m from his position. Long moments passed before he watched the globe descend slowly towards the earth and blink out of sight. Having alerted his two fellow conspirators, they were able to turn around just in time to see the globe disappear. In Germany that same summer, a land artist named Lars Uwe was constructing crop circles near his home at Ittig, Westphalia, when he twice encountered a ball of light that was so bright he had to cover his eyes.

Two powerful flashes were also witnessed by circlemaker Rod Dickinson and three others when out constructing a crop formation in Wiltshire one clear night in early August 1994. Among those present was a radio reporter who was recording the event for future broadcasting. Unfortunately, however, he had his equipment off when both flashes occurred. Another circlemaker named 'John', who started constructing circles and formations for the first time in 1994 and was also present with Dickinson at the last mentioned incident, experienced two further incidents of this nature later that same week. On the first occasion he and two helpers were puzzled by a series of bright flashes that twice came from bushes at the edge of the field in which they were carving out a new formation in heavy rain. They occurred 15 to 20 minutes apart in brief bursts, lasting only a few seconds at a time, and were accompanied by a strange 'crackling noise'. Those present described this curious phenomena as like 'flashes of light produced during arc welding' and as 'a ball of white light flashing (*i.e.* pulsating) on and off'. Thinking the flashes might have been caused by some kind of electrical equipment shorting out due to the heavy rain, the company returned to the location in daylight but found no simple explanation to account for these curious effects.

Soon afterwards John and a friend were again out constructing a formation, this time in fine weather, when after four hours in the field another localised light burst occurred. On this occasion, John had become overwhelmed by a strong sense of foreboding shortly before the close-proximity flash took place. So much did this incident affect him that he decided they should leave the field without completing the formation. John, who was responsible for a number of major pictograms in Wiltshire during 1994, has pointed out that these three quite separate incidents occurred in formations placed in the same general vicinity and, in his case, turned out to be the final three he was involved in the construction of that summer.(3)

If such claims are to be taken seriously, then it implies that the mere construction of crop circles and crop formations could catalyse the appearance of aerial light phenomena, such as momentary flashes and more sustained lightforms, as well as other strange effects, simply by creating some kind of intangible disturbance in the immediate environment. Reports of strange lights seen by hoaxers could, of course, be purely coincidental, or it might be that the witnesses involved are misidentifying natural or man-made phenomena in the rush to complete their clandestine handiwork. This is possible; however, there is one further component to this debate which brings us back to the work of Wilhelm Reich and throws new light on the relationship between the strange effects reported at both man-made crop circles and prehistoric sites - and this is the orgone accumulator.

The Orgone Solution

Reich experimented much with the orgone energy accumulator - the device designed to concentrate the production of orgone energy. It works on the principle that orgone is attracted to and absorbed by organic matter, a process that Reich likened to the effects of static electricity on rugs, nylon and hair (indeed, he believed this was a manifestation of orgone itself).(4) Metallic (*i.e.* inorganic) substances likewise attract this universal energy, but then quickly repel it. Reich could not say how the metal achieved this flow (indeed,

PLATE 9. Wilhelm Reich's orgone accumulator. The effects associated with multi-layered accumulators match those experienced by visitors to both crop circles and prehistoric monuments such as earthen mounds and stone barrows.

most electronics engineers say this theory is complete nonsense), although he believed that the alternating layers allowed the energy to only move inwards, thus setting up the accumulator as a kind of orgonomic greenhouse, accepting and generating energy.

As we saw in Chapter 1, the orgone accumulator was found to cause an assortment of adverse physiological effects included dizzy spells, headaches, nausea, sore throats and a complete draining of bodily vitality.(5) Furthermore, those operating cloudbusters - which incorporated the use of a multi-layered accumulator - would often experience such DOR-related effects as dehydration, diarrhoea, nausea, severe pains in the 'solar plexus', shivering, throat dryness and vomiting.(6)

So why should a simple box cause such adverse effects? The only possible answer is that the energy excitation created by the multiple layers of inorganic and organic materials produces some sort of overload of vital energy inside the human body. In small doses this effect could, it seems, be beneficial in stimulating regeneration of bodily tissue and quickening natural healing processes, but in much larger doses orgone energy appears to over-excite the body and, as a consequence, induces physical ill-effects. In this knowledge Reich went on to develop a device known as a DOR-buster which consisted of a long funnel attached to a small, multi-layered accumulator. Its purpose was to function in much the same way as the cloudbuster - drawing excess energy out of the body and into a small accumulator, and thus restoring the bodily energy to a suitable level.

Spinning Lights

Of equal importance to our debate is the observation by users of the orgone accumulator of tiny balls of light, usually blue-green in colour, seen to emerge from the inner surfaces of the multi-layered walls and momentarily spin through the air before disappearing from view.(7) These light discharges appear to possess some kind of nebulous form and are undoubtedly linked to the luminous bions Reich observed in decaying and living tissue, as well as in other substances such as coal and sand. We must also not forget the dots and lines of blue or violet light seen by Reich to emanate from both the metal-lined walls and various objects inside the Oslo basement room he used for the early bion experiments.

Similar bursts of light to those seen in connection with orgone energy are frequently reported in connection with both crop circles locations (see Chapter 26) and prehistoric monuments. Compare, for instance, the below example of luminosities witnessed inside a megalithic dolmen with the yellow-white, lightning-like streaks of light seen to ripple across the metal-lined walls of orgone accumulators by Reich and others.

Light Luminescence at Ancient Sites

The case, quoted in Paul Devereux's major work *Places of Power, Secret Energies at Ancient Sites*, concerns archaeologist John Barnatt and his photographer colleague Brian Larkman who, during the summer of 1979, conducted an extensive survey of the megalithic monuments of Cornwall.(8) On 21 July the two men visited a dolmen named Chun Quoit and following an afternoon survey of the site they set up camp and began a relaxing evening. Deciding to take a further look at the ancient monument, they approached it in darkness and took turns in squeezing between the closely-grouped upright stones and sitting inside the small empty chamber beneath the 2.6 m square capstone. Unexpectedly, both John Barnatt and Brian Larkman were perplexed to witness a unique form of luminescence rippling across the undersurface of the capstone. Barnatt described this phenomena as 'periodic bursts of multi-coloured light (with colours reminiscent of a rainbow) [that] flashed across the stone's surface in short linear bands'.(9) This curious effect continued unabated for some 30 minutes with both men individually observing the strange sight.

Brian Larkman's diary account of the incident contained more subjective detail, with him speaking of seeing what he described as 'a reflection of myself, ghost-like in the shadows of the stone slab opposite'.(10) This effect was in addition to his witnessing of the very real light phenomena and may well have been some kind of visionary side-effect. Such spontaneously induced altered states are, as I mentioned earlier, commonplace at crop circles and have also been reported in connection with orgone accumulators.

The Plughole Effect

Parallels between ancient sites, crop circles and orgone accumulators abound and, what's more, the catalogue of effects reported in connection with each one is also frequently linked with UFO encounters as recorded by Michael Persinger and Gyslaine Lafreniere, among others. These effects include out-of-body experiences, psychic experiences, reality shifts, time distortions and an array of ill-effects that are reported time and time again by UFO witnesses (see Chapter 35), suggesting common ground between all four elements of this curious mystery. Furthermore, at least some of these physiological effects are, as we have seen, connected with so-called fairy encounters of past ages.

Should these perhaps wild assertions prove correct, then I feel the key to explaining this enigma lies in Reich's belief that an accumulator displaces or interrupts the free flow of the 'Cosmic Energy Ocean', and in doing so creates an energy excitation in and around the device. This theory can be explained to some degree by using what I see as a kind of plughole effect, *i.e.* if a plug is removed from a bath full of steady water, the slow drainage and pressure changes would produce untold ripples and vortices that upset the equilibrium of the entire liquid content, especially in the vicinity of the plughole. Placing flattened circles or geometric designs in a field of virgin crop might well be likened to removing the plug from the plughole. If so, then it is remotely feasible that ancient sites, crop circles and orgone accumulators all affect the immediate environment in much the same manner and therefore can and frequently do catalyse, or at least accelerate, the production of very real electromagnetic and paranormal effects. The plughole effect implies that an increased excitation of orgone occurs in the vicinity of such sites, suggesting that - if we invoke Reich's reversed entropy theory - mobile energy forms of a much lesser orgonomic potential would be attracted to these places. Should these energy forms achieve manifestation then it might well explain the presence of at least some of the mysterious lights witnessed in the proximity of both ancient sites and crop circles (others may be due to the sighting of some prehistoric monuments at locations where earth light phenomena repeatedly occurred in past ages and continues to occur today, *i.e.* close to geological faulting and underground mineral deposits. In the

Philippines lights are said to repeatedly ooze from geologically-significant locations known to the local inhabitants as *lugares incantados*, 'enchanted places'(11)).

It might even be argued that crop circles should be seen as temporary or *disposable* 'sacred' sites, available to the public only for a matter of days, weeks or months before they disappear beneath the blades of a combine harvester. Ancient sites, crop circles and orgone accumulators almost certainly function by virtue of the same basic principles, so by studying their individual properties we can perhaps attain a better understanding of their overall nature. One thing is for sure though, it doesn't matter what or who creates crop circles - be it aliens, crop artists, wind vortices or the Mowing Devil - evidence suggests it is their sheer presence that causes the many strange effects that repeatedly surround them, *not* the agency behind their construction.

6

In the Eye of the Dragon

If the side effects of any assumed energy excitation in the environment can for the moment be viewed in terms of Wilhelm Reich's discovery of orgone energy, then the Austrian scientist's belief that alternating layers of organic and metal (i.e. inorganic) substances are necessary to produce a successful accumulator is of the utmost importance to our own understanding of Neolithic and Bronze Age monuments. For it has been pointed out on several occasions that the tightly packed layers so often used in the construction of burial mounds and barrows appear to parallel Reich's multi-layered orgone accumulator.

The first person to refer to Reich's work in connection with prehistoric monuments was author and visionary John Michell in his 1969 classic *The View Over Atlantis*. In this he says:

> From his [Reich's] descriptions of the orgone flow and the ways in which it can be directed, it is difficult not to suspect that this form of energy was known and controlled in prehistoric times. Many of the greatest works of the megalithic builders involve the construction of a hidden chamber set deep within the earth or at the heart of some great artificial edifice. In Britain the chambers of New Grange and those newly discovered at Knowth and Silbury [Hill] are among the finest examples. The huge mounds that cover these secret rooms are not merely piles of earth heaped up at random. They are carefully and purposely constructed in a way which bears direct comparison with Reich's orgone accumulator. The chamber itself is lined with stone covered with a layer of turf and with successive layers of clay and sod. These layers are carefully built up, different types and colours of clay being used at each stage. Finally the whole structure is buried under a great mound of earth.(1)

If these observations are proved correct, then it would make Silbury Hill Europe's largest orgone accumulator (even though it does *not* possess a central, stone-lined chamber). Continuing this theme, in his 1989 book *The Orgone Accumulator Handbook* American orgonomist James de Meo cites the successful use of man-sized orgone accumulators sunken beneath ground level and compares these with both the megalithic 'root cellars' of New England and the Amerindian burial mounds. He also points out that certain burial mounds and prehistoric structures are constructed of 'clay soils or stone of high iron content, covered over with other layers of organic-rich soils or peat.' He falls short of suggesting that these must therefore act like orgone accumulators, but does admit that: 'Some authors familiar with ancient archaeological sites have even speculated that the life energy principles were known and used by ancient peoples.'(2)

So, if earthworks and chambered barrows are to be viewed as prehistoric energy accumulators, then what about other types of ancient monument? Might they serve similar functions? In many cases I feel the answer is yes, but for somewhat different reasons. For instance, the clear gaps below ground level between the often evenly-spaced standing stones of stone circles would give an alternating circular arrangement of organic and inorganic substances that act together to form some kind of invisible field. This effect, seen in association with the circular, egg-shaped or elliptical geometry of the stones, could well constitute an amalgamation of the effectiveness of both the crop circle and the box-like orgone accumulator. Earthen monuments, such as henges and hill-forts might also act as flat-plan orgone accumulators, producing and storing energy in association with their circular banks and ditches.

PLATE 10. Silbury Hill in Wiltshire, Europe's largest man-made mound. Author and visionary John Michell was the first to link its internal layering with Wilhelm Reich's orgone accumulator (author's pic).

Yet all of this brings us back to the reality or not of orgone, or indeed Reich's concept of a primordial ocean of cosmic energy permeating the known universe. Should a mass-free and presumably pre-atomic energy continuum of this description actually exist, then it seems clear that cultures both past and present would have interpreted its invisible presence and effects as constituting the existence of a universal, life-giving force defined almost exclusively in philosophical and/or mystical terms. In places such as China and Japan this mysterious force has always been known as *ch'i*, *ki*, or *qi*, while to the Hindu mystics of India it is known as Prana. In more modern times these same curious effects have been rediscovered by free thinkers such as Franz Anton Mesmer, who in the eighteenth century saw this life energy in terms of 'animal magnetism', and Karl von Reichenbach, a nineteenth-century German scientist, who, inspired by Mesmer's work, proposed the existence of a universal force called 'Odyle' or OD.

The Two Breaths

Viewing the characteristics and qualities of the landscape in terms of the presence of an alleged terrestrial energy is best understood by looking at the age-old beliefs of indigenous cultures who have accepted the existence of such natural forces for thousands of years. For example, the so-called geomancers or earth diviners of the Chinese *Feng-shui* (pronounced *fen-shway* and meaning 'wind and water') tradition recognise *ch'i* as the universal life-force. Its name means 'two breaths', a term expressing its dualistic nature, its so-called Yin and Yang components - one female and the other male, one negative and the other positive. In *Feng-shui* these twin aspects are symbolised by the white tiger and azure dragon, whose misty breaths weave together to become one harmonious life-essence existing in all living things. *Ch'i* has also been used

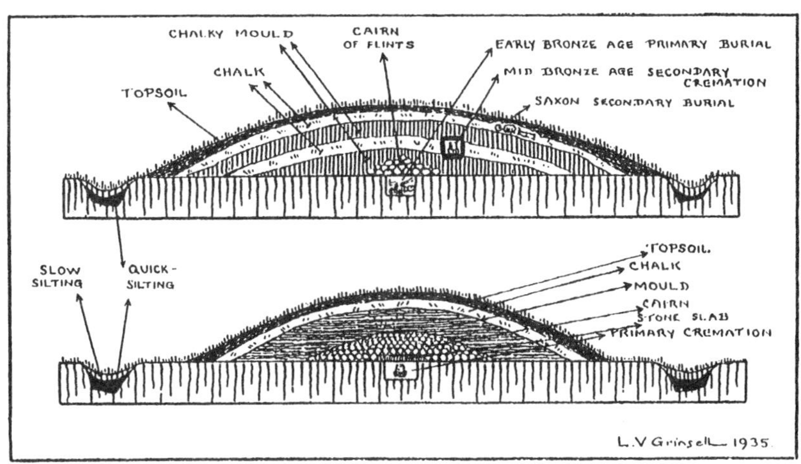

FIG 8. Cross-section of two basic round barrows showing the layering employed in their construction. Other examples from around the world incorporate more complex layering effects involving levels of flints, grasses, reeds, even bones (pic: L. V. Grinsell).

for many centuries in eastern healing practices, such as acupuncture, as well as in martial arts, where it is utilised to focus, sharpen and project the physical power of the body.

To the *Feng-shui* geomancers *ch'i* exists in different concentrations upon the earth's surface and flows (or discharges) from place to place along winding paths known as *Lung-mei* or 'dragon veins'. Through ritualistic attunement and the use of magnetic instrumentation, these highly skilled men are able to predict the nature of the *ch'i* present at a location. They also believe there are different conditions involved with the accumulation, direction and flow of the 'two breaths'. These include the topography of the surrounding landscape and the presence of water - factors that had to be considered when siting prospective new buildings or monuments. Great care would be taken to construct new towns in strict accordance with ancient *Feng-shui* principles in the belief that by regulating the flow of *ch'i*, the quality of life would also be enhanced. Landscaped settings, such as the *zen*-influenced gardens of Kyoto, Japan, were created with the specific purpose of accumulating, enhancing and channelling the natural *ch'i*, and today we refer to the study of this age-old earth divination as geomancy.

The Earth Mysteries

Since the 1960s the inexplicable effects of any pre-supposed energy continuum have been seen by dowsers and supporters of the earth mysteries, *i.e.* those interested in the ancient technology and wisdom of prehistoric monuments, as 'earth energy', 'ley energy' (after the concept of leys or 'ley-lines' proposed during the 1920s by Herefordshire man Alfred Watkins) or, simply, 'the energy'. Unfortunately, such terms are inappropriate as they are all based on the assumption that these energetic effects are focused primarily around prehistoric monuments and mostly-unproven alignments stretching between distant sacred places.

Fuelled by the conflicting and quite subjective interpretations of this elusive 'earth energy', Paul Devereux, editor of *The Ley Hunter* journal, launched a major scientific project in late 1977 to determine not just its recordable existence, but to decide its place in physics today. The Dragon Project, as it became known (after the connections between dragons and lines of energy in *Feng-shui* geomancy), conducted extensive field research over a several-year period at prehistoric monuments across Britain, with more extensive, long-term experiments being conducted at the Rollright stone circle situated on the Warwickshire/Oxfordshire border. Early results clearly indicated that many ancient sites were indeed hotbeds of detectable anomalies; however, these were not anomalies relating to some intangible universal energy, simply unaccountable ultrasound pulses, variations in the background radiation levels and subtle shifts in the geomagnetic field.

A summary of the results obtained by the Dragon Project was first highlighted in an article written by scientific archaeologist and lecturer Don Robins and published in *New Scientist* during 1982.(3) They were expanded in Robins's 1985 book *Circles of Silence* and in Devereux's *Places of Power, Secret Energies at Ancient Sites,* published in 1990. Both authors concluded that prehistoric man was fully aware of geophysical anomalies relating to both time and place and skilfully enhanced and perpetuated their presence by using an advanced knowledge of stone and earthen building techniques. The inexplicable effects induced by such locations would have made them places of ancient power where shamanic practices, such as the achievement of astral flight and altered states of consciousness, were perpetuated through ceremonial magic and dreamtime experiences.

Paul Devereux discovered no new scientifically-detectable 'energy' and so, in consequence, put into doubt the very existence of not just the so-called 'earth energy' of the dowsers and ley hunters, but also the *ch'i* of the Eastern geomancers, the *prana* of the Indian mystics and any other interpretation of this intangible life force - including Wilhelm Reich's orgone energy. Indeed, in respect to Reich's orgone research, Devereux's view is, simply: 'Forget it. It's just another name for another unknown.'(4)

Yet to any dowser, psychic or open-minded earth mysteries researcher, hitherto undiscovered terrestrial energies are not just an unquestionable reality, they are both detectable and visible to those who have the gift of second sight, in other words those with a psychic sensitivity. What's more, they *are* scientifically verifiable as the following report from Japan seems to show.

Channelling Ch'i

Recent experiments undertaken by a consortium of eminent physiologists and medical scientists at the Department of Physiology of the School of Medicine at Showa University in Tokyo, have demonstrated that certain talented individuals with the ability to channel *ch'i* through the palms of their hands can create to order bio-magnetic field strengths 1,000 times stronger than those normally detected in the human body. To make sure that the delicate magnetic field detection system - which included a pair of coils with 80,000 turns and a high sensitivity amplifier - were not producing machinery artefacts, the subjects were asked to 'switch off' the flow of *ch'i*, at which the visible oscillations on the screen suddenly stopped. When the subjects were again asked to channel *ch'i*, the instrumentation registered a reaction once more.

To produce such responses in the bio-magnetic field, a bio-electric current equivalent to this reaction would have been required. Yet when the scientists tested the subjects to see whether such an electrical current was indeed present, they were astonished to find there was no increase at all in bio-electrical activity. This implied that the individuals were defying the laws of physics and producing incredibly strong bio-magnetic fields by substituting the necessary bio-electric current with some kind of X-factor - an energy source seemingly beyond the detection of scientific instrumentation. Was this X-factor the elusive *ch'i* of the Buddhist mystics and the *Feng-shui* geomancers? The physiologists of the University certainly accepted this possibility, for their final report on the experiments concluded that 'the extraordinary large bio-magnetic field strength might be originated from "Qi" energy [as referred to] in the oriental medicine or in the oriental traditional philosophy.'(5)

For *qi*, or *ch'i*, substitute the term animal magnetism, bio-energy, earth energy, ether, Odyle, orgone, plasma energy or prana, call it what you want - they are all expressions representing the same X-factor behind the mysterious energy reactions detectable either by scientific instrumentation or by the subtle processes of the human body.

If this is true, then what is this elusive X-factor, and what causes its manifestation in the real world? Could it be the displacement, destabilisation and excitation of some kind of primary energy continuum laying beyond the realms of scientific detection? As previously stated, Reich came to accept that the 'Cosmic Energy Ocean' was simply a medium by which other more primary forces such as gravity and electromagnetism were brought into focus. He also concluded that orgone acted as a vehicle for the conveyance of light and could thus be observed in this way, *i.e.* as the blue-green bions seen under the microscope, the spinning balls of light observed inside accumulators or the various other strange light manifestations found to be associated with orgone energy. On this matter he said:

> We may assume that the OR energy ocean which fills all space is the carrier of the vibrations related to light. However, the relationship seems to be a much closer one. *The OR energy unit itself,* as it develops from and sinks back into the OR ocean, emits light, *strongest and sharpest at the peak and weakest during the period of rise and fall* [Reich's emphasis].(6)

By measuring the subtle shifts or discharges perceived as the result of the presence of orgone, Reich believed he could calculate the displacement or excitation of the energy 'ocean' itself - *implying that the only way we can really perceive the energy continuum is by studying its apparent echoes.*

So, can we define this energy continuum in terms of modern-day quantum physics? I feel we can.

The Superforce Theory

In metaphysics orgone can be equated with the concept of quintessence, the fifth element, ether, but in physics it can be recognised as the so-called Fifth Force, the much sought-after superforce that quantum mathematicians have long believed to be the binding factor behind the primary forces governing space-time. As early as 1922 equations were put forward by the German mathematician Theodor Kaluza which unified electromagnetism with gravity by demonstrating that they were both outward manifestations of a five-dimensional superforce. Four years later in 1926 a Swedish physicist named Oscar Klein was able to incorporate Kaluza's ideas into a workable quantum theory.(7)

Re-evaluations of the Kaluza-Klein or Unified Field theories by quantum physicists during the 1980s have strongly supported the concept of a superforce, but not one existing across five dimensions as envisaged by Kaluza - one embracing 11 different dimensions, no more, no less. To these people the universe was created in an 11-dimensional state with no distinction between matter and force, only a pure multi-dimensional energy source, linked by some scientists with the concept of zero point energy (zpe) and the 'dark matter' now thought to fill the otherwise empty universe. Once this energy started to disperse after the Big Bang, some of the dimensions curled in on themselves, creating matter in the form of particles or wave vibrations. At the same time they produced what we know as the forces of nature, which are the readily identifiable manifestations of the original superforce.

This is the currently held view concerning the construction and mechanics of *our* universe. So, is this 11-dimensional or multi-dimensional superforce the pre-atomic energy continuum proposed by Wilhelm Reich during the 1950s? I think the answer is firmly yes. If so, then the energy continuum will be the only force that remains constant in all dimensions - those we know and those we will perhaps never know, even though they *must* co-exist with our own space-time and be present with us here and now. Only the loudest echoes of these other dimensions can ever be registered by us, and these we almost certainly view in terms of anomalies of physics, astral domains, paranormal phenomena and highly subjective emotionally-based experiences which are, as I demonstrated in the previous chapter, frequently reported in association with crop circles, orgone accumulators, prehistoric monuments and the UFO phenomenon.

The True Dragon

Earth mysteries exponents have always cited the existence of the *Feng-shui* geomantic tradition, with its belief in *ch'i*, as evidence of earth energies criss-crossing the landscape and connecting ancient ritual sites. Indeed, I have used the analogy myself in this present chapter. However, like *ch'i*, the concept of earth energies appears to be an all-encompassing solution for a multitude of strange effects that remain unexplained or paranormal simply because we have never before recognised either the presence or the importance of a multi-dimensional energy continuum.

And yet if we had all looked deeper into the *Feng-shui* tradition we would have seen that *ch'i* itself is purely the outer manifestation of a much more primordial force or matrix known as *shan,* the dragon, delineated by topographical features of the living landscape such as hills, mountain ridges, rivers and streams.(8) This concept is of paramount importance to the *Feng-shui* geomancers, for they say that without the arteries, veins and water ducts of the dragon, there is no way its blood, its breath and its tears, *i.e.* the different forms of *ch'i*, can flow.

So if *ch'i* is an expression of the life energy, then the concept of *shan* suggests that the practitioners of *Feng-shui* may well have recognised long ago the presence of an energy matrix or continuum that allows the manifestation of primary forces, such as electromagnetism, gravity and light, and is today seen by quantum physicists in terms of the Fifth Force, superforce or Unified Field theory.

This then is the *true* spirit of the dragon.

7

A Guiding Light

On Thursday, 9 July 1992 I stood in a crop formation at Sompting, Sussex, (the one nicknamed the Spectrum logo) and decided to test Trevor James Constable's bioform hypothesis. According to his books he would stand on a rocky prominence in a desert region and simply use the power of the mind to draw 'critters' into some kind of recordable manifestation, be it photographic or purely visual. Knowing that crop circles had been frequently linked with photographic anomalies of the type achieved by Constable, I wondered what might occur if I was to use a simplified form of his so-called Star Exercise in association with a little creative visualisation.

For the occasion I set up my Nikon FG20 SLR camera fitted on a tripod with a standard 50 mm lens focused on infinity, the intention being to take a sequence of time delay photographs. This done, I positioned myself in the centre of the circle and visualised a spiralling vortex of white energy rising upwards into the air. Following this exercise I pictured tiny balls of light cork-screwing down towards the circle. In this way I hoped to create the necessary environment to draw any bioforms into manifestation and hopefully record the results on 200 ASA Kodak Ektachrome colour slide film.

After some five minutes of visualisation I walked back to the camera and pressed the time delay button. I then returned to the circle and continued the meditation. After hearing the camera click, I left the meditation again and took two further time delay shots, this time with me standing behind the camera lens. The exposure on this bright, but cloudy day was f.5.6 at an estimated shutter speed of 1/250th per second.

The matter was then forgotten until I collected the processed slides from Photofen (now Pegasus Photographic Laboratories) of Leigh-on-Sea, Essex, a commercial processing company run by my colleague Gary Bond. I flicked through each in turn and was perplexed by what I found. On the first of the three shots taken during the meditational exercise in the Sompting crop formation - the only one showing me standing in the circle with my arms raised - there was a horizontally placed, grey-green elliptical mass in the sky directly above my head. It was shadow-like in appearance with a definite colour graduation towards the centre in green, blue, indigo and, finally, violet.

The anomaly was distinct and clear, even on the small slide, and enlarged prints only increased its objectivity. What's more, this flattened, oval shape bore a striking resemblance to the very similar photographic anomaly caught on camera by John Langrish above Knap Hill, Alton Barnes, in July 1991 - the only difference being its slightly different colour graduation.

Logical explanations failed me. The anomaly was certainly not an emulsion blemish as the slide was studied under a microscope on my return from the processing laboratory. The only possible solution either Gary Bond or I could offer was an out-of-focus insect passing close to the lens as the shutter opened and closed. Although this solution posed certain problems, it seemed to be the only one we could offer.

Psycho-interactive Processes

If photographic anomalies like the one taken at Sompting do represent unmanifest energy forms, then it implies that these unseen masses exist on the fringes of the electromagnetic spectrum and can be coaxed into recordable appearance through psycho-interactive processes, just as Constable believed. The physics behind such a wild concept is still beyond even basic theory, although what slim evidence we do have suggests that energy forms appear to register their presence in accordance with the electromagnetic frequency ranges they penetrate, whether as a radar trace, a photographic image, a noticeable geomagnetic shift or as a visual sighting. Very

PLATE 11. The photographic anomaly caught above a crop formation at Sompting, West Sussex, by the author in July 1992. This picture went on to inspire the foundation of the Orgone 93 project later that year (author's pic).

occasionally UFO sightings coincide with blips on radar, or instrumental responses on the ground, but in most cases just one of these aspects is present, indicating its existence only in certain very specific areas of the electromagnetic spectrum. Another familiar aspect of the UFO phenomenon is its ability to pulse, flicker and blink on and off, and this too suggests short-term penetrations across only very specific frequency ranges, whether they be visual or otherwise.

These ideas are borne out by the rainbow-like colour changes frequently reported in association with UFO sightings. Aerial lightforms will be seen to change from blue to turquoise, gold, orange and then finally red before becoming black absorptive bodies as they appear to pass into the infrared frequency range which is, of course, invisible to the naked eye. Some are seen to blink out completely before reappearing and reversing the whole colour sequence, starting with black and then shifting from red to turquoise, gold and then finally back to blue again.(1) Such colour changes have earned these extraordinary lights the title 'rainbow fairies' in the eyes of remote Philippino communities.(2)

A further example of this effect was recorded on film during the reported sighting of a large luminous, oval-shaped object observed by three women from a remote cabin in the Nord-Osterdalen valley of Norway during the early hours of Saturday, 3 August 1991. It was seen to blink on and off at regular intervals and one of the women managed to video just one of its brief flash-like appearances before the batteries gave out. No

PLATE 12. John Langrish's photograph of an elliptical blob, similar in colour graduation to the one in Chris Trubridge's own picture, seen here above Knap Hill, just north of Alton Barnes in July 1991. Nothing was seen at the time (pic: John Langrish).

explanation was ever forthcoming to account for the presence of this aerial lightform, viewed for a total of two hours and also possibly seen by a local farmer.(3)

When the resulting video was examined a distinct crackling sound could be heard at the exact moment the object appears, implying some kind of outside interference. Since video cameras are generally well insulated against electrical noise, this crackling could represent some kind of electrical discharge emitted by the phenomenon observed. More importantly, when the recording was played back in slow motion, the single appearance of the aerial flash turned out to be two quite separate bursts of light, clearly indicating that the object was pulsing in and out of manifestation while emitting electrical energy only when visible to the camera eye.(4)

Project Hessdalen

The idea that UFOs are sometimes present in our skies without being seen is obviously a matter of speculation. It does, however, have some scientific support. Following increased reports of UFO sightings in the remote valley region around Hessdalen in eastern Norway from December 1981 onwards, a multi-national research team was set up in 1983 to scientifically monitor this unique aerial phenomenon - the first time that a programme of this nature had been conducted whilst the phenomenon was still being observed on a regular basis.

Between 21 January and 26 February 1984, Project Hessdalen, as it became known, recorded no less than 188 sightings of mysterious light sources, many of which were subsequently dismissed as misidentified man-made or natural phenomena. Of those sightings left unexplained some were said to have appeared as constant lightforms, either in the daylight or in the night sky, while others pulsed in regular or irregular sequences or continually changed their pattern of movement. Still others were described as changing direction or shifting in altitude. Some were even described as looking 'like many light-sources "tied together"', usually in different colour sequences. Anomalous recordings were made on various different kinds of instrumentation, some in association with clear visual sightings. This included radar traces and noticeable shifts in the geomagnetic field. The team also took a series of striking colour photographs, many of which remain as some of the most baffling aerial luminosities ever captured on film.

The results of the first season at Hessdalen convinced the team to return to this remote mountainous region in 1985. With increased support from a number of scientific institutes, as well as from the military, the project monitored the area from 13 January through till 27 January. This time the observation team made no significant sightings at all, which was obviously a great disappointment. However, during this same period they did obtain a number of 'instrumental recordings' comparable with those made the first year in connection with clear visual sightings.(5) This suggested that the sources responsible for the production of the mysterious lights between 1981 and 1984 were still present in 1985, but now only in an invisible state. This suggests that the phenomenon may have existed just outside the visible spectrum, or that its rate of pulsation had rendered it invisible to the naked eye. Evidence of this possibility was recorded on one occasion in 1984 when radar traces matched a visual sighting on the ground. To quote from the Project Hessdalen technical report compiled by Erling Strand:

> One of the three times the light was followed with the eyes and was seen as a reflection on the radarscreen at the same time and direction, there were reflection [sic] every second sweep. But the light was seen all the time. Could it be that... the light does not reflect radar waves all the time? Only sometimes? The same thing happened a couple of times when we didn't see the light: reflection every second sweep.(6)

This curious anomaly, which demonstrates the unpredictable nature of the UFO phenomenon, suggests that although the light observed on the ground remained constant in the visible spectrum, it appeared to be producing a radar trace only every *second* sweep of the dish. On other occasions the presence of unseen energy forms were registered as regular pulsations on the radar screen, even though they did not achieve manifestation inside the visible spectrum.

Earth Light Consciousness

Another important facet of the Hessdalen phenomenon was the soberly reported way in which it would appear to react or respond in a purposeful or intelligent manner. On several occasions the aerial lights appeared to 'play' with the project observers during their night-time vigils in near constant arctic temperatures. For instance, on Sunday, 12 February 1984 a slow moving light with a regular pulsation was seen crossing the sky. A high-powered laser was trained on its position and in response it changed its flashing sequence from flash... flash... flash... to flash, flash... flash, flash... flash, flash. Once the laser was switched off, the light resumed its original pattern. The experiment was repeated *four* times by the observers, and on each occasion the light reacted in the same way.(7) Later that same night another unidentified pulsating light responded in exactly the same fashion, producing double flashes when the laser was trained on it. This time the exercise was repeated no less than *five* times before the light moved out of sight. By the end of the 1984 season, lights had responded to laser signals on a staggering eight out of nine occasions.(8)

Project director Leif Havik became acutely aware of the playful character of the phenomenon after one small red light unexpectedly moved around his feet on leaving the caravan HQ during the evening of Monday, 20 February 1984.(9) The event was witnessed by two independent observers and remains unexplained. Havik also discovered that unidentified lights would invariably catch the observers off-guard, usually when they were either loading their cameras or when their equipment was out of reach. This situation eventually prompted the team to leave their cameras behind when going for night strolls as they knew this would invite a better response from the lights.(10) Coincidental problems of this type continually dogged the progress of scientific teams attempting to photograph the Loch Ness monster during the 1960s.

Many cases exist where manifested light sources appear to tease, even play with the witnesses, like some kind of simple animal response. Paul Devereux has discussed this so-called 'earth light consciousness' in his book *Earth Lights Revelation*, while this current book also records a number of examples of this unique and highly significant behaviour on the part of the phenomenon. If light consciousness, as I shall refer to it, is a real possibility, then it intimates at some kind of psycho-interactive exchange taking place between the minds' of the witnesses and the lightforms being observed. If the human brain can truly interact, communicate even, with pure energy, then how might such a wild process be explained in scientific terms?

If UFOs are the product of energy manifestations created or severely altered through intense oscillations in the flow of the energy continuum, then it is possible that they attain a form of complex information exchange through a process known in quantum physics as non-locality, or non-local interaction.

UFo

Non-locality

Energy Non-locality

This particular theory, put forward during the 1960s by John Bell of CERN, the European laboratory for particle physics in Geneva, contends that every particle in the universe is one half of a pair, a so-called virtual pair. These matter-antimatter pairs are deemed to split out of nothing, move away from each other and then, after an unspecified time, rejoin and annihilate their partners. I understand that because the net energy used is zero, they comply with the normal 'energy conservation rule'.

Although this theory might not sound earth shattering to you or me, whole new ideas are now emerging which suggest that the universe is simply one huge virtual split across 11 dimensions, bringing us back to the superforce or Unified Field theory as an explanation for the existence of a multi-dimensional energy continuum.

Non-locality works because it does not matter where in the universe the other half of a virtual pair is located, it must automatically respond to its partner in a manner that can only be described as 'atomic telepathy', a subject discussed in a February 1994 issue of *New Scientist*.(11) If this is true, and there is mounting support for this concept, then it implies an *instantaneous* transfer of information.

There is no doubt that quantum theories such as non-locality and the multi-dimensional superforce are potential keys to unlocking the mysteries of the paranormal, while at the same time re-writing the laws of physics. What's more, science writer John Gribbin has summed up these revolutionary new theories by suggesting that the topography of space-time is far more complex than we could ever have imagined 'with wormholes and bridges connecting different regions' in a series of non-local signalling routes, transferring quantum electrodynamic information instantaneously.(12) If you apply such concepts to the idea of light consciousness, then it means that individual communication between virtual pairs could replicate the temporal functions governing human consciousness, primary intelligence and memory storage.

Di force

These revolutionary new ideas open new doors concerning the relationship between the human mind and the unseen world. Could it really be possible to draw unmanifest UFOs - the alleged bioforms of Trevor James Constable - into some kind of recordable manifestation using subtle, mental processes such as meditation and mystical practices? Constable thought so, and as a consequence used his so-called Star Exercise to record the presence of apparent unseen energy forms on photographic negatives. I half-heartedly attempted a similar mental exercise at the Sompting crop formation in July 1992 and was truly amazed by the results. So, if I could achieve a photographic anomaly of this calibre in just 10 or so minutes of half-hearted exploration, what could a co-ordinated, multi-disciplinary team achieve over a much longer period in an area currently producing a high level of UFO-related events? Were we on the verge of finding a way of putting Constable's highly contentious work to the test once and for all?

The Project Conceived

The idea of a serious research project appealed to me for a number of reasons. Since the publication of *The Circlemakers* in July 1992 some researchers had called into question many of the theories put forward within its pages. Despite the revelations exposing the vast percentage of modern-day crop circles and crop formations as illegal land art, my interests still lay in the many strange effects still being reported at such locations. As there appeared to be so many parallels between the electromagnetic and paranormal events recorded in connection with not just crop circles, but also orgone accumulators, prehistoric monuments and UFOs, a full understanding of this relationship was essential.

Fuelled by these thoughts I announced preliminary plans for a project to study the relationship between these different subjects at the City Circles Symposium at Conway Hall, London, on Saturday, 26 September 1992. For the occasion I tried to gather together as many people as possible who I knew wanted to try and demonstrate the role played by orgone in both the earth mysteries and the UFO enigma.

Unanimously it was decided to go ahead with the project which I quickly christened 'Orgone 93', as it signified the binding factor behind its many aims and intentions, while recording its year of inception. What's more, in occult circles the number 93 possessed certain numerical values relating to the coming aeon of mankind. It therefore seemed highly appropriate for our own purposes!

Before the exact aims of the project were finalised, a decision had to be made on where exactly it should take place. We needed an area currently producing a high level of UFO-related events and paranormal activity - somewhere classed in ufology as a 'ufocal' or 'window area'. It would also have to constitute what might be described as a ceremonial or ritual landscape, *i.e.* an area containing a high number of Neolithic, Bronze Age and Iron Age monuments, earthworks and field systems in a good state of preservation. In addition to this it needed to be easily accessible to those taking part (most lived in or around London) and a place of interest to the various different mysteries communities, otherwise no one would be particularly interested in the project's results.

Only one location fitted all the criteria, and this was the picturesque downland around the towns of Devizes and Marlborough in Wiltshire, and in particular the agricultural landscape surrounding the small village of Alton Barnes where, since the arrival of its first crop formation during the summer of 1990, a number of unidentified aerial luminosities had been reported by residents and visitors alike.

As to when the project should take place, the vote was unanimous. Orgone 93 would conduct a two-week period of experimentation during the second half of July 1993, when the highest level of UFO-related activity could be expected in the area.

Having made the choice of time and location for Orgone 93, the next step was to completely familiarise ourselves with the area's archaeology, geology and history of anomalous events. Even though this would obviously take some months, it would allow a total perspective of the environment in which the project intended to carry out some of the most adventurous experiments ever conducted in the name of parapsychology.

8

The Wiltshire Mystery

From Christmas Day 1964 on until the end of the 1970s the quiet town of Warminster in Wiltshire symbolised the hopes and desires of those seeking an extra-terrestrial solution to the UFO enigma. It became the Mecca of ufology with the summits of local hills such as Cley Hill, Cradle Hill and Starr Hill becoming its open-air temples.

Over 15 years of weekly and often daily 'skywatches' produced literally hundreds of visual sightings of unidentified lightforms, many of which were eagerly catalogued in the popular hardbacks and pulp paperbacks penned by Warminster journalist Arthur Shuttlewood. I refer the reader to such classics as *The Warminster Mystery* (1967), *Warnings from Flying Friends* (1968) and *UFOs, Key to the New Age* (1971), all of which capture the ambience of this other-worldly relationship between a Wiltshire market town and alleged visitors from out of space.

Most common were reports of curious aerial lights of different colours seen traversing the night sky. There were, however, many other far stranger reports as well, such as the nocturnal sound of stones beating down on local house roofs, the appearance of strange alien entities and the discovery of unexplained ground markings. Even if the vast majority of cases quoted by Shuttlewood can be explained away, this still leaves a large number of reliable reports of mysterious lights seen in the night skies, in particular accounts by both residents and visitors alike of a luminosity known locally as the Warminster 'Thing' or the 'Amber Gambler'.

Upton Scudamore

Like so many other UFO investigators during the 1970s, I can vouch for the reality of the Warminster phenomenon through personal experience, for it was here that I witnessed a small globe of light one cold night in 1976. The date was Saturday, 9 October and with me was fellow UFO investigator Barry King, his two brothers and one of their friends. We had left London by car late on the Friday evening and had entered Warminster around two o'clock the next morning. Later that day we would visit Avebury, Silbury Hill and Stonehenge, among other places, but at the time all we wanted was to find a suitable location to spend the night.

Not knowing the town, we found ourselves leaving on the A350 Westbury road and, after a couple of miles of aimless driving, came upon a secluded farm track, opposite a lane leading to Upton Scudamore village. It looked ideal for our purposes so we dipped the headlights and took a chance.

It was an extremely foggy night, with visibility down to between 100 and 200 m. To our left were stark, silhouetted trees, while to the right were low trimmed hedges. Unexpectedly, we became aware of an intensely bright light emerging from the wall of fog across the fields to our right. It was the size, shape and colour of a motorcycle headlamp, and every few moments it would gently bob up and down as if the 'motorcyclist' was navigating the ploughed furrows. Gradually it drew nearer and nearer, but for some reason a sense of 'normality' overtook us, for aside from the occasional comment, or the passing glance, we merely ignored its presence and continued our search for a suitably-spooky place to park the car. In the end, we decided not to investigate the light as we assumed it was probably the farmer coming to throw us off his land, despite the late hour.

The track eventually curved to the right as it ascended a slight slope, giving us a clear view of the small sphere continuing its movement at right-angles to our earlier course. After passing across the track it appeared to rise slightly and was finally lost from view among the trees.

PLATE 13. Crop circle and UFO-related graffiti on the side of a concrete barn at the summit of Cradle Hill, Warminster, where mysterious lights and other strange occurrences have frequently been reported since the mid-1960s (author's pic).

After breakfast the next morning we checked the ploughed field for any signs of muddy motorcycle tracks. Not only were there none to be seen, but the low hedgerow along this stretch of trackway had no accessible spot where a vehicle might have left the field.

Cradle Hill

I thought no more of the matter until January the following year when I purchased the latest book by Arthur Shuttlewood, entitled *The Flying Saucerers*. I was intrigued to find it contained an account of just such a mysterious 'ghost light' being seen upon Cradle Hill - which, I later realised, is less than half a mile directly up hill from the position we saw our own light. Shuttlewood described it as a Will-o'-the-Wisp with the appearance of a 'circular lantern' or 'cycle headlight'.

Unlike us, Shuttlewood and his two colleagues had run towards the luminous ball, prompting it to change in shape from a sphere to an ovoid before jerking up and down like a yo-yo. It then shot upwards and weaved from side to side with the three observers in close pursuit. After chasing the poor light through copses, gates and hedgerows, it was finally lost from view in the direction of the army range at Imber. Its apparently intelligent actions and shape-shifting abilities led Shuttlewood to conclude that it was 'surely no earth contrivance' and undoubtedly not of 'human construction.'(1)

These two accounts are samples of the type of aerial luminosities generally witnessed in the Warminster area. The reference in each case to the light sources appearing like a 'circular lantern' or a 'motorcycle headlamp' is commonplace in historic cases of this nature. For instance, they were terms used regularly by witnesses of the recurring light phenomena seen near the Warwickshire village of Burton Dassett during the 1920s.(2) The way the light source appeared to evade capture in the second case also suggests it should be classed as an example of light consciousness.

Window Areas

Since the 1970s the focus of attention concerning UFO 'window areas', *i.e.* an area of increased UFO activity, has been predominantly northwards, yet the gradual rise of interest in the crop circle enigma during the 1980s has allowed some UFO communities to turn their attentions back towards the south of England, and in particular the two neighbouring counties of Hampshire and Wiltshire - an area delineating part of the old Saxon kingdom of Wessex.

By the summer of 1988 this new-found interest had begun to focus on the rich agricultural landscape making up the Kennett Valley, the Marlborough Downs and the Vale of Pewsey in Wiltshire - areas of rolling chalk downland and sloping field systems, bordered by Beckhampton to the west, Devizes to the south and Marlborough to the east. This region is also one of the most densely populated ceremonial landscapes in Britain, with Late Stone Age and Early Bronze Age stone and earthen monuments located on hill-top summits everywhere the eye turns. Of these, the most well-known ancient sites are Silbury Hill, Europe's largest man-made mound, the huge megalithic henge complex at Avebury and various impressive long barrows such as the example at West Kennett. Along the axis of the Pewsey Vale Downs is a wall of ancient defences consisting of Neolithic and Bronze Age hill-forts, earthen encampments, the Wansdyke ditch and other assorted earthworks, while at the northern end of the Kennett Valley lies Windmill Hill, an early Neolithic causewayed camp occupied around 3700 BC and containing later Bronze Age barrows.

The presence of so many prehistoric monuments in the proximity of crop circles and crop formations led many (including myself) to assume some kind of direct connection. It also led others to re-open the debate as to whether there was a connection not just between UFOs and crop circles, but also between UFOs and ancient sites. This last avenue had been explored during the 1960s by early ley hunting pioneers and earth mysteries researchers such as Philip Heselton, John Michell, Paul Screeton and Tony Wedd. Such a connection had also been suggested by Arthur Shuttlewood as well as by another Warminster man, David Holton, who as early as 1968 proposed that 'etheric' energies released from the soil - particularly from 'tumuli, plague pits, graveyards and battlefields' - were responsible for the production of the UFOs appearing around his home town. Unfortunately, as with Constable and many other believers in a terrestrial answer to UFOs, Holton's thought-provoking ideas were completely ignored by the UFO community.(3)

Mary Freeman

Speculation concerning the links between prehistoric monuments, crop circles and the UFO phenomenon took a dramatic turn during the late evening of 13 July 1988 when a woman named Mary Freeman experienced a significant UFO event just beyond the Avebury complex. It occurred as she was driving out of Avebury along the minor road that cuts through the Kennett Avenue of standing stones and joins the A4 Marlborough to Beckhampton road (SU110688). Unexpectedly, she became aware of a huge amber-coloured light in the base of the clouds. From its underside came a tube-like beam of bright white light that appeared to strike a position south of Silbury Hill. Mary later related how whilst the object was in view small objects, such as a packet of cigarettes and a notebook, inexplicably leapt into her lap.(4)

Mary Freeman had recently become acquainted with a local medium named Isabelle Kingston to whom she conveyed details of her UFO experience that same night. Two days later, a reporter from the *Marlborough Times* received a telephone call to say that a series of five crop circles, a so-called quintuplet set, had appeared in a field south of Silbury Hill. Within eight weeks of this first crop circle event at Beckhampton, no less than 51 other circles (many unfortunately of human manufacture) had appeared within seven miles of this location.

Isabelle Kingston had been waiting for a sign from the alleged extra-terrestrial intelligences with whom she believes she is in communication. They had told her to watch out for a sign that would demonstrate the importance of Silbury Hill both to her satisfaction and to that of the outside world. This prediction, whether real or not, has led some crop circle cynics to dismiss Mary Freeman's initial UFO sighting as either a figment of her imagination or the creation of Isabelle Kingston. Such an assumption need never have been made, for it seems that the Kennett Valley, east of Beckhampton, has long been associated with the appearance of mysterious aerial lightforms, as the following cases demonstrate.

Avebury, 1978

One excellent example of an unidentified aerial object seen in the vicinity of Avebury came to my attention in January 1983. It was conveyed to me by Heather Peak Garland, a mature Avebury resident who has lived in the village, amid the circles of tall standing stones, throughout her entire life. She vividly recalls how on the evening of 5 November 1978 she witnessed an unusual sphere of light near her home in the High Street. The time was approximately nine o'clock and Heather had just stepped into the cold, late autumn air to take her collie dog for a walk. As usual, she entered the grass enclosure containing the tall stones forming the henge's south-western perimeter (SU10126975) and continued her casual stroll. With the dog close behind, Heather followed the line of the huge earthen ditch before noticing something like a full moon floating through the air. On looking closely she saw that the 'moon' was, in fact, a soft, yellow-white orb of light, gently drifting towards her position from the direction of Beckhampton in the south-west.

The luminous globe was approximately 1 to 1.3 m in diameter and was said to have resembled a 'floating air balloon'; it was definitely *not* a firework. In silence, it moved gracefully over the tops of the trees and the earthen henge's perimeter wall, before turning on to a right-hand course above the standing stones. It then lost height and finally came to rest on the grass - a distance of no more than 100 m from where Heather stood open-mouthed. Here it simply extinguished like a light bulb.

As a countrywoman, Heather is completely familiar with the night sky, so she is unlikely to have made a mistake about what she viewed that night in 1978 - 10 years before the first quintuplet set of crop circles appeared opposite Silbury Hill on 15 July 1988.

Avebury Trusloe, 1981

In Chapter 4 I cited the story of the Yatton Keynell schoolmaster who told his pupils - including the young John Aubrey - that one evening in 1633 or 1634 he had chanced upon a 'fairy ring' on the downs where a number of fairies were going round and round, singing 'and making all maner of small odd noyses'. The downs 'beyond Chippenham' where the schoolmaster is said to have encountered this curious light display are likely to have been those beyond the village of Cherhill, between Calne and Beckhampton, which was also the scene of another mystifying episode in 1981.

The case in question features a respected antique clock repairer from Pewsey who, at his own request, wishes to be known only by his first name of Henry (full name and address on file). He was 26 at the time and the month was either July or August. On the evening concerned Henry had decided to take a brisk stroll across the Cherhill Downs, between Beckhampton and Cherhill, in the company of his friend Toby. Leaving their car in a tree-enclosed lay-by on the A4 Calne to Beckhampton road, opposite a dirt track bordering fields belonging to a farm in the nearby Avebury Trusloe, they climbed a path towards an ancient trackway known as the Old Bath Road (SU06926958) sometime between 18.00 and 19.00. A few minutes later, Henry caught sight of a small bright object emerging onto the northern ridge of Cherhill Down, some 200 to 300 m from their position. Out of the corner of his eye he then watched as it rapidly approached on a course coincident to the Old Bath Road, apparently hugging the contours of the land at a height of no more than 1 to 1.3 m off the ground. Within 50 m of where they stood, Henry realised the object was in fact a flattened, silver-white ellipse, or 'disc', some 15 to 20 cm in diameter. With this realisation, he called out to his friend just as the moving light vanished from sight. Unfortunately for Henry, Toby only saw a fleeting glimpse of the bright object, yet it was enough to confirm the objectivity of his friend's experience.

Henry, who might be described as a psychically-sensitive individual, feels that what he saw was a tangible object, some kind of 'hardware'. Furthermore, the sighting left him with the rather uncomfortable impression that the object had been 'conscious' of his presence and had 'deliberately' vanished the moment he went to alert his colleague. In other words, it was a conscious, thinking entity in its own right.

PLATE 14. The henge at Avebury, Wiltshire, where Heather Peak Garland saw an earth light in November 1978. Why are ancient sites so often associated with the appearance of mysterious aerial lights? (author's pic)

Lights in Folklore

Aside from the above examples, local folklore appears to preserve stories of strange lights seen in past ages within the Kennett Valley, many of them being recorded by writer Kathleen Wiltshire who spent most of her life collecting folk tales, ghost stories and legends across the county. For example, in her essential book *Ghosts and Legends of the Wiltshire Countryside*, published in 1985, she recounted the story of a man who had to pass through some woods near West Kennett on his way home from work each night. On one occasion he became inexplicably lost in the darkness and was almost at his wit's end when a strange light suddenly appeared before him and guided the poor fellow to safety.(5)

Elsewhere in the same book, Kathleen Wiltshire speaks of a phantom funeral procession that was witnessed on more than one occasion upon the Wansdyke close to Tan Hill, between the parishes of All Cannings and East Kennett.(6) It was said to have been heralded by the appearance of eerie glowing lanterns, which are clearly portrayed in the illustration of the procession that accompanies this account. Similar fairy processions are recorded in connection with at least one other section of the Wansdyke.(7)

Also of probable relevance to this debate are the various accounts of phantom black, or indeed white, dogs said to haunt certain locations - usually prehistoric barrows - on the downlands and moorlands surrounding the Kennett Valley. These are very often said to appear at night and to possess 'eyes of burning coals'(8) or 'eyes as big as saucers'(9), suggesting perhaps the recurrence of some kind of glowing light phenomenon at such places. One such story speaks of a ghostly white dog with red ears that enters the West Kennett long barrow with a 'priest' on the longest day, while another account speaks of a similar white dog with glowing eyes that 'peers from beneath' a megalithic dolmen known as the Devil's Den, close to the village of Fyfield.(10)

FIG 9. The Wansdyke's ghostly funeral procession witnessed on at least two occasions on Tan Hill, near All Cannings, Wiltshire, this century. Its approach is said to be heralded by spectral lamps of the sort depicted in this line drawing of the procession included in Anne Wiltshire's 1985 book *Ghosts and Legends of the Wiltshire Countryside.* Are these lanterns folk memories of earth light appearances like those seen in the area today? (pic: Anne Wiltshire/Colin Venton, Melksham)

Other strange stories included in Kathleen Wiltshire's extraordinary books may also help us to understand the paranormal potential of the Wiltshire environment. However, for the moment we must return to our investigation of the mysterious light phenomena that has accompanied the proliferation of crop circles in the Beckhampton, Devizes and Marlborough area since Mary Freeman's initial sighting back in July 1988.

Isabelle's Prediction

1989 saw the appearance of many more crop circles in both Hampshire and Wiltshire, so much so that the 1990 summer season was eagerly awaited by the growing crop circle community, which either consisted of ardent UFO believers or supporters of the meteorological-based solution to the mystery proposed by Terence Meaden.

As summer approached, Isabelle Kingston was asked to recommend a likely location for a nocturnal crop watch in the hope of capturing a circle being made by supernatural processes. Her psychic communicants indicated that the fields below the Pewsey Vale Downs, in the parishes of Alton Barnes and Alton Priors, should be watched as circles would appear here soon. For several nights the fields in question were observed from a vantage point close to Adam's Grave on Walker's Hill without any success. Having given up this location in favour of other more productive sites, no one noticed when, just two weeks later, on the night of 12 July 1990, Alton Barnes became host to the most dramatic crop formation to date. More extraordinary still, on that same night a second, virtually identical pictogram appeared below the western edge of Milk Hill, some 1.5 km from Adam's Grave.

Alton Barnes is 7 km south of Avebury and until this time was virtually unknown to the outside world. This all changed with the arrival of its extraordinary landscape pictogram - carved out in wheat at a location known as East Field. In the first month literally thousands of visitors flocked to see this wonder of our times. Aerial shots of the formation were broadcast world-wide, while the rock group Led Zeppelin even featured it on the front cover of an album. Luckily, the tenants of Alton Barnes Farm, David, Tim and Polly Carson allowed people to enter the field in question, charging a nominal fee of £1 for the privilege. This was by far the best policy as it regulated the flow of visitors and made entering the crop circles an adventure in its own right (the majority of the money earned from this venture went to a local church hall and a nearby school).

As might be expected, the pictogram produced a number of useful anecdotes including stories of altered states of consciousness, geomagnetic anomalies and the observation of mysterious lights seen in the vicinity of East Field. Of these, the best example involved Rachel Martineau, the wife of crop circle researcher John Martineau.

Rachel visited the pictogram in late July, and soon after her arrival around midday she began feeling unbearably hot and quickly experienced a thumping headache. She also felt a pulling in the pit of her stomach (the solar plexus region) at which point she said she looked up and saw what she later described as 'red flashing things', like streaks of lightning overhead. It was then that her eyes beheld a strange object hanging over the standing crop beyond the circle, some 3 to 6 m away from her position. Looking at it closely, she saw it was either doughnut or blood cell-shaped and around 1.3 to 2 m in

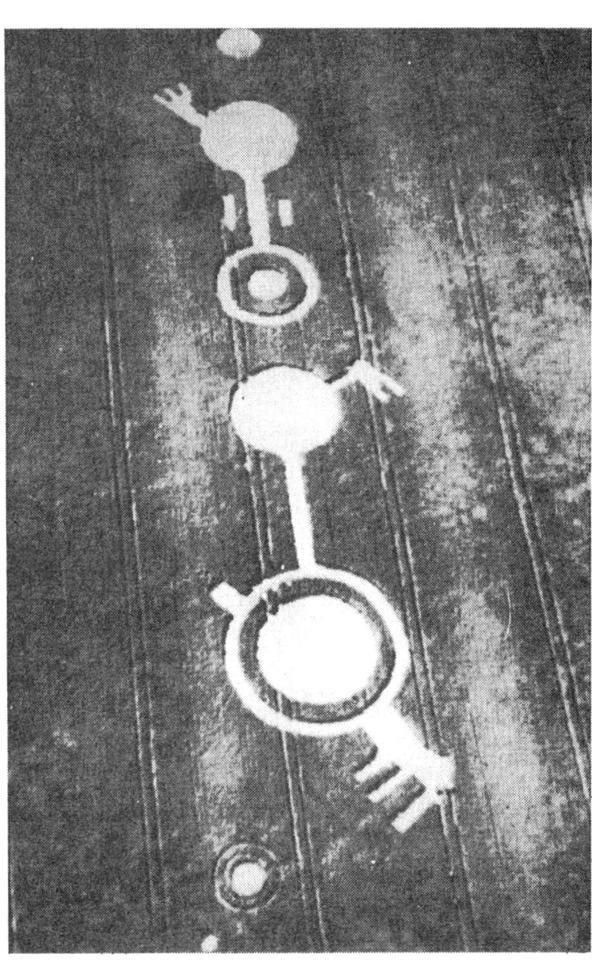

PLATE 15. The Alton Barnes crop formation of 12 July 1990. Its presence drew thousands of visitors and an assortment of curious events, including ill-effects, strange lights and altered states of consciousness. No one has as yet come forward to claim responsibility for its construction (pic: Busty Taylor).

diameter. It appeared to be composed of thousands of 'sparkly' lights, which she likened to 'glow-worms', each one writhing about in a huge 'living mass'. The mysterious object then grew in size and appeared to swing from side to side as it shifted position slightly. After some three to four minutes of observation, the glowing mass started diminishing as it receded backwards, gradually picking up speed until it was lost from view behind the tree-lined slope on the western edge of East Field (in the direction of Walker's Hill).

Even while the strange phenomenon was in sight, Rachel began to experience further adverse physiological and psychological effects. Aside from the intense headache which, she said, was 'all over' her skull, she felt 'shakily' sick and suffered acute dehydration. Upon leaving the formation she needed to consume large amounts of liquid before her body could regain a sense of stability. The other ill-effects wore off gradually, but on her return to Bristol later that day she apparently witnessed two glowing orbs, described as 'big orange beach-balls', that bounced along the road towards her and her husband, who was unfortunately unable to see them.

Rachel readily accepts this last incident was subjective in nature, and had probably been induced by her earlier encounter with the floating energy mass at Alton Barnes. This too may have had a partially subjective element to it, for she recalls that other people in the crop formation had not appeared to respond to the object's blatant presence. Over the years Rachel says she has visited a large number of crop formations, but has never since experienced anything quite like what she did in East Field that day in July 1990.

What I find most interesting about this case is that all the ill-effects reported by Rachel match exactly those reported by operators of cloudbusters during the 1950s. Intense dehydration, stomach problems in the solar plexus region, headaches and nausea are all symptoms linked with the presence of DOR (see Chapter 1).

Strange Illnesses

Rachel Martineau was not the only person to experience such ill-effects after visiting the Alton Barnes crop formation. Heather Park Garland - the witness to the floating globe back in 1978 - visited East Field with a friend and gained entry into the pictogram not long after its arrival. She marvelled at its majestic beauty before making the return journey to Avebury. That night she was afflicted by inexplicable flu symptoms that persisted for two whole days. She said it was like constant 'sea-sickness', adding that she had been frequently forced to steady herself during bouts of uncharacteristic giddiness.

Linking the unexpected illness with her visit to the crop formation, Heather contacted her friend and asked him if he was well. He said he was, but that a neighbour who had visited the crop formation that same afternoon was also now suffering from acute nausea. Heather nonchalantly offered me this information during a visit to her home in 1992. She had no idea that others had reported similar illnesses following visits to crop circles. Her story I take very seriously for, as I mentioned earlier in connection with her UFO sighting, she is a countrywoman in tune with every aspect of rural life and is not liable to flights of fancy.

Anecdotes such as these are meaningless on their own, but the more you ask around, the more they can be found. When strong patterns begin to emerge it becomes difficult to simply dismiss them out of hand. Both Rachel Martineau and Heather Peak Garland suffered physiological effects after visiting the huge Alton Barnes crop formation, yet neither knew anything of the other's experiences.

Some crop circle researchers believe the 1990 East Field pictogram was constructed by a group of youths calling themselves the United Bureau of Investigation (UBI), an accusation they have vehemently denied to the author on many occasions.(11) Regardless of who, or what, constructed this unique landscape design, its sheer presence had a profound, zen-like effect on many of its visitors. Why then did its presence cause such adverse physiological effects, similar in every respect to those experienced by visitors to the Barbury Castle formation the following summer? What was it that made these particular examples of clandestine land art so special? Obviously far more knowledge of the area was needed before questions such as these could be answered to any sort of reasonable satisfaction.

9

Euphoria

Among the visitors to Alton Barnes during the long hot summer of 1990 was 30-year-old Stephen Alexander and his wife Janice, from Gosport in Hampshire. Fired by a casual interest in the crop circle enigma the couple visited the two-week old pictogram in East Field during the afternoon of Thursday, 26 July.

In the blazing heat, they surveyed the circles and corridors of fallen wheat before deciding to make the long climb to the top of Walker's Hill, where the earthen remains of the Adam's Grave Neolithic long barrow are to be found. Arriving at the summit, they continued along the ridge of the Pewsey Vale Downs until they reached the westerly edge of Milk Hill. In a wheat field below them to the south-west they could see the crop formation that had appeared the same night as the example carved in East Field.

The Milk Hill Video

Having descended the hill-slope to an estimated height of 250 m (SU09856387), Alexander used his video recorder to film both the pictogram and the surrounding landscape. It was at this point that the camera eye picked out something unusual in the wheat field directly below, at an estimated distance of 300 m from their elevated position (SU09556397). On the resulting video, Janice is heard to ask her husband 'What's that?' as he begins to film what might just turn out to be the best evidence yet for the existence of earth light phenomena.

The film shows a small white light source moving among the heads of the corn at an estimated speed of between 6.5 and 11 km per hour. Its characteristics are erratic - sometimes its pace is constant, yet at other times it appears to flicker or reflect sunlight before slowing down and blinking out of sight. It then reappears, remains motionless, before repeating the same process in a random fashion as it passes through the crop, possibly even cutting a swathe on occasions. In a matter of some 30 seconds it completes an entire circle, having crossed tractor tram-lines at right angles and having followed their course at other times, all without any possible indication as to the light's origin.

Pulsing, flashing, flickering and shining are all words appropriate to describe this anomalous light which appears to bear a diameter of no more than 20 to 25 cm. To say the phenomenon seen is spherical would be inappropriate as it seems to have been more a contained light burst than a solid object.

After completing its wide circle the phenomenon meanders it way across the wheat field towards the west, with Alexander continuing to film all the time. The viewer then hears the couple going through various possible explanations for this inexplicable light source. A bird, a balloon, even tinfoil are all suggested as they attempt to rationalise this bizarre sighting. On two occasions the ambling light comes to a stand-still for so long that the video recorder is switched off. It is only switched back on when the object decides to continue its erratic journey.

The phenomenon then continues its westerly course at an increased speed of something between 15 and 30 km per hour, with the light source appearing to retain its original magnitude. At a distance of some 850 m from the observers, the flickering, pulsating light is seen to leave the wheat field, cross over a trackway and enter a second field (SU087639) - this one in the process of being ploughed out by a tractor. The viewer then sees the farm vehicle reaching the end of the field and turning 180 degrees, before coming to a halt just as the light source passes some 75 to 100 m north of its position.

'The tractor's stopped,' Janice is heard to say.

PLATE 16. The view from the western edge of Milk Hill across to Clifford's Hill and Rybury Camp. In the field below, Stephen Alexander and his wife Janice witnessed and videoed a pulsating white light that was also seen by tractor driver Leon Besant (author's pic).

At this point the light is much more difficult to study, although it still appears to be at a height of no more than 1 to 1.3 m off the ground. Retaining its faster speed, the diminishing light then leaves this second field and quickly crosses a third and final field before it begins to ascend the lower slopes of Clifford's Hill, some 1.25 km from the observers. It then ascends the fairly steep hill without any effort whatsoever, although by now its pulsations are becoming less obvious and less frequent. The phenomenon is then seen climbing the earthen henge that marks the boundary of Rybury Camp (SU08406395), the Neolithic encampment crowning the summit of Clifford's Hill, 1.5 km from Milk Hill.

Momentarily, the light is then seen pulsating rapidly as it makes for the prehistoric camp's curved, central plateau. Here is it lost from view for the last time, yet whilst Alexander continues filming his wife is heard to say 'It's gone... No, it's not - it's going up in the air.' The camera lifts upwards but certainly to the camera eye the apparent vertical ascent of the faint light cannot be seen, a fact audibly confirmed by Alexander who says: 'Can't see it on here.'

Janice claims she could actually see the light rising into the sky, emitting intermittent flashes before it was finally lost from view. Even at this late stage in the sighting, Alexander was still attempting to rationalise the light source by suggesting it might be a balloon. Quite rightly, Janice is heard to point out that if it was a balloon then it would have risen into the air long before now. The video recording ceases at this point, ending the observation. In total the light was filmed for five whole minutes, although during this period it is to be remembered that the video recorder was switched off twice during times of inactivity. This might account for another minute or so, giving a total time of six minutes observation. From the moment it began its westerly course to the point it was last seen on the encampment's central plateau, the light had covered a distance of around 1100 m in just 106 seconds - implying an average ground speed of 10.37 m per second.

The observed phenomenon is not that impressive. More important is the movements it makes and the length of time it is in view, all the while keeping a regular distance from the ground and continuing its chosen course without interruption from either the wind or any physical obstacles. Its mannerisms might almost be described as purposeful, yet not intelligent. From my own repeated viewing of the resulting video I would strongly suggest that the anomaly is not a mistaken balloon, nor a bird or a piece of tin foil reflecting the sunlight; all these explanations are inadequate to explain the full qualities of the light source under question.

The Tractor Driver

In the months that followed Stephen Alexander presented his video evidence to various crop circle researchers in the hope that they might find it worthy of further investigation. It was Colin Andrews, co-author of the best-selling book *Circular Evidence*, who finally tracked down the farm worker that was driving the tractor when the light source had sped past en route to Rybury Camp.

His name is Leon Besant and, at the time, he was employed by Cannings Cross Farm, situated on the Alton Barnes to Devizes road. In an interview given on video to German magazine editor Michael Hesemann, he said he had been 'rolling' the field on the date in question when he turned to see 'a silver glinting light' that was 'flying around in the corn, on top of the corn'. He then spoke of stopping the tractor to gaze at the light source as it entered the next field. On returning to the farm that evening he told his work colleagues of the sighting, and as a consequence was ribbed constantly for a whole week. Having had enough, Besant dropped the subject completely until Andrews came along six months later and showed him Stephen Alexander's extraordinary film. Apparently, his work colleagues then changed their tunes, implying that they had always believed him! I have been able to confirm this entire story with the farm, although it seems that Besant has now left his position as a farm employee and is currently living with his family in Trowbridge, Wiltshire.

The Phenomenon Observed

With reference to his interview with Hesemann, Besant seems to have found it difficult to describe the phenomenon he observed. After saying it was about the 'size of a beach ball', he hesitates before going on to say that it was 'like glint(ing), like silver, like tin foil-you blaze in the sun, like blazing light... (like) a constant glint. I couldn't make it out. I don't know what it was.'

Despite this uncertainty Hesemann had no hesitation in deciding that the object observed was 'a small metallic reflecting disc', like the 'unmanned probes, (or) telemeter discs' of UFO lore. This somewhat subjective conclusion was partly based on the apparent findings of video 'experts' at Nippon Television who had supposedly studied the film at some length. According to Colin Andrews in an interview given to camera for Hesemann, the Japanese had apparently concluded that the object recorded on video is: '... less than six inches in diameter, (and) reflecting, most efficiently... white, bright light - sunlight - off of its surface.' Andrews goes on to say that: 'the object is moving through the heads of the plants, parting the wheat as it moves around... and indeed appears to be showing quite an interest in the crop circles that were already there then. It is a most important piece of film.'

All this may be so, but according to Stephen Alexander, what Andrews failed to mention was that the Japanese video experts also found that the glinting object appeared to have no material substance other than as a pure source of light. In other words, in between flashes the object *ceased to exist*.

Furthermore, a belief that the phenomenon observed was in fact reflecting light, and not producing light, is based on the preconceived assumption that it was a metallic object of extra-terrestrial origin. Such an interpretation is completely misleading, for Alexander simply referred to what he saw as 'a shining object', while the farm worker could only describe it as 'like blazing light... a constant glint.' Indeed, in a letter to me dated Thursday, 18 February 1993 Alexander, having recently read *The Circlemakers*, asked whether the object he saw could have been an orgone-related energy form. Such a supposition seems very likely indeed. Irregular pulsations penetrating the visible ranges of the electromagnetic spectrum could conceivably result in the type of phenomenon videoed by Stephen Alexander in July 1990. It might also explain the object's apparent lack of substance in between its irregular light pulsations.

Rybury Camp

The earth light's interest in the Rybury prehistoric hill-fort, situated beyond the summit of Clifford's Hill, also poses further questions. Earthworks such as Rybury might well act as efficient orgone accumulators producing gross displacements in the localised energy continuum. Should this assumption prove correct, then by employing Reich's reversed entropy theory (*i.e.* that orgone flows from lower to higher concentrations) it suggests that any unmanifest energy form, if seen as a condensed mass of orgone, would be attracted like a magnet to locations such as Rybury Camp. On reaching its destination the bioform would either be absorbed into the existing energy matrix present at the site or deflected - like an object approaching a planet's orbit - onto a new energy beacon elsewhere in the landscape. Should the nature of the light source remain unexplained, then its course from the base of Milk Hill to Rybury should be plotted in the greatest detail to see whether its movements corresponded to unseen geophysical features such as the geomagnetic field, sub-surface rock strata and underground water deposits.

Lights at Lockeridge

Not 12 hours after Stephen Alexander filmed his dramatic video sequence on Milk Hill, 30-year-old lorry driver Gary Williamson began his weekly run from Alton Barnes to London.(1) On reaching the outskirts of Lockeridge (SU14506730) around 04.00, he noticed a group of three intense white lights out of the open window on the driver's side. They formed a horizontal line and appeared to be positioned above the northerly end of West Woods, some 400 m south-east of the road (SU15256725). Williamson stared at them in awe, knowing that, despite having lived in nearby Alton Barnes all his life, he had never seen anything quite like this before.

The three lights were estimated to have been around 8 m apart and about 25 m above the tops of the trees. No noise was heard, and after some three to four minutes the lorry entered a built-up area and the lights were lost from view, having remained stationary throughout the sighting. Williamson is certain they were not lights from army helicopters, early morning stars or military flares.

Later that morning a huge pictogram, similar in design to those that had already appeared at Alton Barnes and Stanton St Bernard on Thursday, 12 July, was discovered in a wheat field positioned between the long barrows of East and West Kennett. It was aligned directly on nearby Silbury Hill, and in similar with the two previous examples, the identity of its manufacturers remain a mystery.

A Euphoric Summer

The interest Alton Barnes attracted during the 1990 summer season prompted circles enthusiasts to return again the following year. By mid June 1991 there were skywatchers on many local vantage points, such as the summit of Adam's Grave, the edge of East Field and the car-park beneath the Knap Hill Neolithic encampment. Night after night the entire area bubbled with nocturnal activity. There was a euphoric feel in the air, almost as if something of immense importance was about to happen. It was becoming clear that the large area collectively referred to as 'Alton Barnes' - which in fact takes in the parishes of Alton Barnes, Alton Priors, Lockeridge, Stanton St Bernard and Woodborough - was fast emerging as a major centre for supernatural activity and a new Mecca for UFO activity and extra-terrestrial contact akin to Warminster in its heyday.

The John Holman Video

Among those eagerly awaiting some form of aerial activity in the skies above Alton Barnes was John Holman, convener of the Yorkshire and Humberside branch of the Centre for Crop Circle Studies (CCCS). Overnight on Saturday/Sunday, 22/23 June 1991, Holman, his son Robin and another observer named Leigh Winstone were walking along the Ridgeway path as it follows the length of Overton Hill towards the A4 road, close to the Neolithic post-hole monument known as the Sanctuary. The time was just before 23.24 and the sky was clear. The ground was slightly damp and the weather was turning distinctly cold with a slight wind blowing up. Looking towards the southern horizon,

PLATE 17. Chris Trubridge's photographic anomaly caught above the Adam's Grave long barrow, near Alton Barnes, Wiltshire, in July 1991. Nothing was seen at the time. In the colour original the circular blob graduates inwards from yellow, through to orange, red and then finally black (pic: Chris Trubridge).

Holman noticed a 'flickering red glow' said to have resembled a 'diffuse' aerial 'fire' above what he later realised was Milk Hill. It was not distinct, he said, but relatively diffuse, and after just a few seconds it simply vanished from view. The aerial glow then reappeared in the same position and subsequently repeated this sequence on several occasions.

Reaching a suitably elevated vantage point (SU11916898), the group of three came to a halt and scanned the skies as Holman noticed a star-like point of white light appear above the position of the diffuse glow. It then winked out almost immediately only to be replaced by the appearance of a bright orange 'sphere' of light. Alerting the others, Robin Holman aimed the video camera and filmed the unidentified object hanging low over the southern horizon.

The bright orange object was filmed for only six seconds before it simply blinked out of sight and was not seen again. The resulting video shows a bright oval-shaped light, orange in appearance, with a three-quarters moon seen clearly above it. Still photographs show the colour differential between the anomalous object and the moon, which appears to have been about 50% larger in size. According to Holman's estimates, the orange light was positioned low over Milk Hill some 5 km away, close to where Stephen Alexander had filmed his own anomalous light only 11 months earlier.

Leigh Winstone had been able to observe the strange object through 8 x 25 binoculars and believes he detected two dark patches on the light sphere. He later spoke of its colour as being yellow, even though both the video evidence and Holman's witness testimony suggests it was orange. The object's size was estimated at around 23 m in diameter, while freeze-framing the video reveals that it blinked out of view across just two frames, showing it disappeared in approximately 2/25th of a second. Pains-Wessex Schermuly of Salisbury, the company who supply parachute flares to the military for use on Salisbury Plain, viewed the video in July 1991 and, after due consideration, were confident that 'this event was *not* a Pains-Wessex flare [their emphasis]'.(2)

The 'Cloud' Extra

Aside from the strange photographic anomalies already mentioned in Chapter 3, a further, much more baffling example from the summer of 1991 was presented to me by artist and photographer Rod Dickinson. With a casual interest in the crop circle mystery, he had visited Alton Barnes on or around Friday, 9 August. During the early afternoon he viewed the huge 'key' formation to be seen that summer on rising ground due south of East Field, located in the neighbouring parish of Alton Priors (SU115621).

The weather was pleasant and sunny and Dickinson used a new roll of Kodak Gold 100 colour film to record details of the picturesque design's long corridor and swirled circles of fallen crop. He took 12 separate shots of different angles, each frame being 'bracketed' two or three times to ensure at least one suitable exposure at the end of the day. With the sun behind him, he used fast shutter speeds of between 1/125 and 1/500 of a second.

Dickinson says no more was thought of the matter until the film was developed and he noticed something highly unusual in the resulting prints. Frame Nos 6, 7 and 8 all show the same thing - a landscape shot looking north-east along the corridor towards a large swathed circle of fallen crop. Beyond this is open countryside with the easterly edge of the Pewsey Vale Downs visible on the horizon. In the sky are a distinctive array of scattered clouds climbing towards the top of the picture. This feature, along with the movements of the three visitors at the eastern end of the formation, makes it clear that

PLATE 18. The first of the three shots taken by artist, circlemaker and photographer Rod Dickinson of the crop formation that appeared in July 1991 at Alton Priors, Wiltshire. Note the position of the three visitors against the second and third shots in the sequence, taken no more than one minute apart (pic: Rod Dickinson).

PLATES 19 & 20. The second and third shots in the sequence taken by Rod Dickinson of the crop formation at Alton Priors in July 1991. The second frame appears to contain an extra 'cloud'-like object that was not seen when the picture was taken. Could you explain this anomaly? (pics: Rod Dickinson)

these bracketed shots were taken within a minute or so of each other, *i.e.* just long enough for the photographer to wind on the film and set up the camera again.

With these facts in mind, Dickinson has pointed out that in the second of the three shots - and in this one alone - there is an extra 'cloud', yet a cloud with peculiar characteristics. Positioned centrally in the frame, it is shaped like a slightly curved cigar and hangs in the open sky at a 45-degree angle above the Pewsey Vale Downs. Its 'underside' bears a distinct dark area, suggestive of curvature and shadow, and beneath this is a diffuse grey mass similar in consistency to a thick cloud. It differs from the surrounding clouds in that it has a much greater density, shape and colour, and its angle is contradictory to those around it. Furthermore, there is not even a hint of this 'cloud' on either of the frames taken before or after this one - nor does it appear in the frame that follows, No 9, which shows a slightly different perspective of the same view. Dickinson saw nothing at all when the photographs were being taken.

Certainly, the picture does not show any kind of common meteorological occurrence or any recognisable photographic artefact. These opinions are also shared by photographic expert Gary Bond, who studied each picture using Adobe Photoshop software and a Solitaire 8TD imaging camera. No obvious trickery appears to have been involved, although hardware similar to that used by Bond to study the pictures could *easily* create such effects, so this possibility cannot be ruled out.

Rod Dickinson informs me that shortly after his visit to Alton Barnes in August 1991 he began rolling his own - in other words he became a nocturnal land artist creating his own crop circles, initially in his own home county of Dorset and then during the 1992 and 1993 summer season in the crop circle capital of Wiltshire. In spite of his clandestine antics, Dickinson claims the cloud extra is a genuine photographic anomaly given to me in good faith for research purposes. I can only accept his word until such times as I know otherwise.

Light Beams and Crop Circles

Just as controversial was the alleged sighting around 03.00 on Friday, 12 July 1991 of a luminous column seen to descend onto Knap Hill by night watchers encamped on the western edge of East Field. The vertical shaft apparently emanated from the base of a dark cloud, and on making contact with the rounded cap of the Neolithic camp, it was said to have broken into rays of light which dissipated into the base of the hill. 11 km away at Hackpen Hill, unaccountable animal disturbances were reported around the very same time while a local teacher was said to have witnessed an unidentified aerial .luminosity. The next morning a fresh crop formation was discovered at the base of Hackpen Hill, directly beneath the watchful eye of a white horse hill-figure.

Hackpen Hill was once a traditional haunt of the fairy folk, as may be seen from a curious tale recorded in the seventeenth-century by antiquarian John Aubrey. He was told by an elderly gentleman named Ambrose Browne of 'a hinde [that] goeing upon Hack-pin with corne' that was led a merry dance by the fairies to the village, for it was firmly believed these infernal spirits inhabited the location. It was also said that 'a shepherd of Winterbourne Basset' went upon Hackpen Hill and reported that the ground did open up and he was taken into 'strange places' underground, where music was being played on viols and lutes. Nothing good came of the shepherd's visit to the fairy mound, for it was said that 'never any afterwards enjoy themselves.'(3)

More intriguing were reports during the evening of Tuesday, 16 July 1991 of strange lights being seen in the sky above Silbury Hill, near Beckhampton. From a nearby layby crop watcher Brian Grist and two of his colleagues saw a series of strange, pulsating lights from midnight onwards. By one o'clock they had become so unnerved by their aerial observations that the watch was abandoned. Other lights were apparently reported by independent witnesses, and the warden of Barbury Castle, an Iron Age encampment some 8 km north-east of Beckhampton, was said to have heard a colossal roar and a low humming sound at 03.30 that morning. At first light the huge, now famous crop formation with a triangular ground-plan was found etched in wheat below the northern slopes of the Iron Age encampment. Dr Terence Meaden visited the site and, after due consideration, pronounced it man-made. In spite of this assessment, it was here that Oliver Stummer, Adrian Dexter and my partner Debbie Benstead all fell ill after entering inside the formation. To this day those responsible for this remarkable mandala

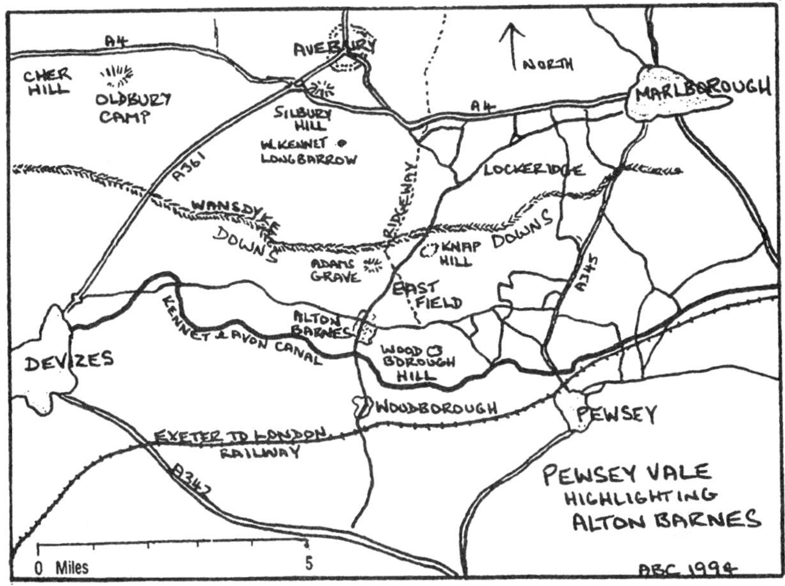

FIG 10. Map showing Alton Barnes and the Vale of Pewsey, scene of so many UFO sightings since 1990.

in corn have never come forward, so the mystery continues.(4)

Hoaxing Revelations

The euphoria instilled by the events reported during the summer of 1991 was effectively shattered in early September by the revelations in the *Today* newspaper concerning the circle-making exploits of Southampton sexagenarians Doug Bower and Dave Chorley.

Despite this disconcerting situation, which had been inevitable for some time, it seemed clear that reports of unidentified aerial phenomena in and around Alton Barnes, Beckhampton, Devizes, and even Warminster, had been on the increase since the arrival of the first great pictogram in July 1990. Yet as we knew from Heather Peak Garland's earth light encounter of November 1978, Henry's sighting of a small luminosity on the Cherhill Downs in 1981, and other accounts of mysterious lights seemingly preserved in local folklore, exotic phenomena of this sort were not new to the area.

What *was* new were the crop formations and the sudden influx of people brandishing cameras and video recorders at the ready. So, was this the reason for the sudden increase in reported UFO sightings? Or were there other, more complex answers? In the wake of the recent hoaxing revelations from the likes of Bower and Chorley, 1992 was going to prove crucial to our understanding of the inexplicable luminosities appearing with ever growing frequency in the rich agricultural landscape around Alton Barnes.

10

Nocturnal Lightshows

The Centre for the Search for Extra Terrestrial Intelligence (CSETI) is an American organisation that believes in the existence of alien hardware visiting the earth from elsewhere in the Galaxy. Motivated by one Steven M. Greer MD, CSETI's intentions are to pave the way for open contact and liaison between mankind and extra-terrestrial cultures. Part of their programme is to prepare fully-paid-up clients for an eventual space flight on board an alien vehicle.

Steven Greer has added an extra category to the vocabulary of ufology by introducing what he terms a close encounter of the *fifth* kind. This, he suggests, is where some form of conscious, two-way communication is achieved between us and the aliens out there. To achieve these aims Greer and a trained group of suitable individuals will go wherever there has been a dramatic increase in UFO sighting reports. This could be anywhere in the world, and once on site they will set up high-powered lasers and attempt to mentally communicate with unseen alien intelligences. With an open mind, the chosen group will then use co-ordinated meditation to reach out with their thoughts and attempt to 'vector' 'structured spacecraft' into the area.

Despite the outlandish nature of CSETIs' alien roadshow, Steven Greer is no fool. He is a shrewd businessman and an able campaigner for the ET cause. Furthermore, his group meditations at locations throughout the world have resulted in some truly remarkable sightings that can in no way be simply ignored or put down to the imaginations of those taking part. At places such as Gulf Breeze, near Pensacola on the south Florida coast, as well as in the vicinity of the extinct volcano and sacred mountain of Popocatepetl in Mexico, Greer and his associates have achieved visual sightings of a number of unidentified objects following the employment of creative visualisation and meditational practices.

Project Starlight

Steven Greer was introduced to the British crop circle scene by author Colin Andrews, and following a series of communications between the two men it was decided that a CSETI team should position itself in Alton Barnes for a period of 10 days during July 1992 under the name Project Starlight. Through the cooperation of farmers David, Tim and Polly Carson, Greer was able to secure the lofty heights of Woodborough Hill for his other-worldly exploits. Capped by a dark clump of tall spindly trees, this prominent local landmark lies 1.2 km south-east of Alton Barnes. From its grass summit clear views can be gained across East Field to Adam's Grave, Knap Hill and Golden Ball Hill (its enigmatic name inspired by floral associations, not mysterious happenings). To the south stretches the Vale of Pewsey and beyond that the rising downs marking the commencement of Salisbury Plain.

Sceptics might argue that Greer had laid himself wide open to hoaxing activities by allowing supporters such as Colin Andrews to publicly announce that a UFO event of great significance would take place in Wiltshire during the last week in July, an obvious reference to the assumed success the CSETI team would achieve during their stay at Alton Barnes. Despite such reservations, from Tuesday, 21 July through to Thursday, 30 July, it was a common sight to see CSETI's three lasers projecting beams onto low clouds in the night skies above Alton Barnes.

The group's concerted efforts attracted a number of British participants and as their first week progressed there were three claimed sightings of mysterious lights seen moving about the area. The last of these, a prominent orange glow witnessed around 00.45 on Friday, 24 July was videoed by Reg Presley, the singer with rock group The

PLATE 21. Woodborough Hill, the site chosen by Steven Greer and his CSETI team for Project Starlight in July 1992. Its names may well derive from the Saxon god Woden (author's pic).

Troggs, who had joined the CSETI team for the evening. Apparently, the object remained in view for approximately five minutes and a helicopter was seen to approach just before it veered off in a northerly direction. Having spoken to Presley and CSETI member Ed Sherwood on this matter, it seems this object was unlike anything they had ever seen before and was definitely *not* an army flare. Further strange lights were also witnessed after this orange light had disappeared.

During the evening of the Friday/Saturday, 24/25 July, Greer and his colleagues - which included Colin Andrews - apparently witnessed 'a spinning structure, with blue-green, red and white lights, that were spinning around its periphery'. At the time they were inside a crop formation directly below Woodborough Hill. The sighting prompted Greer to state: 'It was at this point that I was convinced that we had a "lock on" with a structured spacecraft of non-terrestrial origin. I believe that it is the same craft which later visited us on the night of July 26th...', a reference to what took place just 48 hours later.(1)

Like a Christmas Tree

Despite the witnessing of further amber-orange lights during the night of the 24/25 July, and again on the following night, it is the incident on the night of Sunday/Monday, 26/27 July that is of the greatest interest to our understanding of the Alton Barnes phenomenon.

Following various minor sightings of strange lights, the rain began to fall heavily, bringing with it an encroaching fog and forcing the assembled group to abandon their activities, which were being conducted from a crop formation situated at the base of Woodborough Hill. The time was shortly after midnight and, on returning to their vehicles, those still remaining decided to park up in a small lay-by on the concrete track running between the Carsons' residence at Old Manor, Alton Barnes, and the Woodborough barns, located on the southern side of the hill. In one car sat Steven Greer and his friend Dr. Sandra Small, and in the other vehicle, parked behind, were art teacher Chris Mansell and his girlfriend Annick Nevejan, who had both arrived only an hour beforehand. The rest of the party had decided to call it a day and return to their respective beds or guest houses.

It was at this point that Chris Mansell noticed an unidentified mass of lights in a south-westerly direction.(2) They appeared out of nowhere and as his eyes adjusted to the sight he could make out that it was in fact 'a long strip of coloured lights which appeared to be revolving from left to right changing colour from red through white to green'. Mansell quickly calculated it to be no more than 33 m off the ground and around 600 m south of their position, somewhere in the vicinity of the Woodborough canal bridge (SU11376070) which straddles the Kennet and Avon Canal. Instantly, Mansell leapt out of his car and in the pouring rain rushed across to alert Greer and Dr Small, both of whom promptly emerged into the open air.

All four watched as the revolving mass of lights moved slowly and quite silently in a south-westerly direction for some three to five minutes. As it did so, the strange object lifted away from the skyline giving Mansell, 'the first complete indication... that it was a free floating thing, and that it wasn't on the ground.' As it continued its course, Greer held out his hand and quickly estimated that the object's comparative size was 40 mm at arm's length.

It was then that the curious aerial phenomenon gently flipped onto its side to reveal a further sequence of lights in red, white and blue-green, with three further orange lights centrally positioned in a triangular configuration. This new sight prompted Greer to remark: 'My God, it looks like a Christmas tree.' According to Mansell, this is indeed what it looked like - the lights of a Christmas tree, although those on the 'under-belly' were evidently much dimmer than those on the side.

Using binoculars, Mansell relayed details of what he could see as Greer switched on an audio cassette. Ironically, CSETI's photographic and video equipment had been taken back to the guest house by another member of the party, so no hard evidence was gained of the event.

The slow-moving object was then seen to temporarily pass behind a clump of trees before recommencing its journey. Shortly afterwards one of the three orange lights making the triangular configuration detached itself from the main group and drifted into the fog before rejoining the central mass. Similarly, a red light was then seen to detach itself from the cluster of lights and move to the east before returning to its source. Three further red lights then detached themselves and moved off to the west before rejoining the main formation.

All of the party later reported feeling 'an electrical charge, a tingling' sensation as the phenomenon was in sight, and there was also talk of a compass belonging to Steven Greer going haywire.

The CSETI director then decided he would try to communicate with the light cluster, so he quickly grabbed a high-powered flashlight from his car. Using this he signalled twice to the object. To everyone's amazement, a light at the apex of the formation flashed twice. Further attempts prompted similar imitative responses, confirming to them that the first reply had not simply been a coincidence.

The whole episode lasted for between 10 and 15 minutes and totally shook up all those present, including Greer himself. Soon afterwards the CSETI co-ordinator began referring to this event as the 'near landing' of a 'structured metallic craft'. To quote from his report entitled *Close Encounters of the 5th Kind: Contact in Southern England, July 1992* prepared following his visit to England: 'The significance of this event can hardly be overstated. This event constitutes a close range, close encounter of the 5th kind with a clear interactive component. It appears that the CSETI team was successful in vectoring in a spaceship to its location...'(3)

Light Clusters

Such were the conclusions drawn by Steven Greer. However, Chris Mansell is a little more open minded on the matter. In an interview with the author on Sunday, 1 August 1993 he admitted that: 'In my kind of limited opinion at the time the only way I could see of making those lights... (was) some kind of structure for them to be mounted upon... Having said that, and having seen many accounts of things that have happened since.... I wouldn't be surprised if somebody came to me and said it was a collection of energies, as opposed to a metal, hammered-together craft. In fact, I would rather it was something as subtle as a collection of energies than a hammered together craft...'(4)

Mansell is comfortable with the idea that what he witnessed was a complex arrangement of lights clustered together by some kind of unknown force field. Such light clusters were seen in the skies over Hessdalen in Norway between 1982 and 1984. Here they were described as a 'kind of light that looked like many light-sources "tied together", usually with different colours. It looked as if they had a fixed distance to each other all the time. These lights could be down in the valley, but were mostly seen at the same height as the nearest mountain.'(5) Does this not adequately describe what Greer, Mansell *et al* saw that night in July 1992?

In addition to this, one light cluster seen over Hessdalen was even described as appearing like a set of Christmas tree lights,(6) similar words to those used by Greer to describe the phenomenon he observed at Woodborough in July 1992. For him to subsequently refer to this aerial light display as a 'structured metallic spacecraft' is simply absurd.(7)

By the late summer of 1992, aerial luminosities had taken over as the most important phenomena occurring in the Alton Barnes landscape, and disco lights or not, nothing was going to prevent people from coming forward to report some of the most extraordinary sightings ever recorded in this part of rural England.

11

Tawsmead Stirs

The CSETI team continued to witness unusual aerial phenomena - generally balls of orange light - until their departure for the United States on Friday, 31 July 1992. Yet by their own admission, none of these sightings were as spectacular as the 'near landing' during the early hours of Monday, 27 July. Very few believed the strange accounts emanating from the Greer camp, despite the large number of witnesses involved, and like it or not, their controversial activities appeared to be paying dividends for other people watching the skies above Alton Barnes as well.

John and Julie Wakefield

One independent sighting from this period came from John Wakefield, 25, and his partner (now his wife) Julie, 26, who were part of a group of four dedicated crop circle enthusiasts who took up temporary residence in Alton Barnes at the beginning of the 1992 summer season. Having befriended Tim and Polly Carson, the tenants of Alton Barnes farm, they were asked to monitor any nocturnal activities occurring on the estate and, when the crop formations did occur, co-ordinate visitors wishing to enter East Field. John Wakefield and his friend Nick Riley were instantly recognisable by their long, dreadlocked hair, for which reason the group were often referred to as 'the Dreads' or 'the Hippies'. However, they are astute, intelligent and sincere young people with a healthy attitude towards both the UFO and crop circle enigma.

At around 22.15 on Tuesday, 28 July 1992, John and Julie Wakefield were seated in their Landrover, positioned on the bend of a small lane at West Stowell, between Alton Barnes and Wilcot (SU13746208), watching the southern horizon. Suddenly they noticed an intense orange glow above Wilcot Withy Bed, a wooded area beyond the Kennet and Avon Canal, some 1.4 km south-south-west of their position.(1)

Clambering onto the roof of the vehicle to obtain a better view, the couple quickly identified the light as a large orange orb slowly bobbing about in the low sky. Its size, from the height of the trees, was estimated to be around 11.5 m diameter.

The fiery light source then appeared to come to a halt and remain stationary for an estimated five minutes. It was at this point in the sighting that something occurred that might seem difficult to swallow, yet, if correct, could prove crucial to our understanding of light consciousness.

Watching the otherworldly object, Wakefield mentally asked it a simple question. With the words 'Are you what I think you are?', his mind returned to another UFO sighting he, Julie, Nick Riley and the fourth member of the party, Chris Hitchen, had experienced on their very first journey from Manchester to Alton Barnes one night in late July 1990.(2) It had occurred on a country road near Wyre Piddle in Worcestershire and had begun when the exterior lights of Wakefield's old Landrover had flickered before finally fading completely. At the same time he and Nick Riley, who was seated in the passenger seat, noticed that the vehicle's dashboard lights had also dimmed out.

As the vehicle was diesel powered, the engine was unaffected by this electrical failure, but without headlights Wakefield could not see a thing so he pulled the Landrover over and came to a halt. Curiously, the electrics then returned, and readying themselves to set off again, John noticed a mysterious moving light some 1 km in front of them. It possessed an electric-blue core with a fluorescent white corona, and its comparative size was said to have been as big as a full moon. Without faltering, it made an enormous loop in the open sky and disappeared. Their excited yells alerted Julie and Chris Hitchen who had been asleep, at which point the light source reappeared and made the same circular manoeuvre before vanishing a second time, on this occasion with all four of them as witnesses.

Nothing further occurred, so the journey continued. None of the group had seen anything quite like this light before and it is fair to say that its appearance had a profound effect on all of them, especially as they were on their way to see the Alton Barnes crop pictogram. Following two summers of visiting crop circles in Wiltshire, all four decided to leave Manchester and settle in Alton Barnes on a semi-permanent basis (where all four still live to this day).

Now, in 1992, John and Julie Wakefield were being confronted by a mysterious aerial light that, like the one seen in Worcestershire two years earlier, challenged their conceptions of mundane reality. Were the two objects linked? Were they one in the same? He had to know.

Immediately after Wakefield posed his loaded question, the stationary orange ball was seen to disgorge 'a small orange thing' estimated to have been approximately 2.5 m in diameter. It moved away from the main luminosity on a right-hand, westerly course and proceeded to make a wide clockwise loop before returning to rejoin the main light source. As it commenced this long manoeuvre, the couple heard the dogs and cattle at nearby Draycot Farm and West Stowell Farm making a dreadful din. Until this point they had made no noise at all, leading them to associate this sudden aural commotion with not only to the proximity of the aerial light display, but also to the unexpected appearance of the small satellite object. All this was seen by John Wakefield as an outright response to his earlier question.

On completion of its circuit, the tiny orange ball was enveloped by the main object, shortly after which it began to descend slowly into the trees, illuminating the upper branches as it was gradually lost from sight.

Climbing into the Landrover, the couple continued to watch the trees for some five minutes before the same or a similar object appeared again above the very same woods. As before it bobbed up and down for a few seconds before settling into a stationary position. Stepping outside, they watched closely as the orange ball hung motionless for a further three minutes, before it once again descended out of sight.

Afterwards the couple moved slowly along the Wilcot road towards Alton Barnes. Wanting to tell someone about the sighting, they stopped off at the farm's silage pit, situated on the southern edge of East Field (SU11706225). They had hoped to catch John Langrish who, with his wife and young child, had been parked up here for a week or so. Unfortunately, Langrish and his family were not around, so they returned to their vehicle, ready to continue the journey.

It was then that they noticed the same or a similar object, this time above Tawsmead Copse (SU126618), an extensive wooded area some 700 m south-east of them and 1.5 km north-west of Wilcot Withy Bed, the scene of their two previous sightings. They watched in astonishment as the fiery globe rose out of the trees, illuminating the tree-tops as it climbed silently into the air. Reaching a height of around 10 to 30 m above the tree-tops, the spherical light moved off in a westerly direction towards Alton Barnes. It then came to an abrupt halt and simply hung in the sky glistening brightly.

Then something unexpected occurred. An army helicopter approached from the north, to be quickly joined by two others, one from the east and another from the west. As they approached, the fiery light began a slow southerly course, blinking out as the first helicopter neared it. All three helicopters then encircled the area where the ball had last been seen, before seemingly losing interest and flying out of sight.

The whole episode had taken place between 22.15 and 22.35, giving a total of 20 minutes in all. There had been no sound at all from any of the orange globes, and left firmly in the minds of John and Julie Wakefield was the belief that the mysterious aerial phenomenon they had observed on three occasions that night was the product of some non-human intelligence, a conclusion drawn from the blatant response to Wakefield's pertinent question.

Having listened to the couple retell this story on more than one occasion, and having grown to know them as friends, I can find no grounds to doubt what they saw. They recall the night sensibly and soberly, and openly question the nature of what they witnessed. Their observations bears some striking similarities to the CSETI sighting of two nights earlier, especially the apparent psycho-interactive response from the phenomenon and the manner in which the small satellite detached itself before rejoining the main object.

The couple later spoke to a Mr Bryant of Draycot Manor Cottages, close to where the light had appeared, and he confirmed that between 22.00 and 22.30 on the night concerned his dogs had uncharacteristically barked incessantly for some minutes, and that he could not account for their actions.

Many other people later came forward to verify many aspects of these sightings, including some of those taking part in the CSETI operations at the base of Woodborough Hill, south-west of Tawsmead Copse. This included Ed Sherwood who not only witnessed the final orange ball from a crop circle in South Field, Alton Priors, but can confirm its interception by the army helicopters. Indeed, he claims that army helicopters appeared to take more than a passing interest in the lights observed during the CSETI operations, and states that he saw them approach aerial luminosities on no less than *six* separate occasions that summer.

John and Julie Wakefield are more than certain that what they witnessed on three occasions, and at two separate locations that night, was not an illuminated balloon of some kind as some sceptics have suggested.(3) If so, then I believe this case to be an important example of light consciousness which served to convince the witnesses of the phenomenon's very real ability to respond to their thoughts in an interactive manner. The sightings also appear to include tentative evidence of animal agitation among both domestic and farm animals, a situation that might well have recurred just three nights later.

The Trench Video

The excitement thrown up by the more or less nightly light displays in the Alton Barnes area during the presence of the CSETI operations did not lessen after their departure on Friday, 31 July.

The early hours of Saturday, 1 August saw another sighting of a bright orange ball in the vicinity of Tawsmead Copse. The witnesses this time were Steve and Gillian Trench, and their 14-year-old son Steven, of East Ham - all members of the London UFO Studies Group who had recently begun to take an active interest in the crop circle mystery. Reports of new crop circles had drawn the couple to Alton Barnes in the hope that they might catch a glimpse of an aerial anomaly of some kind.

In an interview with the author on Tuesday, 10 November 1992, Steve and Gillian Trench spoke of how they had arrived at East Field around 02.10 BST, following an evening in nearby Beckhampton and a late night skywatch on Adam's Grave. By a strange coincidence, that evening they had met and spoken separately to Stephen Alexander and John Holman - both of whom had previously produced videos of unidentified light sources in the Alton Barnes area.

Reaching their car, parked in a layby on an elevated section of road north-west of East Field, they climbed the hill and parked just beyond a set of temporary traffic lights (SU11506366). As they stepped out of their vehicle, the family noticed a bright pin-point of white light motionless above Tawsmead Copse, some 2 km south-south-east of their position. It was seen to move from left to right, but was quickly eclipsed by the sight of a much larger orange sphere of light that appeared directly above the trees. According to the witnesses, it was pulsating rapidly and appeared to be spinning on its vertical axis. At first the Trench family thought the smaller white light had transformed into the much larger fiery globe, but then they noticed the tiny white light vanishing out of sight in an easterly direction. Already Gillian had reached for the video camera - an AKAI PVS-C40F camcorder - and was filming the event, catching the last moments of the two objects together as Steve Trench began studying the light display through 10 x 50 binoculars. He described the main object as 'a clear sphere with many lights inside spinning, turning and rotating very fast'(4) - words similar to those used by Rachel Martineau to explain the object she had seen hanging above the East Field crop formation in July 1990.

The orange orb was clearly below the level of the distant horizon, eliminating the possibility of it being a distant object, and, as with the Wakefield's sightings of three nights before, the light gave the appearance of dancing up and down and zig-zagging from side to side. For a total of 11 minutes the object was filmed by Gillian who hand-held the camera for the first eight minutes before placing it on a tripod for the remainder of the sighting.

Five minutes into filming, the object is seen to dip out of sight, only to re-emerge in a new position. Although the luminosity does not increase its overall brightness during the sighting, it does fade from view on several occasions. Its final act is to rise steeply before apparently plunging behind the tree-line around a mile or so beyond Tawsmead Copse. It did not re-appear.

Bird Reaction?

The only possible strange effect the Trench family noted in connection with the proximity of the orange ball was the commotion made by the birds of the neighbourhood about half-way through the sighting. It was so noticeable that their son openly mentioned this unexpected cacophony, which apparently lasted for a few minutes before dying away completely (this incident is not recorded on video). At no other time, either before, during or after the sighting had any other bird song been registered by them. Whether this commotion was linked with the appearance of the light source is impossible to say, although it is to be remembered that John and Julie Wakefield had reported a similar, uncharacteristic animal reaction during their own sightings. It is also perhaps important to remember that birds react to such natural phenomena as full-moon eclipses, believing them to be the first stirrings of dawn.

Aerial Flashes

Following the departure of the fiery globe, Steve, Gillian and Steven Trench moved on to East Field where they found John and Julie Wakefield, Nick Riley and other individuals seated inside their caravan.(5) The youths had not seen anything themselves as they had been facing in the opposite direction. The Trench family stayed with the group until around 05.30, during which time they apparently witnessed several electric-blue flashes on both the eastern and western horizons. They did not appear to be storm related and the sky was described as mostly clear throughout the rest of the night. Although the Wakefields confirm these flashes occurred, they did not place any special importance on them as they occur so often (see Chapter 26).

Assessment of the Trench Video

Having examined the Trench family's video at some length, I can find no reason to doubt the couple's description of the observation or to conclude that what they saw was a gas-filled balloon. The camera recorded the incident on a 10X zoom lens set on a low, four lux light level. From what I can see, the pulsating light source diminishes in brightness during the recording, often leaving only an audible commentary for several seconds at a time. The light is seen by the viewer to jig about, both up and down and sideways. Much of this can be put down to camera-shake, yet even allowing for this, it does appear as if the object made some quite rapid movements on occasions. At one point the recorder's auto-focus can be heard winding as if attempting to follow the light's sudden advance towards the position of the camera. Throughout the recording, the couple pass sober comments on what they can see with the naked eye. Quotes such as 'It's so hard to keep track of it', and 'It's going up' or 'It's gone into the trees' add to its authenticity.

Another Tawsmead Video

The Trench video was the second reported film of mysterious lights taken at Alton Barnes that summer. Around 23.50 on Saturday, 9 May circles enthusiast Kerry Blower had stood with friends by the silage pit on the edge of East Field (SU11706225) and filmed two or more pulsating light sources hanging above Tawsmead Copse.

Copies of the film clearly show a double-sectioned light source in white and orange. This is quickly joined by a second, virtually identical light that appears slightly above and to the right of the first example. The two lights are then seen together before the first fades out quickly, leaving the second object to continue its display. After some seconds it increases in magnitude until it becomes a much larger, ill-defined light mass. At one point the upper dome appears to possess a dark spot that gives the impression that the whole thing is rotating on its vertical axis. Towards the end of the video the remaining light seems to disappear and reappear some three times, an effect suggesting that it was momentarily passing behind shifting clouds.

No obvious explanation comes to mind to explain Kerry Blower's short video sequence. However, all that can be said with any certainty is that this particular episode so early on in the season, acted as a clear portent of the events that were to plague Tawsmead Copse for the rest of the summer.

Despite the existence of these inexplicable video sequences, such efforts can only be treated as anecdotal evidence as no frames of reference can be discerned in the darkness, not even any stars. This means that from a sceptic's point of view, they could have been taken anywhere at any time. Only good daylight video evidence, such as that obtained by Stephen Alexander in July 1990, can ever really help our cause.

12

Bouncing Balls

Among the cases that cannot be put down to illuminated balloons are two that involve white globes of light seen by lone witnesses on the roads outside Alton Barnes during the late summer of 1992. The first of these took place between Alton Barnes and Honey Street during the night of Sunday, 23 August 1992. The single witness to this event was crop circle researcher Paul Vigay who had just left other skywatchers on East Field, having decided to call it a day and make the drive back to his home in Southsea, Hampshire.(1) The time was around 23.30, and as he navigated the dark, winding bends he became aware of a bright light source on the road ahead which he immediately took to be a car approaching from the opposite direction (SU10386100).

As he drew nearer to the position of the glow, he saw it was in fact a single white headlamp moving towards him in the centre of the road. It appeared to be travelling at around 50-60 mph and Vigay assumed it to be a motorcycle headlight. Despite this rational assumption, he realised the light was travelling at a height of no more than 45 cm above the road surface.

Fearing he was about to collide with a road vehicle, Vigay slowed down to allow it to pass. Yet at a distance of no more than 3 to 6 m in front of him, instead of swerving to go around his car, the light suddenly veered upwards and hurtled over the roof at a height of around 5 m off the ground. As it passed overhead the engine stalled, even though the headlights were unaffected. Vigay also noticed that the object appeared to be emitting light from all angles, confirming that it was some kind of three-dimensional light source, even though the glow was too bright to allow him to discern its exact appearance.

Five to 10 seconds later, Vigay regained his composure and wound down the window to look behind him. He could see no sign of the object. Concluding he had witnessed some kind of inexplicable light phenomenon, Vigay restarted the car engine and returned to Alton Barnes. No one else had reported seeing anything unusual that night.

Whether or not the car engine was stalled through some kind of electrical interference from the light is impossible to say. Vigay does stress, however, that his vehicle had never stalled before when slowing to a halt, and certainly there are many, many instances of car-stops reported in association with close proximity UFO sightings from all around the world.

Judith Daw

This second example of a small globe of light seen at near ground level, comes from a woman named Judith Daw who lives in the village of All Cannings, 3 km east of Alton Barnes. She is the wife of a local farmer and possesses no particular interest in either crop circles or UFOs, making her two separate observations of unusual lights that much more significant to our study. The first occurred sometime between the hours of 01.00 and 02.00 one morning in July or August 1992.(2)

At the time, Judith was driving home to All Cannings after a night out in Trowbridge. With her in the car was her husband and a family friend, both of whom had fallen asleep on the journey. As they passed between the villages of Allington and Stanton St Bernard, just 4 km out of Alton Barnes, Judith took a corner and saw Cannings Cross Farm looming up on the right-hand side. It is owned by her husband, although the family also own a house at All Cannings, which was where they were heading on this occasion.

With the farm still some 350 m away, Judith saw a bright light source emerge onto the road in front of her. It had come from the proximity of the farmyard and was described as resembling a 'motor-cycle headlight' (a term we have met with before on several occasions). As Judith slowed down the car she watched in puzzlement as the light ascended the uphill track towards a disused chalk pit. It moved with some speed and seemed to be bobbing up and down gently (another familiar attribute of this phenomenon). Judith finally lost sight of the light as it disappeared behind dense undergrowth.

On reaching the position the light had crossed the road, Judith glanced up the track but saw nothing, and by the time she had comprehended her predicament, she realised that both her husband and the friend were still asleep. She also knew that the track in question is difficult to navigate and is rarely used at night by farm vehicles.

Judith emphasised that what she observed moved 'too fast' for it to have been a vehicle of some sort, especially as it had virtually 'bounced' across the road before entering the track. It was points such as these that had convinced her that she had witnessed some kind of unusual phenomenon.

One interesting aspect of this case is the direction in which the light was seen to take. To the left of the track, just metres away from where it was last observed, is the site of an important Iron Age settlement dating back to *c.* 500 BC. It is unique to the area and is believed by archaeologists to have belonged to the same culture that built the Glastonbury lake villages in the neighbouring county of Somerset. Further along the track, some 750 m past the chalk pit, is the summit of Clifford's Hill, beyond which is Rybury Camp, the point of attraction for the pulsing light source videoed by Stephen Alexander two years earlier. This now meant that we had two quite independent cases of mysterious light sources being drawn towards this prehistoric hill-top location, each from different directions. Interestingly enough, the highest point of Tan Hill, which lies due north of Clifford's Hill, was once known as the Devil's Church. Devil-associated place-names usually derive their origin from either prominent topographical features or repeated accounts of supernatural occurrences, almost certainly the appearance of mysterious lights. The prominence marking the location of the Devil's Church is not an obvious landmark, so could a supernatural connotation be applicable here? One possible clue is

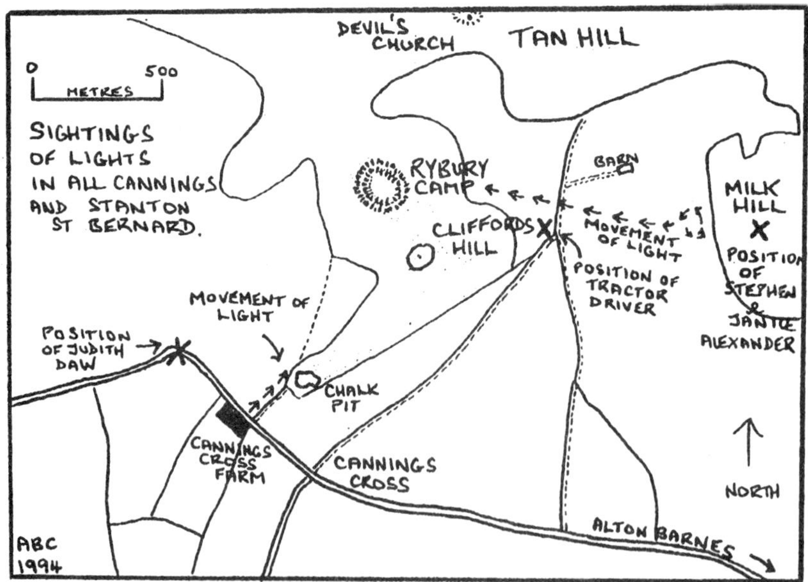

FIG 11. Map showing Cannings Cross Farm and nearby Rybury Camp on Clifford's Hill. The positions of the mysterious phenomenon videoed by Stephen Alexander in July 1991 and seen on the Devizes to Alton Barnes road by farmer's wife Judith Daw in 1992 are marked.

PLATE 22. The base of Clifford's Hill, near Cannings Cross Farm, All Cannings, where the mysterious ball of white light was seen by local woman Judith Daw in 1992 (author's pic).

the story recorded by Kathleen Wiltshire of the spectral funeral procession heralded by glowing lanterns and said to have been seen passing along the Wansdyke at the point where crosses Tan Hill. Did this account indeed preserve some folk memory of very real light phenomena observed in this area during past ages?

Kitty Candlestick

At the north end of All Cannings village lies All Cannings Bridge which straddles the Kennet & Avon Canal, opened in 1809. Before the end of the eighteenth century this area of land was known either as Cannings Marsh or Candle Marsh. This last variation is curious, for it is not simply a corruption of the Cannings Marsh place-name which is known to have existed in this form since the eleventh century when the Anglo-Saxon Chronicle records a Danish raid taking place here.

Candle prefixes to place-names are generally interpreted by ethnologists as locations, usually fields, where Candlemas celebrations occurred on or around February 2nd each year. Yet in the case of Candle Marsh, this cannot have been the case for obvious reasons. Furthermore, there is no evidence of Candlemas festivities ever having taking place in All Cannings. This therefore leads us to postulate a possible connection between the place-name Candle Marsh and the appearance of *Ignis Fatuus*, the 'foolish flame' seen generally in marshy areas and known also as the Corpse Candle. Of even more interest is the knowledge that in Wiltshire ghost lights were once known by the name Kitty Candlestick, while in the neighbouring county of Hampshire they were known as Kitty-in-the-Candlestick.(3)

Strengthening the case for a connection between Candle Marsh and the appearance of earth lights is the fact that the small moving light witnessed on the Devizes road by Judith Daw followed a field boundary that begins at the canal, close to where the

FIG 12. A Will-o'-the-Wisp light seen here above a swamp. Such phenomena may well account for the Candle Marsh place-name near All Cannings. In Wiltshire mysterious lights were always known by the name Kitty Candlestick.

old Candle Marsh was once situated, and terminates approximately 800 m away at Cannings Cross Farm, the location of Judith's night-time sighting.

The Water Meadows

Neither was this Judith's only sighting in 1992. That autumn she witnessed two bright white lights conducting unusual manoeuvres above trees at a locality known as the Water Meadows, 900 m due east of her home at All Cannings (SU08426200).

Unable to sleep one morning between the hours of 03.00 and 04.00, Judith sat up in bed and noticed the lights out of the window. She watched them for an estimated 15 minutes as they moved back and forth at great speed before rapidly coming to a halt and quivering in the air. These movements were then repeated several times before she decided to close her eyes and go back to sleep.

Judith is sure the lights were not army Gazelle helicopters which regularly use the area for low level manoeuvres. She also points out that the noise of their engines can easily be heard in the still of the night. On this occasion, however, she heard no noise at all.

Water meadows are thin strips of agricultural land divided by irrigation ditches adjoining local streams. Those at All Cannings have not been used for farming purposes for many years, although the parallel running strips of land are still to be seen. In past centuries this area would have been extremely marshy and may once have formed part of Cannings Marsh. A connection with marsh-related light phenomena is therefore possible in this case as well.

Why Alton Barnes?

Presented in the last five chapters are various examples of mysterious lights being seen in and around Alton Barnes since the appearance of the first crop formation in East Field during the summer of 1990. We also know that mysterious lights had been seen in the area during the 1980s, the 1970s, and possibly even further back than this if local folklore is to be believed.

If we accept both the witness testimonies and the video sequences as evidence of some kind of hitherto unidentified phenomenon present in the Alton Barnes area, then are we to assume that it has always been present and that the sudden influx of visitors has simply brought these sporadic sightings to the public's attention? Perhaps the whole of Britain experiences a similar level of paranormal activity, yet because of the lack of available witnesses much of it goes unreported and unrecorded. This *is* possible, although I doubt it very much as this would tend to suggest that any highly-populated area would produce an increased number of UFO sightings, and this is simply not the case. London, for instance, with its many open parks and expanses of water, produces a very low sighting average.

Why then was Alton Barnes producing an above average quota of UFO sightings? Was it simply the influx of visitors into the area, or were there other more complex reasons? It was time to take an in-depth look at the local geology to see whether this could throw any light on the matter.

13

A Geological Perspective

There appears to be an intrinsic link between what we know today as the UFO phenomenon and localised geological factors, including the presence of sub-surface water, rock faulting and mineral ores, subtle shifts and disturbances in the geomagnetic field and the occurrence of earthquakes and tremors.

If these findings are correct, then a basic knowledge of local geology is essential to our understanding of locations where UFO events tend to occur. As an example of the rewards such research can offer, when Paul Devereux conducted an extensive survey of the light phenomena being reported in and around the Wiltshire town of Warminster, he discovered that the only two surface faults in the whole of the area - the Warminster fault and Longleat fault - both skirt the southern base of Cley Hill, one of the principal locations noted for its UFO sightings. Furthermore, the Warminster fault continues eastwards beneath both the town and Cradle Hill, where mysterious lights also appeared with frequency during the 1960 and 1970s.(1) As a consequence, the sheer existence of these parallel-running faults helps us understand the apparent proliferation of paranormal and UFO-related events in the Warminster area.

Findings such as this made it essential for Orgone 93 to conduct a careful geological study of the Vale of Pewsey.(2)

The Valley Basin

The low-lying basin making up the Pewsey Vale is bordered to the north by the east-west axis of the Marlborough Downs, known locally as the Pewsey Vale Downs. Further downland defines its border to the south, and beyond this is Salisbury Plain, used extensively for military purposes. The valley itself is almost entirely composed of sedimentary rocks deposited by the sea during the Cretaceous period, somewhere between 93 and 65 million years ago. Of these the three principal rock strata are, in order of age and depth (or superposition), Gault Clay, Upper Greensand, chalk and various types of chalk rock. Covering the surface layers in many areas, particularly in the basin itself, are deposits of more recent mud and clay.

As a whole, the rolling downland of southern England is considered to have been formed around 20 million years ago by enormous buckling caused through intense tectonic pressure. As the land bulged and folded upwards it created what are known as anticlines. Exposed strata pushed upwards by these convex anticlines eventually became so stretched that they fractured. The resulting cracks and hollows made the upper surfaces of the anticlines vulnerable to harsh weather and erosion, meaning that the exposed chalk layers gradually disintegrated until each striation was transformed into a vast concave basin. This is how the Pewsey Vale was formed.

A considerable amount of the Pewsey valley basin now consists of Upper Greensand which, as the name suggests, is a form of green sandstone - its colour coming from a mineral with very slight radio-active properties known as glauconite. Into this lower basin there also appeared deposits of alluvium, gravel and hillwash, all being either washed down from the upper levels of the downs or left behind by receding glaciers during the various ice ages.

Where the arable land rises to reach the base of the undulating Pewsey Vale Downs there are layers of Lower Chalk varying in depth from between a 0.5 to 3 km. As the downlands continue to rise, the Lower Chalk gives way to a layer of Melbourn Rock before reaching the much higher Middle Chalk levels. Some of these slopes display white horse hill-figures such as those of Alton Barnes, Pewsey and Westbury. Less frequently the Middle Chalk is superseded by bands, or outliers (*i.e.* island-like rock outcrops) of

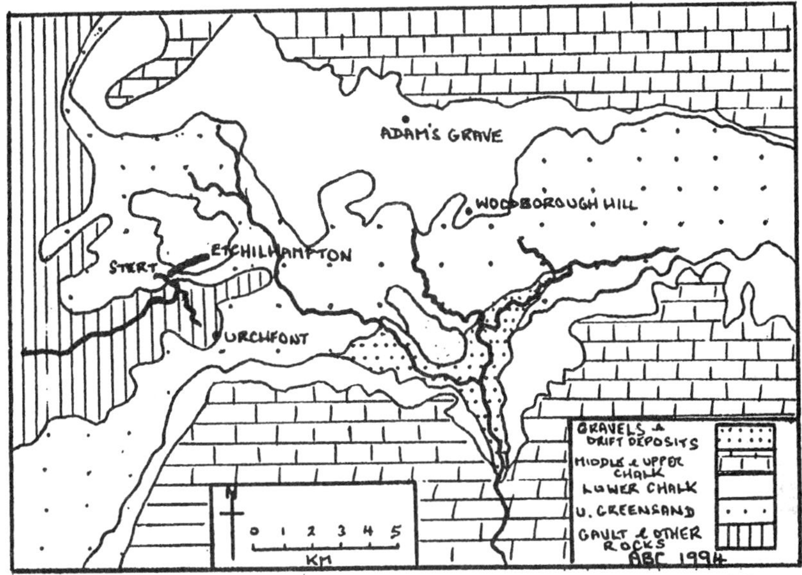

FIG 13. Geological maps of the Pewsey Vale. Above, an aerial view, showing the Etchilhampton-Stert fault, and, below, a cross-section showing the apex of the anti-cline.

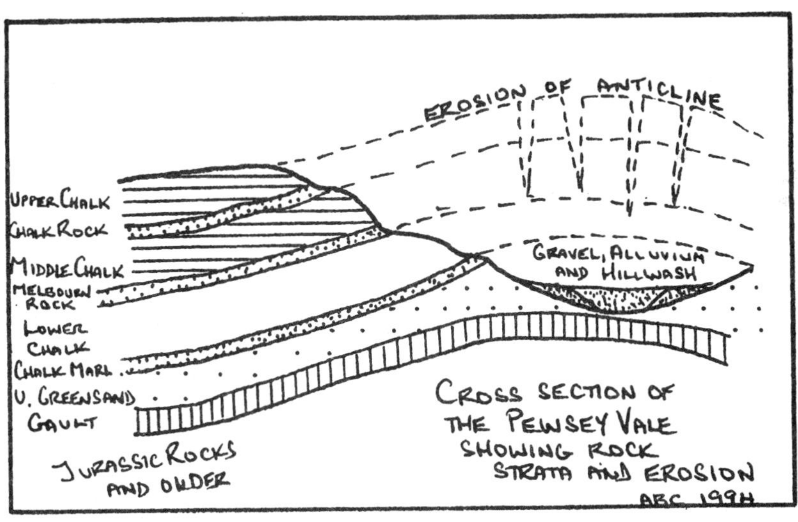

Upper Chalk. If these are over 300 m in height they are sometimes capped with summits of clay-with-flints. Many of these outliers later became sites of prehistoric occupation either in the Neolithic or Bronze Age periods. This includes the forts or encampments at Oliver's Castle near Devizes, Knap Hill and Golden Ball Hill above Alton Barnes, Martinsell

Hill near Pewsey and Rybury Camp on Clifford's Hill. The undulating escarpments and rolling character of the downlands are due mainly to the permanence of the Melbourn Rock and Middle Chalk which erode much more slowly than the softer marls and clays.

Alton Barnes, along with Stanton St Bernard to its west, sits on Lower Chalk. Yet intruding into the eastern side of Alton Barnes, mostly in the adjoining parish of Alton Priors, is a narrow strip of Upper Greensand which starts in Woodborough and traces the southerly course of a stream that rises amid a series of natural springs located in Church Meadow, close to the 12th-century church of All Saints, Alton Priors.

Wiltshire Faults

Faults occur where rock formations have been displaced either vertically and/or horizontally, owing principally to tectonic stress in past ages (some are, of course, still active today). They can either be exposed at ground level (surface faulting) or they may exist underground (sub-surface faulting). The amount of displacement is known as the throw, and the greater the throw the larger the fault. The only way to detect sub-surface faults is through inconsistencies recorded in the depths and placement of different rock strata, something usually only detected when either wells or bore-holes are dug. Yet even when this occurs, only an approximation of the extent of the fault can be determined unless more bore holes are made further along the suspected axis of the fault. On geological maps faults are shown as thick blue lines placed generally between the boundaries of different rock strata that would not border each other under normal geological circumstances.

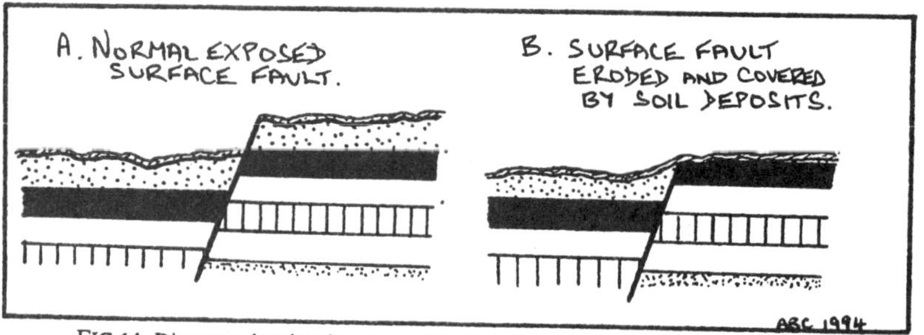

FIG 14. Diagrams showing the nature of faulting. Left, after tectonic stress has caused a noticeable throw and, right, after weather and erosion has covered its presence.

In south-west Wiltshire there is one major fault. This is the Mere fault which starts in the village of West Knoyle and continues due west, passing south of Mere and Zeals before entering the neighbouring county of Somerset. The Mere fault's vast 185 m down-throw on its northern side brings together outcrops of Upper and Middle Chalk in line with much older (and usually much deeper) Corallian Beds and Kimmeridge Clay of the Jurassic age.

Towards the end of the nineteenth century, the area of Mere Down, north-east of the town of Mere, was traditionally associated with curious lightforms viewed in terms of the marsh-related Kitty Candlestick. In one account a 'light as big as [a] plate' was seen going to-and-fro across the downs 'like a flash of lightning', according to an issue of *Notes & Queries* dated 4 April 1891.(3) Mere Down is not close to the axis of the Mere fault; however, its proximity does indicate a possible connection with the appearance of the mysterious lights. Warminster is just 13 km north-north-east of Mere.

There are a number of smaller faults in the county. The local geological map shows one with a south-west trend in deep Jurassic beds at Rowde, some 3.5 km west-north-west of Devizes. There is another between the villages of Quemerford and Bromham, south of Calne, while a third example exists in the Middle Chalk at West Lavington, 8 km south of Devizes. It runs roughly parallel to the A360 road for about 2 km and its presence is identified by a 30 m vertical displacement in the rock faces on either side of the main road.

Between West Lavington and Alton Barnes there is just one fault. It bears a south-westerly axis and runs for approximately 2 km between the villages of Stert and Etchilhampton, which lies 6 km south-west of Alton Barnes. The Stert fault only has a small throw and is detectable on the surface. Other than these examples the Pewsey Vale, and Wiltshire in general, is relatively free of faulting and suffers very few earthquakes and tremors.

Also worthy of mention are the so-called listric faults, caused principally by landslips, and the much smaller faults noted by geologists in exposed chalk cliffs along the Marlborough Downs. One of these has been observed in railway cuttings north-east of Whitefield in the Og Valley,(4) while another is recorded at Poulton Down, south of Rabley Wood.(5) Landslip-linked faulting can almost certainly be found along the Pewsey Vale Downs, particularly where quarrying has upset the natural erosion of the hill-side.

Warminster Geology

By way of comparison, the geology of Warminster - 25 km south-west of Alton Barnes - is very similar to that of the Pewsey Vale, with chalk on the north-east of the town and Upper Greensand to the south-east. Cley Hill, where two surface faults have been noted by Paul Devereux, is made up of Lower Chalk with outlying bands of Middle and Upper Chalk on its summit. It is therefore very similar to the many outlying summits of the Pewsey Vale Downs.

Aside from the presence of faulting at Mere and Warminster, there seems to be no obvious correlations between surface or sub-surface faults and the manifestation of unusual light phenomena in the Wiltshire landscape. The areas bordered by the Quemerford or West Lavington faults, for instance, are not exactly noted for their UFO activity, suggesting that if local geology *does* play a role in the production of anomalous lights in the Pewsey Vale, then other localised factors were also involved. One suggestion could be the tiny landslip-linked faults. If they are to be found on the Pewsey Vale Downs, then it is conceivable that they could produce low level stresses and strains in local rock strata, but surely not enough to catalyse the production of aerial luminosities.

Wiltshire Hydrology

Looking at the rock strata of the Marlborough Downs, the Kennett Valley and the Vale of Pewsey, the only obvious factor that could play some role in the production of lightforms is the ability of the Upper Greensand and chalk beds to act as highly efficient aquifers, carrying underground springs and streams, due to the impermeable Gault Clay directly beneath them. Aquifers or water-bearing rocks can occur in shallow valley basins or on hill-slopes where the water becomes trapped by much later clay deposits. Most of the valley's rainfall sinks into the ground and flows slowly towards its low-lying basin which at its lowest level is known as the Pewsey Lake.

The appearance of UFOs in association with bodies of surface and sub-surface water has been noted again and again. In the past, poorly-drained marshes and swamps were areas traditionally associated with mysterious luminosities that in Britain were known under an assortment of quite baffling names such as *Ignis Fatuus*, *i.e.* 'foolish flame', Hopping Jack, Jack o' Lantern, Joan a' Wad, Spunkie, Will-o'-the-Wisp, etc. In Victorian times it was fashionable to explain away this curious phenomenon as the misidentification of marsh gas - trapped methane that could spontaneously ignite into a flickering blue flame. Although this is an interesting concept, and one that still prevails, methane is not known to spontaneously ignite under normal circumstances and, what's more, many of the aerial lights viewed over marshes are very often seen to move *against* the prevailing wind in a manner suggesting purposeful motivation. Like ball lightning, these illuminated spheres belong to an altogether different category of phenomena. In the previous chapter I noted the Candle Marsh place-name near the village of All Cannings and suggested that it might have gained its appellation from the appearance of mysterious lights known by the colloquial name of Kitty Candlestick. If this supposition is correct it implies a clear link between water deposits and aerial luminosities in this county.

It is also important to remember that in Reichian physics decaying organic matter, like that found in marshes and swamps, was believed to produce a rapid acceleration in the excitation of orgone energy, a factor that may well be linked with the production of moving lights at such locations.

In more recent times man-made reservoirs and deep water-filled pits have become the focus of strange light phenomena. I have noted this connection on a number of occasions in my home county of Essex - the most recent example being the curious series of events that have plagued the night-time anglers at the secluded, man-made fishing reservoir of Totham Grove at Great Totham, near Maldon in Essex (see Chapter 26). Large, man-made bodies of water such as dams, reservoirs and lakes appear to create adverse pressure on the rock strata, which in turn causes a proliferation of minor tremors in the immediate area.(6)

Reich saw bodies of water as locations of accelerated orgone activity and used fast-flowing underground springs to discharge the DOR that built up during cloudbuster operations. Constable also recognised the apparent relationship between UFOs, orgone bioforms and bodies of water after studying the Tully reeds case of January 1966 and the UFO-linked scorched circles found on North Island, New Zealand, during 1969. The phenomenon's apparent affinity for bodies of water led him to refer to UFOs as 'cold, contractive, water-hungry energy'.(7)

If man-made bodies of water do catalyse the production of sub-surface tremors and, by virtue of this, paranormal phenomena, then it is reasonable to suggest that the vast volumes of water stored in Wiltshire's Upper Greensand and chalk layers might also play some role in the production of aerial luminosities. If so, then this would make sense of UFO appearances not only in the Kennett Valley, the Marlborough Downs and the Pewsey Vale, but also in the area of Warminster. However, the presence of water can in no way explain the apparent cycles or peaks of UFO activity noted in such regions.

The Aquifer Attractor

In the *The Cerealogist* No 5, Winter 1991/2, an article by Brian Grist entitled 'The Aquifer Attractor' suggested a relationship between the presence of aquifers and the distribution of crop circles and crop formations in the downlands of southern England.

Grist pointed out that porous bed-rock would invariably be covered with a thin layer of well-drained soil, making it ideal for the cultivation of grasses or cereal crops. This meant that a large percentage of Britain's grain was cultivated in regions, such as Wessex, where aquifers proliferate. Invariably the most favoured locations of aquifers, *i.e.* hill-slopes and shallow valley basins, are localities that crop circles seem to favour most. Grist also noticed that circles began shifting closer to the edges of aquifers during the dry spells of 1989 and 1990, leading him 'to wonder whether or not their placements might in some way be influenced by the relative position of sub-surface water levels at the time the events occurred.'(8)

The article goes on to say that an aquifer 'is rendered attractive (as a crop circle site) on account of its sub-surface water courses.' Water, Grist argues, is a conductor of electricity and could act like a magnet for an electrically-ionised vortex of the sort proposed by Terence Meaden. Where the knowledge that the greater majority of all crop circles found are of man-made manufacture leaves Grist's thought-provoking hypothesis, I do not know, but it does show that the efficiency of the Upper Greensand and chalk as aquifers has already been linked with the predominance of paranormal activity in Wiltshire.

As in the case of geology, the hydrology of Wiltshire appeared to play a part in our quest to understand the nature of Alton Barnes' paranormal potential. This new knowledge could now be weighed against any results achieved either by ourselves or by others during our two-week study of the area. These could then be matched against more transient geological events, such as earth tremors and geomagnetic shifts registered during this period. Only then might we be able to truly determine the relationship between geophysical events and UFO activity of the sort recorded in the earlier chapters of this book.

14

A Psychic Interface

From the evidence accumulated so far it would appear that, before the discovery of the first crop formation in East Field during July 1990, the observation of unidentified aerial lights in the Alton Barnes area occurred only very sporadically. However, after Steven Greer had set up his CSETI operations on the summit of Woodborough Hill during the second half of July 1992, reports of inexplicable light sources seen locally increased dramatically and continued to occur long after the team's departure from England.

If this assessment is correct then what, if anything, were the CSETI team doing to catalyse UFO activity in a way not seen before in the Alton Barnes area? Steven Greer's answer would probably be that the sightings were the result of structured spacecraft responding to his nightly attempts at 'non-local' communication. In my view, the truth of the matter is somewhat different, for it is possible that CSETI's psycho-interactive communications stimulated the localised energy continuum to such a degree that, as a by-product, it produced various sightings of unidentified lightforms in an area already prone to such activity.

Count-down at Cader Idris

Other examples where induced psycho-interactive events have led to the manifestation of unknown lightforms do exist. For instance, during 1982 my colleague Graham Phillips convinced a party of questing associates that they should spend midsummer's night by a pool on Cader Idris, a mountain near Dolgellau in Wales. Among those present were earth lights author Paul Devereux and a number of my closest friends, whose word I trust implicitly.

Phillips - who is now an author and historian - had received psychic information suggesting that an event of paranormal significance would occur at precisely one o'clock in the morning, midnight GMT. It would be viewed, he said, from a vantage point half way up the mountainside, close to a rocky lake, set between jutting cliffs of ancient volcanic rock. All waited patiently, and when one o' clock came the party had split up, with Devereux and two others standing by a small camp-fire and another person scanning the horizon with his back to them.

As they completed their count-down to the appointed time, Devereux and those standing next to him saw a tiny blue-white globe of light come from the vicinity of the sheer rock face and pass directly overhead. The fourth person caught sight of the light in mid-flight and all turned to watch as the glowing sphere zoomed out of range behind a nearby ridge. Its size was estimated at between 30 and 60 cm in diameter, and it had appeared at *exactly* one o'clock. At the time Devereux, who often relates this tale at lectures (but omits the circumstances of its appearance!), kicked himself as his book *Earth Lights* had just gone to press! The case was subsequently quoted in *Earth Lights Revelation*.(1)

Graham Phillips has been responsible for several similar events where quite clear unexplained aerial luminosities and paranormal incidents have been witnessed by disinterested individuals following psychic calls to be at a certain location at a certain time.

Mary Jones and the Egryn Lights

Another extraordinary example of apparent light consciousness seems to have occurred amid the small, isolated communities situated between the towns of Barmouth and Harlech in Merionethshire during the Welsh Religious Revival of 1904-5. Its phenomenal rise coincided with the observation on a great number of occasions of mysterious lights seen in the proximity of the religious gatherings, particularly in the vicinity of the Egryn

Chapel where the remarkable 'Merionethshire seeress' named Mary Jones would conduct emotionally-charged services of an evangelical nature.(2)

Although mysterious lights of varying colours, shapes and sizes were witnessed in the region by residents, visitors, London reporters and independent third parties, it is clear that Mary Jones appeared to have a kind of personal relationship with the luminosities, which she saw as 'Heaven-sent' signs from God. A good summary of this apparent relationship appeared in the March 1905 issue of *The Occult Review*, which, along with the Society for Psychical Research, took a special interest in the curious events surrounding the Welsh seeress.

> The 'star' and 'lights' appeared for the first time on the night that Mrs Jones commenced her public mission at Egryn. The star was heralded by a luminous arch, of the character of the *Aurora Borealis*, one end resting on the sea, the other on the hill-top [a distance of well over 1.5 km], bathing the little chapel in a flood of soft effulgence. The star soon after appears, its light flooding the chapel itself. Ever since then, up to the middle of February, the star and the lights have always accompanied Mrs Jones' mission. The star invariably heralds the lights, and when they come it disappears. The star seemed to rest above particular houses, whose roofs are thrown out in bold relief amidst the surrounding darkness. When this occurs in the Egryn district a convert or converts invariably turn up at the next meeting from that particular house; when it occurs at a distance the house is the one selected for the Revivalist's temporary lodging. Similarly it glows placidly on the roof of the chapel where her service is held, and when it does so the spiritual character of the meeting is very marked. On two occasions only, so far as I know, has the star or light stopped short of the chapel fixed for the service - and on each occasion the service proved a frost.(3)

Over the winter months of 1904-5 the phenomena observed in and around the Welsh hills surrounding Egryn included 'a large square of light', 'a big flame', 'a rainbow of vapour', 'a solid bulb of light', 'balls of fire', and 'columns' or 'pillars of fire', seen in colours varying from blue, to blood red, brilliant copper and dazzling white. More curious were the reported visions that accompanied the appearance of the lights. These included manifestations of winged angels and Christ crucified, as well as one account of instantaneous transportation to paradise!(4) In contrast, there were also cases of a mysterious man-in-black, thought to be the devil in disguise, who appeared in full view of assembled groups before transforming into a phantom black dog and vanishing from sight.(5) A full account of these extraordinary events can be found in Kevin and Sue McClure's invaluable 1980 publication *Stars, and Rumours of Stars* (see also Chapter 35).

Paul Devereux also deals with the 'Egryn lights' in *Earth Lights Revelation* and demonstrates that of the 21 geographically positionable sightings studied, all occurred within 700 m of the major Mochras fault running between Harlech and Barmouth. Of these, 17 were within a 300 m distance, while 10 were found to have occurred within just 100 m of the fault.(6) Furthermore, the Egryn Chapel - over which the lights were regularly seen - is situated just 100 m from the Mochras fault, while Llanfair Chapel, the scene of further light sightings, is positioned directly on it. If these cases represent genuine paranormal events, then these statistics strongly support the assertion that geological faults play a major role in the manifestation of aerial luminosities.

The evidence for Mary Jones' relationship to the 'Egryn lights' clearly suggests that the phenomenon was visibly responding to her evangelising efforts, as well as to the more general events surrounding the religious revival. Mrs Jones appears to have been the key to this unconscious interaction, probably through her personal belief that the 'star' and the accompanying 'lights' were divine confirmation of the success of her mission. Kevin and Sue McClure acknowledge this personal relationship in *Stars, and Rumours of Stars*, when they observe:

> I have never heard of poltergeist events on this scale, though travelling lights have been reported. Certainly Mrs. Jones's mental state seems closely related to that of catalysts in poltergeist cases; similarly her kind of emotional and bleak devotion is such as I have encountered among those who claim to be magicians. The lights, whether 'real' or subjective, were an effective and consistent means of Mary

Jones' achieving her ambition of conversion and Revival. They went where she went, appeared where she had been and, supposedly, where she was going... I can only imagine that whatever the nature of the lights, they would probably have had no existence at all without Mary Jones' own wish and intention that they should exist. Religion is perhaps, the most powerful channel for natural psychokinesis, magic, miracle, or whatever one may call it, open to the Western world.(7)

The Power of Meditation
Could it be possible that, without realising it, the emotionally-charged meditational practices used by Steven Greer and his CSETI team were having similar effects? In other words, they too were drawing aerial luminosities into manifestation. In the case of the Woodborough light cluster seen overnight on 26/27 July 1992, this apparent psychic interface was seemingly confirmed when a high-powered flash-light was used to obtain responsive replies from the object observed, replicating the results repeatedly obtained by the Hessdalen team using a laser during 1984.

Having worked with both psychically-sensitive individuals and meditational practices for 15 years, I felt it would be important to try and see whether the results of the CSETI team could be reproduced under controlled conditions. Alton Barnes seemed the most obvious choice to conduct such an operation as it appeared to be at its peak of paranormal activity and had already seemingly produced excellent examples of this phenomenon.

Meditational practices
In an attempt to gain results similar to those achieved in July 1992 by Steven Greer's CSETI project, a series of co-ordinated meditations would be used by ourselves. Each would include so-called path-working techniques in which those taking part are taken on a mythic journey using creative visualisation. The meditations employed would also need to feature set archetypes and symbols based on presupposed belief systems considered to be associated with crop circles, prehistoric ritual monuments and the UFO phenomenon. Once chosen, a particular belief system would be picked for each meditation so that the results of the experiment could then be weighed against the use of a selected archetype. In this way the project would gain some idea of the effectiveness and potency of each archetype in respect to not just the environment in question, but also the mental agility of the individuals involved.

I also decided that every meditation should include blatant imagery featuring balls of light, either coming down from the sky or rising out of the ground. In the mind's eye these would be seen to act in an intelligent manner buzzing around the group, posing for the cameras and interfering with the monitoring equipment - the human traits we wanted to impress upon any presupposed energy forms in our attempts to coax them into registerable manifestation. By doing this our minds would hopefully cause additional fluctuations and reverberations in the surrounding environment that might affect the monitoring equipment in some way.

After careful consideration, the following three archetypes were chosen for use:

Archetype i - Alien entities, using the popular notion of the so-called 'Greys', the alleged intelligences associated by many with not just the UFO phenomenon, but also with the abduction scenario gaining popularity in the United States at this time. Their short, spindly bodies, long grey faces and large black eyes have made them the most evocative archetype in the subject of ufology for many years. For a classic representation of the 'Greys' see the cover illustration of Whitley Strieber's best-selling book *Communion*.

Accompanying this archetype would be the obvious image of structured metallic spacecraft as popularised by the misconceptions of the flying saucer craze of the 1940s and 1950s. Despite man's own technological advances in the past 50 years, the extra-terrestrial space vehicle has continued to be seen in terms of the flying saucer-shaped UFO, as may be judged by the quite bizarre photographs produced during the 1970s by Swiss UFO contactee Billy Meier.

Many crop circle enthusiasts believe that the formations are etched out by alien technology of the sort associated with both the Greys and/or the structured metallic spacecraft conceived of by Steven Greer and others.

Since an extra-terrestrial explanation for the UFO phenomenon is by far the most

PLATE 23. The face of a 'Grey' painted by artist and circlemaker Rod Dickinson. This striking archetype is currently the most potent in the minds of those seeking an extra-terrestrial solution to UFOs, alien abductions and the crop circle enigma (pic: Rod Dickinson).

potent in the minds of man, the use of this archetype was going to be essential to our own experiments.

Archetype ii - Ancestor spirits, using the belief most prevalent among supporters of both the earth mysteries and the psychic questing subject that the prehistoric places of Britain possess *genius loci*, *i.e.* guardian spirits, usually ancestral spirits connected with the locality in question. These are thought to be attached to sites such as long barrows, stone circles, sacred springs, tumuli and ancient trees, as well as many pre-Reformation Christian structures.

Genius loci can also be seen as geomythic or totemic entities, such as fabulous beasts, elemental beings and the fairy folk of Celtic and Norse tradition. All these various types of spirit form have been associated in past ages with the appearance of mysterious lights, particularly in the vicinity of prehistoric monuments.

Archetype iii - the Goddess, after the James Lovelock concept of Gaia, the collective expression of a living earth. The steady rise in popularity of the Goddess archetype over the past two decades has come as a kind of spiritual response to the gradual destruction of the planet by mankind. From the women peace protesters of Greenham Common to the moving words of the Hopi Indians of Arizona or the Kogis of Colombia, we are gradually coming to terms with the idea of a thinking, living earth of which we are all a part. In turn, this has paved way for the gradual re-emergence of the Goddess under a multitude of different guises, encompassing archetypal concepts from such diverse cultures as ancient Egypt, Iron Age Europe, Phoenicia, Sumeria and the classical world.

Many Goddess worshippers have seen the dramatic increase in crop circle appearances as a sign of eschatological change brought about by our misuse of the planet - the 'Mother is crying' idea of the Hopi indians. Paul Devereux's earth lights theory has also helped awaken the idea that unexplained luminosities are the product of Gaia herself.

The Cone of Power

Before any archetype can be used in a meditation, those taking part are asked to construct what is known as the 'cone of power'. This is a visualised beehive-like cone of electric-blue light drawn like a blanket around the outside of the group, who will either stand or sit in a circle. The purpose of this imagery is to focus the psychic mind by using the cone both as a barrier to the outside world and as a wall of protection on a psychological, and possibly even a psycho-magical level. It also acts as a point of common unity among those taking part and is believed by mystics to establish both the circle of meditators and the site itself as a potent energy beacon. Using Reich's reversed entropy theory, this would suggest that, as a high potential of orgone, the meditation would draw in other less-potent energy forms from the immediate environment - like moths to a flame. It was this same basic principle that both Van Tassel and Constable used to draw down UFOs during the 1950s.

Psychic Experiments

The conducting of meditations as an active ingredient in a scientific project was almost entirely new to this field. The Dragon Project had invited dowsers, practising witches and psychics to visit the Rollright stone circle and interact with monitoring equipment whilst conducting some form of ritual communication with the guardian spirit of the site. This approach had unfortunately led to conflicting views and responses, forcing Devereux to drop this aspect of the project. Despite this set-back, on a number of occasions known psychics visited the Rollright Stones and gained clear responses from instrumentation when others failed to gain a response at all.(8) Another example where psychic sessions were successfully used to produce tangible paranormal results under scientific conditions was the SORRAT group, founded in 1961 by the late Dr John G. Neihardt to study psychokinetic effects. Its aims were to gain the co-operation of the 'spirit' world in an attempt to demonstrate the reality of psychic abilities to the scientific community. At the SORRAT headquarters at Skyrim Farm, near Columbia, Missouri, USA, members would perform seances in which they would request help from spirit guides attached to one or other of the mediums in attendance. Once contact had been made, the spirit entities would then be asked to conduct certain tasks, usually under control conditions inside a hermetically-sealed, glass-fronted tank known as the mini-lab. Among the quite startling results they obtained were video recordings of metal rings being joined together, messages being 'automatically' written onto paper with a pencil, objects appearing or disappearing in full view of the camera and the manifestation of small 'grapefruit'-sized balls of light.(9)

The startling video evidence and witness testimonies of those who witnessed the SORRAT group in action are truly remarkable and should have gained more attention from the outside world than they actually did. Unfortunately, the whole affair was seen as one big hoax by the sceptics of the American parapsychological community, leaving SORRAT to be cast quietly into oblivion.(10) Despite these allegations, the SORRAT experiments showed that psychic communication *can* be successfully combined with scientific exploration. Thankfully, Orgone 93 was not looking for evidence of a spiritual existence, it wanted only to demonstrate that the human mind can affect any presupposed energy continuum and, through this, the physical environment, using belief-orientated, psycho-interactive processes.

15

Pointing at the Sky

Both Reich and Constable successfully used cloudbusters to affect aerial light phenomena, for which reason it was decided that our own experimentation should also include the use of such a device. We would employ it solely for the purpose of stimulating the localised environment in the hope that this would accelerate the appearance of UFOs, whether in an invisible or visible state. Like a group of meditators, a cloudbuster appeared to act as a beacon of high orgone potential, thus increasing the chances of localised energy-related activity, something Constable proved to his own satisfaction.

During 1993 the only operational cloudbuster in the United Kingdom belonged to Tony Beddoe, the founder of ORTEC, an organisation dedicated to the study and development of orgone technology, based at the West Usk Lighthouse in Newport, South Wales. Beddoe was also a senior lecturer on product design and innovation at Gwent College of Higher Education in Caerleon-on-Usk and had made a 12-year study of Wilhelm Reich and his work.

From the outset Beddoe offered his expertise and knowledge to the Orgone 93 team and agreed, in principle at least, to deploy his cloudbuster in Alton Barnes for the duration of the experiments. It soon became apparent, however, that this could prove problematic for a number of reasons. Firstly, rumours of its imminent use in the Vale of Pewsey quickly reached the ears of local farmers who became concerned that its presence might interfere with the ripening of crops at a crucial stage in their growth. Their belief in the reality of the cloudbuster's capabilities was unshakable, partly due to the connections I had drawn between crop circles and orgone energy in *The Circlemakers*. Secondly, it seemed that the idea of a cloudbuster stationed in the modern-day crop circle Mecca had not been greeted too kindly by certain groups and individuals. By the spring of 1993 two people had independently warned me of planned sabotage attempts on Orgone 93 equipment while the experiments were in progress (thankfully, this was not to take place). Why anyone should want to sabotage our work was difficult to imagine.

It was with these points in mind that Tony Beddoe agreed to construct a much smaller orgone engineering device (OED) based on the same principles as the cloudbuster, yet designed only to affect the immediate environment, not the local weather! The OED, or mini-cloudbuster as it became known, consisted of six long steel tubes held together with steel brackets that terminated in two small orgone accumulators. From this trailed hollow cables which were to be earthed in a fast-flowing water source. The whole device was eight feet long and needed to be mounted on a large tripod to give it full support and manoeuvrability.

Painted in black, the device looked more like a ghostbuster than a cloudbuster! What's more, in an attempt to ensure he was not affected by any presupposed DOR when the device was in operation, Beddoe would always dress in black leather, with thick army boots, a flying helmet and special ultra-violet detecting goggles - making him look more like a First World War air-ace than an orgone engineer!

The prospect of working with a scaled down cloudbuster genuinely excited the team, although it had to be remembered that this was no toy. Operating a cloudbuster required not only considerable skill, but also a detailed understanding of Reichian physics, for misuse could, it seemed, lead to the build up of DOR in the immediate vicinity of the cloudbuster. This in turn might result in the operator suffering an assortment of adverse physiological effects as described in Chapter 1.

Such statements might seem a little over-dramatic when you think of a cloudbuster as simply a collection of hollow tubes connected to a few cables and an orgone accumulator, but to some operators these warnings have become a living nightmare. For

PLATE 24. Tony Beddoe readies his Orgone Engineering Device (OED) or 'mini-cloudbuster' during an Orgone 93 experiment in July 1993 (pic: John Horrigan).

example, on 6 December 1954, Reich's research assistant, Robert A. McCullough, was using a cloudbuster at Reich's establishment at Tucson, Arizona, when he apparently became aware of the presence of DOR being drawn through its tubes. This subjective impression, he concluded, was confirmed by the Geiger counter which steadily rose to give readings of 700 counts per minute! At the same time he experienced a 'sour' taste in his mouth described as 'a very bitter taste, much stronger than usual and *tasting like offal* [Reich's emphasis].' Without further warning McCullough suffered 'a crippling sensation in his right leg' followed by paralysis down his whole right side. At the same time Reich claimed the radio was producing a continuous static noise, and in conclusion he put the whole incident down to DOR from an unseen Ea or UFO caught in the line of the cloudbuster.(1)

Despite the trauma of this horrific incident, the pain had eased enough for McCullough to return to the cloudbuster the next day. Unfortunately, he found that every time he tried to use the device the crippling sensation returned. So severe did this illness become that McCullough was forced to leave Tucson.(2) The doctors said McCullough had suffered a stroke, and even today he still drags his right foot.

Trevor James Constable speaks of a similar incident that took place in December 1971 when he was using his own form of cloudbuster during a weather control experiment in southern California. A visitor to the site became excited when he realised that a strange light had appeared in the area of the sky where the device was being directed. In that same instant there was a sharp crack as a bluish burst of light hit the tube on which the man rested his hand. His whole right side was jolted by the shock, leaving him temporarily paralysed for some minutes. The pain apparently brought tears to his eyes and made him feel as though every nerve in his body had been 'irradiated'.(3)

During the early 1950s, Reich's own daughter Eva would become violently ill when pointing a cloudbuster at the mysterious aerial lights that lingered in the skies above Rangeley, Maine, while the late Jerome Eden was said to have been 'hit by a light beam from a UFO' when operating a cloudbuster in December 1971.(4) Furthermore, America's most well-known cloudbuster operator, James de Meo, believes that in the wrong hands these innocuous-looking devices can actually cause considerable damage, not just to their operators, or to bystanders, but to the entire eco-system in the area in which they are being used.

Clearly, great care was needed when using a cloudbuster, whatever the true nature of its alleged capabilities. Even though our own example would be used by Tony Beddoe only to 'stimulate' the immediate environment, the warnings of experienced cloudbuster operators such as Constable, Eden and de Meo were not to be ignored.

16

Monitoring the Unseen

Probably the most important element of Orgone 93 would be its ability to carefully monitor each experiment using available scientific instrumentation. Changes in the background readings during either the experiment or a control period were to be matched against any achieved photographic evidence, any unexplained visual sightings made or any subjective psychic experiences reported by those taking part. All this was essential if we were to fully comprehend how each individual component of the project might register possible intrusions or changes in the energy continuum at the location in question.

Other similar monitoring programmes had been conducted in the past by groups such as the Dragon Project during the late 1970s, early 1980s, and Norway's Project Hessdalen during 1984 and 1985. Among the many objectives of the Dragon Project had been the prolonged monitoring of known energies at prehistoric sites in the hope that repeatable patterns might be discerned. Only after several years did this painstaking work enable the construction of a comprehensive picture of the energy fluctuations at the sites concerned. Aside from the monitoring programme, another inter-connected facet of the Dragon Project was the collating of anecdotal stories from the many volunteers who spent long periods of time at the sites concerned. These subjective paranormal experiences provided enough raw data to produce undeniable patterns of what appeared be occurring on a subtle level at such locations. In turn, the corresponding patterns allowed a greater understanding of the results obtained through more orthodox means.

As with the Dragon Project, Project Hessdalen did not dismiss the various anecdotal stories recorded by the members of its team or told to them by independent witnesses. It is also known that in the wake of the various instances of light consciousness experienced by the team during 1984, the project directors sought the assistance of Scandinavian parapsychological groups in the hope that psychically-talented individuals might be able to either communicate with or remotely view aerial lightforms. This followed in the wake of various alleged predictions from psychics concerning the appearance of UFOs in the Hessdalen region during 1982-3.(1)

In order to take the subject one step further Orgone 93 needed to go beyond the parameters set by both the Dragon Project and Project Hessdalen. Despite the obvious drawbacks concerning money and the long catalogue of aims already cited, our own intentions were to try and combine the use of the OED with both meditational work and the monitoring of known energies at locations in and around Alton Barnes. It would also be important to catalogue any other unusual events that might occur in the same area during the same period. In this way any fluctuations or signals registered on the monitoring equipment could then be assessed with respect to the activities either generated by ourselves or occurring independently of our own presence in the area.

It was therefore clear that we needed sensible scientific instrumentation that would both suit our requirements and fulfil the criteria of the proposed monitoring programme. With this in mind enquiries were made and one by one instruments did eventually come our way, and by the summer of 1993 the following equipment had either been secured or promised:

i. an ex-Ministry of Defence Radiac Mk II Geiger counter. This huge bulk, looking like something that might have been used at Aldermaston during the 1960s, utilised an analogue meter to register counts per second (cps) in alpha, beta/gamma combined or x-rays, although for our purposes it was to be used only to monitor background levels of beta/gamma radiation. This was supplemented by another Geiger counter on loan from its maker, Rodney Hale, MIEE, C Eng., FR Met S, an electronics engineer of high standing with his own company of 24 years based near St Albans, Hertfordshire. He had been heavily involved in the technical side of the Dragon Project back in the 1980s, while in 1992 he had participated in the CCCS-backed Project Argus and in early 1993 he was engaged in supplying equipment for the organisation's current research programme entitled Operation Relate (Research into Electromagnetic and other Terrestrial Effects). Hale's own instrument, made by his company Melford Designs, incorporated three built-in Geiger-Muller tubes and an LCD display which records counts per minute (cpm).

ii. an ultrasound detector. Anomalous bursts of ultrasound had been recorded on a number of occasions in the proximity of the Rollright stone circle in Oxfordshire during the Dragon Project, especially around the point of dawn. Before the late 1970s anecdotal stories had appeared to connect inaudible sound waves, such as ultrasound and infrasound, with the uncharacteristic reactions of animals and birds at ancient sites, prompting a serious investigation into this highly intriguing area of study.(2)

By the early 1990s it had also become clear that uncharacteristic animal reactions to the presence of crop circles and crop formations might also be connected to the presence of either ultrasound or infrasound.(3) It was therefore imperative that we monitored for ultrasound at selected locations in the Alton Barnes area. For this reason I purchased a basic multi-band Gnometec detector that could well be tuned to cover a frequency range of between 30 kHz and 85 kHz. Any signals would produce audible emissions either through a tiny loudspeaker or via headphones.

This basic detector was supplemented by the use of a second device made by Rodney Hale and calibrated to two specific frequencies - 26 kHz and 40 kHz, which could be combined together to give one signal. Any sounds registered by the device were displayed by an analogue meter using a comparative scale of between 0 and 100.

iii. an electro-static volt meter. This instrument measures the electro-static voltage of the air potential produced by ionisation. It has been suggested that the build up and discharge of electro-static energy at ancient sites may well be linked with localised weather conditions,(4) while in ufology it is considered that the mechanical and electrical problems experienced by motor vehicles during close proximity UFO encounters could be the result of powerful electrical discharges and/or electro-static interference.

iv. a very low frequency (VLF) radio receiver. This instrument, a Model WR-3 designed to listen to radio emissions between 50 Hz and 11 kHz, was kindly donated to Orgone 93 by Conversion Research of Descanso, Arizona.(5) A similar instrument had previously been used by American earth lights researcher Edson C. Hendricks to monitor the possible relationship between whistlers - the sound of lightning colliding in the upper atmosphere - and the manifestation of mysterious lights at Marfa in Texas.(6) The results of these ground-breaking experiments led Hendricks to suggest a correlation between the appearance of spooklights and the occurrence of whistlers.

All monitoring equipment would be operational for a full 10 minutes before and after each 20-minute experiment, ensuring a suitable control period in every instance. Most of the apparatus would be operated by members of Earthquest, an earth mysteries and psychic questing group I ran in my home town of Leigh-on-Sea, Essex. Although Orgone 93 could in no way be described as a 'scientific' project, it would be conducted in an objective manner in the hope that the energy effects we had so long taken for granted in connection with meditational practices could now be demonstrated to a scientific community. If we could achieve this aim alone, then it would be an major addition to our understanding of psycho-interactive processes.

17

The Eye of the Camera

Since photography would be another important aspect of the project, an understanding of the mechanics of the visible light and infrared ranges of the electromagnetic spectrum was essential. For example, what exactly is the electromagnetic spectrum? Well, in simple terms it is the range of known energies detectable by scientific instrumentation. These include cosmic rays, gamma rays, microwaves, radio waves, ultra-violet and infrared (IR) radiation, x-rays, as well as visible light. All these are normally measured either by their frequency or wavelength, usually using units of Hertz (Hz) or Nanometers (nm) respectively.

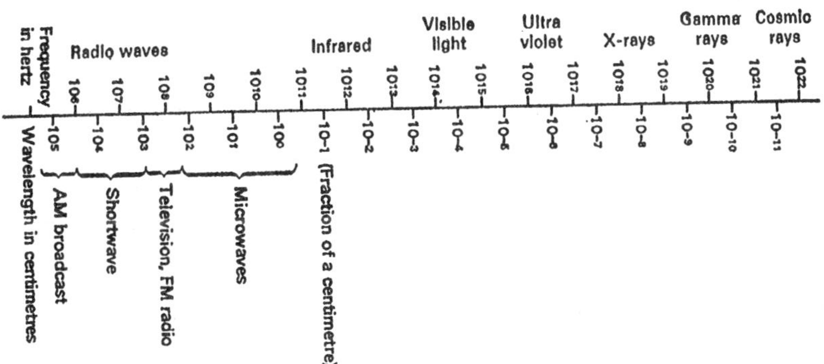

FIG 15. The electromagnetic spectrum. Many UFOs probably exist in a multi-dimensional state beyond the realms of the visible spectrum.

The manifestation of light is determined by the frequency ranges accessible to us humans. Visible light begins at around 380 nm, with the colour violet, and decreases in frequency, passing blue, blue-green, green, yellow-green, yellow, orange before finally becoming red at around 700 nm. The naked eye receives the full frequency range of the visual spectrum, enabling our brain to see colour. Other energies can affect us in different ways, while many lifeforms have shifted or extended colour ranges that push into regions either side of our own visible spectrum. For instance, some lifeforms can see into the ultra-violet (UV) range, which lies beyond the violet end of our visible spectrum, while others see more into the IR range, which lies beyond the red end of the spectrum. Photography allows us to 'see' frequency ranges that would otherwise be inaccessible to the naked eye. By using different sorts of films, lenses and filters, cameras can also record objective imagery well beyond the visible spectrum.

Infrared Photography

The IR range of the electromagnetic spectrum is a form of heat radiation which normal panchromatic film emulsions cannot detect. Special extra-sensitive films are necessary for

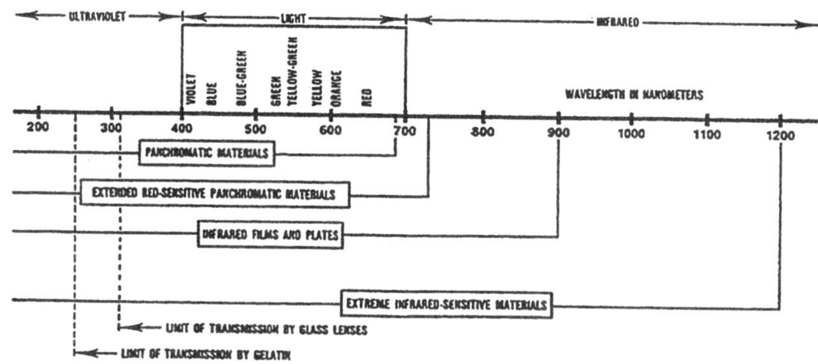

FIG 16. The electromagnetic wavelengths governing the parameters of infrared, visible light and ultra-violet photography. Can film emulsions really record the presence of unseen energy forms?

this purpose, and these usually extend the visible range from between 380 and 715 nm to between 380 and 900 nm. Other types of IR films can even reach as high as 1200 nm. Beyond these wavelengths photography is only really conducted using electronic means.

Filters are used to block out unwanted visible light which, if allowed to reach the unexposed film, will only confuse or cancel out the IR imagery as it reacts with the sensitive emulsion. These filters are manufactured by international companies such as Cokin and Hoya, although for many years it was the Kodak Wratten glass and gelatin filters that were used for this type of photographic work. They include the translucent red gelatin filter No 25 and the deep red filters Nos 87 and 88A for black and white work, and the deep yellow filter No 12 for colour work. Some photographers use no filters at all.

From ASSAP, the Association for the Scientific Study of Anomalous Phenomena, Orgone 93 was able to secure the loan of a video camera with an IR-sensitive Vidicon tube for the duration of the experimentation. This enabled us to record each session, as well as the control tests, in the hope that any anomalous IR imagery captured on the still camera would also be reproduced on video tape.

Ultra-violet Photography

After some years of working with the IR range, Constable turned his attentions to combined IR and UV photography which he found also produced some quite striking photographic effects. To achieve these results he used the opaque Kodak Wratten glass filter No 18A which prevents the entire visible spectrum from entering the camera, yet allows both the IR and UV frequency ranges to reach the film emulsion. Using Goethe's bipolar conception of colour, Constable concluded that the visible spectrum was not linear, as displayed in illustrations, but circular. He suggested that behind the light spectrum was a separate 'reverse' or 'dark' spectrum, utilising normally invisible IR and UV light. In here, he believed, his bioforms or 'critters' could be photographed using the No 18A glass filter.(1) This allows bright sunlight to penetrate through as a diffuse crimson hue. Naturally, we wanted to try and incorporate UV photography into Orgone 93 but this, unfortunately, posed one major problem. UV rays are electromagnetic waves between 200 and 400 nm. The emulsion of normal panchromatic film is sensitive not just to the visible spectrum, but also UV rays down to approximately 300 nm. However, conventional optical glass and plastic lenses prevent UV radiations entering a camera in the same way that sun-glasses or polarisers block out the sun's rays. This is a necessary practice as UV radiations would otherwise bleach out or over-expose any normal daylight imagery etched onto the emulsion.

Only a lens made of fluorite rock crystal, or a camera needing no lens at all, can be used in UV photography. The Japanese photographic giants Nikon manufacture an expensive crystal lens, the so-called UV-Nikkor 105 mm f/4.5, used principally for medical purposes as UV radiation highlights bodily bruising invisible to the human eye. UV photography also captures hidden features in plant and animal life, although special short-wave UV films are necessary to 'see' frequency ranges below 300 nm.

Although I already owned a Kodak Wratten glass filter No 18A, the Nikon flourite crystal lens cost a cool £1500, making it an impossible addition to our project. In the end we opted instead to use a cheap second-hand Praktica LTL camera body which my colleague John Horrigan converted into a simple pin-hole camera able to carry the valuable glass filter. Early experiments showed that although the camera took reasonable photographs in bright sunlight, extremely long exposure times would be necessary if we were to use it for IR and UV photography. Unfortunately, this was the best we could do on an extremely low budget, although even from the outset I had my reservations over the probable efficiency of this process.

Anomaly Photography

Timing is, according to Constable, extremely important. He suggested that first light was the best time to produce photographic anomalies. The Dragon Project also found that more monitoring anomalies occurred at ancient sites around the point of dawn than at any other time of the day. Since producing photographic anomalies was going to play such an important role in Orgone 93, we finally decided to conduct experiments twice daily - at the point of dawn and at midday GMT (Greenwich Mean Time), *i.e.* 1pm BST (British Summer Time).

I did not relish the thought of getting up at around four o'clock each morning to climb steep hills in the pre-dawn air, and I knew this sentiment was shared by the rest of the volunteers. However, if we were to achieve any real results, then this seemed to be the only solution - so it would *have* to be done.

The Photographic Section

London-based electronics engineer Roger Wilkins and his partner Judi Smith, who co-edits a journal on alternative sciences entitled *Journeyman* agreed to co-ordinate the project's photographic section. The couple had been drawn into actively researching the concept of atmospheric energy forms after digesting Constable's essential book *The Cosmic Pulse of Life*. Inspired by its array of IR photographs showing alleged bioforms or 'critters', they spent one early morning at Hackpen Hill on the Whitehorse Downs of Berkshire trying to duplicate Constable's results.

Using Kodak HIE high speed black and white film and a Wratten gelatin filter No 88A they photographed the empty sky above a low tumulus before returning back to London. The finished results showed a small circular black 'blob' when printed on no less than three separate frames, all depicting the same area of sky. These apparent photographic anomalies aroused the couple's curiosity enough to ensure their participation in Orgone 93.

After much discussion with them concerning finances and time factors, we agreed that video cameras should be used both for IR and visible light work throughout the entire two weeks of experimentation. Still pictures in IR, UV and visible light would also be taken at five-minute intervals before, during and after each experiment - meaning a total of nine shots per camera per experiment. All HIE high speed IR-sensitive black and white film exposed during our own experimentation would be developed on the premises. This would help keep costs to a minimum while allowing us to keep track of how the project was doing, giving us the chance to either alter or update the timetable of experiments as and when necessary. All colour films would be processed and studied by Gary Bond and his colleagues at the Pegasus Photographic Laboratory.

This left one last necessity in respect to the photographic section. The chances were that the English weather would not be too kind to us, so we needed a camera hide in which to place the line of cameras. To this end John Horrigan constructed a home-made device using pieces of tarpaulin removed over a several-day period from industrial skips left near his home in Leigh-on-Sea! Everything was set, all we needed now were locations to conduct the project and these, as you will see from the next chapter, had to be chosen carefully.

18

Choosing the Sites

Ancient places, holy hills, sacred mountains and water sites all appear to produce electromagnetic, paranormal and other forms of paranormal effects similar to those recorded in association with both the orgone accumulator and, it seems, the modern-day crop circle. If we were therefore to try and understand the reasons why such places appear to possess the power to create or induce such phenomena, then these considerations would need to be borne in mind when selecting the sites for our own intended experimentation. In addition to this, the chosen sites would need to be within a few miles radius of Alton Barnes to ensure that early morning journeys were made that much more palatable to the volunteers involved, and any localised background readings would remain relatively constant for each experiment. With these factors in mind, five sites were finally chosen:

i) **A Water Site (SU10846220).** For this we would use the Broad Well, the bubbling springs that rise from the Upper Greensand levels situated on the edge of Church Meadow, Alton Priors, and form a stream that flows south to join the Christchurch Avon. Hidden amid a tree-lined enclosure between field boundaries, these ancient springs rise on the Alton Barnes farm estate owned by New College, Oxford, and leased, through E. & A.G. Stratton, to the Carson family of Old Manor, Alton Barnes.

In the past the Broad Well was known as the *Brade Wyll*,(1) as well as the Bridewell,(2) a name very possibly recording the site's early Christian sanctity. St Bride or St Bridget is the Christianisation of a much earlier Celtic goddess of the same name who signified the fecundity of the land and presided over the sacred springs and holy wells which later became known as Bridewells. Even though the Broad Well has no known folklore attached to it, I saw no reason why a potent spring-head such as this should not have been a site of both domestic and religious importance in prehistoric times.

Less than 200 m south-south-east of the Broad Well is the twelfth-century church of All Saints, Alton Priors, now sadly no longer used for regular services. A late medieval building known as the Priory, located just beyond All Saints church, is reputedly haunted. On no less than three separate occasions exorcisms were conducted here by a local parish priest in the hope that it would rid the building of a malevolent poltergeist. Less than a hundred metres away is the final stretch of the Ridgeway which is also reputedly haunted. Recently this same spot has also been the scene of localised aerial flashes, a familiar feature in circle-making exploits and UFO lore.(3)

Next door to the Priory is the 18th-century Old Manor, which has had its own fair share of mysterious happenings. On one occasion an inexplicable shaft of light was seen to pass through the kitchen by several people, while unaccountable footsteps have been heard on the stairs.

ii) **A Hill-top Site (SU11846141).** For this we chose Woodborough Hill situated on the eastern edge of Alton Priors. Iron Age strip lynchets may be discerned on the hill's raised slopes and in 1992 it was, of course, the setting for Steven Greer's CSETI operations. The Woodborough place-name may derive from the woodland that originally surrounded the hill, although some sources believe it originates from the hill's association with Woden, the all-seeing Saxon god of the underworld. A few hundred yards north-east of Woodborough Hill is the extensive woodland known as Tawsmead Copse - the scene of many mysterious lights in recent years. Both locations are on land belonging to the Alton Barnes estate. As with East Field and most of Alton Priors, both Woodborough Hill and Tawsmead Copse lie on Lower Chalk.

iii) **An Ancient Site (SU11386340).** For this we chose Adam's Grave, the remains of the Neolithic long barrow capping Walkers Hill, 1.25 km north-north-east of Alton Barnes. It is also known as 'Old Adam', and can confidently be equated with the *Wodnes beorh* (Woden's barrow) of the *Anglo-Saxon Chronicle* where battles were allegedly fought in AD 592 and in AD 715.

To the north-west of Adam's Grave, on the southern slopes of Milk Hill, is a white horse cut in 1812 by Alton Barnes farmer Robert Pile. At the base of Walker's Hill is the Ridgeway track, and between here and the long barrow Kathleen Wiltshire records that the clear sound of ghostly horses have been heard on occasions.(4)

On the other side of the Ridgeway is the Neolithic causewayed camp of Knap Hill upon which a mysterious luminous column was seen to descend in July 1991. Below both Adam's Grave and Knap Hill is East Field, the scene of various crop formations and other mysterious happenings since 1990. Like the rest of the Marlborough Downs, Milk Hill and Walkers Hill are composed of Middle Chalk, although the highest level of Milk Hill is composed of an outlying deposit of clay-with-flints.

iv) **A Crop Formation (SU03346000).** For obvious reasons the chosen location could not be predicted in advance. Seeing that East Field, and Alton Barnes in general, had been graced with classic examples of this phenomenon since the advent of the pictogram in 1990, it seemed a fair chance that there would be more in 1993. Two land artists had already offered to roll us an example or two for the project, but this did not seem to convey the spirit of the thing, for it was likely that part of a crop formation's mystique lay in the knowledge that its manufacturer, human or otherwise, remains unknown.

As it turned out, Alton Barnes produced no examples of crop formations of any merit until the night of Saturday/Sunday, 21/22 August 1993, just days before harvest time, when a simple design turned up in East Field. As a consequence, an experiment was conducted in the hexagonal configuration of six circles adjoined to a seventh central circle by thin radial spokes to be found by mid July below Etchilhampton Hill, 8 km south-east of Alton Barnes and just 500 m from the Stert-Etchilhampton fault.

v) **A Control Site (SU10806235).** For this we chose, rather conveniently, the back garden of Brown's Cottage, our rented accommodation in Alton Barnes. Although it was only 150 m north-north-west of the designated Water Site, I decided this was sufficient distance for any control tests to be carried out without any obvious interference from other localised factors. It was also close enough to the sites already chosen to reflect the background readings of the area in general. Geologically speaking, Brown's Cottage lies on Lower Chalk, very close to the narrow strip of Upper Greensand that enters the parish from the direction of Woodborough.

The Avebury Experiment

One further location was required for an open-house experiment we intended conducting at the very end of the two-week period. Its purpose was basically to find out what sort of effect an extremely large number of people would have on the environment if they took part in a synchronised meditation at a prehistoric site in conjunction with the use of the OED. The only possible site that could be used for this purpose was the Avebury megalithic complex, which lies 7 km north-north-west of Alton Barnes. As Natural Trust property it is open to the general public and there is easy access to the village by car or coach as well as adequate facilities to buy food and drink.

Crop circle researcher Roland Pargeter had organised a major conference to be held in Glastonbury, Somerset, from Friday, 30 July to Sunday, 1 August 1993. During the first day conference goers were to embark on a coach journey to the Vale of Pewsey and the Kennet Valley in the hope of seeing some crop formations. I suggested that as part of the trip the 50 or so people on the coach should visit Avebury and take part in the experiment following a short introduction by myself. Pargeter readily agreed to this proposal, sealing the final details of the project's schedule.

By the beginning of June 1993, the foundations of the project had been laid and everything was in place for the commencement of experimentation on Saturday, 17 July. Yet before it could start in earnest, we needed to conduct certain preliminary experiments to familiarise ourselves, not just with the monitoring equipment, but also with the various sites to be used. In the end, the first of these two Sunday excursions to Alton Barnes proved to be more memorable that we could ever have imagined.

19

The Golden Ball Anomaly

The first preliminary experiment took place on Woodborough Hill during the afternoon of Sunday, 13 June 1993. It was a bright sunny day and the original intention of this lazy visit had been to inspect the location to make sure it was suitable for our purposes.

The group, consisting of ten people, had earlier completed a meeting at The Waggon & Horses public house in nearby Beckhampton, and having obtained permission from Tim and Polly Carson to enter the Alton Barnes farm, our vehicles followed the concrete track to the Woodborough barns. From here we climbed towards the copse of tall trees crowning the south-eastern edge of the hill. The weary party rested in the hot sun before deciding to conduct an impromptu meditational exercise around 16.00. Rodney Hale and Judi Smith said they would take photographs from the sidelines whilst the rest of the group came together in a circle and used the same visualisation I had employed in the Sompting crop formation the previous summer. This consisted of 'raising' the cone of power and then visualising a column-like thread of light rising up from its apex. We then imagined our point of consciousness climbing with the thread as it punched a hole in the clouds and continued into the upper atmosphere.

At this point in the meditation I asked everyone to try and mentally draw any presupposed atmospheric energy forms down towards our position on the ground. These we visualised as glowing spheres of light encircling our group. They were then seen withdrawing back from whence they came. The imagined column or thread of light was also withdrawn and the cone of power dismantled. I decided against the use of any archetype on this occasion as this then kept the whole meditational exercise plain and simple.

Judi Smith used a Canon A35F camera to take photographs of our visit to Woodborough Hill. It has a programmed AE shutter fixed at 1/125th of a second and was loaded with Kodak Gold 100 ASA print film. In all she clicked off 19 photographs that afternoon, 14 of which were taken during the meditation. The timing of these shots was random, based solely on her own intuition. The exposed film was developed the following week at a postal photographic laboratory and on studying the final prints she was surprised to find a clear anomaly on just one photograph showing the Pewsey Vale Downs taken during the meditation.

Having established that the anomaly was not a chemical blemish, she studied the print closely. It showed a fuzzy black object with no set shape and no distinct edges hanging over Golden Ball Hill, just east of Knap Hill. No other print bore even the slightest trace of a photographic artefact in any way, shape or form.

During the week commencing Monday, 21 June, Gary Bond of Pegasus was able to scrutinise both the print with the anomaly and the other pictures taken that day on Woodborough Hill. His first reaction was to admit that the anomaly was not a distant object, such as a bird or an aircraft, since the object seen was fuzzy and the rest of the picture was sharply in focus.

If not a bird or a plane, then the only logical explanation for the photographic anomaly was an insect passing close to the lens - the same solution I had offered for the object caught on film at Sompting the previous year and for the object captured above Knap Hill by John Langrish in July 1991. Although the insect theory remains a plausible possibility, it does pose various fundamental problems.

Yet whatever its explanation, the fact that we could so easily obtain such clear photographic anomalies begged the question of what we could expect to achieve in two weeks of constant experimentation.

We were to find out soon enough.

PLATES 25 and 26. Above, Church Meadow, Alton Barnes, the chosen Water Site in the Orgone 93 experimentation of July 1993 (pic: Orgone 93). Below, an anomaly caught on film above Golden Ball Hill by Judi Smith on Sunday, 13 June 1993 using a Canon A35F camera with a programmed AE shutter fixed at 1/125th of a second and Kodak Gold 100 ASA print film. Does this picture show a large bee or an unseen energy form? Inset, computer enlargement of the anomaly (pic: Judi Smith).

20

A Catalogue of Strangeness

Despite early set-backs, the Orgone 93 experiments were conducted without fail twice daily for 12 whole days. A full diary account was regularly entered onto a word processor and this provided us with a comprehensive log of the two week's proceedings. It is too long to quote in full, so I present here only the days most relevant to the results discussed in the subsequent chapters.

The following pages will, I hope, give the reader some idea of the mystifying incidents that befell the group during the period of experimentation. The text also includes one or two thought-provoking anecdotes, as well as a few subjective feelings on what the early results appeared to represent on a day-to-day basis. These, I believe, you will find of interest in the light of the many inexplicable sequence of events that surrounded Alton Barnes in the days that followed these comments.

Thursday, 22 July 1993. Experiment 10. Midday GMT. Hill-top site. Meditation using archetype ii. Six people took part, viz. Debbie Benstead, Jason Cormick, Lisa Dawkins, Kerry Horrigan, Anne Mowling and myself. 12.55 start.

For the first time the meditation employed the use of ancestor spirits as the selected archetype. After raising the cone of power we went in mind to the grassed-covered remains of Adam's Grave, which we imagined as a gateway made of stone slabs leading down into the otherworld. At this point I called upon the ancestor spirits and asked everyone to visualise prehistoric men and women, dressed in various different costumes, emerging into the open air. We then built an arc-like bridge of light between Adam's Grave and Woodborough Hill, and used it to draw the procession towards our position. Once in our presence they were seen first to encircle us and then to release balls of light from their hands. These were seen to spiral around our own cone of light.

Having completed the exercise, I reversed the imagery and returned the ancestor spirits back across the land bridge to Adam's Grave, where they returned through the darkened gateway into the otherworld. I then closed down the circle.

Everyone taking part said how strongly they were able to follow this particular meditation. They explained how vividly they had seen the ancestor spirits, as if they *had* actually been there with us on Woodborough Hill. One or two gained imagery outside of that specified by myself and for some minutes there was much talk about the success of this meditation, as opposed to those featuring either the 'Greys' or the Gaia archetype.

Some four minutes into the meditation John Horrigan recorded a noticeable rise in the radiation count. This high level persisted until the final minute of the meditation when it fell to the same low level recorded during the first control period. Video footage shot by cameraman Paul Shobbrook clearly showed that as I called forth the ancestor spirits, asking them to join us on the hill, the wind increased quite dramatically - the timing was so precise it is eerie to watch. This effect did not occur at any other time during the meditation. Furthermore, the sudden wind gust occurred five minutes into the meditation - one minute *after* the background radiation level began to rise. Is there a connection?

The quite clear results of this lunchtime experiment on Woodborough Hill inspired me. It was apparent that the conditions had been correct in every respect, making me wonder whether this had been connected with our use of ancestor spirits as the chosen archetype for the meditation. Those taking part felt more at home with this type of imagery, simply because they actually *believed* that ancestor spirits inhabited the ritual landscape of Wiltshire. In their minds we really were inviting them to join our meditation. Such feelings generate belief-related emotion of a kind I feel sure is connected with the potency of psycho-interactive processes.

For these reasons I decided to again use ancestor spirits at the Water Site the following lunchtime in place of the scheduled archetype.

Friday, 23 July. Experiment 12. Midday GMT. Water Site. OED with meditation using archetype ii. Six people took part, viz. Sue Chapman, Anne, Debbie, Kerry, Lisa and myself. 12.50 start. The meditation was a basic re-run of the ancestor spirit visualisation of the previous lunchtime. It was also the first time we had used the OED in conjunction with a meditation since Experiment 1.

Once again we saw crowds of Neolithic and Bronze Age figures emerge from Adam's Grave and walk across a bridge of light to join us, this time in Church Meadow. On their arrival, we visualised them dancing around our circle accompanied by rhythmic drumming, vocal chanting and foot stomping. As their ceremony grew to a crescendo we imagined light balls emerging from ancient sites all across the downs. We saw them gather together overhead and begin to encircle our group, as if motivated by the dancing of the ancestor spirits, who, I suggested, were calling upon their own ancestors through ritual worship. Once the exercise had been completed, the procession was despatched back to the otherworld via Adam's Grave.

As we came out of the meditation Anne had tears in her eyes due, it seemed, to the very strong emotions generated during the meditation. She said she felt like she could have stayed with these people forever; the sensations were intense, she admitted. Lisa said she felt a strong pressure upon her body, the only meditation this had occurred to date. Others reported similar physiological effects. I felt sure this was the most potent meditation we had conducted to date and anticipated some good results.

A short-term rise in the background radiation was recorded, although much less than the previous lunchtime. On developing the infrared film used during the experiment, Roger Wilkins noticed no less than five photographic anomalies on a shot taken 15 minutes into the meditation at 13.15 (Roll 4, Frame 15). The best of these is a solid ball (black when printed) in front of a cloud in the area where Beddoe had been directing the OED only minutes beforehand. Another blob can be seen below and to the right of this same cloud. Others, far smaller, are to be seen elsewhere in the frame. These were by far the largest and most pronounced photographic anomalies produced so far.

Monday, 26 July. Experiment 15. Dawn. Hill-top site. OED only. 05.10 start. The sky was clear and there was a clean, fresh feel to the environment; it had also rained overnight. Tony Beddoe used the OED to perform a circular 'draw' overhead Woodborough Hill, while the rest of the team monitored from the summit. No unusual sounds were noted on the VLF receiver, but there were two whistlers registered - one during the first control period and another during the experiment itself. The electrical interference was also particularly loud for some reason. At 05.37 I saw something very strange. Whilst listening to the VLF radio receiver on top of Woodborough Hill, I happened to be looking across the fields towards the north-west when I noticed a black object tumbling slowly over the heads of the corn. It was about 300 m away, close to the base of a field I later discovered was known as the Crates. It looked like a piece of card - some one and half foot square - turning on its horizontal axis.

The object was in view for the count of three before it simply vanished from sight. Having assumed it had fallen into the crop, I digested what had occurred and then realised there was no wind at all - it was a perfectly still morning. I then assumed that the tumbling object was a large bird, so I waited for it to re-emerge from beneath the level of the ripened crop. It never re-appeared, and after some 20 minutes of constant watching I realised I may have witnessed something unusual. I could offer no other explanation for this curious observation which, I must stress, was fully visible, not some clairvoyant impression. Shortly after 06.00 I gave the field one final glance before leaving the hill.

It later transpired that a visible light, colour 'intuitive' shot taken by Judi Smith at 05.21, produced a small photographic anomaly alongside the clear silhouette of a bird. She did not notice any midges or flies in the vicinity of the camera bank.

Experiment 16. Midday GMT. Hill-top Site. OED and meditation using no archetype. Eight people took part. A series of minor mishaps prevented the experiment from starting until 13.15. Joining Tony Beddoe at the OED was business associate Mike Collen and his wife, Shirley.

PLATE 27. No less than five dark blobs can be seen in the sky above Church Meadow in this black and white, IR shot (Roll 4, Frame 15) taken during Experiment 12 of Orgone 93 on Friday, 23 July 1993. Are they all air-bells? (pic: Orgone 93)

Moments before the commencement of the first control period, Austrian crop circle researcher Oliver Stummer, who had been attending the lunchtime experiments since the beginning of the previous week, experienced something quite odd. Sheltering from the light drizzle beneath the western end of the large clump of trees crowning the summit, he unexpectedly saw a bright burst of yellow light emanate from a horizontal position some 10 m away from him. It appeared to come from the direction of the camera hide, situated at the base of the hill (flashguns were not in use). Accompanying this incident had been a growing awareness of some kind of presence located above the copse of trees. Unnerved by what he could sense, Stummer decided to leave the hill-top and stand next to the camera bank and OED. He thought no more of the matter, although he did mention the incident to Judi Smith.

At approximately 13.20 the battery powering the IR video camera failed without explanation and at around 13.25 Paul Shobbrook's battery belt, powering his video recorder, dropped its charge from 14 to 11.5 volts, something that only normally occurs through some hours of continual filming (it later resumed its original charge).

Shobbrook's problems caused the meditation to be temporarily aborted, although somehow the message to stop did not reach the camera bank at the base of the hill. This was just as well as at 13.29 an IR shot (Roll 5, Frame 12) produced a huge black, circular anomaly which appears to be hanging above the western end of the copse - exactly where Oliver Stummer had experienced the bright flash of light only 14 minutes beforehand.

Two further photographic anomalies turned up on negatives taken during the same experiment - one is a visible light, colour shot taken at 13.43 and the other is an IR shot (Roll 5, Frame 18) taken at 14.01, some eight minutes after the completion of the meditation. This second black and white picture shows a white streak in the approximate vicinity of the VLF radio receiver. Having studied the negative at great length, this streak does not appear to be the result of an emulsion blemish, although this has to remain the most lightly explanation.

John Horrigan recorded a slight rise in the background radiation count during the meditation, and Johnny Merron recorded an air potential of 400 V/metre throughout the entire experiment. This is extraordinarily high in comparison with previous readings.

Tuesday, 27 July. Experiment 18. Hill-top site. OED with meditation using archetype iii. Five people took part. 13.00 start. The meditational imagery focused on the British goddess Elen, favoured in the earth mysteries as a guardian of the sacred ways and as the female intelligence of the land. We visualised her on the hill releasing spheres of light from the ground beneath her feet.

The final IR frame at the end of the second control period (Roll 5, Frame 36), taken at 13.40 shows a small, circular photographic anomaly in approximately the same position as the anomaly caught on camera at 13.29 the previous lunchtime. A visible light photograph taken at the beginning of the meditation at 13.16 also shows a small anomaly (orange-black when printed) directly above the hill.

As with our visit to Woodborough Hill the previous lunchtime, Johnny Merron recorded an extremely high air potential of 400 V/metre throughout the entire experiment. In contrast, the background radiation count was low.

Wednesday, 28 July. Experiment 20. Midday GMT. Water Site. OED and meditation using archetype i. A total of 11 people took part, viz. Debbie, Lisa, Duncan Bittle, Grace Carey, Jason Digby, Richard Ward, Sean York and myself. 12.50 start. For this meditation, the largest so far, we were joined by Graham Hancock, author of the international bestseller *The Sign and the Seal*, his partner Santha and their young daughter.

For the visualisation we used extra-terrestrial imagery blended together with visions of coloured globes of light seen circling around the assembled group. At the end of the meditation both Graham Hancock and his wife Santha complained of acute dizziness and headaches; both immediately retired to Brown's Cottage to recuperate. Whether these effects were simply the result of their participation in the experiment remains unclear; certainly neither were experienced in this type of meditational practice.

On developing the IR black and white film taken during the experiment, one shot timed at 13.05 (Roll 6, Frame 13) was found to contain two fairly large anomalies, one in

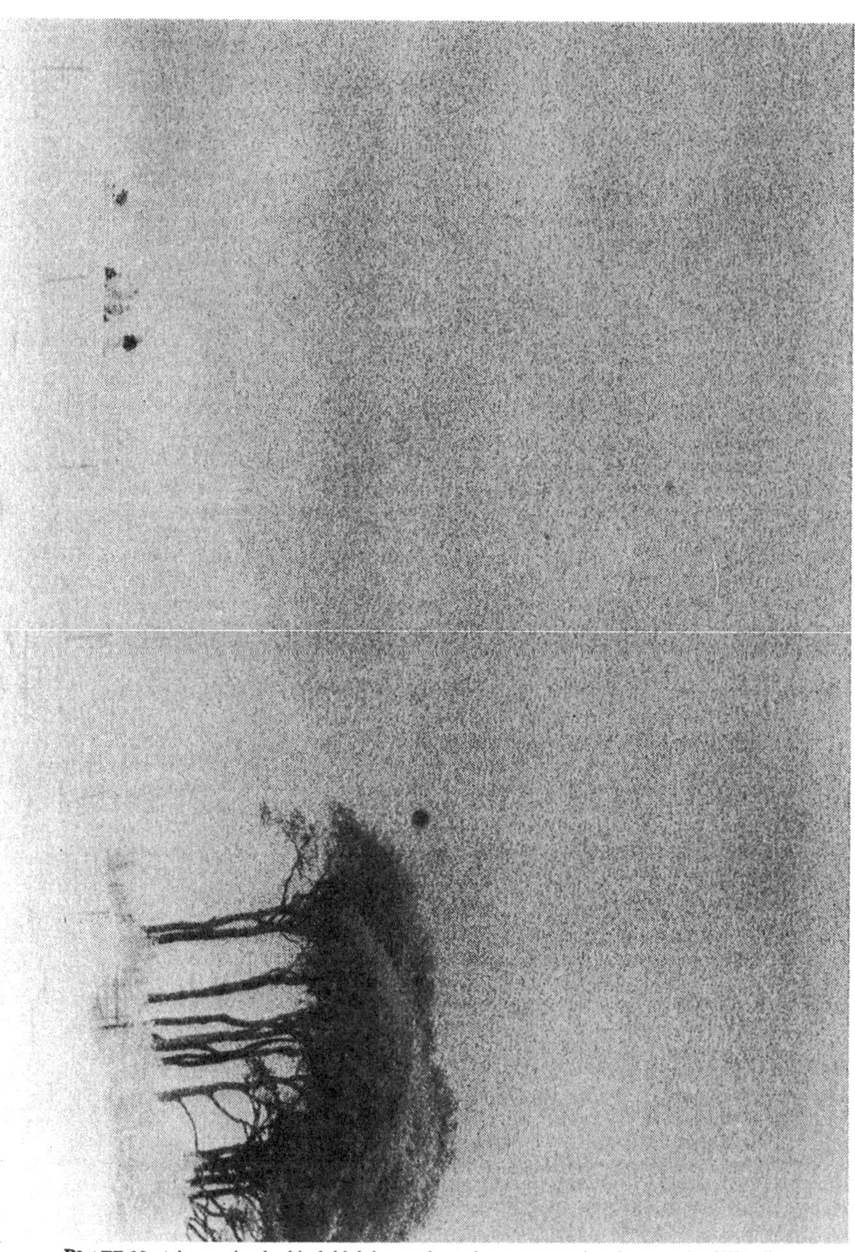

PLATE 28. A large, circular black blob hangs above the trees crowning the summit of Woodborough Hill during Experiment 16 of Orgone 93 on Monday, 26 July 1993. Minutes before this black and white, IR picture (Roll 5, Frame 12) was taken at 13.29, Oliver Stummer had stood below the same tree and experienced a bright flash of light followed by an overwhelming sensation of a presence nearby (pic: Orgone 93).

the area of sky being worked on by the OED and another off to the left of the picture. The first mentioned has a short, stubby tail trailing towards the right-hand side. In addition to this, an 'intuitive' colour shot (Frame 17) taken by Judi at 13.02 displays a much larger anomaly in the same area of sky as the IR anomaly with the tail. The strangest feature of this colour anomaly is that on each side of its main body is what appears to be a bright blue, tube-like protuberance.

Thursday, 29 July. Experiment 21. Ancient Site. OED with meditation using archetype i. Four people took part, viz. Grace, Kerry, Lisa and myself. 05.20 start. Yet another bleak morning on Adam's Grave with the weather like a dull, winter's day on Dartmoor. There was a thick misty cloud sweeping across the hill-top as well as bitterly-cold wind gusts. The 'Greys' visualisation was repeated once again.

The radiation count was extremely erratic and the VLF radio receiver picked up a series of 'thump'-like sounds at irregular intervals. Rodney Hale, who had also joined us for the day, recorded the same thumps on his own VLF receiver. No ultrasound emissions were reported on either receiver.

On development of the IR black and white film something very strange was noticed. One frame taken during the meditation at 05.50 (Roll 6, Frame 29) shows a tiny anomaly between my back and the VLF radio receiver. The next shot (Roll 6, Frame 30), taken at 05.55, shows a somewhat larger, circular anomaly on the top of the aerial attached to the VLF radio receiver; its positioning begs explanation.

Experiment 22. Midday GMT. Crop formation at Etchilhampton. Meditation using no archetype. Five people took part, viz Duncan Bittle, Grace, Kerry, Debbie and myself. 13.00 start. The use of this same visualisation had resulted in the oval photographic anomaly caught above the Sompting formation in July 1992, so I hoped it might prove equally as rewarding in a different crop formation.

Rodney Hale and Johnny Merron reported that the air potential varied between 20 and 60 V/metre from circle to circle. Johnny Merron sketched a ground-plan in an attempt to record the various readings.

On development of the IR black and white film we found that the third shot (Roll 7, Frame 4), taken at 13.11, during the first control period, displayed a tiny anomaly in the air above the circle.

Friday, 30 July. Experiment 24. Midday GMT. Avebury complex. 13.30 start. Meditation using no archetype at the Avebury complex. For our final experiment we were joined by around 60 people attending the Glastonbury crop circle conference organised by Roland Pargeter. Tony Beddoe positioned himself with the OED next to the large megalith known as the Devil's Chair, located in the south-eastern quadrant of the henge, while the meditation was conducted in the centre of the nearby stone circle.

Nothing unusual occurred, although the orgonomic temperature differential deteriorated during the meditation, but rose slightly during the second control period. The electro-static air potential was particularly high, for some reason. Furthermore, the VLF radio receiver recorded a short, sharp buzzing noise during the experiment, as well as one further prolonged sound during the second control period. This was almost certainly caused by some kind of localised radar interference. No photographic anomalies were produced during the experiment.

In conclusion, I felt the general atmosphere was not right for a co-ordinated meditation. Even though some people got something out of it, many others simply wanted to join their colleagues in the pub after the long journey from Glastonbury, suggesting that their minds had not been in the correct conducive state for a meditation of this sort.

This final exercise at Avebury completed the two-week period of experimentation. Throughout this time those responsible for the various different aspects of the monitoring programme were made to complete the daily report form, sometimes a little reluctantly. In the end, however, this provided us with a basic sample of the overall results and trends. These were, of course, supplemented by hand-written readings made in individual field books, much of which would need considerable scrutiny before any real sense could be made of what had really taken place during those tortuous two weeks in July 1993.

21

Does the Camera Never Lie?

With unfaltering conviction, Roger Wilkins and Judi Smith controlled two video cameras and three still cameras throughout the entire two weeks of experimentation - dedication that resulted in over 16 hours of video footage and 18 reels of exposed film.

Every other day Wilkins would develop and print the infrared-sensitive black and white films in a converted bathroom at Brown's Cottage, Alton Barnes. For this he used Kodak HC110 dilution B developer recommended for the development of the Kodak HIE high speed IR-sensitive film used in the experiments. Wilkins added local tap water to the liquid solution and this in turn was introduced to a standard developing tank. Agitation of the tank's vertical spool was carefully conducted once every 30 seconds, the time prescribed by Kodak. On removal from the tank, the resulting negatives were then hung up to dry before being scrutinised in greater detail. The meticulous procedures adopted by Roger Wilkins, and by Gary Bond in Leigh-on-Sea, failed to prevent the appearance of a large number of clear photographic anomalies.

Infrared Photographs

Against all expectations the seven reels of IR film produced no less than 26 inexplicable objects on 18 separate photographs - 25 as dark circular forms when printed and one white 'glow-worm' streak captured during Experiment 16 on Monday, 26 July 1993. Two of the dark 'blobs', as they became known to us, sported short, fireball-like tails.

Before we could make any assumptions concerning these photographs, it was imperative that we eliminated any possible logical explanations for the presence of the anomalies. In the case of the black, circular blobs the only nagging doubt in our minds was that they were not photographic anomalies at all, but 'air-bells', air bubbles or pin-holes, produced when tiny pockets of air remain attached to the exposed film during development. This results in a tiny area on the resulting negative where the chemical fails to react with the emulsion, causing a transparent spot that turns black when printed. Against this possibility, however, were the meticulous precautions taken by Wilkins to avoid such problems and the anecdotal stories reported in respect to the experiments in question, *i.e.* the events surrounding Experiments 12 on Thursday, 22 July and Experiment 16 on Monday, 26 July. There was also the dark anomaly positioned on the aerial of the VLF radio receiver in one of the photographs taken during Experiment 21 on Thursday, 29 July.

Gary Bond, who had agreed to analyse any photograph presented to him, initially suggested 'air-bells' as the explanation for these anomalies. However, he also doubted that as many as 25 'air-bells' could result from the use of just seven films, especially if the prescribed developing instructions had been followed satisfactorily.

The 'Air-bell' Solution

The appearance of air-bells on photographic negatives is not a common fault, and every professional photographer I have spoken to says that they have never suffered from this problem, even when using IR-sensitive film. In an attempt to learn more about this subject Roger Wilkins and Rodney Hale conducted a series of experiments during August and September 1993. They hoped to produce air-bells using the same type of IR-sensitive film and the same developing solution as that used at Alton Barnes in July that year (see Appendix II - The Air-bell Experiments). The results of this work have shown that under certain circumstances dark circular blobs and more obvious black pin-holes can be created under normal photographic conditions. However, although many of these blobs bear similarities to our own photographic anomalies, the air-bell solution is by no means

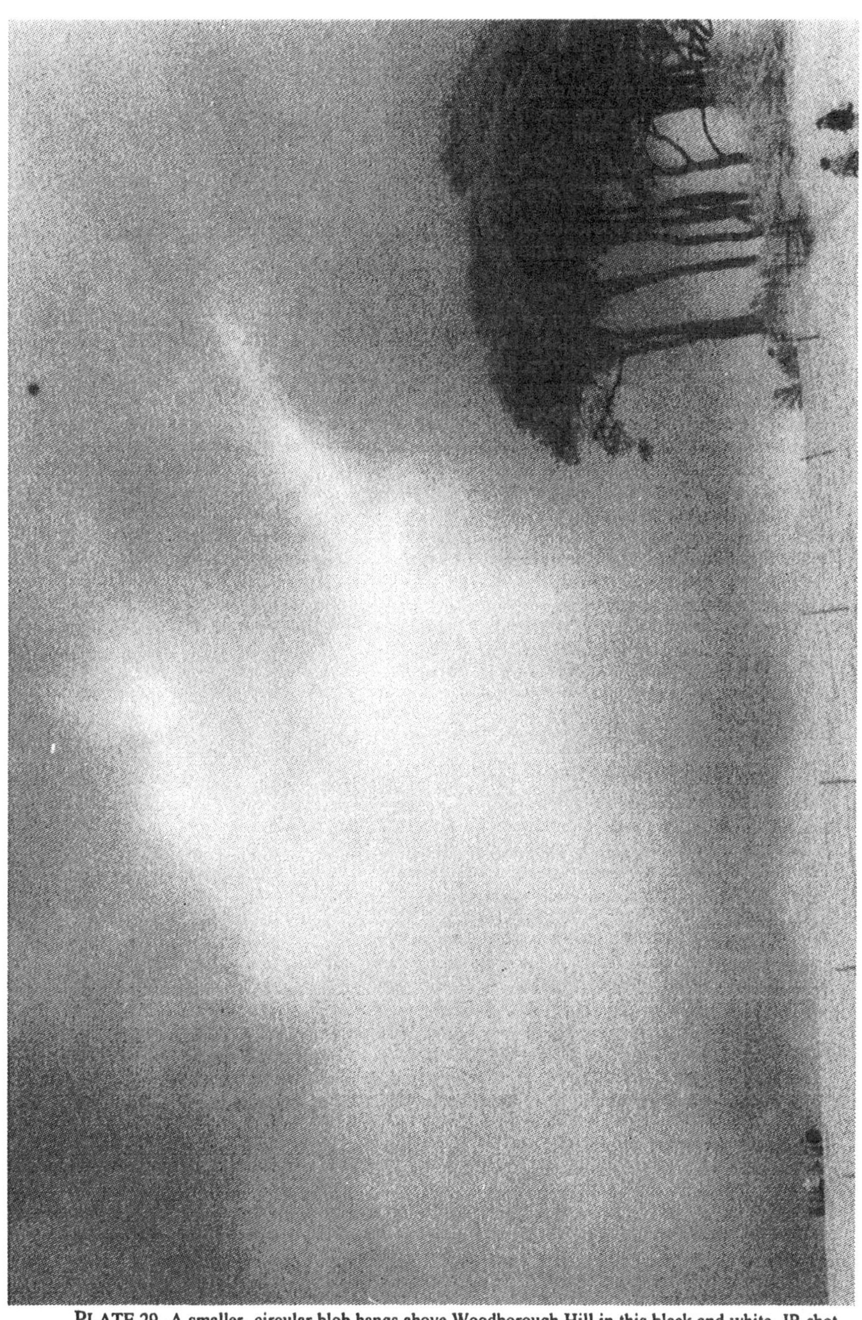

PLATE 29. A smaller, circular blob hangs above Woodborough Hill in this black and white, IR shot (Roll 5, Frame 36) during Experiment 18 of Orgone 93 on Tuesday, 27 July 1993. The previous lunchtime had produced a much larger circular anomaly over the same tree (pic: Orgone 93).

cut and dry. A question mark lingered over the true nature of the black and white anomalies obtained during Orgone 93.

Visible Light Anomalies
Using visible light film Orgone 93 obtained eight photographic anomalies, five using Johnny Merron's Ricoh SLR camera during the regular experimentation and three as 'intuitive' shots taken by Judi Smith with her own camera. Only two of these examples came near to matching the black and white photographic anomalies, and this was the orange-black blob captured on camera at 13.16 during Experiment 18 and the white circle and hemisphere seen in the sky on the photograph taken at 13.43 during Experiment 16.

The only logical explanation I could offer for the anomalies on either picture was blemishes on the negative caused through chemical stains. Against this solution was the simple fact that Wilkins had checked both negatives with an eyeglass and could find no trace of raised blemishes where the marks appeared on the frame. Furthermore, the orange-black anomaly was similar to the examples produced by both John Langrish and Chris Trubridge at Alton Barnes during the 1991 summer season.

The six remaining examples taken during the period of experimentation showed indistinct fuzzy shapes, usually elliptical in appearance. Of these, no less than five might be explained as small insects passing in front of the lens, leaving us with the picture taken at 13.02 on Wednesday, 28 July during Experiment 20.(1) The photographic anomaly in question bore a remarkable similarity to the example achieved at Woodborough Hill on Sunday, 13 June during the first initial experiment and, as previously mentioned, displayed a blue, tube-like protuberance each side of its main body.

In September 1993 Gary Bond was finally able to study the picture's original negative using the company's Macintosh Quadra 950 computer. The results were truly amazing. The computer software was easily able to pick out the anomaly's two light blue protuberances which continue to remain a complete mystery. Despite this, there must remain a distinct possibility that, like the other five examples already discussed, this picture in fact shows an insect of some sort. Yet on a visual basis alone, Gary Bond remains unconvinced by this theory, adding light-heartedly that the anomaly looks like no insect he knows! Certainly, the computer enhancements failed to convince anyone of the insect verdict.

Ultra-violet Photography
The UV photographs conducted with a pin-hole camera, shielded by a Kodak Wratten 18A glass filter, proved totally inconclusive. Long exposure times and blurred pictures made any interpretation of resulting imagery virtually impossible. Of the six rolls of film used in the experiments, none produced anything recognisable as an anomaly.

Future experiments with UV photography must involve the use of a fluorite crystal lens which, unlike its standard glass counterpart, allows UV light to enter the camera. Using this in conjunction with the correct filter mechanism would result in sharp photographs. Only then could any resulting imagery be studied in greater detail.

Video Results
The meditation, or the position of the meditation during control tests and OED experiments, was videoed for the entire 40 minutes by Roger Wilkins and Judi Smith from a distance that varied according to which site was in use. In the case of Woodborough Hill it was approximately 50 m when meditations were in progress, although this distance increased to approximately 200 m during OED experiments, which necessitated the camera bank being located close to the base of the hill. In the case of the Water Site, the distance was approximately 10 m, while at Adam's Grave, owing to the steep incline the distance was reduced to between 5 and 10 m.

The 16 hours worth of video footage produced by the end of the 24 experiments did not reveal any anomalies of any sort, which was obviously a great disappointment. We had dearly hoped that the black and white IR-sensitive camera on loan from ASSAP might have been able to tell us more about the photographic anomalies achieved during the different experiments.

Yet, if nothing more, these video tapes stand as testimony that the 24 experiments were carried out in the manner described in this book.

PLATE 30. Black and white, IR shot (Roll 6, Frame 13) depicting the scene in Church Meadow, Alton Barnes, during Experiment 20 of Orgone 93 at 13.05 on Wednesday, 28 July 1993. Notice the two dark anomalies in the sky, one above and to the right of the meditators and the other off to the far left of the frame. A colour shot taken at 13.02 showed a further dark anomaly in a similar position as the right-hand circular blob (pic: Orgone 93).

PLATE 31. Colour shot (Roll f, Frame 17) taken at 13.02 showing the Orgone 93 meditation in Church Meadow, Alton Barnes, on Wednesday, 28 July 1993. Above a tree on the right-hand side is a small dark anomaly which, on the original colour print, possesses a curious sky blue protuberance on either side of its body. These are clearly visible on the enlargement and therefore beg explanation (pic: Orgone 93).

The Future

Orgone'93 was able to achieve photographic results closely matching those obtained by Trevor James Constable with the help of Jim X. Woods in the Californian desert during the 1950s. The only real difference between his pictures and ours was that we had critically examined each one and assigned it a logical solution. Unfortunately, however, there was no golden envelope we could open to reveal whether we had been correct or not in our assumptions.

Stereo photography was the only way forward. Using such equipment would, in theory, eradicate the problem of air-bells, emulsion blemishes and raindrops all in one go. Most important of all, with the application of mathematics the distance of any feature in a stereo picture could be accurately calculated - meaning that objects close to the lens, such as insects, could easily be identified. After much searching a Pentax stereo adaptor was acquired in early 1994 and plans were made to use it in a further round of experiments at Alton Barnes that summer. Only after these had been completed and the results made known would we be able to determine, once and for all, the true nature of the photographic anomalies so easily caught on film since the 1940s.

22

Ultrasound

Ultrasound detectors respond to friction caused by human movement and the wind rustling through leaves up to a distance of approximately 50 m. Initially this confused some of the Orgone 93 team into believing we were getting genuine readings from unseen sources, but after a few minutes of familiarising one's self with the instrument's capabilities the brain easily associates the flickering of the needle with mundane activity. With these points in mind, the results recorded by my colleague Johnny Merron, who had previously worked with the Dragon Project, simply beg explanation, for on the first six mornings Rodney Hale's ultrasound detector produced off-scale readings at a frequency of 26 kHz. This signal would last for between 30 seconds and several minutes, after which the needle would generally settle down to display only random readings between 0 and 30 on the relative scale. If the detector was switched across to its second frequency of 40 kHz as the off-scale readings were occurring, the needle would simply drop back down to 0 and return to readings of 100+ the instant it was switched back to 26 kHz.

Furthermore, during Experiment 11 at Adam's Grave on Friday, 23 July 1993, Merron recorded random pulsing during the first control period, *i.e.* before dawn, and then shortly after the commencement of the main experiment, which straddled the period of sunrise, the needle rose and remained off-scale for around 30 seconds before falling away to nothing. Checks to make sure the instrument was still functioning proved positive, suggesting that the 100+ signal was genuine.

As early as Experiment 1, Merron had suggested that the off-scale signals could be due to 'feedback' caused by the detector itself. However, the repeatedly high signals around dawn convinced him that this explanation was simply inadequate to explain the strange pulses.

Rodney Hale, who joined us for the day on Friday, 23 July, listened to Merron's account of this abnormal ultrasound pulsing and concluded it was probably due to over-sensitivity on the part of the instrument. He adjusted the device accordingly and in the remaining seven days of experimentation the problem never recurred. Indeed, after this date the detector registered virtually no ultrasound emissions at all, even from mundane sources.

Despite Hale's assurances, I had my doubts concerning the over-sensitivity solution for the early morning, off-scale readings. The sheer fact that they had taken place, with two exceptions, around the point of sunrise at all three sites being used suggested this was genuine pulsing recorded at a frequency of 26 kHz. Had the device not been re-set, then I believe the same readings would have continued in a similar fashion for the rest of the two-week period.

Supporting this contention is the knowledge that, using a wide-band ultrasound detector during the autumn of 1978, the Dragon Project obtained similar 'ultrasonic pulsing over the dawn period in the immediate area of the King Stone', close to the Rollright stone circle in Oxfordshire. Strangely enough, these same signals could not be recorded inside the ring of stones - an effect described by project co-ordinators Paul Devereux and Don Robins as the 'zero-field effect'. The following February early morning signals were also recorded in the circle as the overall pulses appeared to grow stronger. This activity gradually declined following the Spring Equinox until 'virtually no activity was recorded at all' by early summer. Subsequent work was conducted to verify these findings, leading to the supposition that the cycles of pre-dawn and dawn ultrasound emissions appeared to be linked with both the lunar phases and sunspot activity.(1)

Aside from the off-scale readings recorded by Orgone 93, some days also produced constant ultrasound pulses at regular intervals of anything between 2 and 5.5

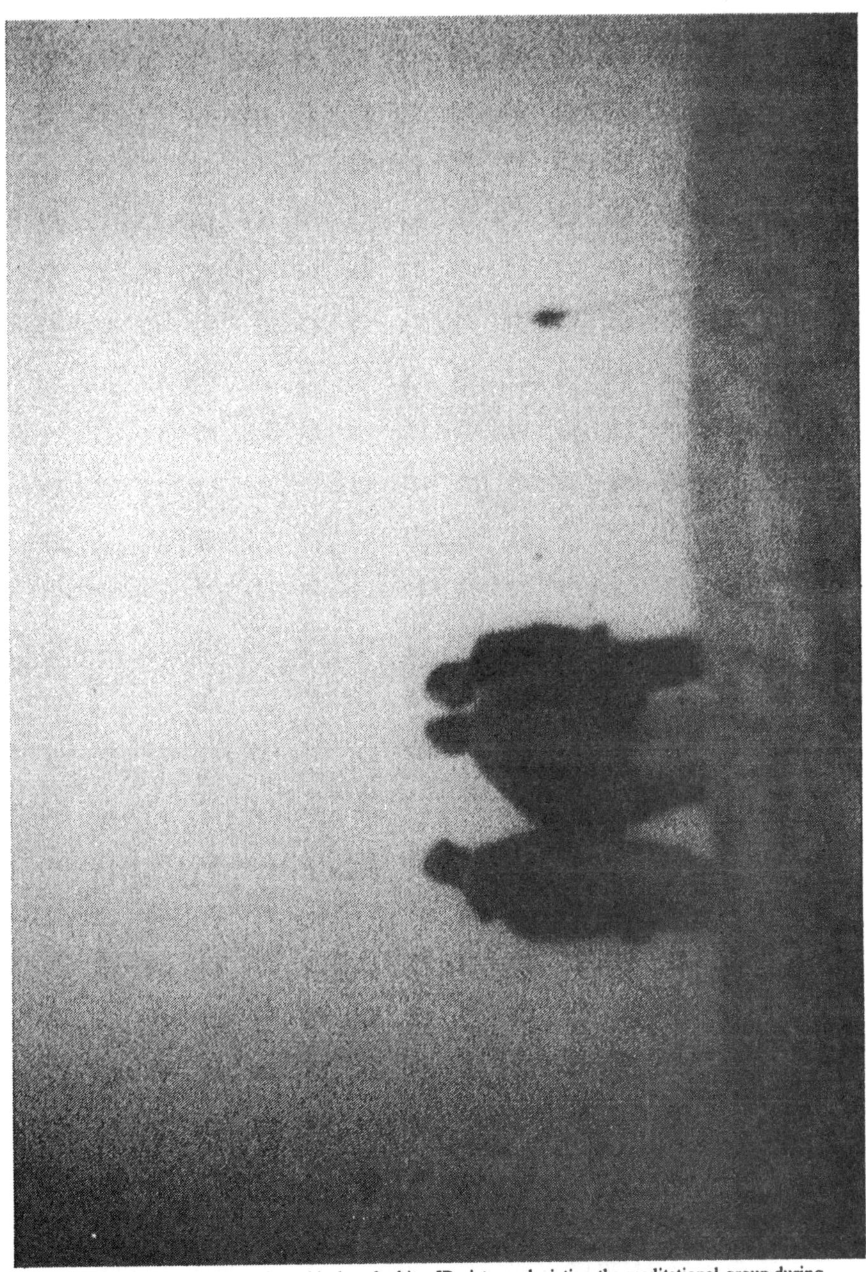

PLATE 32. The first of two black and white, IR pictures depicting the meditational group during Experiment 21 of Orgone 93 at Adam's Grave on Thursday, 29 July 1993. This shot (Roll 6, Frame 29), taken at 05.50, shows a tiny circular grey blob between the back of the right-hand meditator (the author) and the VLF radio receiver fastened to a bamboo pole.

PLATE 33. The second of two black and white, IR pictures depicting the meditational group during Experiment 21 of Orgone 93 at Adam's Grave on Thursday, 29 July 1993. In this shot (Roll 6, Frame 30), taken at 05.55, a circular black anomaly can clearly be seen on the tip of the VLF radio receiver's telescopic aerial. Is this simply an air-bell? or does this photograph show an unmanifest energy form visible only to IR photography? (pic: Orgone 93)

seconds. For instance, throughout the entire duration of Experiment 10 on Woodborough Hill at lunchtime on Thursday, 22 July, Johnny Merron recorded regular pulses of between 0.25 and 0.5 seconds every 5.5 seconds at a frequency of 26 kHz, while during the dawn control tests at Adam's Grave on Friday, 23 July the other multi-band detector, which was normally quiet, picked up regular pulses every 1.5 seconds at the slightly higher frequency of 80 kHz. Similar readings were recorded for the entire duration of the control tests on Adam's Grave around sunrise on Wednesday, 28 July. There is no readily-available solution to this problem, although it is our belief that these regular pulses, which were only recorded sporadically, probably originate from an unidentified local transmitter.

Orgone 93's photographic and monitoring programmes produced an assortment of quite baffling anomalies, yet they seemed to pale into insignificance when compared against the controversy that surrounded its radiation results, and it is this matter that we must address next.

23

Raising the Radiation

In Britain, background radiation detectable at ground level is almost entirely made up of cosmic radiation and radio-active isotopes in the earth, rocks, soil and atmosphere. Different regions produce considerable variations in the ambient count depending on an assortment of uncontrollable factors, especially local geological factors. In parts of Cornwall, for instance, the sub-surface geology and radon gas emissions will ensure greater background counts than, say, the Vale of Pewsey or the Marlborough Downs with their sedimentary deposits of chalk and greensand.

Airborne radioactive isotopes can also cause temporary fluctuations in background radiation, as can many other less obvious factors such as the movement of people and electronic noise in the instrument. All these factors had to be taken into account when assessing the final results achieved through the use of our own Geiger counter.

Before the commencement of each experiment John Horrigan would set up the Radiac Mk II Geiger counter some 10 to 15 paces from the position of the meditation and, after giving the instrument five minutes to settle down, he would log the ambient beta/gamma count once a minute for the entire 40-minute session, sometimes longer. Once the experiment was under way no one was allowed to approach the Geiger counter, other than those who had already been present during the first control period, and no apparatus was permitted to be moved. These efforts enabled us to build a comprehensive picture of the fluctuations that might be expected in the Vale of Pewsey during the month of July.

A Controversial Discovery

The clear initial results of this tentative research had not been anticipated. On nine separate occasions the Geiger counter indicated that the background count had increased, sometimes quite noticeably, during the period of meditation. This went against all expectations and was further highlighted when the sequence of readings were plotted as graphs.

The possibility that the background count should increase during meditational exercises seemed difficult to equate with our understanding of orgone energy and the energy continuum as a whole. Reich, for instance, appeared to believe that the background radiation count would actually *decrease* in the proximity of an orgone accumulator.(1)

Having reviewed these controversial results, both Rodney Hale and Roger Wilkins cast grave doubts on the reliability and efficiency of the old Radiac Geiger counter, and as a consequence of his suspicions, Wilkins dismantled the instrument and examined its components. His conclusions were that the delicate Geiger-Muller tube, although still functional, was so old that it should be replaced at the earliest possible convenience. What's more, due to inherently poor voltage regulation, the device produced either exaggerated readings or, in some cases, no readings at all. This therefore explained some of the more erratic count rates obtained during the experimentation; however, Wilkins also stated that these findings did not necessarily invalidate the repeated, and often sustained, radiation rises obtained during the periods of experimentation.

Where, then, did this leave the readings so diligently logged by John Horrigan? Fortunately, not all was lost, for although the Radiac counter might not have been able to record the true counts per second, its needle did appear to register the localised trend over a prolonged period, so its readings could not dismissed out of hand. Moreover, the cavalry was just over the horizon.

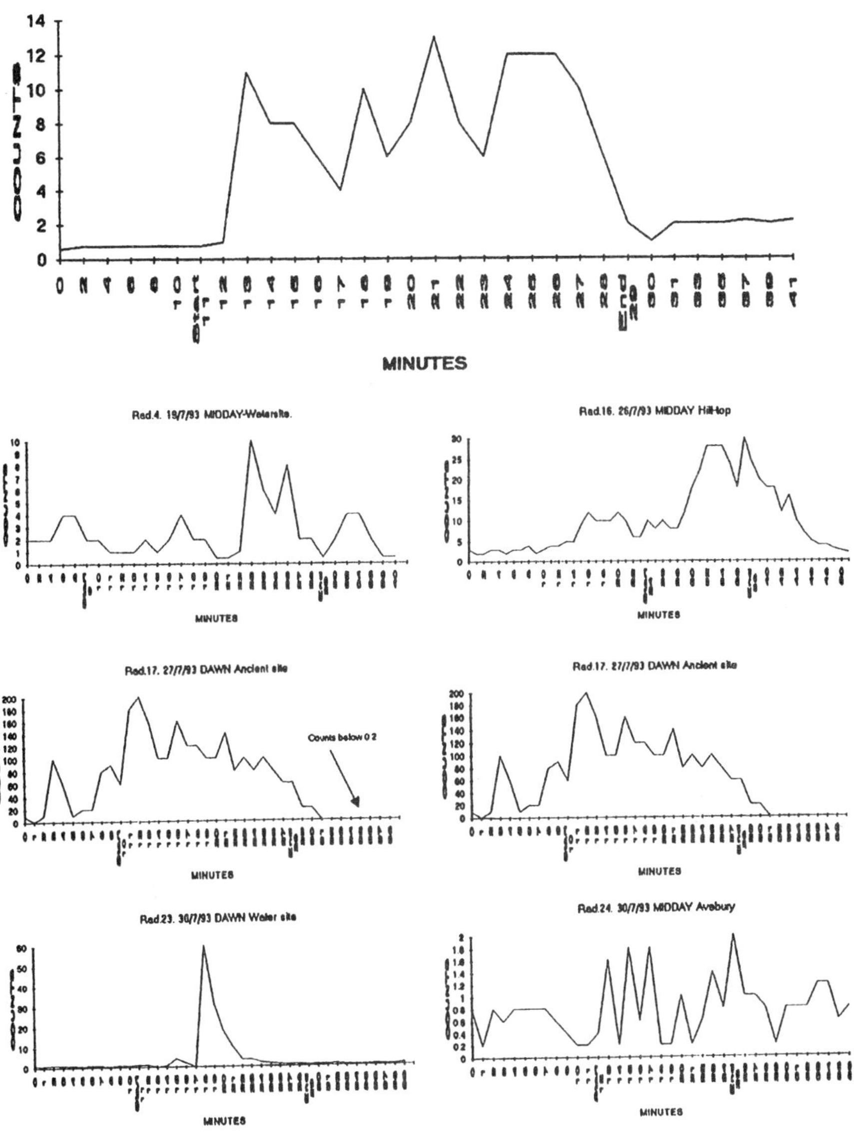

FIG 17. Seven examples of the peculiar radiation rises registered on the Radiac Geiger counter coincident to the meditations conducted during Orgone 93 experimentation in July 1993 (pics: John Horrigan).

Much of what follows might seem a little tough-going to some readers; however, as you will see, confirmation of Orgone 93's radiation results is of paramount importance to our understanding of not just psycho-interactive processes, but also the possibility of the mind being able to affect such things as unseen UFOs existing in the atmosphere.

Computer Confirmation
Rodney Hale made two one-day visits to the Orgone 93 experiments at Alton Barnes. The first of these, on Friday, 23 July 1993, he recorded the radiation counts per minute (cpm) on his own triple-tubed Geiger counter during Experiment 12 at the Water Site, which produced a small rise in the background count on our own Radiac set. To our relief Hale's own counter also registered a noticeable rise during the meditation. In a report dated 17 October that year, Hale confirmed that on 23 July he obtained 'a higher count rate for the period of the meditation', therefore parallelling the results obtained by our own Geiger counter. He also fed this data into a computer and used a cumulative summing method to bring out the above and below average count rate to show the overall trend. This too confirmed the rise recorded during the meditation period, a result Hale openly described as 'very clear and startling', even though he advocated further work before coincidental natural variations could be ruled out.(2)

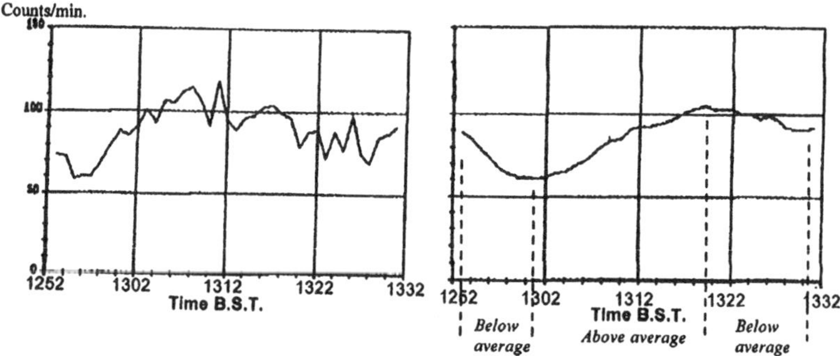

FIG 18. Left, a graph showing the radiation rise recorded on Rodney Hale's triple-tubed Geiger counter coincident to the meditation conducted during Experiment 12 on Friday, 23 July 1993. A small rise was also recorded on the Radiac Geiger counter at the same time. Right, the cumulative trend graph of the same experiment (pic: Rodney Hale).

Inspired by these new findings, I arranged for members of Earthquest, the earth mysteries group I run in Leigh-on-Sea, Essex, to take part in a further meditational experiment. Many of them had been present at the original Orgone 93 experiments and were happy to follow up this work in whatever way they could. The session finally took place on Sunday, 28 November 1993 in the function suite of a public house where the group meet on a regular basis for both lectures and meditations. In attendance was Rodney Hale, who monitored the whole experiment using a computer-linked Geiger counter positioned on the edge of the circle of meditators, and John Horrigan, who took manual readings from the old Radiac Geiger counter positioned some 10 paces away from the group.

Two meditations were conducted, the first - from 12.54 to 13.14 - featured the same ancestor spirits imagery used so successfully at Alton Barnes, whilst the second one, from 14.05 to 14.27, featured extra-terrestrial-based imagery. The results were not stunning by any means, although the resulting graph did highlight certain unusual characteristics as Rodney Hale pointed out in his summary report of the occasion:

> The eye can detect a possible difference of activity (on the resulting graph) just before and for most of the (first) meditation, but nothing special can be noted for the second period of meditation.(3)

Using the cumulative summing method to show the overall trend, Hale went on to construct a second graph which showed that:

> ... a period of above average gamma count rate started with the call for the first meditation and was sustained for most of that first period. The second period is rather lost in the general change which occurred over the three hours recorded, *i.e.* a somewhat below average count rate for the first two hours followed by a sharper period of above average for most of the last hour. With tongue in cheek one could say that the two calls for meditation both marked a turning point in the count rate!(4)

This last remark refers to my call for everyone to sit in a circle and relax their minds in readiness for the up-coming meditation. Oddly enough, the Radiac set showed no noticeable change in the beta/gamma count, almost certainly confirming Roger Wilkins' view that the Geiger-Muller tube was now no longer usable.

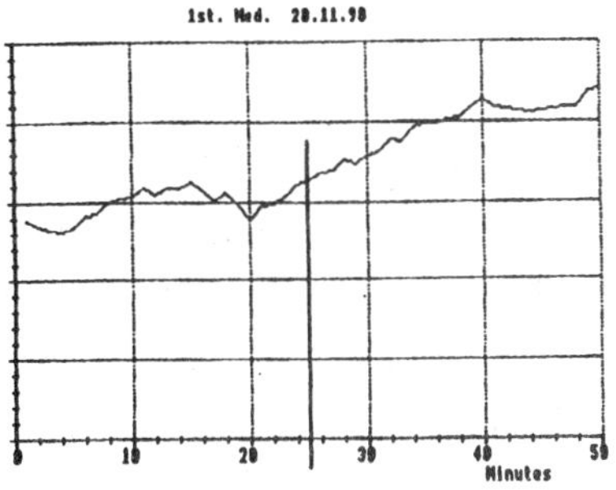

FIG 19. Cumulative trend graph showing the first meditational experiment conducted with the Earthquest group at Leigh-on-Sea, Essex, on Sunday, 28 November 1993 (pic: Rodney Hale).

The Ridgeway Quest

Since belief-orientated emotion appeared to play some part in the efficiency of psycho-interactive processes, I realised that if this process could be combined with more serious ritualistic practices out in the landscape, then it might just be possible to obtain an even clearer picture of such activity. I therefore jumped at the chance of combining further experimentation with a proposed walk along the entire length of the prehistoric Ridgeway track, conceived and organised by John Horrigan on behalf of the Earthquest group.

The aim of this pilgrimage was to traverse the entire length of the Ridgeway from its point of commencement in Oxfordshire to its modern-day place of termination at Alton Priors in Wiltshire, a distance of some 136 km. The trek was to begin on Friday, 1 April 1994, Easter weekend, so it was agreed that on their arrival at Alton Priors, those walkers still standing should take part in two meditations - one featuring both the Ridgeway and ancestor imagery, and the second featuring no fixed archetype. At the same time other members of the Earthquest team would monitor the location for possible electromagnetic or paranormal anomalies.

Control Experiment

By way of a control experiment to the up-coming Ridgeway quest, a preliminary session was conducted at Rodney Hale's home at Bricket Wood, near St Albans, Hertfordshire, on Sunday, 27 March 1994. Some 17 Earthquest members attended - 14 taking part in the first meditation and 15 in the second. An assortment of instrumentation was placed inside the circle of meditators to monitor fluctuations in different regions of the electromagnetic spectrum.

All readings from the session were fed directly into three separate computers over a four-hour period commencing at 13.30 and ending at 17.30. The two 30-minute meditations - one at 15.00 and the other at 16.39 - featured, in the first instance, a path-working exercise involving both the Ridgeway and the same ancestor spirit imagery used at Alton Barnes the previous summer, and in the second instance, and by way of a control, an unplanned visualisation featuring Victorian children at play. In addition to the main session, a second four-hour period of monitoring was recorded by Hale following the group's departure around 18.00.

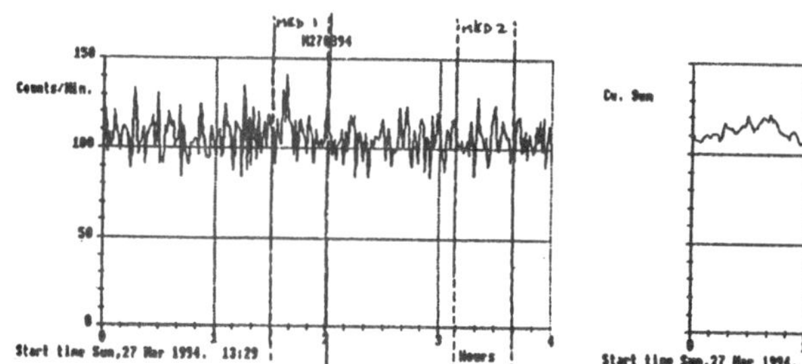

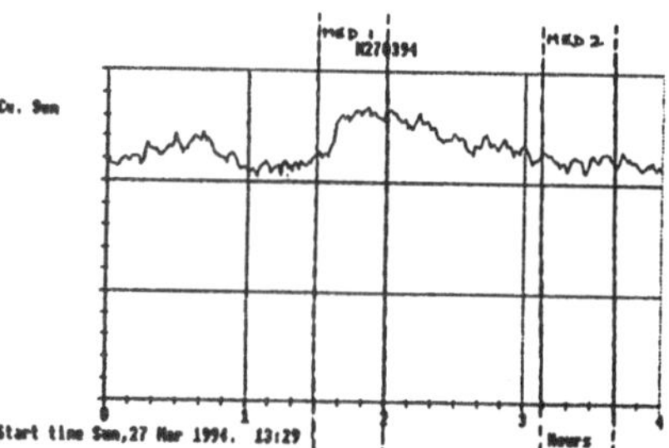

FIG 20. Left, graph showing the radiation count rate during the first 'ancestor spirits' meditation at Bricket Wood on Sunday, 27 March 1994. Right, cumulative trend graph for the same experiment. The sudden increase coincides with the group 'raising the cone of power' (pic: Rodney Hale).

The Highest Count

The radiation count recorded during the first meditation showed a substantial increase some five minutes into the meditation - a point coincident with the raising of the cone of power. The final graph revealed a sudden burst of activity which continued for some six to seven minutes before slowly settling back down again. A second graph using the cumulative summing method to represent the overall trend of the readings confirmed this sudden rise around five minutes into the meditation. In his technical report of the session, Rodney Hale summed up the abnormal radiation rises in the following manner:

> The main feature is a burst of high activity shortly after the start of the first meditation... Some gentle rises and falls are normally present, although the second 4 hour period presents an unusually quiet picture... The highest count/min (for the whole session), 141, occurs just the once during thc first meditation. Using the standard statistical test for a normal distribution of the 240 one-minute counts carried out during the four hour period, the calculated chance of a count of 141 occurring is one in 5000, and we had to find it in the meditation period!(5)

The Walk

The clear radiation rise recorded during the first meditation was enough to boost the morale of the Earthquest team, particularly those gearing themselves up for the start of the Ridgeway quest just a few days later.

Despite atrocious winter conditions during the entire five-day period, six out of the seven individuals who embarked on the walk managed to endure three whole days before being forced to abandon their journey some 65 km short of Alton Priors (it was completed in September 1994). Having finally reached their destination point by alternative means, the group then gathered in Church Meadow, Alton Barnes - the Water Site of the Orgone 93 experimentation - during the afternoon of Tuesday, 7 April 1994. Several other members of the Earthquest team were also present to help with on-site monitoring.

The first meditation was conducted between 15.08 and 15.28 by John Horrigan and featured visualised highlights of the Ridgeway quest. A 15-minute control period then followed before the start of the second meditation at 15.43. This time those individuals not operating monitoring equipment also joined the circle, making a total of 11 meditators. The theme of the creative visualisation was to attempt to influence the instrumentation and to draw down 'energy forms' into some kind of registerable manifestation using light channelling techniques alone.

A total of 83 radiation readings, timed at 66-second intervals, were registered on a small, twin-tubed Jupiter counter. These were later compared with 60 similar readings recorded the previous afternoon at the same location using the same instrument. As on previous occasions, Rodney Hale fed this information into a computer and analysed the results. And, as before, there was a noticeable burst of radioactivity around the beginning of the first meditation which did not recur during the second session, and was not present in the readings of the previous day.

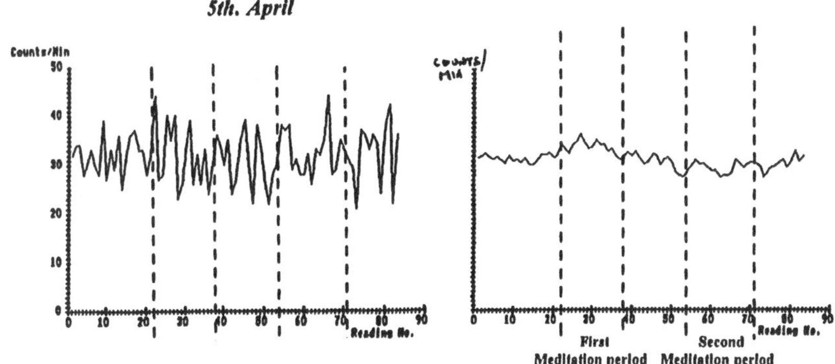

FIG 21. Left, a graph showing the radiation count rate during an experiment with the Ridgeway walkers at Alton Barnes, Wiltshire, on Tuesday, 5 April 1994. Right, the cumulative trend graph of the same event (pic: Rodney Hale).

Statistical Confirmation

In a report dated 15 April 1994,(6) Hale used these latest results to re-examine all seven meditation sessions monitored either with his own triple-tubed Geiger counter or by the Jupiter counter. By adding together the corresponding counts per minute for each control period and meditation, he was able to discern an overall trend emerging for the first time. A graph displaying the grand total of counts recorded for all seven sessions revealed a distinct rise in activity, beginning just before the start of the meditation and climbing steadily throughout the rest of the session. Only on completion of the meditational period does this increased level begin to subside. A second graph representing the general trend for all seven sessions further supports these findings.

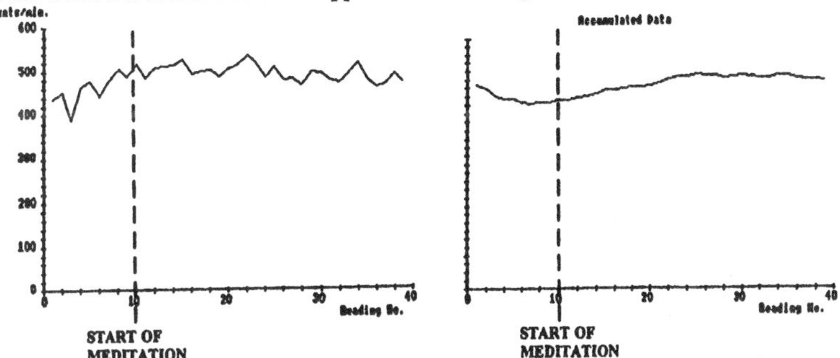

FIG 22. Left, a graph showing the combined radiation counts of seven separate experiments conducted under the guidance of electronics engineer Rodney Hale between July 1993 and April 1994. It confirms that meditation-linked experiments appear to produce an increased count rate on Geiger counters. Right, the cumulative trend graph for the same experiments only further confirms these findings (pic: Rodney Hale).

Hale then made a series of calculations based on the total counts recorded during the first four minutes of each meditation against the total counts recorded during the first four minutes of each initial control period. On *all seven occasions* the statistics showed clear increases in cpm during the first four minutes of the meditation. In Hale's own words these figures indicated 'a persistent, and sometimes strong, trend of increased radioactivity starting some minutes before the actual start of the meditation.'

It was too early to speculate on how exactly the human mind might be able to increase the localised radiation count; indeed, according to the laws of physics it is impossible. Yet perhaps there was another answer. What if unconscious, psycho-interactive processes are able to focus on the radiation counter being used and force the ionisation of gas in the Geiger-Muller tube to produce *false* readings in the absence of increased radioactivity? It seemed a tantalising possibility and one that both Rodney Hale and Roger Wilkins were prepared to consider as cautious electronic engineers. If so, then was there any outside evidence to suggest this was indeed the case?

The answer is yes...

Focused Human Attention

Between 1977 and 1979 William A. Tiller of the Department of Materials Science and Engineering at Stanford University began experimenting with 'focused human attention', or psychokinetic (PK) effects, in association with something he referred to as a gas discharge device, which bore remarkable similarities to the processes employed in a Geiger-Muller tube.(7)

Although dismissive of many of the exotic claims made in the name of high voltage or Kirlian photography, Tiller became convinced that behind the normal bio-electrical discharges was a 'novel phenomenon' that increased the amplitude of the observed effects.

Having proposed that this 'novel phenomenon' was generated naturally by the human body, Tiller constructed a gas-filled discharge detector designed to interact with a human subject's bio-electrical field to give an increased count rate when the applied voltage exceeded a certain level. The detector was similar to a Geiger-Muller tube in that it was perpetually poised to produce a volley of so-called 'microavalanches' when ionisation occurred inside its gas-filled cell.

For the intended experiments it was decided that during the first five-minute period the subject would simply sit or stand 1 m from the detector, the so-called WOH (without hands) mode, during which time the resulting count rate would be recorded. For the next five-minute period the subject, while remaining in the same position, would place his or her hands above the device's grounded electrode and, without touching it, focus their mind on increasing the counting rate - the so-called WH (with hands) mode. During the final five-minute period the subject would resume his or her original position and await the completion of the experiment as further readings were taken.

Repeated experiments with thousands of subjects over a three-year period admirably demonstrated that when a person brought his or her hands close to the grounded electrode, there would be an intermittent and sometimes sustained increase in the count rate, even though the applied voltage of the subject remained less than the breakdown voltage of the detector, ruling out the likelihood of this being a simple capacitance effect. Anyone was apparently able to achieve this effect; young, old, students, non-students, healers or non-healers, it didn't seem to matter. Indeed, it appeared that anyone with the ability to focus their attention appeared to produce the best results. However, sometimes no one would be able to achieve an increased count rate for periods of up to several days at a time, and yet no correlations were ever found in respect to matters such as rain storms, lunar phases, etc.

Many tests were conducted to try and find a more orthodox explanation for these anomalous results (this included placing dummy hands over the detector charged to potentials of up to several kilovolts DC), but nothing appeared to have the same effect. There is not the space to go into the many tests the research team conducted in an attempt to rule out the possibility that more obvious effects, such as capacitance and heat, were responsible for the increased count rates. For us it is the unexpected results they obtained which are of more importance to our own debate, for it seems that on some occasions, when the system was left running for an hour or so on the WOH mode, if one of the subjects entered the empty room the detector would begin a burst of activity before settling back down to zero again. Tiller also reported that:

> On other occasions, when in another part of the lab discussing other topics while the system was running in the WOH mode with zero or only a few counts recorded, if attention suddenly turned to matters concerning the cell, the detector would often begin chattering and produce a substantial number of counts. It was dramatic events like these that made us suspect a possible mental influence on electron microavalanche development in the gas.(8)

As a result of these curious discoveries, Tiller set up two further experiments to test the authenticity of this apparent 'mental influence effect'. In the first instance a subject would stand or sit before the detector in the 'without hands' position for the first five-minute period. He or she would then spend the next five minutes attempting to influence the device to give an increased count rate using no hands, just mind-power alone - the so-called WM 'with mind' mode.

The results of these extraordinary experiments were quite remarkable. The revised experiments showed that a subject did not need to place his or her hands around the detector to obtain an increased count rate; *one had only to use the mind*. Furthermore, it appeared that when hands were placed around the grounded electrode and the subject focused his or her concentration on other matters, *i.e.* simple arithmetic, no increased count rate would be recorded. Even more startling, when a subject was placed inside a faraday cage (which blocks out all electromagnetic interference) and focused his or her mind on a detector contained inside a further faraday cage some 3 m away, a substantial increased count rate was still recorded, strongly suggesting that, in Tiller's words, a 'nonlocal' phenomenon was responsible for this apparent 'mind/matter' interaction.(9)

Although Tiller points out two major differences between the processes involved with his gas discharge device and a Geiger-Muller tube, it seemed clear that since both use gas-filled cells poised in readiness for an ionisation event, they can both be influenced by non-local processes. Moreover, Dr Roger Taylor, who first brought Tiller's work to my attention in May 1994, visited Stanford University in July of that year and spoke at length with Tiller himself. Dr Taylor gave him details of both the Orgone 93 and subsequent Earthquest experiments and was happy to accept the possibility of the human mind affecting the count rate of Geiger-Muller tubes. Although Tiller's original work was brought to an abrupt close when his equipment was stolen by one of his students, he said that others are now experimenting with similar devices and that hopefully they will be able to attain similar results. Further liaison between Tiller and ourselves is planned in the future.

Tiller's three-year study of focused human attention goes a long way to validate the possibility of radiation anomalies like those achieved by Orgone 93 and the Earthquest group on various occasions between 1993 and 1994. Yet if this was the case then it implied that what we had seen on so many occasions were not increases in the ambient radiation levels at the locality involved in the experimentation, but increased counting rates produced inside the Geiger-Muller tubes caused by unconscious, non-local interaction. This meant there was every possibility that the old Radiac Geiger counter really had registered genuine discharge events even though the device was poised on the edge of break-down; indeed, perhaps this was a significant factor in itself, for had it been working properly during the initial round of experiments then I believe there is every possibility that we would never have noticed these clear counting anomalies. Maybe an element of uncoordinated chaos is essential to the success of such experimentation.

These are important realisations. Quite obviously, more radiation tests, both indoors and out in the landscape, were planned for the summer of 1994. Yet even at this stage in the proceedings, it seemed clear that if the human mind could affect instrumentation and/or the environment through focused human attention, then it made the possibility of using similar non-local processes to draw unseen bioforms into manifestation that much more appealing to the outside world.

24

The ORANUR Effect

Orgone researcher Tony Beddoe was given the job of finding a way to measure the orgonomic potential or excitation of the pre-supposed energy continuum during the periods of Orgone 93 experimentation. Various ideas were put forward and in the end he decided to use a multi-layered orgone accumulator for this purpose. The alleged temperature difference between this and the outside air could, it seemed, enable Beddoe to establish the orgonomic tension of the environment - an idea gleaned from the work of Wilhelm Reich. This effect, referred to by Reich as To-T (*i.e.* To - Temperature inside the accumulator, T - temperature outside) was particularly noticeable during hot sunny days when it was believed that the sun's influence increased the orgonomic potential at ground level. Yet on dull, stormy days Reich would generally find that the temperature differential was either greatly reduced, or it disappeared altogether.

In the aftermath of the ORANUR experiments of 1951-2, Reich discovered that instead of producing positive temperature differentials (PTDs), the Institute's accumulators would display a clear negative temperature differential (NTD), *i.e.* it would be colder inside the box than in the open air. At first Reich could not understand why this should be, but as the atmosphere above Rangeley, Maine, grew ever bleaker, and the Institute's staff started suffering from ill-effects likened to radiation sickness, he came to believe that NTDs were connected with the over-excitation of orgone in the immediate environment - the so-called 'ORANUR effect' which resulted in the production of atmospheric DOR.

Much later Reich concluded there was a clear connection between abnormal NTDs in his accumulators and the proximity of nuclear facilities and power plants. Moreover, Beddoe points out in his Orgone 93 report that American orgone specialist Joel Carlinsky '... recorded this effect in the vicinity of radioactive materials. (And that) ORTEC has also recorded small negative differentials close to VDUs.'(1)

The accumulator used in the Orgone 93 experiments was 22 cm square with an outer casing of wood and inner layers of rock wool and steel wool. It had an opening just large enough to take a standard thermometer, electronically linked to a second external thermometer bearing an LCD that displayed both the accumulator's internal temperature and the ambient air temperature. The box was painted black and this had immediately received much criticism, since some heat absorption would undoubtedly occur; white would presumably have been more preferable. When necessary, Beddoe would cover the box with a thick black cloth and attempt to keep it away from direct sunlight. He would also leave the accumulator in the garden of Brown's Cottage to ensure that any temperature changes would not be due to its sudden transference into the open air.

The second problem was that any recorded temperature changes could not be compared against a control. A blue polystyrene box constructed by Beddoe for this purpose proved totally impractical and had to be abandoned at a very early stage in the experimentation. In addition to this, changes in the exterior temperature would cause a lag inside the multi-layered box, meaning that the two thermometers could not be expected to equalise for anything up to 30 minutes. Indeed, a proper control would not just have been desirable, it was essential to the objectivity of the experiments.

Despite these unforeseen set-backs, Beddoe meticulously recorded the temperature differential between the accumulator and the outside environment for the whole duration of the experimentation. Nothing really unusual occurred until Experiment 4 at the Water Site on Monday, 19 July 1993. Around the start of the first control period Beddoe recorded an unusually abnormal temperature differential of -8.5 degrees C. This decreased to -8.9 degrees C. during the meditation, but then increased to -3.9 degrees C.

during the second control period. Weather-wise, there was a 50% nimbus cloud cover, with the wind increasing during and after the meditation.

These early results completely baffled Beddoe. Never before had he seen such unusual temperature differentials, a fact which alarmed him slightly as in orgonomic terms this indicated a 'contaminated' or 'over-excited' environment. NTDs were an indication of the alleged ORANUR effect, so high readings such as these suggested that the environment was being over-excited by some external influence, probably man-made in origin. More significantly, this unusual environmental condition appeared to diminish quite dramatically during and after the meditational period.

Experiment 6 on Woodborough Hill at lunchtime on Tuesday, 20 July again produced an abnormal NTD that reached -8.5 degrees C. during the first control period, before increasing to -4.2 degrees C. during the meditation and -0.5 degrees C. during the second control period (the cloudbuster was not in use). The weather at the time consisted of a high cloud-base with south-westerly wind gusts during and after the meditation. Following this experiment my partner Debbie suffered severe flu symptoms, acute nausea, a persistent headache, a sore throat and an unaccountable metallic taste in the mouth. She also developed two small warts on the little finger of her left hand which remained for several months.

All these ill-effects have been associated by the likes of Constable, Eden, DeMeo and Reich with ORANUR conditions and a DOR-poluted environment, suggesting that Debbie, as a psychically-sensitive individual, had suffered an over-excitation of bodily energy caused by an unstable environment around Woodborough Hill that lunchtime. Although warts are seen by orthodox medicine as a type of virus, homoepathy teaches that they are energy-related complaints and can be treated as such.

More strange readings were recorded during Experiment 10 on Thursday, 22 July on Woodborough Hill. The following lunchtime, during Experiment 12 at the Water Site, we used the OED together with a meditation for the first time since day one. This was also the second occasion that we employed ancestor spirits as the selected archetype in a meditation. Beddoe noted that the weather during the first control period was calm, with cumulus, high stratus and cirrus clouds overhead. There were also low winds. An abnormal NTD was once again recorded, and yet despite the use of the OED the average readings decreased from -1.4 degrees C. during the meditation to -2.2 degrees C. for the second control period. During his use of the OED, Beddoe became dizzy, nauseous and developed a dry throat. To overcome these effects Beddoe bathed in salt water in the hope that this would decrease the presumed over-excitation of energy inside his body, and this did seem to do the trick.

As previously discussed, the black and white, infrared-sensitive film used during this experiment produced a single frame containing no less than five globular anomalies seen in the sky above Church Meadow. This was the highest number achieved on any one photograph during the entire period of experimentation. Furthermore, the largest anomaly was in the area of sky being 'worked on' by the mini-cloudbuster. The fairly decent weather that week had also brought with it a sticky humid atmosphere, and shortly after the conclusion of our experiment heavy rain began to fall, even though most of the sky was still relatively free of clouds. This situation may or may not explain the clear PTDs recorded during both experiments the following day, Saturday, 24 July.

PTDs were again recorded during the dawn experiment using the OED on Woodborough Hill on Monday, 26 July (the occasion I saw the dark tumbling object above the crop in Tawsmead field). This all changed, however, during Experiment 16 on Woodborough Hill that lunchtime when Oliver Stummer witnessed the bright flash of light and curious voltage drops were independently recorded by Roger Wilkins and Paul Shobbrook.

In the slight drizzle, Beddoe had focused the OED on the dull and cloudy sky from a position at the base of the hill, just beyond the camera bank. With him were Mike and Shirley Collen, business associates who had come to observe the OED in operation. Almost from the start Beddoe had begun registering peculiar temperature differentials which fell from +3.3 degrees C. during the first control period to -7.0 degrees C. during the second control period, and this was despite the fact that the external temperature actually *rose by 5 degrees C.* These curious readings tended to support the idea of a subtle shift taking place in the local environment - from one of relative stability to one of over-excitation. It also indicated a particularly changeable environment that was seemingly deteriorating by the minute. Furthermore, even before the thermometers began to display a highly abnormal NTD, both Tony Beddoe and Mike Collen began to experience severe head pressure. In Beddoe's case this developed into a dry throat - the second time this had occurred in a matter of days.

Both Beddoe and myself were baffled by these results and concluded that the atmospheric tension was building once again. At that time I was also unaware that an extremely high air potential of 400 V/metre had been recorded on Woodborough Hill, or that the IR photography would produce two clear anomalies that lunchtime.

PLATE 34. Tony Beddoe operating the mini-cloudbuster during the Orgone 93 experimentation in July 1993. Can this simple device enhance the energy excitation of the environment? (pic: Nel Bat)

No temperature differentials were recorded during Experiment 17 on Adam's Grave at dawn on Tuesday, 27 July, but Experiment 18 on Woodborough Hill that lunchtime once again produced a highly abnormal NTD. Using the OED, Beddoe later recorded that he had felt 'dizzy, light headed,' and had experienced a 'bitter taste, stomach ache, [a] tightening of [the] chest, [and] back ache...' during the session. As on previous occasions, this implied some kind of environmental excitation. Remember too that during this experiment an extremely high air potential of 400 V/metre was again recorded and a dark photographic anomaly appeared above the copse of trees that crowns the hill for the second day running.

From Wednesday, 28 July till the end of experimentation on Friday, 30 July, Beddoe recorded quite normal temperature differentials, suggesting that the environment had become more stable. Why this should have been so is beyond our grasp, since there appeared to have been no obvious change in the weather pattern. It was still cloudy, with the odd rain showers and the occasional period of sunshine. It is, however, worth noting that from Monday, 26 July till the end of the second week, Beddoe used the OED for one or more experiments each and every day. Although this device was only meant to stimulate the immediate environment, perhaps it might have played some role in dispersing the apparent ORANUR effects noted at different stages during the two-week period of experimentation.

The only exception to the above pattern was the experiment conducted with the Glastonbury conference goers at Avebury on Friday, 30 July. Here an abnormal NTD was again recorded. However, as this was our only experiment at the location it is difficult to assess whether these readings were typical or not.

A Pattern Deduced?

Despite the lack of a control, the pattern that emerged with respect to the use of an orgone accumulator as a means of measuring the orgonomic tension of the environment appeared clear. At times when it displayed a highly abnormal NTD an assortment of monitoring and photographic anomalies also occurred, while those of a psychically-sensitive disposition experienced ill-effects. In Beddoe's case this would occur during the use of the OED. On three occasions (Experiments 4, 6 and 10) it also seemed that, coincident to the meditation taking place, the NTD was severely reduced, suggesting a possible connection between the two. It is also to be noted that all three of these experiments produced clear radiation anomalies hinting, once again, at the possibility of mind interaction with the environment.

If this is so, then the steady reductions in the NTD recorded during the meditations could mean that the visualisations were helping to enhance the *quality* or *richness* of the local energy matrix surrounding the site concerned. The concept of healing the landscape using meditational or ritualistic practices has, of course, been the belief of psychics, mystics and shamans since time immemorial. Could this process therefore help us to understand the energy cycles at power sites such as stone circles and barrows, or at locations or zones where UFO sightings are a frequent occurrence? Despite obvious draw-backs, a study of alleged environmental tension using Reichian physics warranted further attention and this we would re-address in the round of experiments planned for the summer of 1994.

Before evaluating the rest of the controversial results obtained by the Orgone 93 team, it is necessary to trace and record the many other strange events which befell Alton Barnes during the period of experimentation, for only then can we truly begin to make sense of what occurred during those final two weeks of July 1993.

25

The Monitoring Game

At the same time that the participants of Orgone 93 were bedding down in readiness for another pre-dawn start, many others were either switching on their monitoring equipment or preparing themselves for night-time vigils at local vantage points in and around Alton Barnes.

As in previous years the area produced a multitude of unusual events throughout the height of the summer, many of them occurring during the last two weeks of July. Before we go on to detail the nature of these coincident events, it might be helpful to set the scene by mentioning just some of the incidents reported prior our on arrival in Alton Barnes on Saturday, 17 July 1993.

Crop Formations

The nocturnal land artists were slow to take advantage of the ever ripening fields of Wiltshire during the summer of 1993. Between Beckhampton and the Marlborough Downs there were very few crop formations to be seen by early July. Then overnight on Saturday/Sunday, 10/11 July, some joker rolled flat a huge ring of crop straddling three fields at the East Kennett/West Overton T-junction, while further along the same road the same person or group left a set of three circles, each with comma-like spurs. The circular arrangement made by this formation gave it the appearance of three sixes grouped together - an obvious play on the number's occult significance. Those who first entered this formation the following morning found lumps of badger fur hidden beneath the fallen crop, leading them to speculate a sinister motivation behind its clandestine construction.(1)

Project Relate

On the same night that the ring and three circles appeared, the CCCS-backed Project Relate began monitoring from two separate locations at Alton Barnes under the watchful eyes of Rodney Hale, Simon Lyons and Dr Roger Taylor. Its intentions were to monitor electromagnetic and other terrestrial effects in the hope that the results could be correlated with any crop circle events or aerial luminosities reported in the Alton Barnes area during this same period.

The Relate equipment consisted of a mains-linked computer recording geomagnetic shifts, earth or ground currents and the presence of microwave radiation. It was operated from the Old Manor, the home of Tim and Polly Carson, in Alton Barnes. This was supplemented by a battery-operated 'black box', positioned initially in Tawsmead field, which dealt with the recording of airborne sounds, underground seismic sounds, earth or ground currents and VLF radio signals. The monitoring work of this dedicated group is of the utmost importance to our own research as it ran parallel with the Orgone 93 experimentation.

The first inexplicable result achieved by the Relate equipment occurred during the early hours of Sunday, 11 July, just hours after the mains-linked computer was switched on for the very first time. Between 04.25 and 05.02, a period of some 37 minutes, it registered four strange earth current pulses - one sustained signal followed by three matching smaller peaks.(2) On discovery of these recordings, which were completely outside the expected ambient variation in earth currents, there was much excitement as that same night the large ring and so-called 666 formation had been constructed just outside the village of East Kennett, some three miles north-north-east of Alton Barnes.

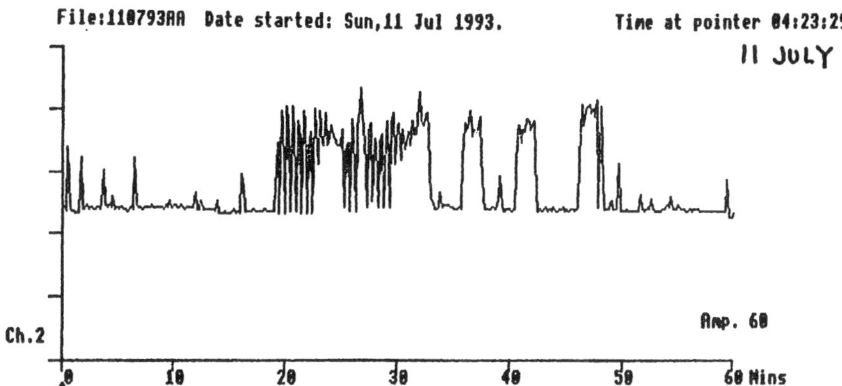

FIG 23. Above, graph showing the inexplicable earth current pulses recorded during the early hours of Sunday, 11 July 1993 by the Relate computer positioned at Alton Barnes. Compare these to the almost identical earth current traces recorded by the same equipment during the early hours of 5 August 1993 (pic: CCCS/Relate).

It seemed too much of a coincidence that the number and size of the crop circles should exactly match the sustained pulses received by the Relate equipment, even though the likelihood of the circles being man-made was suspected from the outset. It was also known that neither the stomping of feet, nor the rolling flat of crop would have had any noticeable effect on the production of earth current pulses.

Alton Barnes and nearby Woodborough come under the Newbury division of Southern Electricity, who produce earth currents when switching over the main electrical grid system during a fault. With this knowledge in mind, Rodney Hale was able to ascertain from Kevin Small of the Business Support Unit that the above mentioned earth current pulses, along with another set of identical signals to be described in Chapter 27, were in no way connected with their work, leaving unknown military activity on Salisbury Plain as the only possible explanation.

Paul Hailey and the 'Zebedee' Whistle

Another monitoring programme operational in Alton Barnes was the one put together by electronics engineer Paul Hailey. He had volunteered his services to the Relate team before the season commenced and as a consequence conducted his own specialist work under the CCCS's banner. His monitoring took place for 13 days between Sunday, 11 July and Friday, 23 July, and for a further four days between Friday, 30 July and Monday, 2 August.

Hailey's own equipment consisted of a multi-track tape recorder with conditioning amplifiers programmed to record the audio section of electromagnetic signals, as well as earth probe signals, seismic pulses, quiet radio signals at around 100 MHz and audible sound. There was also a channel for timing pulses. This mass of equipment was run from a converted dormobile with the overall purpose of recording possible evidence of localised paranormal anomalies, whether circular or otherwise.

Hailey established his base at the secluded silage pit on the southern edge of East Field, just off the Alton Barnes to Pewsey Road. Each night he would return to his van sometime before midnight and then monitor constantly through till dawn. However, it was to be nine days before Hailey was to achieve his one and only sequence of inexplicable events. On the night of Monday/Tuesday, 19/20 July, Hailey began monitoring as normal around 23.00. Nothing unusual occurred until 23.59 when he unexpectedly heard a very peculiar modulated sound that cut across the various channels recording the sensors and ground probes located outside the vehicle. The noise lasted for just 1.5 seconds and to all intents and purposes sounded like the curious whistle made by Zebedee in the children's programme 'The Magic Roundabout'!

Alerted by this mysterious sound, Hailey quickly checked the tape recorder to make sure it was still functioning properly. Finding no obvious fault, he turned and glanced out across East Field and immediately noticed an unidentified pale white light at an estimated elevation of 25 degrees, travelling due east between two clouds directly above Knap Hill, some 1.6 km north of his position. It stayed in view for between 20 and 30 seconds before blinking out, giving Hailey enough time to conclude that it was not an aircraft, an illuminated balloon or a satellite. There was no sound accompanying this sighting, a fact confirmed by the exterior microphone. The time recorded for this incident was 00.02 and the night was calm and devoid of any obvious wind.

From that day on until the completion of his monitoring programme, the same curious whistle did not repeat itself and no further unidentified aerial luminosities were seen, meaning that the incidents on the night of July 19/20 were the only obvious anomalies recorded by Hailey. There was, however, many, many hours of tapes for each of the various channels which would have to be studied before any final judgements could be made.

On his return home, Hailey established that the Zebedee whistle was in fact created by the tape recorder inexplicably running backwards and re-recording what was already there. Similar effects can occur during a power supply black-out, like that caused by lightning, thereby suggesting that in this case the whistle was the result of an as yet unknown disturbance to the equipment. Hailey was able to simulate the whistle without too much difficulty and was therefore satisfied that he had achieved a suitable explanation for this occurrence. Yet why the tape deck should have hiccuped on this one occasion remains a mystery. Having designed, developed and put together his own instrumentation, Hailey could safely say this disturbance was unconnected to the tape deck's power supply, for as he put it himself:

> Although the signal is heard clearly on nearly all tape channels, it does not appear on the graphs, due to its nature. The tape reversed direction for two seconds during recording, (and) this is a normally 'impossible' situation. The deck has no push-button facility for reverse direction recording, all recording is in one direction only. The fast rewind condition must have occurred spontaneously, and although this effect was reproducible by interfering with the 'tape tensioning' arms, the actual cause of the malfunction is unknown. The fact that timing markers (recorded to tape during on-site recording) were two seconds short for this period, prove that a reverse tape travel did occur for a time.(3)

To confuse matters even further, when checking the seismic readings for the night concerned, Hailey discovered that an anomalous pulse had been recorded at just after 00.00, *i.e.* between the time of the tape recorder malfunction and the appearance of the pale white luminosity, some two minutes later. The height of the resulting spike indicated that it had lasted for some seven seconds and was about half the strength of the signal produced by a passing car. It apparently takes the form of a vibration of around 3 cycles per second.

Hailey could find no logical explanation for this seismic disturbance, although its presence between the tape anomaly and the sighting of the luminosity must raise the question as to whether there is a link between these three, quite separate incidents.

Magnetic Bursts

From the early hours of Sunday, 11 July through till the night of Monday, 19 July the

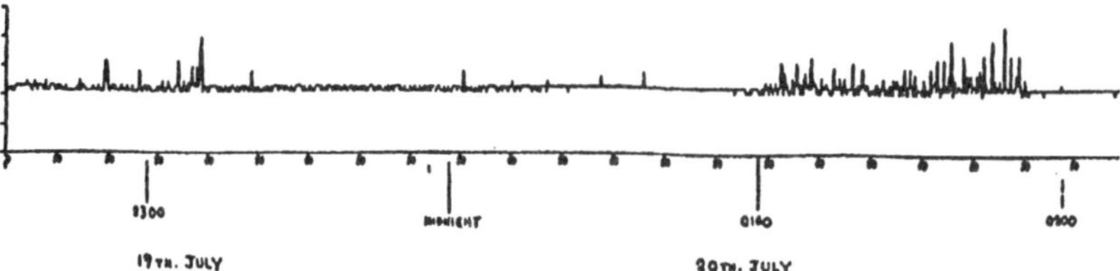

FIG 24. The unaccountable 'change in the trend' within the geomagnetic field recorded by the Relate equipment between 01.00 and 01.50 on Tuesday, 20 July 1993, just one hour after Paul Hailey's 'triple' event on East Field (pic: CCCS/Relate).

Relate team's monitoring equipment recorded no obvious anomalies. Then, between 01.00 and 01.50 on Tuesday, 20 July, the mains-linked computer registered an unaccountable 'change in the trend' within the geomagnetic field - the only major burst recorded during the whole of the three-and-half-week monitoring programme.(4)

What exactly this occurrence represents is not easy to ascertain, although the fact that it took place just one hour after Paul Hailey's 'triple' event is difficult to overlook. This cluster of inexplicable events hints at the fact that something significant occurred at Alton Barnes overnight on Monday/Tuesday, 19/20 July and that this shift was recorded by both Paul Hailey and the Relate equipment.

Other than these alleged incidents, as well as various claims of mysterious lights being seen locally, life was pretty quiet for local skywatchers until the night of Monday, 26 July when the fun really began, both on the ground and in the air.

26

The Big Flash

Certain sections of both the crop circle and UFO communities believed that Monday, 26 July 1993 would herald an event of immense supernatural significance. Such predictions were almost certainly influenced by the fact that there had been notable 'paranormal' occurrences in and around the Alton Barnes area on this day in previous years. For instance, in 1990 Stephen Alexander made his famous video of the moving light from the edge of Milk Hill and a giant 'key' pictogram, aligned on Silbury Hill, appeared that night at nearby East Kennett. On 26 July 1991 a second dramatic 'key' formation - considered by some to be among the best ever - was again discovered at East Kennett, while in 1992 Steven Greer, Chris Mansell *et al* witnessed the anomalous light cluster from a position on the concrete track close to the Woodborough barns. With these incidents in mind, common sense suggested that in 1993 a similar event might occur locally, and this is indeed what happened.

Ball-like Core

That night, despite the constant drizzle and low cloud-base, a number of crop watchers braved it onto local vantage points around the Alton Barnes area. One such person was rock musician Reg Presley. He was standing in Knap Hill car-park with a small group of people and a local television crew hoping to catch an aerial luminosity on film.(1) Just after midnight, at a time put at between 00.10 and 00.15 Presley says he caught sight of an inexplicable white light appear somewhere over Woodborough Hill, 2.3 km south of Knap Hill. As it moved rapidly out of sight in a westerly direction, he quickly used his flashlight to alert the television crew who were waiting some 50 m away. Just as they left their equipment to respond to Presley's call, a second bright light flashed across the southern sky heading in a westerly direction, either in or just below the cloud-base. It was in view for less than a second, but in that time Presley saw that the source of this earlier flash was a white elliptical mass. The television crew also registered the presence of the flash as they walked across to Presley.

Soon afterwards the television crew gave up for the night, leaving Presley alone with a few friends. Just over an hour later another, much greater flash occurred. Presley says it appeared either overhead or just beyond Woodborough Hill and apparently possessed a bright circular core as large as the moon. This quickly extinguished from the centre outwards, leaving only a tiny white pinpoint of light that vanished as the landscape was plunged back into darkness. In his opinion this circular mass was the *source* of the big flash which, he says, illuminated not only the entire landscape, but also the interior of the low cloud-base. Glancing at his watch just after the event, Presley noted the time was 01.20.

Most intriguing of all was the alleged colour of the aerial flash, for Presley believes it was distinctly blue, possibly even turquoise. It was definitely not lightning, he stresses, for despite the drizzle, there was no sign of any storm activity that night.

Sven Reuss and his friend 'Tier', two German crop circle enthusiasts from Frankfurt, were also in Knap Hill car-park when the big flash occurred. They confirm the time as 01.15 and also spoke of the aerial light burst possessing a ball-like core.(2)

Other people who saw the bright flash included American circles researcher Nancy Talbot, and John Martineau, who were both standing on Woodborough Hill at the time. Martineau later spoke of it possessing a greenish hue and occurring behind Woodborough Hill, not over it.

Another interesting account of the aerial flash that tends to confirm Martineau's recall of the incident came from Nick Riley, who was seated in a small caravan on the eastern side of the Woodborough barns, south of Woodborough Hill.(3) He was fortunate enough to have glanced out of the vehicle's only window just as the burst of light took place. He said it originated from the vicinity of a now lost round barrow known as Swanborough Tump (SU13106007), 1.8 km south-east of Woodborough barns.

Like both Presley and Martineau, Riley described the flash as distinctly blue-green, or turquoise in colour, not white like 'normal lightning'. He said it left an after-image in the eyes, like a photographic negative, during which time he said he could plainly see the distant Pewsey Road on which Swanborough Tump is situated.

PLATE 35. The view across to Tawsmead Copse, left, and Woodborough Hill, right, from Adam's Grave during the summer of 1992. It was beyond Woodborough Hill that the big flash occurred around 01.20 on Tuesday, 27 July 1993 (author's pic).

The Power Failure Mystery

Overnight on Monday/Tuesday, 26/27 July there was also an electrical power failure in Alton Barnes. When exactly this occurred and for how long it lasted is unclear, although the following morning there were signs everywhere. Tim and Polly Carson at the Old Manor, Alton Barnes, said they awoke to find the LCD on the electric alarm clock flashing the incorrect time. The Relate team's computer, positioned in an upstairs room at the farm, had also ceased to function, while an electric alarm clock belonging to Malcolm Emery, the farm's dairy worker, who lives opposite the Old Manor, also malfunctioned. More importantly, David Carson, who lives 200 m away from the Old Manor at the Old Rectory, was rudely awoken somewhere between 01.00 and 02.00 by the sound of his answerphone replaying old recorded messages stored on its tape, something it only does when there has been a momentary power failure. He is quite sure of the time, and says he spoke to other residents of Alton Barnes the following day and they too confirmed that a power failure had taken place. Unfortunately, no one kept a record of what happened that night as the power failure was only seen as significant once news of the big flash began to spread.

Electrical Blackout - the Official View

Alton Barnes is served by a low voltage (240 volt) network originating from a series of local transformers.(4) In turn, these are fed by a high voltage (11,000 volt) 'feeder' system located at the nearby Pewsey sub-station. With this information as a backdrop, I was able to ascertain that no fault, whether sustained, *i.e.* a temporary closure of the mains system, or transient, *i.e.* damage caused either by birds or wind-born debris, had occurred in any of the areas concerned for the 48 hours in question. Indeed, if a power failure *had* taken place, whether momentary or otherwise, then it would have 'tripped' the circuit breaker at Pewsey sub-station. If this had occurred, then it would have been recorded in a maintenance log kept by Southern Electricity, and this was empty for the two days concerned. Furthermore, they stated that no reports of any apparent power failures were received from members of the public in Alton Barnes, Woodborough or anywhere else in the region during this period.

Clearly there was some kind of discrepancy here, for a power failure *did* occur in Alton Barnes between 01.00 and 02.00 on Tuesday, 27 July 1993, and the fact that it had almost certainly accompanied an event featuring an enormous aerial detonation cannot, I feel, be ignored.

Meteorological Conditions

What then was the source of the big flash? According to a spokesman (name on file) at the meteorological office at RAF Lyneham, the weather at midnight on the 26 July consisted of constant light drizzle with a full cover of stratiform clouds at 500 feet, while the visibility was said to have been anything between 15 and 25 km, which is exceptionally good.(5) After this time the thick cloud-base had begun to break up slightly, with *no reports of any thunderstorm activity*. He also pointed out that an altogether different cloud characteristic would have been necessary to produce storms - one involving cumulo-nimbus clouds, which were simply not present that night. Although this weather report was made at Lyneham, some 18 km north-north-west of Alton Barnes, the same weather conditions would have certainly prevailed in the nearby Pewsey Vale.

Localised Light Bursts

Inexplicable airborne flashes have, as I have already noted, been witnessed before in the Alton Barnes area. They were seen following the videoing of an orange light source above Tawsmead copse by the Trench family during the early hours of Saturday, 1 August 1992. John Wakefield informs me that, in addition to the huge airborne flashes, close range light bursts have also been witnessed locally. For example, around midnight on Sunday, 26 December 1993 he left the Old Manor in the pouring rain to return along the concrete track to the Woodborough barns. Reaching a position close to the ill-defined earthworks marking the final stages of the Ridgeway path, he was unexpectedly dazzled by a bright blue-white flash of light with a ball-like core. It had occurred some 30 m in front of him and was said to have been at a height of around 10 m. An hour or so later his friends Nick Riley and Chris Hitchen saw a similar flash when driving past the same position.

I have also spoken to others who have been witness to similar light bursts in the same area, and I was myself witness to a huge aerial flash that occurred above Knap Hill during the late evening of Saturday, 30 May 1992. At the time I was standing by the barn on the edge of East Field (SU12306233) in the company of Robert Irving, a crop circle sceptic and circlemaker, his friend Pam Price and my partner Debbie Benstead. The instant the flash occurred we all clearly heard a peculiar noise emanate from a position just metres away from where we stood. It seemed to be over the wheat field and resembled the sound of a fishing reel being cast very quickly. It lasted for around two seconds before ceasing abruptly. The peculiar noise then restarted around 30 m to our right, still over the crop, and then in a matter of some 20 seconds it repeated its performance some three to four times as it appeared to curve around in an arc and was heard one final time in the field on the opposite side of the deserted Pewsey Road. No one could offer any simple explanation for this unusual event.

If it was the sound of some unseen bird, then it had almost certainly been triggered into flight by the aerial burst of light. Returning to our cars, we promptly drove up to Knap Hill only to find its car-park empty. No one appeared to have been sky-watching this early in the season.

Aerial Detonations in UFO Window Areas

I also witnessed a more localised flash at the base of Glastonbury Tor in Somerset in the pouring rain late one night in the mid-1980s, and aerial flashes of this sort are not uncommon both at prehistoric sites and in areas of increased UFO activity. For instance, just before the commencement of a UFO 'flap' in West Yorkshire during October and November 1981, a series of aerial flashes were seen in the vicinity of Wyke Woods, close to the Woodside housing estate, between the towns of Bradford and Halifax. So sure was local earth mysteries researcher Paul Bennett of the connection between these mysterious light bursts and the subsequent UFO events that he summarised the situation with the following words:

> What seems to happen is that before a UFO wave occurs the entire sky gets lit up, only for a second or two, but definitely bright enough to read by. Then the burst instantly dies and perhaps a few minutes later another 'flash' will occur - its nature echoing the first, or previous, one.(6)

Wyke Woods produced luminosities which bore remarkable similarities to the type of aerial phenomena which has been repeatedly associated with Tawsmead Copse since the summer of 1992. The West Yorkshire flap was seen as part of the overall wave of sightings that had haunted the Pennines of Lancashire and Yorkshire since the mid-1970s.(7)

The Totham Elf

Periodic flashes were also reported in the wake of an important earth light encounter by an angler at the secluded, man-made fishing lake of Totham Grove at Great Totham in mid-Essex during July 1992. Most of these light bursts occurred above the lake itself, but some appeared to come from the vicinity of a nearby medieval church. Further enquiries revealed a spate of earlier poltergeist-linked incidents surrounding lone fishermen out by the reservoir late at night. Knowledge of these occurrences had led some anglers to place the blame on an impish entity referred to as the 'Totham elf'.(8)

The indirect link between elemental beings and unexplained flashes is interesting here, for there is some evidence to suggest that in past ages the fairy folk were believed to have been the cause of such phenomena. This suggestion comes from a book entitled *Rambles in Western Cornwall by the Footsteps of the Giants, etc.*, written by J. O. Halliwell and published in 1861. In here it points out that: 'Sometimes the fairies throw a light before his (the traveller's) face that completely dazzles him, and leads him backwards and forwards, without allowing him to make any progress in his journey.'(9) Although this statement could simply refer to a form of earth light phenomena, I do feel localised light bursts are intended as well.

Aerial Flashes at Hessdalen

A similar aerial phenomenon was also reported by the research team monitoring the remote mountainous region near Hessdalen in Norway during the now famous UFO flap of 1984. For example, on Sunday, 26 February observers witnessed a massive flash in the sky moments before a mysterious 'spotlight' was directed towards the ground.(10)

Furthermore, airborne flashes continue to be seen in and around Hessdalen, some in direct association with UFO events. A prime example of this clear relationship occurred on Thursday, 16 October 1987, the night of the Great Storm in southern England. Three adults and a child were travelling by car along a mountainous road some 10-15 km out of Hessdalen when, at 19.20, they witnessed 'a bright flash of light which illuminated the [clear, dark] sky towards Alen [some 10 km to the NW].' It was said to have been greenish in colour, and was followed just one minute later by a second flash. Each one lasted for between 3-4 seconds. Several minutes earlier the observers had witnessed 'several' what they described as star-like balls of light pass overhead at great speed, and in the wake of the two flashes they also encountered a further aerial object said to have been shaped like a shining green prism with 'four legs underneath'. The witnesses said it flew towards them, before briefly coming to a halt and then ascending into the open sky. All four percipients in this case experienced a notable head pressure both during and after the observation of the strange object.(11)

Egryn Light Bursts

Evidence of anomalous flashes occurring in historical UFO 'window areas' at times of increased sighting activity can be found in the accounts of the strange lights that accompanied the evangelism of 'Merionethshire seer' Mary Jones during the Welsh Religious Revival of 1904-5. One story gleaned from the *Proceedings of the Society for Psychical Research* for December 1905 speaks of a Mr B. Redwood and his assistant from the *Daily Mail*, who had travelled to Egryn in the hope of demonstrating that the luminosities were, in fact, a form of atmospheric electrical phenomena. To this end they installed 'most delicate instruments capable of being influenced by any extraordinary electrical condition of the atmosphere' at a position on the Egryn Hills where lights had recently been observed. Following an uneventful evening without any unusual incidents, the two men were unexpectedly witness to a very spectacular aerial event described as follows:

> ... suddenly in the northern sky a brilliant flash appeared, and shortly afterwards a second one, the first flash being followed by a distinct report. This light appeared momentarily, and did not seem to partake of the characteristics of lightning, but was peculiarly like the illumination produced by a magnesium flash lamp.
>
> Our delicate instruments did not respond in the slightest degree, and what these flashes really were it is impossible to conjecture.(12)

Earlier that night the sky had been clear, with the moon visible. It had then rained heavily, although at the time when the aerial flashes occurred the weather was said to have 'improved'. The fact that the instrumentation failed to respond to the aerial flashes tends to confirm they were not storm related.

The similarities between the above examples and the occurrence of airborne flashes at Alton Barnes during the early hours of Tuesday, 27 July are self evident.

Airborne Flash Correlation?

Lending even further weight to the fact that an event of significance did occur overnight on Monday/Tuesday, 26/27 July 1993 is the knowledge that the Project Relate equipment recorded various strange anomalies that same night. As already noted, their mains-linked computer positioned at the Old Manor was put out of action by the mysterious power failure. However, the battery-operated black box, situated close to Woodborough Hill, continued to function, which is just as well as between 23.00 and 00.00 it recorded various inexplicable sounds, the first being two unexpected audible noises on its earth current channel. The first signal sounded like 'a needle being dragged across a record', while the second example consisted of a 'whistle of varying pitch lasting for two or three seconds.'(13)

Aside from these curious intrusions, a further inexplicable sound was recorded on the underground microphone. Rodney Hale described this in his report as a 'doomph'. The other two channels - recording airborne sounds and magnetic variations - recorded nothing unusual, ruling out the likelihood of these noises being the result of a tape fault. Nothing like what was recorded overnight on Monday/Tuesday, 26/27 July was repeated *at any other time* during the entire period the Relate equipment was in operation, emphasising the probable significance of these strange sounds.

Electro-static clues?

The only possible clue to the Alton Barnes big flash is the dramatic increases in the electro-static air potential recorded on Woodborough Hill during both Experiment 16 at lunchtime on Monday, 26 July and Experiment 18 at lunchtime on Tuesday, 27 July. On each occasion the electro-static volt meter displayed constant readings of 400 V/metre, as opposed to the usual background level of around 100 V/metre in normal dry weather.

In contrast, extraordinarily low readings were picked up during the dawn experiment at the Water Site on Friday, 30 July. During the first control period readings of -50 V/metre were recorded. This lowered to -200 V/metre during the meditation, before returning to -60 V/metre during the second control period. Extreme negative air potentials of this order are only normally associated with adverse meteorological conditions such as dust-storms, rain-storms and thunderstorms which were not present at the time.

Powerful electro-static effects have long been associated with electrical malfunctions during close proximity UFO encounters. If this theory is correct, then the highly unusual electro-static readings recorded on Woodborough Hill might also be linked to the inexplicable drops in charge noted in the battery belt used by cameraman Paul Shobbrook and in the car battery used by Roger Wilkins to power the IR-sensitive camera during Experiment 16 (which, as we know, also produced various photographic anomalies). If it *can* be established that a link exists between the abnormal electro-static readings and these quite separate events, then the early morning power failure at Alton Barnes also begins to make sense.

Paul Hailey related how during the many nights he spent monitoring inside his converted dormobile he would occasionally see minor bursts of light in the cloudy skies above East Field. He is sure these discharges were not storm-related but electro-static in origin, so is it possible that an increased air potential can lead to the strange aerial light bursts witnessed in UFO 'window areas'. In spite of this attractive solution, it hardly seems likely that simple electro-static anomalies can themselves produce massive airborne flashes of the sort witnessed at Alton Barnes on Tuesday, 27 July 1993. Nor can they have caused the voltage drops experienced by the Orgone 93 team the previous lunchtime, or the anomalies recorded by the Relate black box, or the subsequent power failure that accompanied the big flash. On the other hand it *is* possible that all these effects are by-products of a much more primary occurrence influencing the area and creating an assortment of side effects. Perhaps the presence of a multi-dimensional energy continuum of the sort proposed in this book can help us understand these subtle patterns of activity.

A Natural Explanation?

No scientific explanation has yet been established to account for this curious natural phenomenon, although a connection with earth light phenomena and various geophysical factors is highly likely. Accounts suggesting that the big flash possessed a ball-like core is strong evidence in support of this view.

If unaccountable airborne flashes are really to be connected with the manifestation of UFOs, then it is important to remember that although geophysical factors might be partially responsible for the production of lightforms at ground level, many other factors must contribute to their appearance in the upper atmosphere. Constable envisaged his bioforms or ether ships as 'fish in the ocean of atmosphere', existing undetected in the stratosphere and achieving sizes of anything from that of a coin to 'at least half a mile in diameter'.(14) His revolutionary concepts were more-or-less inspired, yet new evidence emerging from a NASA research team and a US military spy satellite might help us to understand not only Constable's amoeba-like 'critters', but also the light bursts witnessed at locations and zones associated with UFO activity.

In July 1993 - the same month that the big flash took place at Alton Barnes - geophysicists and scientists from the NASA Research Center in Mountain View were able to video 'giant glowing shapes and weird columns of light' reaching from the top of a Midwest thunderstorm to 'the edge of the atmosphere'. According to the *San Francisco Chronicle* of 25 September 1993 the light anomalies were recorded by a research team aboard a DC-8 plane following the progress of thunderstorms feeding the great floods that swept across America that summer.

'They were not really what I expected.' admitted Professor Eugene Wescott, a geophysicist at the University of Alaska's Geophysical Institute in Fairbanks. 'The first one looked like a crown with three or four spikes from the base... another [looked] like a big jellyfish and another maybe like a huge carrot.'(15)

The NASA scientists, once again headed by Professor Wescott, were back in the skies watching for unusual phenomena above thunderstorms in June and July 1994. This time they were able to monitor and photograph two distinct types of short-lived aerial light displays. The first, described as giant, blood-red 'jellyfish' with mushroom-like tops more than 96 km high and blue 'roots' or 'tendrils' extending down some 64 km, are referred to as 'sprites'. A colour photograph of one of these red 'sprites' caught above a thunderstorm in the US Midwest on 3 July 1994 was released to the international media. In the UK it was published in the 11 August issue of *The Independent*.(16) Accompanying this spectacular photograph was a smaller image of a second type of phenomena observed by the team and referred to as 'blue jets'. These apparently originate in the centre of storms and rise to heights of about 40 km in a narrow cone at '300 times the speed of sound'.

The difference in colour between the red 'sprites' and the 'blue jets' Professor Wescott puts down to varying 'atmospheric constituents at the heights at which they appear.' On the night of 1 July alone the NASA scientists recorded no less than 46 'blue jets' and 6 'sprites' in just 30 minutes. The intense thunderstorms are thought to be behind the occurrence of these new natural phenomena. The 'sprites', which last for only a few thousandths of a second and travel at half the speed of light, are considered to be the result of electrical discharges passing between the tops of the cloud and the upper atmosphere. However, the blue jets, which last up to one tenth of a second, are more difficult to explain as they 'travel too slowly'. It seems that Space Shuttle astronauts have reported seeing 'sprites' in the past and, according to Professor Wescott, they could well have been witnessed from the ground.

Even further confirmation of the existence of previously unknown natural phenomena comes from a tantalising article in *The Times* newspaper of Wednesday, 19 January 1994. It reports on recently declassified information concerning unaccountable airborne explosions registered by US military spy satellites in the upper atmosphere - with at least three of the 136 detected since 1975 occurring over Britain. In force they are said to compare with the equivalent of 1000 tonnes of TNT and yet they are being seen as a form of unknown natural phenomena. According to a British astronomer named John Mason these aerial detonations could have been mistaken for UFO events, since they are thought to have been visible from the ground as 'huge bursts of light', parallelling the words of Professor Wescott. Most intriguing of all is the scientists' belief that much of the energy released from these explosions occurs in the infrared range of frequencies.(17)

The above accounts confirm that we are dealing with airborne light phenomena of an entirely unfamiliar nature. Might these aerial displays be seen as macrocosmic manifestations of the same primary energy responsible for the production of terrestrial earth lights, as well as the microscopic blue-green energy vesicles seen by Reich to discharge from decaying tissue and spin out from the interior walls of orgone accumulators? I think the answer is very likely to be yes.

27

The Cosmic Joker

From midnight through till around two o'clock on the morning of Wednesday, 28 July 1993 the skies above Alton Barnes seemed alive with an assortment of curious luminosities. Yet unlike the euphoric reactions to the big flash of just 24 hours beforehand, what occurred on this night was seriously overshadowed by the acts of those attempting to cast doubt and uncertainty on any event seen as supporting a supernatural solution to both the crop circle and UFO enigmas.

In March 1993 John Wakefield, Nick Riley *et al* had discovered the remains of a large red balloon close to the Woodborough barns, just south of Tawsmead Copse and Woodborough Hill. There had also been indications that during this same period someone had been using a large orange balloon in the vicinity of the barn on the southern edge of East Field. A local shepherd purportedly saw a group of men with cameras and tripods acting suspiciously, as if they were attempting to photograph their handiwork. Long after the end of the 1993 summer season, stories began to circulate implying that known crop circle sceptics, who were themselves illegal crop artists, had been releasing luminous balloons with a 1 m diameter from a position between Alton Barnes and Stanton St Bernard from around 01.30 on 28 July 1993. This location had been chosen in the knowledge that, when airborne, the balloons would be carried down wind towards the skywatchers situated at local vantage points.

This disconcerting information adequately explains the sightings of various pale green lights seen overnight on Tuesday/Wednesday, 27/28 July 1993 by at least four groups of witnesses positioned around East Field. Although I can completely understand (but cannot condone) the draw of illegally manufacturing crop circles and crop formations at the dead of night in the name of art or psychic communication, this understanding does not extend to the deliberate creation of aerial luminosities. Such acts can in no way be seen as extensions of the artistic talents of those concerned, simply outright deception and trickery aimed at making a mockery of a subject that relies heavily on the accuracy of witness testimony to further its knowledge of the phenomenon under study.

Hedge-hopping Globe

Despite the light-hoaxing activities, there did seem to have been some sightings on the night of 27/28 July 1993 that were *not* illuminated balloons. The first of these occurred on the A4 Beckhampton to Marlborough road, sometime around midnight. The sole witness to this event was Mike Saunders, an earth mysteries enthusiast from Dagenham, Essex.(1) At the time he had just left the Avebury stone complex and was on his way to the Swindon junction of the M4 motorway - a route that would take him through the town of Marlborough. Some 10 minutes into his journey, as the vehicle passed through open countryside between the villages of Fyfield and Manton, Saunders unexpectedly caught sight of what he took to be a 'yellow globe' passing across his line of vision from right to left, *i.e.* from south to north. It appeared over a hedge and at its closest point was said to have been no more than 20 feet away from his car.

As the 'globe' left his line of vision after some 10 seconds in view, Saunders glanced down at the dashboard clock and noted the time was exactly midnight, an unnerving coincidence which convinced him that he should put his foot down and simply carry on the journey.

A Weather-linked Phenomenon over Knap Hill

The luminous balloons were released to float above East Field between 01.30 and 02.00 on the morning of 28 July, and once those responsible had satisfied themselves that their games had achieved the desired results, they departed the area. Yet then, at around 02.30, something quite strange occurred. Christian Kaese and his colleagues from the German FGK scientific monitoring group from Lower Saxony were positioned on the road by Knap Hill with representatives from a British UFO group. Little interest was shown at first when the low cloud-base directly above them started to unfold like a funnel to reveal a clear hazy sky with one or two stars visible. Yet then all watched in amazement as a white light appeared ahead and grew immediately in brightness until it had reached a magnitude greater than any normal star. It then shot away at a tremendous speed *beneath* the cloud cover towards the east, along the axis of the Pewsey Vale Downs. Kaese later said it moved so fast that it was viewed only as a long streak.

Furthermore, after the light's disappearance, the open sky directly above them continued to clear for some 20-30 seconds until they could plainly make out the stars of Cassiopeia. It then gradually closed up until just two to three minutes later there was a total cloud cover once more. So curious was Kaese over the nature of this aerial anomaly that he checked the weather conditions that night with Thruxton airfield in the nearby county of Hampshire. They revealed that at the time of the sighting, *i.e.* 02.30, there had been an 8/8th cloud-base at 300 m across the whole of the region, confirming the peculiarity of the funnel-like opening that had appeared in the clouds above Knap Hill for such a short time. The possibility of a relationship between the unexpected cloud conditions and the appearance of the bright aerial light is difficult to ignore.

Further East Field Activity

In the wake of the multi-witness events reported during the nights of Monday/Tuesday, 26/27 and Tuesday/Wednesday, 27/28 July, the days that followed produced further stories of unusual lights being seen in the vicinity of East Field. Steve and Gillian Trench, and their 15-year-old son Stephen, who had videoed the orange pulsating light above Tawsmead Copse in July 1992, were back sky-watching overnight on Wednesday/Thursday, 28/29 July. Around 22.30 they were standing in a small recess situated on the south-west corner of East Field when they noticed a small, golfball-sized blue globe rise up from the standing crop just 10 m away from their position.(2) It quickly climbed to a height of around 4 m before 'floating' northwards towards Knap Hill. Reaching for the video camera, Gillian openly voiced her disappointment at not having seen it earlier with the words: 'I wish it would come back so I could film it better!' At that very moment, she claims, the object came to a halt and returned towards their position where it proceeded to remain still for several seconds. It then resumed its original course and was finally lost from view somewhere above the centre of the field. Apparently, when a torch was shone on the object's spherical shell, it just seemed to 'absorb' the torch-beam and had no reflective quality whatsoever.

Both Gillian and her husband concluded that this tiny globe had responded to their verbal request for it to pose for the camera. They feel certain it had been conscious of their thoughts and had acted in an apparently intelligent manner.

Coincident Spikes

Project Relate's mains-linked computer system and battery-operated black box monitored the Alton Barnes area throughout July and into early August. Following the inexplicable sounds recorded on the black box's earth current channel overnight on Monday/Tuesday, 26/27 July, no further anomalies were reported until the night of Thursday/Friday, 29/30 July.

Without warning, Relate's computer equipment recorded a spike-like pulse simultaneously on all four of its channels, *i.e.* those monitoring earth current pulses, magnetic field variations and microwave emissions. Unfortunately, this was the one occasion when the computer mysteriously failed to log the time of the event due to a malfunction. However, the position of the spikes on the resulting graphs indicated that the event had taken place sometime between 23.00 and 00.00 on Thursday/Friday, 29/30 July.(3)

These results may or may not have some bearing on the fact that at around 01.30 on the morning of Friday, 30 July, astrologer and crop circle researcher Leonie Starr watched a group of tiny green balls of light dancing up and down in the north-west corner of East Field as she had stood on the summit of Woodborough Hill.(4) As an experienced Alton Barnes skywatcher, Leonie could give no explanation for what she saw, even though sceptics immediately dismissed her sighting as either misinterpreted hoaxing activity or the beams of distant torchlights.

The last reported sighting which is of any interest to our catalogue of data occurred between 21.42 and 21.45 on Saturday, 31 July. Andrew Buckley, a graphics designer from Cheshire, was standing on the eastern slope of Knap Hill with several other observers when he caught sight of a 'bright, oval-shaped object' appear above Tawsmead Copse.(5) All watched as it began moving off slowly towards the north-east at a fairly high angle. It was estimated to have been around 3.5 km distance and was completely soundless. After some three minutes it disappeared from view just beyond the summit of Knap Hill. Buckley was able to video the last 60 seconds of the sighting which he has since spent much time trying to analyse and evaluate with the limited resources available to him. He is positive that what he saw was not an aeroplane or a balloon of some sort.

Earth Currents

As we know, the very first unaccountable signals registered by Relate's computer monitoring equipment were the four earth current pulses recorded between 04.25 and 05.02 on Sunday, 11 July, the project's first night of operation. This, of course, was the same night that the huge ring and so-called '666' formation appeared at East Kennett, just 5 km north-north-east of Alton Barnes.

No similar earth current pulses were recorded again until Wednesday/Thursday, 4/5 August, Relate's very last night of operation, when an almost identical set of spikes - one long sustained signal and three shorter peaks - were registered between 06.33 and 07.04.(6) Despite these signals being strikingly similar in appearance, it must be pointed out that the graphs display only cumulative readings made from the greatest recorded amplitude across a period of 10 whole seconds, meaning that - although the spikes are sustained - the actual second by second readings might have told a slightly different story.

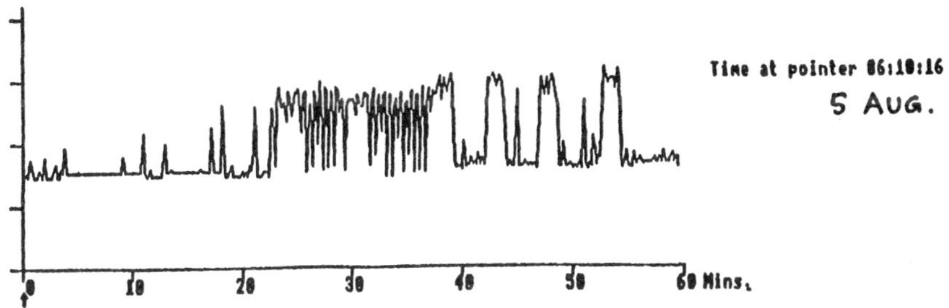

FIG 25. The mysterious earth current traces recorded between 06.33 and 07.04 on Thursday, 5 August 1993 by the Relate computer positioned at Alton Barnes. They matched a similar set of traces registered during the early hours of Sunday, 11 July, Relate's first night of operation. But what was their origin? (pic: CCCS/Relate)

Once again, Southern Electricity, who produce earth currents when switching their main electrical grid system in response to a fault, could offer no simple solution to explain these curious traces. Indeed, the Business Support Unit at Newbury was just as perplexed as Rodney Hale was as to the source of the strange pulses. As suggested earlier, the only lines of enquiry left open is with the Ministry of Defence on Salisbury Plain.

The Cosmic Joker

Unfortunate mishaps and strange coincidences, or synchronicities as they are known in Jungian psychology, were frequent during Project Relate's three and a half week period of experimentation. Add to this the chance recording of two virtually identical sets of earth current pulses - one during the first night of operation and the other registered during the very last hour of the project and the word 'coincidence' appears to take on a new meaning. Indeed, in the case of the second recording, the computer was switched off for the final time *just minutes* after the anomalous signals were unknowingly recorded. Should this final sequence of earth current pulses not have been noticed, then those registered overnight on Saturday/Sunday, 10/11 July would have assumed a warped significance. They would have undoubtedly been linked with the nocturnal appearance of the large crop ring and the three smaller circles of the '666' formation constructed at nearby East Kennett that same night. Since no crop circles turned up on the night when the *second* set of readings were recorded, then we can safely assume that the earth current pulses were *not* linked to the manufacture of any crop formations, man-made or otherwise.

Such synchronicities are common in the study of the earth mysteries and were recorded in earnest by the late cryptozoologist and mysteries writer F.W. Holiday during his extensive investigations of Loch Ness during the 1960s.(7) Such irritations we must not question, for to ponder on them too deeply would be to evoke the paranoid within us all, and in doing do so we would only convince ourselves that the Master of Synchronicities, the Cosmic Joker himself, was out there somewhere having a laugh at our expense!

28

Anomaly Count

During the last two weeks of July 1993 one day produced more anomalies in and around Alton Barnes than any other, and this was the 24-hour period between dawn on the 26th and first light on the 27th. The catalogue of strangeness began at 05.37 during the early morning OED experiment upon Woodborough Hill with my visual sighting of a black tumbling object seen over the heads of corn in the field known as the Crates.

Our return visit to Woodborough Hill for Experiment 16 at midday turned out to be quite an extraordinary affair. Over a period of just 45 minutes we achieved two photographic anomalies in black and white, two further examples in colour, two inexplicable cases of battery voltage drops, Oliver Stummer's visual sighting of a bright flash, a further radiation rise linked to the conducted meditation, and an abnormal negative temperature differential, which may or may not have been linked with the noticeable dry throat and head pressure reported by Tony Beddoe and Mike Collen after using the OED. Furthermore, the electro-static air potential on the summit of the hill had, as we have seen, increased from 100 V/metre that morning to a constant 400 V/metre (this high level was recorded again on our return to Woodborough Hill the following lunchtime). These readings were highly unusual since rainy days usually *reduce* the air potential, not raise it.

Finally, at a time estimated at between 23.00 and midnight on the 27th, the Relate black box, positioned close to Woodborough Hill, recorded unique anomalous sounds on both the earth current channel and the underground microphone, hinting at some kind of localised geomagnetic disturbance. The fact that the airborne flash and subsequent power failure had occurred within just two hours (maybe even as little as 75 minutes) of these recordings cannot, I feel, be ignored.

The clear indications are that some sort of subtle change was taking place at Alton Barnes between first light on Monday, 26 July and the early hours of Tuesday, 27 July, and that this shift was both monitored by scientific instrumentation and visually recognised by observers on the ground.

A Geological Solution?

If our findings are correct, then they beg the question: what occurred to allow this subtle shift to take place? Geological factors are almost certainly associated with the manifestation of unidentified aerial luminosities. Such factors probably include the build up of tension around a fault prior to an earth tremor and/or subtle shifts in the geomagnetic field, caused when changes occur in the upper atmosphere due to the influx of solar wind.

The electro-static readings recorded on Woodborough Hill, as well as the probable geomagnetic disturbance registered by the Relate black box, appear to confirm this clear geophysical link. However, as yet, I can find no direct evidence to show that any major geological event played an active role in creating the anomalous events of Monday, 26 July 1993. The British Geological Survey at Edinburgh recorded no abnormal geomagnetic activity between the 26 and 28 July and no seismic tremors were registered in Britain on Monday, 26 July. The only tremor that might have had some bearing on the proceedings occurred at Chipping Sodbury in the county of Avon at 03.52 GMT (04.52 BST) on Wednesday, 28 July. Although it only measured 1.9 on the Richter scale, it might just have been felt by the inhabitants of the town; Chipping Sodbury is 25 miles from Alton Barnes.

The fact that two genuinely unexplained observations of mysterious lights occurred here just hours before the Chipping Sodbury tremor is difficult to overlook. However, the evidence to connect the two is too slim to pursue any further. Had the crop circle sceptics not been sending up luminous balloons that night, then perhaps we might have been able to gain a better perspective of the phenomenon's links with any geophysical activity during this period.

Meteorological Observations

Some researchers of the UFO enigma have recognised correlations between the appearance of unexplained luminosities and various meteorological conditions, such as the proximity of storms, the fall of rain and the humidity at the time of the sighting. As with geology, this too might produce tensions and stains, although this time in the atmosphere. So could any meteorological factor have played a role in the day's dramatic events?

Following the OED experiment on Woodborough Hill at dawn on Monday, 26 July, I recorded the following words in the Orgone 93 diary: 'Subjectively, both Tony and I feel the torrential rain from dawn onwards on Saturday has cleansed the environment of any DOR build-up, giving it a fresh start. Many anomalies occur during or after such releases of meteorological tension.'

These words were written following a noticeable build-up of hot, clammy weather towards the end of the previous week. We had all become lethargic, yet with this had come the overwhelming feeling that something was about to occur - a situation possibly confirmed by the abnormal negative temperature differential (NTD) recorded at the Water Site at lunchtime on Friday, 23 July. The following day had brought with it the torrential rain which had cleared by nightfall, taking with it the hot, muggy weather. In its place was a sense of freshness and tense expectancy. This 'fresh start' had continued until Monday lunchtime when Beddoe again recorded an abnormal NTD at the base of Woodborough Hill. Accompanying these unusual readings were the ill-effects he experienced when using the OED that lunchtime, and from a clear sky with no wind at dawn, the weather had rapidly deteriorated into a dull, overcast sky with intermittent drizzle and a westerly wind.

It is also intriguing to note that the only times I recorded whistlers during the two-week period of experimentation were at lunchtime on Friday, 23 July, the day that produced the second highest anomaly count, and at dawn on Monday, 26 July. Although whistlers are natural occurrences, they are not frequent, and, as I have previously explained, their presence has been linked by Edson C. Hendricks with the appearance of mysterious lights at Marfa, Texas - results that had initially prompted me to include the use of a VLF radio receiver in our own experimentation. A further study of the relationship between whistlers and the UFO phenomenon is, I believe, essential.

If such meteorological occurrences were in any way responsible for the subtle shifts and environmental tensions that led to the anomalous events on Monday, 26 July, then their exact involvement is still to be defined. However, on an intuitive, subjective level it was clear that these environmental tensions enabled us to predict that something out-of-the ordinary was about to occur.

Predictions

It should also not be forgotten that members of the crop circle and UFO communities were expecting a paranormal event of importance to occur on Monday, 26 July 1993, following the significance of this date in previous years. Unconsciously, this knowledge would have been with me when I saw the dark tumbling object above the field known as the Crates and Oliver Stummer witnessed the bright flash on Woodborough Hill. Perhaps the collective awareness of this date's importance acted as a non-local catalyst to heighten, if not produce, some of the day's inexplicable events. I believe this is very possible, although I do not believe it is the whole answer.

It must also be asked what effect the Orgone 93 experimentation had in catalysing any of these events. The OED was used on its own at dawn on Monday, 26 July, while at midday it was used in association with a meditation. Moreover, a possible meditation-linked radiation rise was recorded during the lunchtime experiment on Woodborough Hill. Does this then suggest that some kind of psycho-interactive process might have been taking place? It is possible that the combination of the OED and meditation together acted as a further catalyst to increase the probability of paranormal events occurring in and around Alton Barnes on Monday, 26 July 1993. If so, then I believe that on this one day alone Orgone 93 came close to fulfilling its aims.

Conclusions

Orgone 93 carried through its objectives and liaised with the many other activities occurring in and around Alton Barnes during the summer of 1993. With this eclectic data I was able to piece together a comprehensive picture that appears to show that when our own project was obtaining noticeable results others were doing so as well. If the Alton Barnes area had not been monitored by so many different groups and individuals, then we would probably have been left with just a few insignificant electromagnetic anomalies and the odd anecdotal story, nothing more.

There were no multiple-witness UFO sightings or close encounters with alien beings during the Orgone 93 experimentation, nor any feats of paranormal capabilities beyond the realms of comprehension, just a collection of verifiable incidents that beg explanation, and in many cases fit a gradually emerging picture supporting the existence of non-local or psycho-interactive processes, unknown energy forms and a multi-dimensional energy continuum. Furthermore, the in depth research that accompanied the more active elements of this project certainly helped demonstrate that the village of Alton Barnes, and the Vale of Pewsey in general, had been producing a high level of inexplicable events since the summer of 1990.

Crop Circle Correlations

1993 was a pretty poor year for crop circles and visitors to Wiltshire were, on the whole, disappointed by what they saw. Despite this, I found it intriguing to see that of the three examples that appeared within an 8 km radius of Alton Barnes between Sunday, 18 July and Saturday, 31 July, two were first noted the morning *after* days of high anomaly activity. I speak here of the seven-circled formation at Etchilhampton, first noticed on Tuesday, 20 July, and a lengthy pictogram discovered at West Kennett on Saturday, 24 July. Whether anything should be read into this connection is difficult to say, although it is known that some of the more serious minded circlemakers responsible for this type of clandestine crop art are motivated by both intuition and a very real belief in the UFO phenomenon.

Aside from these quite tenuous connections, we found no real links between the anomalous events recorded either by ourselves or by any other party and the appearance or proximity of any crop circle found during the summer of 1993. This was a disappointing result for those who have actively supported this curious and aesthetically-pleasing enigma for so many years, including the Relate team who had hoped to use monitoring equipment to confirm the supernatural origin of crop circles.

More important today is the rich agricultural landscape that in recent years has played host to not just crop circles, but also to an assortment of inexplicable aerial luminosities. Whether the human perpetrators of the crop circle enigma are aware of it or not, their handiwork has acted as visual beacons drawing inquisitive and open-minded people back to an ancient ritual landscape that is itself a rich source of mystery and imagination. It is with these thoughts at the forefront of our minds that we must strive to understand the true relationship between ourselves and the unseen world recognised and marked out in the past by our distant ancestors.

29

Orgone 94

Throughout the winter months of 1993 a careful eye was kept on the inexplicable events continuing to take place in and around Alton Barnes. Probably the most important UFO event to occur after the departure of the crop circle and UFO enthusiasts at the end of August 1993 featured local man Malcolm Emery, a dairy worker on the Carson's farm.(1) On the evening of Thursday, 4 November he was driving out of Alton Barnes on the Pewsey Road with his wife and two children (SU12006225) when at 19.40, as their vehicle drew level with Tawsmead Copse, which lay some 600 m to the south-south-east (SU126617), Emery clearly saw a fiery globe of orange light hanging low over the trees. All watched the bright luminosity for between two and five seconds before Emery was forced to abandon the sighting in favour of other, more immediate, matters such as slamming on the brakes to avoid the car in front of him! As he turned his head once more, he saw the light blink out of sight. As a resident of Alton Barnes for 22 years, Emery is wholly familiar with the local terrain and is unlikely to mis-identify either man-made or natural phenomena.

The same, or a similar fiery orb, was seen above Tawsmead Copse just two nights later by a local woman (who does not wish to be named) as she drove between Pewsey and Alton Barnes.(2) She said the object was so bright it illuminated the tree-tops. Moreover, on Monday, 21 February 1994 Malcolm Emery again saw the orange ball hanging motionless above Tawsmead Copse as he drove between Alton Barnes and Pewsey.(3) This time it seemed to be down among the trees and further over towards the south-eastern corner of the woods (SU125616). As he concentrated on driving, his wife and daughter Carrie, aged 7, watched as the object turned a distinct blue-white colour before fading from view.

There were further sightings of mysterious lights in the Woodborough Hill area throughout the winter months and so intrigued did I become in establishing the cause of these seemingly inexplicable events that I began investigating Tawsmead Copse and its surrounds with farmer Polly Carson and my partner Debbie Benstead. The fruits of this work were to culminate in some quite extraordinary events during the Orgone 94 experimentation in the last week of July.

As in previous years, crop circles began gracing the cultivated fields of the Marlborough Downs by the end of April 1994. Many were simple patterns carved out in oil seed rape, but these gradually increased in complexity, size and beauty as they transferred first to barley and then finally to ripened wheat. Only the most ardent crop watchers now see these majestic examples of illegal crop art as supernatural in origin. Despite this, the 'croppies', as they have become known, were to seen at Alton Barnes throughout the summer months, either gazing in wonder at the new designs or catching up on the latest gossip at The Barge Inn, Honey Street.

Coincident to the appearance of these creative patterns in crop were, once again, an assortment of aerial luminosities reported by both locals and visitors alike. Some were almost certainly hoaxes or misinterpreted mundane phenomena, yet many others I personally investigated were more difficult to explain and may well constitute important new clues in respect to the nature of the Alton Barnes phenomenon.

Objects of Darkness

One of the earliest, and perhaps one of the most significant, of the 1994 cases occurred during the hot afternoon of Sunday, 12 June. Polly Carson was exercising a horse on the concrete track between the Old Manor and the Woodborough barns around 16.00 when, reaching a dip in the track, the animal suddenly stopped, pricked back its ears and stared

PLATE 36. One of the fake road signs erected by persons unknown on April Fool's Day 1994 between Knap Hill and Alton Barnes. Even though this escapade was undoubtedly a practical joke, it adequately demonstrates the very real association that now exists between Alton Barnes and the UFO enigma (author's pic).

intently. Polly attempted to urge it on, but instead it edged backwards and became highly agitated. Realising that it had seen something untoward, Polly followed the animal's line of sight and was perplexed to see a black ball silently moving over the heads of the crop off to her left at a distance of some 20 m from her position (SU11246143). It was about 25 cm in diameter and gently bobbed up and down before disappearing from view, having been in sight for no more than three to four seconds. It appeared to have been travelling in the direction of Woodborough Hill, which lies some 350 m east-north-east of here.

Polly's first reaction was that it might have been a bird or the head of an animal just visible above the line of crops, so she waited for several minutes but saw nothing more. During this time the horse still refused to budge, and at one stage it even reared up onto its hind legs. Finally, however, it was coaxed forwards and once it had resumed its journey the animal gave no further trouble. On the return journey from the Woodborough barns the horse did not respond at all when it passed the spot where the black ball had earlier been seen.

What Polly was unaware of until much later was that late the previous night, *i.e.* Saturday, 11 June, various people had watched inexplicable bursts of light occurring in the vicinity of Woodborough Hill. Furthermore, late on midsummer's eve crop circle researcher John Martineau witnessed a similar black object rise out of the crops close to the lay-by where Steven Greer, Chris Mansell *et al* had witnessed the light cluster in 1992.(4)

These two sightings of small black objects brought to mind the dark tumbling object I had witnessed moving over the standing crop at the base of Woodborough Hill during the early morning of Monday, 26 July 1993. In similar with these two latest sightings, what I saw had been in view for no more than the count of three. Moreover, all three sightings occurred within 500 m of each other.

Black objects are by no means unique to ufology. Egon Bach in his *Philippine UFOs (St Elmos) of the Volcanoes* describes how floating spheres would be seen to pulse through the colours of the visible spectrum until they became black absorptive objects.(5) On various other occasions dark shadow-like balls were also reported in the Philippines. Like Bach, I consider these colour changes show that the blackness of such objects is due to its presence on the edge of the infrared range of the electromagnetic spectrum. Indeed, Bach blatantly describes these dark absorptive UFOs as 'bottomless sink hole[s] for infra-red radiation'.(6)

The reaction of the horse to the presence of the black ball is also highly interesting since Kathleen Wiltshire, in her book *Ghosts and Legends of the Wiltshire Countryside*, lists several instances where horses have supposedly been 'spooked' by something unseen at locations either in the Pewsey Vale or on the nearby Marlborough Downs. For example, horses were said to 'take fright on the Ridgeway near Chiseldon' and on one occasion, when a lady named Anne Wiltshire of All Cannings was riding her horse on the downs near Tan Hill and the Wansdyke, it 'pricked its ears, stopped and refused to go forward. Upon being urged, it suddenly turned about, and galloped back the way it had come.'(7) Are these animals reacting to unseen energy forms that only their eyes can see? Something inside the infrared range perhaps?

Cherry Red Glow

Many more conventional UFO sightings began to flow in as the summer season got under way. For instance, on the evening of Saturday, 18 June a large orange ball appeared directly above Woodborough Hill and was witnessed by various individuals, including crop watcher Paul Vigay. It was also videoed from an elevated position on Knap Hill by Paul Damon Parsons of the South Wales UFO Research Group.(8) By all accounts the glowing light was in view for so long that those witnessing the phenomenon were forced to assume it was probably a hoax of some kind - whether this was so may never be determined.

There was, however, another more important sighting on Woodborough Hill during the late evening of Tuesday, 19 July, and this we must review in rather more detail. The case features two young people, Tom Trubridge and his fiance Julie Whitear.(9) Trubridge is a quiet, thoughtful and unassuming person with a head for electronics and a deep interest in the crop circle and UFO debate. He is also known to the author. Julie shares his interest in these subjects and is a pleasant, level-headed person.

On the evening concerned the couple had decided to spend the night sky-watching from the summit of Woodborough Hill. It was a good vantage point and as it was on private land they knew it would not normally be frequented by crowds of people; indeed, they found themselves alone up there, a video and a camera by their side in case anything out of the ordinary occurred.

As the night gradually drew in, they gazed northwards across the expanse of East Field. It was a fine clear night, although a little cold, and there was a wind rising. In an attempt to keep themselves warm, the couple huddled together behind a bale of cut grass, facing out towards the clump of tall trees crowning the southern extremities of the hill, a distance of around 50 m from their position. The conversation eventually turned to the price of health food in nearby Devizes, and then, unexpectedly, something strange occurred. At around 23.10 both were stunned to see a dark cherry red glow emerge into view from a position just beyond the line of silhouetted bushes stretching to the left of the copse of trees. Almost as if it was being inflated by some unseen source, the object grew in stages with a series of pulsations until it had reached the diameter of 'a large oak tree' It apparently possessed a solid shell-like surface and was unlike anything the couple had ever seen before.

After some six seconds of viewing this extraordinary sight, Julie at last suggested that they should reach for their camera, at which moment the object rapidly collapsed in on itself until it could no longer be seen. This, as it were, broke the spell and, realising what had just happened, Trubridge started running towards the position where the object had disappeared. As he did so he became aware of a strange 'high pitched sound... like hissing in the back of my head... an electrical chattering or zizzing' that he could feel more in his inner ear than hear audibly. Navigating a barbed wire fence he reached the edge of the hill and gazed out onto the open landscape. The sound had now stopped and there was no sign of life anywhere on the hill.

In his mind Trubridge went over all possible logical solutions, knowing that none, not a balloon, a flare or any form of known natural occurrence could account for the appearance of the cherry red glow. The couple are now unsure of where exactly the object had originated - whether it had emanated from the ground or simply materialised out of thin air *level* with the ground. It had certainly seemed to be at ground level, although its position was very probably slightly beyond the summit of the hill, possibly over its southern slope.

Trubridge is at pains to point out the extraordinary cherry red colour and dark defined shell of the aerial phenomenon which, although self-illuminated, did not project light. Since the sighting Trubridge, who is aware of the idea of UFOs as living energy, has felt quite strongly that the object existed on the very fringes of the infrared range of the EM spectrum - any lower in frequency and he believes it would not have been seen at all. Subjectively, he also feels there was some kind of inter-relationship between themselves and the phenomenon observed, a 'knowing' on its part, almost as if they had been 'invited' to turn their backs on East Field and witness this remarkable event.

Having chatted at length with both witnesses on various occasions about both the incident and its effect on them, I concluded that this was a very important case indeed. The fact that Trubridge felt so strongly that the aerial luminosity existed on the edge of the infrared range is intriguing, especially as he was unaware that two black objects had been seen in the same general area only a few weeks beforehand.

The Eye

At first light the morning after Tom Trubridge and Julie Whitear's sighting on Woodborough Hill on Tuesday, 19 July a brand new crop formation was found in East Field (which already possessed a single circle and a rather crude formation by this date). It consisted of a thick ring with a 75 m diameter enclosing an eye-like ellipse inside a ring, within which was another smaller ellipse and circle.

Perhaps inevitably, this crop formation quickly became known as the 'eye' and, although in my opinion it was made by human hands, it soon became the focus, not only for many hundreds of visitors from all over the world, but also for a number of quite inexplicable incidents, some involving members of the Orgone 94 team.

A Fresh Round of Experiments

Having listened to the many strange stories continuing to emerge from the Alton Barnes

PLATE 37. The scene across East Field towards Tawsmead Copse in July 1994. Faintly visible is the 'eye' crop formation that was discovered just hours after Tom Trubridge and Julie Whitear witnessed a cherry red lightform appear at ground level on Woodborough Hill. (pic: Johnny Merron).

area, in particular Tawsmead Copse and Woodborough Hill, we were, of course, anxious to begin our next round of experiments. These were to be similar in style and content to those of the previous year, yet with a number of minor changes here and there.

A seven-day period between Saturday, 23 July and Friday, 29 July was chosen for our purposes and, once again, co-ordinated meditations were to be the principal focus of attention. Yet having learnt from the successes of Orgone 93, I realised that if we wanted to achieve even better results then the creative visualisations would need to more emotionally based. After much deliberation it was decided that UFO contactee and psychic Ed Sherwood should lead the meditations. He had already achieved success with the CSETI team in 1992 and 1993. His style of visualisation was not dissimilar to the 'no-archetype' meditation used by myself at the Sompting crop formation in July 1992 and then later employed during the Orgone 93 experiments. The principal difference, however, was that after creating a hypothetical column of light between the meditators and the upper atmosphere, the rest of the meditation would be taken up 'healing' global problems, such as the hole in the ozone layer, and sending out an open invitation to any 'extra-terrestrial' intelligences to communicate in some form. By conducting the same meditation again and again at the same spot Sherwood believed that our call would eventually be answered in the form of visual sightings of aerial luminosities and other more subjective experiences. Steven Greer and the CSETI team had used an almost identical form of meditation to 'vector' in 'structured craft'.

In the end we decided to conduct two experiments per day - one at midday GMT, 13.00 local time, and one at dusk. This allowed for a total of 14 experiments - 10 consecutive 'extra-terrestrial' meditations and then, following a day of controls, (as it turned out) two 'terrestrial' based meditations, of which more later. The location chosen for all experiments was Woodborough Hill, which seemed to be the area's central focus for unusual luminosities as well as the site that had scored the highest overall anomaly count during the Orgone 93 experimentation.

As before, it was felt necessary to re-introduce an OED in the experimentation in an attempt to create the correct environmental conditions for the manifestation of energy forms. Orgone expert Tony Beddoe of ORTEC was, once again, called in to co-ordinate this aspect of the project.

Monitoring Programme

Orgone 94's monitoring programme was geared to register any possible environmental or instrumental responses produced in direct association with the meditations. Rodney Hale linked his own triple-tubed Geiger counter with a Psion organiser to enable counts per minute to be automatically recorded in its memory. These were then manually transferred onto report forms following the completion of each experiment. For the first time we were also able to measure subtle changes in the electromagnetic (EM) field using various coils as amplifiers, although more on this in the next chapter.

Other on-site apparatus included an electrostatic volt meter measuring the air potential and the WR-3 radio receiver used the previous year to audibly monitor VLF frequency ranges between 50 Hz and 11 kHz. Each experiment took 50 minutes and consisted of a 15-minute pre-control period, a 20 to 25-minute meditational period and a 10-minute post-control period. The only real difference between Orgone 93 and Orgone 94 was the substitution of the arduous dawn experiment with a much longer evening session beginning at around 21.30, just as the light was beginning to fade. Afterwards many of those taking part would simply remain on the hill for a more informal sky-watch and, sometime around midnight, a further spontaneous meditation.

Electronics engineer Paul Hailey, who had successfully monitored East Field, Alton Barnes, in July 1993, agreed to arrange his own monitoring programme around the Orgone 94 experimentation between the dates in question. In similar with the previous year, Hailey's equipment included a multi-channel tape deck recording incoming data from various pieces of equipment located outside his converted dormobile, parked up close to the north base of Woodborough Hill.

Photographic Section

With only very limited resources, Orgone 94 decided to concentrate on just two areas of photographic investigation - the study of black and white infrared anomalies and visible light colour photography. Of these, the former seemed more important to validate or dispel, so the Pentax stereo adaptor obtained earlier in the year was attached to the camera using HIE high speed black and white film. Unfortunately, despite a lengthy search we were unable to obtain a second stereo adaptor so all colour photography was conducted in mono alone. However, the two cameras were linked by a dual cable release to ensure that the two shots were virtually simultaneous.

An exposure was taken on each camera every fifth minute for the entire duration of each experiment, meaning a total of 11 shots per camera per experiment. Two 'lollipop' marker posts were positioned at set distances of 20 m and 50 m from the camera bank in case any unidentified stereo imagery did appear on film. An idea of fixed distances was essential for calculating the precise distance between the camera and the imagery concerned.

A further SLR camera, loaded with low speed slide film, was used for night-time experiments, while a Panasonic video recorder was used to record all 14 scheduled experiments. Lastly, some (but unfortunately not all) meditations were recorded on audio tape.

The results of the Orgone 94 experiments were, in my opinion, quite astounding as will become clear from the next four chapters. All I ask is that the reader suspends scepticism until they have digested and considered the entire contents of this thought-provoking section of the book.

30

Mind Effects

Unlike the enormous and undoubtedly exaggerated radiation increases visible on the resulting graphs that accompanied Orgone 93 experimentation, the minute-by-minute count rate registered on Rodney Hale's own equipment rarely shows up any visible results at a glance. It is not until one studies the above and below average trend that any real patterns are deduced.(1)

Although the radiation readings on three of the Orgone 94 experiments had to be abandoned due to moisture finding its way into the Geiger Muller tube housing, the remaining nine meditational experiments produced no less than seven visible count rate increases. Furthermore, in six out of seven instances the rise in trend began *before* the commencement of the meditation, sometimes as much as seven to eight minutes beforehand. This pattern had, of course, been noted before, particularly in the graph produced by Rodney Hale from the overall results of seven separate sessions between July 1993 and April 1994 (see Chapter 23). These findings, consistent with the results obtained by Tiller at Stanford University between 1977-9, clearly imply that *simply by thinking about the intentions of the forthcoming meditation* is enough for the human mind to affect the apparatus being used in the experiment.

A preliminary experiment conducted at Woodborough Hill on Sunday, 26 June had produced similar results. The triple-tubed Geiger counter recorded an increase in the radiation count rate during the first meditation alone (another pattern that has been noticed before). This had started some five minutes before the commencement of the meditation - at a point coincident to when the group, already seated in a circle, were being briefed on the contents of the forthcoming visualisation.

The readings taken during two control experiments on Thursday, 28 July did not display the same characteristics as those recording increases during the meditational periods. One showed a slight dip in the overall trend of the count rate, while the other revealed no real changes at all, re-emphasising the importance of the pattern discerned during the meditations. In addition to this, on the few occasions that a smaller, twin-tubed Jupiter radiation counter was also used during an experiment, it tended to confirm the

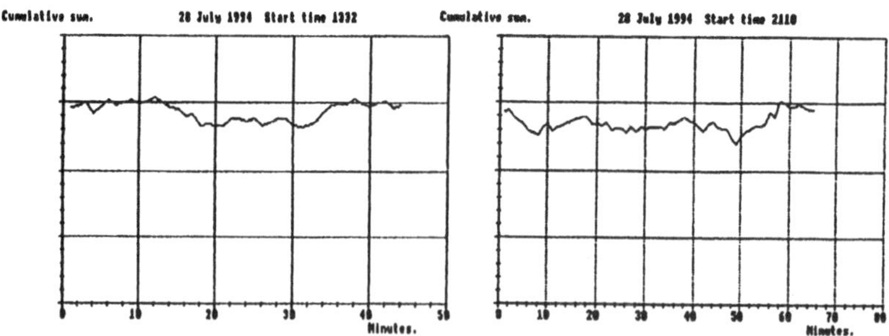

FIG 26. Two cumulative trend graphs showing the above and below average radiation count rates during the two Orgone 94 control tests at lunchtime and dusk on 28 July 1994. Neither show the same characteristics as those obtained during the meditational sessions during the same week (pic: Rodney Hale).

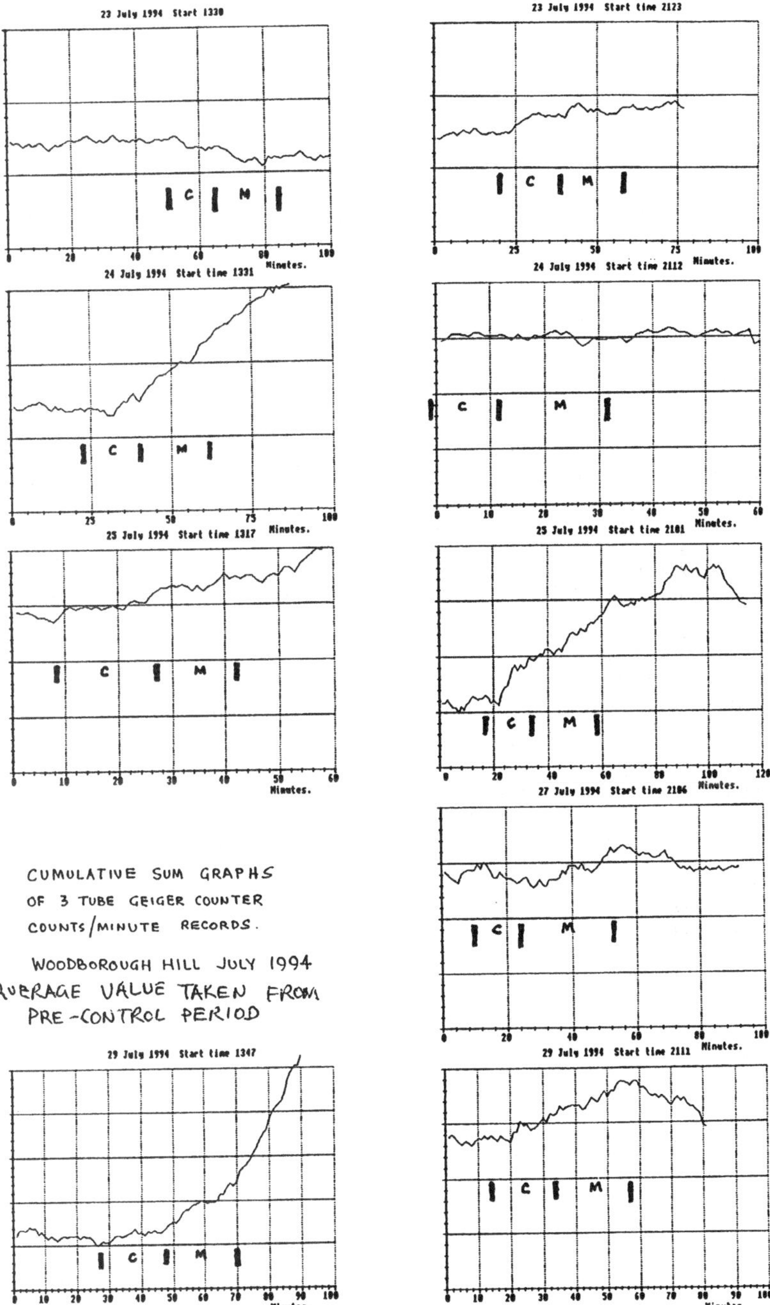

FIG 27. Nine cumulative trend graphs showing the above and below average radiation count rates registered by Rodney Hale's equipment on nine occasions during Orgone 94 in July 1994. Seven display clear increases during meditational periods (pic: Rodney Hale).

results of the main counter.

In September 1994 Rodney Hale fed the total counts recorded for each meditational experiment into a computer and deduced an overall trend for the entire week.(2) Unfortunately, of the nine sessions recorded, one - the dusk session on 24 July - could not be used as it did not meet with the timing criteria necessary (it started too late). The resulting graph displays a now familiar sight, with a steady increase in the count rate beginning some seven to eight minutes before the start of the meditation and then rising continually until the end of the experiment. This suggests that the count rate does not drop at the termination of the meditation, but continues to increase beyond the post-control period. Quite clearly longer post-controls are necessary to follow this trend even further. On a statistical note, a total of 8591 counts were produced during the pre-control periods, against a total of 8973 counts during the first 15 minutes of the meditations, giving an average increase across eight meditations of 4.5%.

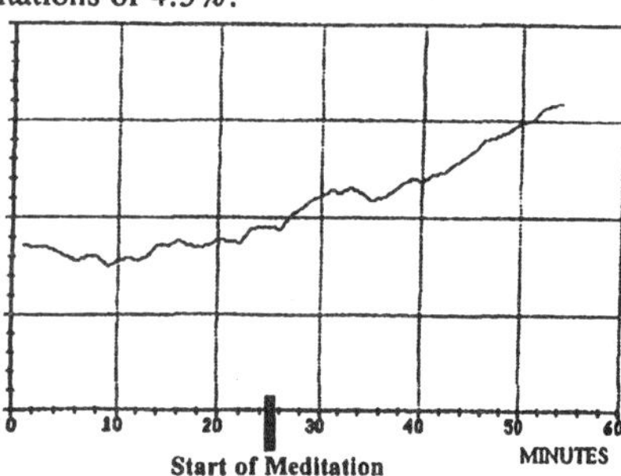

FIG 28. Cumulative trend graph showing the total counts per minute for eight Orgone 94 meditational sessions between 23 and 29 July 1994 using the triple-tubed Geiger counter. Note the increase beginning some minutes before the start of the meditational period, indicating that mental intent may be as powerful as mental action (pic: Rodney Hale).

Little more need be said at this moment about these extraordinary results. They conform very well to an existing pattern and are even further evidence that the human mind can modify the normal count rate of Geiger counters and other such instrumentation through what might only be described as non-local or psychokinetic processes. If one can accept this, then the rest of the project's results must also be assessed with this idca firmly fixed in our minds.

Electromagnetic Activity

The use of metal coils to detect variations in the earth's electromagnetic (EM) field was a new area of study for us. For this Rodney Hale prepared a battery-operated, multi-channel 'black box'. One channel was linked to an ultra-low frequency (ULF) 100-Henry coil acting as an amplifier to measure subtle variations over a fairly wide area. It was located at the end of a 10 m cable away from the meditators, so as not to be disturbed by human movement; this was referred to as the 'background' coil. A second channel was linked via a further 10 m cable to a set of eight coils arranged to measure more localised variations in the magnetic field over a distance of perhaps 0.5 m radius. These were contained in a plastic box, half embedded in the earth and protected by a wooden frame situated on the edge of the circle of meditators; this became known as the 'local' channel.

Similar coils had been successfully used by physicians and scientists at the Department of Physiology of the School of Medicine at Showa University, Tokyo, to measure *ch'i* emissions from the hands of volunteers.(3) In our own case, all signals would be converted to a form suitable for tape recording. After each experiment the used C-100 tapes would either be turned over or removed and marked carefully in readiness for conversion back into electrical waveforms. These were then fed into a computer for final analysis and assessment by Rodney Hale.

Those wishing to participate in the meditations were asked to take their places only *after* the tenth minute of the pre-control period, meaning that the 'local' channel would register a huge burst of activity around this time. After settling down they would link hands in readiness for the off, while two people - usually Debbie Benstead and Ed Sherwood - would lower their own hands down onto the wooden frame covering the 'local' coils. Both channels would then display long periods of relative inactivity until the end of the meditation when the sitters would be politely asked to move out of the equipment's range of detection - their departure creating another recognisable burst of activity. All this made it comparatively easy for Rodney Hale to pick out any uncharacteristic disturbances recorded during meditations and control periods.

Background Bursts

During the entire 14 experiments uncharacteristic disturbances in the EM field were noted only twice on the 'background' channel. The first was a 20-second burst of high frequency activity at 14.29 on Sunday, 24 July, some 19 minutes into the meditation period. Unknown military activity on Salisbury Plain was ruled out as this trace did not appear on any other EM equipment. A similar high-frequency burst occurred at 21.39 during the dusk experiment that evening. This occurred some 14 minutes into the meditation. The origin of this high-frequency activity, with wave cycles between approximately 1 to 10 Hz, remains unknown, although they should, I believe, be reviewed in context with the results achieved using the more 'local' EM apparatus outlined below.

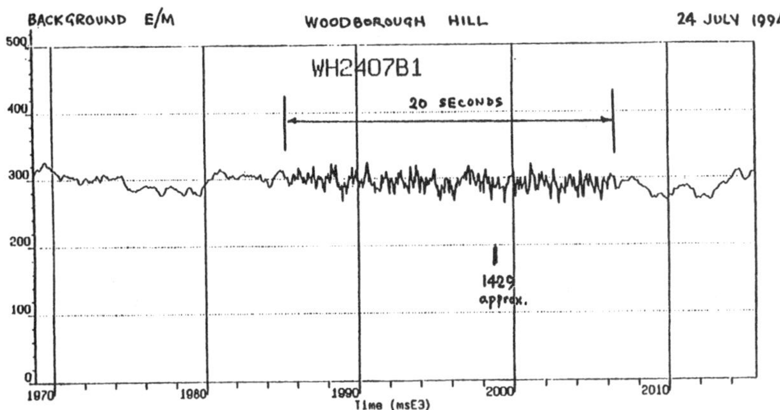

FIG 29. Unaccountable burst of high frequency activity detected by the 'background' electromagnetic coil at 14.29 on 24 July 1994 (pic: Rodney Hale).

Slow Waves

In six out of seven evening experiments long bursts of low frequency oscillations, ranging from 1 to 10 seconds per cycle (i.e. 1 Hz to 0.1 Hz), were found to have occurred for anything between a few short cycles to periods of up to three to four minutes at a time. More importantly, on five out of six of these evenings they appeared coincident with meditations.

The sheer presence of these strange bursts of activity on the 'local' apparatus completely flummoxed Rodney Hale.(4) Having experimented with this equipment before, and being familiar with different types of EM waveforms, he was unable to suggest a cause for this periodic activity. What was the possible cause of such slow waveforms? On average they were around five seconds per cycle which could conceivably have been created by slowly swinging a ferrous metal pendulum back and forth across the path of an EM coil, a feat beyond the capacity of the meditators involved. Another curious fact about these low frequency oscillations was that they only occurred during the evening sessions; not once was there any trace of them during a lunchtime experiment. Why?

Twice - on 27 and 29 July - this low frequency activity started one minute into the meditation and recurred on several occasions before fading out towards the end of each session.(5) Furthermore, on four out of six of the nights concerned, clear radiation increases were also achieved, so might non-local processes have been responsible for this low frequency activity? It is a tantalising, and very real, possibility, but there are two major stumbling blocks that will have to be tackled before any firm conclusions can be drawn.

Our problems start with the dusk experiment on Saturday, 23 July (the very first day of the project). Low-frequency oscillations were found to have appeared some four minutes *before* the commencement of the meditation. At this time the group were wandering across to take their seats following my call to meditation. These distinctive signals continued intermittently until the first minute of the meditation when they gradually faded away. They returned just once, 16 minutes into the meditation, but that was it - no further activity of this sort was recorded until two nights later.

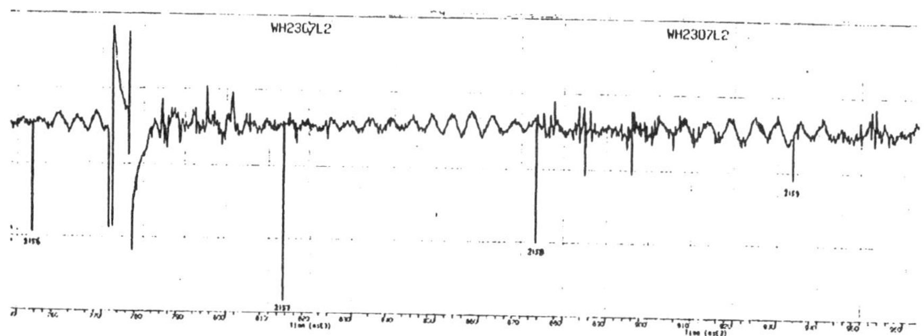

FIG 30. This example of low frequency activity detected on the 'local' EM coils during the dusk experiment on 23 July 1994 began four minutes before the start of the meditation and continued on through till the first minute of the session. Does this lend weight to the idea that intent is as potent as action? The group taking up position is marked by the burst of activity on the left-hand side of the graph (pic: Rodney Hale).

So how might we explain this pre-meditation intrusion? If we return to the patterns emerging regarding the radiation results we can see that on a number of occasions the graphs have clearly shown that count rate increases begin minutes before the commencement of the meditation; indeed, often at a time coincident to the call for the meditators to sit down in a circle and ready themselves for the coming session. I have already suggested that this may well show that *intent* maybe as potent, perhaps even more so, than final *action*. Rodney Hale remains confident that this low frequency activity is in no way the result of movement, especially as it appeared to continue after the meditators had settled down.

So is mental interaction a realistic answer to these EM anomalies? Plotting the occurrence of these strange oscillations on a graph I found that, almost without exception, they occurred during meditations, generally between the first and sixteenth minute. Furthermore, on just two occasions - 26 and 29 July - short bursts of high frequency activity (with cycles between 1 and 10 Hz) also occurred on the local EM equipment. Strangely enough, in both instances it was recorded during the first minute of the meditation, once again intimating at a link between these traces and focused mental activity.

Finally, how can we possibly explain the fact that both the low frequency and high frequency pulsations only occurred on the 'local' apparatus during the evening sessions, never during a lunchtime experiment? Is is possible that the encroaching darkness creates the necessary mental environment to produce these strange signals inside the human mind? Certainly, in psychic questing important meditational work is always left till after sunset as experience has shown that the psychic faculties work better around this time.

There is, unfortunately, one major objection to the idea that all these effects are mind related in some way. During the control tests at dusk on Thursday, 28 July the low frequency activity reappeared. Although fainter, it was still recognisable as the same type of waveform registered on previous days. This was a complete spanner in the works. After some quite startling results on almost every other day, one might even be tempted

PLATE 38. Circuitry equipment monitoring 'background' and 'local' variations in the electromagnetic field on Woodborough Hill during Orgone 94 experimentation. The meditational group are seen in the background. Can the human mind really affect the local environment using co-ordinated meditation? (pic: Johnny Merron)

to suggest that the cosmic joker had been up to his old tricks again. So, were we therefore to conclude that these subtle shifts in the EM field were natural occurrences registered *only* by the 'local' coils, not by the 100-Henry coil monitoring the same sort of changes over a much wider area?

Bricket Wood Experiments

In early August 1994 Rodney Hale conducted a series of control experiments in the back garden of his home at Bricket Wood, near St Albans, using exactly the same 'local' apparatus in an attempt to find out whether he could achieve similar results away from the influence of Woodborough Hill and meditational practices. After several frustrating sessions, Hale finally concluded that it had not been the eight coils that had detected these low frequency shifts in the EM field, but the 10 m length of screened, single core cable! He also satisfied himself that no other part of the equipment, including the tape recorders, was responsible for these bursts of activity; in other words, they were almost certainly not 'machine artefacts' of some kind.(6)

The only negative aspect of this research was that Hale was also able to produce bursts of low frequency activity without the involvement of a meditational group; however, there was evidence to suggest that at least some of this activity had been unconsciously induced by Hale himself.(7)

Despite this unfortunate news, Hale recalled that when the Earthquest group had visited his home on Sunday, 27 March 1994 to conduct two meditational sessions in preparation for the up-coming Ridgeway quest, similar low frequency EM traces had been recorded for 30-second durations during the first few minutes of the meditation; indeed, they had appeared coincident with a noticeable radiation increase. However, on this occasion an entirely different amplifier had been used and the results were fed directly onto computer.

Exp No	Date	Time	Activity	Mins into med/control
01	23.7.94	Midday	Nil	
02	do	Dusk	LF at 21.56-22.00	. -4 to 0 mins
			LF 22.16	. +16 mins
03	24.7.94	Midday	Nil	
04	do	Dusk	LF at 21.32	. +7 mins
05	25.7.94	Midday	Nil	
06	do	Dusk	LF 21.40-43	. +5 to 8 mins
			1 cyc LF 21.47-48	. +12 to 13 mins
07	26.7.94	Midday	Nil	
08	do	Dusk	HF 21.24	. 0 mins
09	27.7.94	Midday	Nil	
10	do	Dusk	LF 21.41-42	. +1 to 2 mins
			LF 21.43	. +3 mins
			LF 21.44	. +4 mins
			LF 21.48-49	. +8 to 9 mins
			LF 21.50-51	. +10 to 11 mins
			LF 21.52-53	. +12 to 13 mins
11	28.7.94	Midday	Nil	control
12	do	Dusk	Slight LF 21.48-50	control: +8 to 10 mins
13	29.7.94	Midday	Nil	
14	do	Dusk	HF burst 21.42	. 0 mins
			LF 21.43-44	. +1 to 2 mins
			LF 21.47-48	. +3 to 4 mins
			LF 21.55	. +13 mins
			LF 21.57	. +15 mins
			LF 22.09-10	. +27 to 29 mins
			LF 22.13	. Post-control: +1 min (group still in position until 22.14)

NOTE: HF refers to frequencies between approx 1 Hz to 10 Hz.
LF refers to frequencies between 0.1 Hz and 1 Hz.

FIG 31. Above, summary of unexplainable 'local' electromagnetic activity during the Orgone 94 experimentation. Below, graphs showing the relationship of both the 'background' and 'local' EM activity to the time-frame of the meditations.

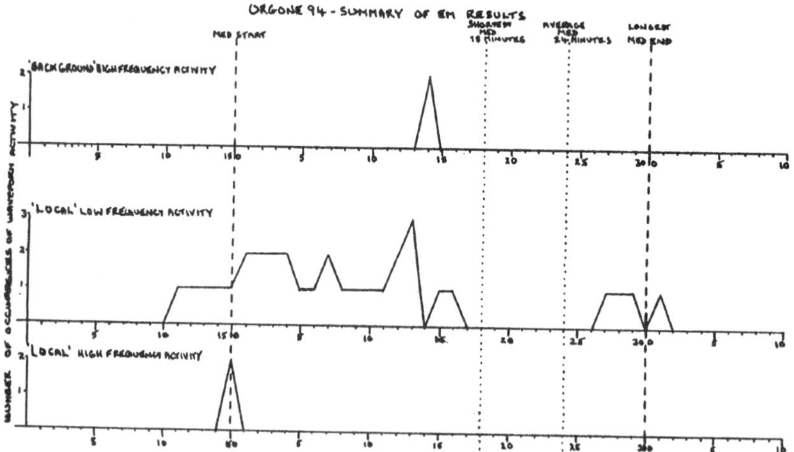

This therefore meant that low frequency oscillations, comparable to those obtained during Orgone 94, had been achieved earlier using completely different apparatus.

In conclusion then, it seemed as though Orgone 94 had recorded a series of low frequency pulses which were probably due to undefined EM activity in the vicinity of the cable that stretched from the equipment to the box containing the coils. This had been positioned amidst the circle of meditators taking part in the experiments, and on four out of the six occasions this activity occurred it appeared coincident with the meditations. On one further occasion it seemed linked with the intention to start the meditation, and on the sixth and final occasion it had occurred very briefly during a control experiment.

So why had it occurred during the control tests? On the evening concerned we had worked the equipment with only a skeleton staff. Debbie Benstead had operated the 'background' and 'local' channels and around the point coincident to when these waveforms occurred the video recording reveals that she was singing along with Lisa Dawkins, who was operating the Jupiter Geiger counter nearby.

This realisation could be important, for on the afternoon of Sunday, 17 July, six days before the start of Orgone 94, Debbie and I had tested the EM apparatus with Rodney Hale in his back garden and we had both taken turns in attempting to focus our minds on its presence. Only Debbie had managed to create a noticeable disturbance on the local channel, and in hindsight this minor activity had produced two low frequency oscillations not dissimilar to those that had appeared with regularity just a week or so later. Was it therefore possible that her joviality and proximity to the equipment had catalysed this characteristic waveform activity? Happiness is an emotional quality that from my own researches has proved to be highly conducive in activating psychic abilities.(8)

None of this does, however, explain the reappearance of the low frequency activity during the trials conducted by Rodney Hale at the beginning of August 1994. We can only assume that either these waveforms occur naturally, or they are the result of Hale's own inadvertent interaction with the equipment, or they are some kind of echo or memory of the results obtained during the earlier experiments and triggered into reappearance by one or other of the first two possibilities.

Breathing in the Mind

Many more experiments will need to be conducted both with and without the involvement of meditational practices to determine the exact cause of this highly unusual EM activity. However, casting caution aside for one moment, if the human mind really can create low frequency oscillations in the localised EM field, then what does this mean to our understanding of psychokinetic abilities? What part of our body could possibly create such a slow rhythmic pulse? Certainly, it is not related to the so-called Alpha, Beta or Theta waves detected in the brain by scientists as these are much higher in frequency.

There is, of course, no obvious answer, but there is just one function of the biological organism that does involve a slow rhythmic pattern that *can* be anything from 1 to 10 seconds per cycle, and this is breathing. Breathing is particularly important to meditational practices and simple breathing exercises are *always* employed before the commencement of a path-working visualisation. Is it possible then that breathing can induce some kind of corresponding brain-wave signal strong enough to affect the localised EM field? If so, then could slow rhythmic breathing be an important key to understanding the nature of non-local processes?

The term *ch'i*, used in eastern mysticism to describe the universal life force, translates as the 'two breaths', a reference, it seems, to its pulsating cycles and patterns in nature. Since we know that *ch'i* might also be the X-factor behind bioenergy effects of the sort recorded by the Japanese physicians and scientists at Showa University, Tokyo, then is it possible that such rhythmic cycles can also be detected in energy-related discharges emanating from the human body and catalysed by focused mental attention? These are thought provoking ideas, but it is time perhaps to move on and assess the rest of the results to see whether they can throw any light on the situation.

31

The Templemakers

For ninety-nine percent of the time the nights at Alton Barnes are like any other, bereft of any unusual aerial activity. One might become momentarily interested in the orange flashing lights mounted on slow-moving combine harvesters returning to their respective farms, or in the high-powered torch beams that periodically scan the distant East Field, or in the multiples of amber-coloured parachute flares that appear with frequency over Salisbury Plain during military operations, or even in the colourful fireballs that streak across the open sky. Yet all these things are easily recognisable to any astute crop watcher.

I mention all this as it is that other one per cent that produces extraordinary aerial displays that leaves me in little doubt that something very significant has been occurring in Alton Barnes in recent years. On no less than four occasions during Orgone 94 inexplicable lights were witnessed in the night sky by one or more of the team. The first occurred around 23.30 on Saturday, 23 July 1994, our first night of operation. Rodney Hale and myself were monitoring an impromptu meditation being conducted by Debbie Benstead, Ed Sherwood and his girlfriend Fiona Johnson. Hale was several metres distance from me when he noticed an orange glow appear some 10 degrees above the south-south-westerly horizon. It seemed to possess a nimbus-like effect around its core and grew rapidly in magnitude before fading out. It then reappeared at the same spot and gave a repeat performance, before vanishing from view for good. These two bright pulsations, which had occurred below the high cloud-base, were visible only for the count of between four and five. As a meditation was in progress Hale had been unable to shout across to me, and by the time he had reached my position the aerial display had already finished. Unfortunately, at that moment I was winding on the film in the camera so saw nothing - an unfortunate coincidence of the sort that recurred with persistence during the week-long period of experimentation.

The meteorological office at nearby RAF Lyneham reported that at 23.00 that evening the visibility had been 8 km with a 7/8th auto-cumulus cloud-cover at 3.9 km, which is very high. By midnight the visibility had increased to 12 km with an additional 2/8th cloud cover at 2.9 km. Based on Hale's account of the incident and the meteorological report for the evening, I concluded that the orange pulsations had occurred slightly to the west of Urchfont Hill, a distance of around 9 km from Woodborough Hill. As an avid astronomer and meteorological expert, Hale is familiar with the night sky and yet cannot suitably explain this occurrence. It seems unlikely to have been the result of an army flare over Salisbury Plain since these are invariably amber-gold in colour and clearly identifiable by their movement and faint smoke trail. Interestingly enough, Sherwood had conducted the meditation after he and Fiona had briefly witnessed a group of three similar orange lights in the same area of sky. Feeling that further activity might occur, he had initiated an open-mind communication in the hope that this would coerce them into manifestation once more. Hale's brief, but baffling, sighting was seen as a response to this act.

That same night crop watchers Tom and Kerry Blower from Cardiff were driving along the road linking Avebury village with the A4 Marlborough to Beckhampton road, when at around 02.30 they witnessed a bright ball of white light moving horizontally amid trees on Waden Hill, close to the Kennett Avenue of standing stones. The following morning a fresh crop formation was discovered just 200 m away from this position - one in which a large number of people subsequently experienced quite disturbing physiological effects including three accounts of alleged black-outs. With this information in mind, the couple were sure that the glowing ball they saw was free moving and not a flare or illuminated balloon of some kind.(1)

Martinsell Hill

Two nights later, at around 22.40 on Monday, 25 July, those remaining on Woodborough Hill after the dusk experiment (which finished at 22.10) had broken into small groups to do their own thing. Sherwood felt sure he could 'see' an 'etheric light' positioned just above the north-east horizon in the vicinity of Martinsell Hill, an Iron Age fort crowning the eastern extremes of the Pewsey Vale Downs (SU178638). He had casually mentioned this to his girlfriend Fiona who had gone to tell Debbie, who was resting alone on the north-eastern edge of Woodborough Hill. Sitting down, the two girls watched silently for just a few minutes when at 22.45 they witnessed an orange light rise into the air above Martinsell Hill and then, after only a few seconds of viewing, make an abrupt right-angle turn towards the east. It continued this course for some three seconds before blinking out of view. Both Fiona and Debbie are confident that what they saw was neither an aeroplane or an army flare - the object's uncharacteristic right-angle turn seemingly confirming this opinion. Sherwood says he has often seen similar orange balls of light appear in the vicinity of Martinsell Hill, which lies just over 6 km distance from Woodborough Hill. Unfortunately, as most people were preoccupied with other more mundane matters at the time, no one else witnessed this curious aerial phenomenon, not even Sherwood himself. Once again, no photographs recorded the event due to its brief duration.

The Great Anniversary and a Repeat Performance

So far the lights-in-the-sky (LITS) had produced fairly low key incidents. Each occurred following hot, though fairly humid, sunny days. No one was making any big claims for what they had seen and neither sighting appeared to have had any direct relationship to the Orgone 94 experiments - something that cannot be said of the following sequence of events which occurred just 24 hours later.

Tuesday, 26 July 1994 had been eagerly anticipated in view of the quite extraordinary catalogue of circles-related incidents that had befallen Alton Barnes in previous years. Ed Sherwood had arranged with GWR Radio of Swindon to broadcast his set 'extra-terrestrial' meditation live around 22.30. This was to be carried via a radio back-pack and a mobile transmitter across south-west England in the hope that it would inspire people to join the meditation either in their homes or at local vantage points. Since Sherwood was involved in our own experimentation, which was not scheduled to finish until around 22.00, it was agreed that he should conduct the GWR meditation from the summit of Woodborough Hill. His exact whereabouts would not, of course, be revealed over the air as this would be seen by some as an open invitation to either join the open broadcast or attempt to ruin it in some way.

The potential of this experiment was enormous. If there was any possibility that the human mind could attract unseen energy forms through open communication then the fact that so many thousands of people would be focusing on this one idea at the very same moment that Sherwood was conducting the meditation on Woodborough Hill, surely increased the chances of tangible results. Moreover, Sherwood had also arranged for several close friends to split into groups of three and follow the GWR meditation from vantage points around the area. I also knew that other, quite separate, groups and individuals, including the CSETI team, would be out on the hills conducting very similar open-communication meditations later that same night.

The earlier part of the day had seen continuous rain, bringing to an end a several-week long period of hot, dry weather. This had forced us to bring out and use the camera hide for the first time that lunchtime, although fortunately the rain had held off for most of the experiment. Nothing unusual had been recorded, even though it is fair to admit that, in similar with the previous year, the noticeable change in local weather had brought with it a tense feeling of expectancy that still prevailed among the team when they returned to the hill around 21.00 that evening.

Yet then the problems began. Rodney Hale's triple-tubed Geiger counter began giving uncharacteristic low readings and later packed up altogether. This we soon realised had been due to moisture creeping inside the head containing the Geiger-Muller tubes during the wet lunchtime session. The screen of the video recorder also displayed the word 'moisture' before cutting out completely, having already failed to work properly that lunchtime. Without either a Geiger counter or the video recorder, there was little with which we could monitor the GWR meditation after our own experiment had been completed. There would be too many people milling around to use the EM apparatus, which left just time exposure photographs to record the event.

Several of Ed Sherwood's colleagues who were to take part in the GWR presentation arrived early and joined the Orgone 94 meditation when it finally got under way at 21.24, with the still cameras facing towards the copse of trees crowning the hill's southern edge. The session finished without incident at 21.48 and after the completion of the post-control period at 21.59, Sherwood began a live interview with the GWR presenter to introduce the evening's proceedings, including the meditation which began at 22.28. This was conducted at exactly the same position as the earlier Orgone 94 session and was for all intent and purposes a repeat performance. Members of our own team joined the group of sitters, including Debbie Benstead and farmer Polly Carson.

My colleague Karl Dawkins and I took time-exposure photographs from within the camera hide using a Pentax SLR camera, its 50 mm lens stopped down to f.11 and focused on infinity. Using Kodak 50 ASA Elite slide film, the camera's automatic setting gave exposure times of anything between five and seven minutes.

The GWR meditation ended at 22.47 and by this time the cloud-base had lowered to just 90 m above ground level, according to the meteorological office at nearby RAF Lyneham. This created a thick mist, hiding the Pewsey Vale Downs and reducing the visibility to no more than a kilometre. Sherwood was once again interviewed by the presenter who invited listeners to call in with their experiences. Then suddenly, without warning, communication was inexplicably lost between the outside broadcast van and the station at Wootton Bassett.

It was then, as GWR attempted to resume its broadcast, that something quite extraordinary occurred. An aerial flash of immense magnitude ripped through the low cloud-base, momentarily illuminating the whole area. At the time, I was looking east and saw this quite plainly. Johnny Merron saw it while inside the camera hide in which he was sheltering and Tony Beddoe witnessed it from the western base of Woodborough Hill. Others, who were still sitting together after having just finished the meditation, also witnessed the flash, but only two people on the hill actually saw its source. One was my colleague Karl Dawkins. At the time, which we recorded as 22.58, he happened to be glancing towards the north, in the direction of East Field, when he clearly saw a 'football'-sized sphere of light appear momentarily before exploding in a massive burst of light without any sound whatsoever. It had appeared almost horizontal to his elevated position on Woodborough Hill, which meant that as the mist had reduced the visibility so much, then the exploding ball must have been positioned at a reasonably low level somewhere in the vicinity of East Field.

From the outset, this incident begged explanation as the low stratus cloud that evening was wholly uncharacteristic of lightning activity. Moreover, the nearby meteorological office at RAF Lyneham confirmed that no storm activity had either been reported or forecast for the night of the 26/27 July. It could also not be overlooked that an almost identical flash with a ball-like core had, of course, been witnessed by Reg Presley and various other crop watchers around 01.15 on the night of 26/27 July 1993, *exactly* one year beforehand. The fact that the 1994 flash had occurred just 11 minutes after the GWR experiment and 59 minutes after Orgone 94's dusk experiment seemed hard to dismiss. Could there have been a direct link between the aerial burst and the open-communication meditations being conducted with so much fervour in the Vale of Pewsey that night?

The following day Sherwood learnt that one of the groups taking part in the GWR link-up - the one situated on the site of the old round barrow known as Swanborough Tump, 1.8 km south-east of Woodborough Hill, had witnessed a group of lights at cloud level which had appeared to come from a 'solid object' with two column-like beams that had reached down like fingers towards the ground. It had appeared to be in the area of Sharcott (SU143595), some miles east of our position. The group, which had included Fiona Johnson's brother Zahari Firebrace, said the columns had revolved around a vertical axis. No one on Woodborough Hill saw this aerial display which had apparently lasted for the entire duration of the meditational period, so no explanation could be offered as to its source of origin.

The following day, Wednesday, 27 July it was discovered that two individuals, Cornelius Crowley from London and Andrew Potter from Reading, Berkshire, had also witnessed the aerial flash of the previous night. In an interview with the author the following evening they explained how they had travelled down from Reading that evening, arriving in Alton Barnes around 21.30.(2) Seeing the 'eye' formation they decided to enter East Field and conduct an open-communication meditation. Having mentally gained permission to enter the formation from its pre-supposed *genius loci*, they proceeded to lie on their backs within the circles and rings of flattened wheat and close their eyes. The meditation went without incident and afterwards both young men lay back and stared up at the bleak sky. It was then, at a time they can only fix at between 22.30 and 23.00, that they witnessed the aerial detonation which they say originated from a position directly above them. However, only Crowley was actually looking upwards when it occurred. Like Karl Dawkins, he described it as a bright ball that instantaneously, and quite silently, exploded to create an airborne flash of immense magnitude.

Crowley estimated the height of the ball to have been around 80 m above the formation, which conforms precisely with Dawkins' own recall of the incident. Independently, Dawkins placed the source of the aerial flash as appearing in line with the position of East Field's 'eye' formation, which was not visible from Woodborough Hill and had not been viewed by him at this time. This was superb confirmation of the objectivity of the event which implied that at 22.58 on Tuesday, 26 July 1994 a bright ball of light had momentarily appeared some 80 m above East Field's 'eye' formation before exploding to create a massive, low-level flash. Surely if this had been some kind of contrived hoax then it would probably have made a loud bang and would have necessitated the involvement of individuals positioned in East Field itself. Certainly, no suspicious activity was reported by Crowley and Potter who appear to have been directly beneath the source of the flash when it occurred.

So what might this 'source' have been? Can we find a suitable solution to this extraordinary event? It is known that aerial flashes of this order occurred in 1993, indeed, on the very same date. Other localised or cloud-level flashes have been reported in the area over the past five years. We also know that Paul Hailey was monitoring the area when the 1994 flash occurred. On completion of his project he examined the resulting tapes for the time period in question, but could find no correlations on any of his channels. This is important, for it does not invalidate the event; far from it, it shows that, in similar with the aerial detonations witnessed over the Egryn Hills in 1904-5, the source of the bright flash was certainly *not* an electrical discharge caused by localised storm activity. Some either a more mundane, or a more exotic, explanation was now needed.

Temporary Temples

During the afternoon of Wednesday, 27 July, before we learnt of Crowley and Potter's viewing of the aerial flash the night before, Debbie Benstead and myself visited the 'eye' formation in East Field for the first and only time it was present. Although we believed it had been manufactured by human hands, we enjoyed its presence for its obvious aesthetic and contemplative qualities. Inside the formation was a party of mostly Japanese tourists over from New York. Their leader, Taoist master Nan Lu - who regularly visits England to sample the crop circles - was jogging and spinning around the formation's different features trying to determine the directional flow of *ch'i* energy.

Shortly after the Taoist had completed his circumnavigation of the formation, which was a sight to watch in its own right, we decided to leave East Field in readiness for the evening experiment. Reaching the outer ring, Debbie unexpectedly doubled up as if in great pain. Trying to regain her composure, she began staggering about and needed assistance to get her away from the site. She immediately complained of dizziness, nausea and a growing headache, and eventually explained how, as she attempted to leave the formation, she had felt as if she had been 'hit' by an invisible barrier of some kind, inducing an instant sense of vertigo that had almost caused her to black out. For some time afterwards she looked pale and did not regain her colour until the late evening.

Nothing like this had happened to Debbie since our visit to the Barbury Castle crop pictogram in 1991, despite the fact that we had entered a number of crop circles and formations since this time. Such physiological effects were, as I knew only too well, a common feature among visitors to such locations, particularly psychically-sensitive individuals like herself. Yet what made the example in East Field different from any other?

PLATE 39. The powerful 'eye' formation that appeared in East Field, Alton Barnes, on 19 July 1994. It presence attracted, not only visitors from all over the world, but also various inexplicable events including various low-level airborne flashes that have so far defied explanation (pic: Johnny Merron).

Although part of this answer probably lay in its design and positioning, we concluded that it had something to do with the influx of well-meaning visitors, such as Nan Lu and his party, who had entered inside this disposable sanctuary during its brief presence in East Field. It is strongly possible that such people generate some kind of energy effect through personal attunement, ritual actions and meditational practices. In a sense, they either purposely or unknowingly excite the flow of the localised energy matrix to such a degree that it becomes a highly-charged temple of 'spiritual' power. If so, then it is feasible that this over-excitation not only induces adverse physiological and psychological effects in visitors, but helps create the correct environmental conditions necessary for the genesis of short-lived balls of light of the kind witnessed on 26 July 1994.

Furthermore, the sheer fact that so many groups and individuals, including Cornelius Crowley and Andrew Potter themselves, were conducting meditational practices in the general vicinity of East Field that night would tend to suggest a direct link of some sort. Could this focused mental activity have been enough to catalyse the sudden creation and destruction of this aerial luminosity? If the answer is yes, then what factors decided its manifestation? Although the electro-static air potential was extremely low for both experiments on the 26th, the weather bore great similarities to that which had prevailed in Alton Barnes when the flash occurred the previous year and when Steven Greer, Chris Mansell *et al* witnessed the light cluster in 1992. In all cases a period of hot, humid weather had been broken by a series of early downpours and then, as the day had progressed, constant light drizzle. Both in 1992 and in 1994 the late evening had brought with it an encroaching mist reducing visibility to just a few kilometres at any one time. Even before the aerial flash occurred we had openly concluded that the night had been ideal for the appearance of aerial anomalies. This recurring weather pattern theme is common in ufology and is something I also feel to be fundamental in the creation of the right environmental conditions necessary to produce the manifestation of both short-term and more sustained lightforms.

A little over 24 hours after the aerial flash of 26 July 1994, an almost identical incident occurred over East Field. It was witnessed by Stephen Alexander and a group of some six other skywatchers positioned in Knap Hill car-park.(3) It seems that around 02.45 on the morning of the 28 July they saw what Alexander described as a 'condensed' flash of light that appeared for about two seconds 'half way up from the horizon'. It was said to have originated from a 'centre point' and to have been 'contained' within a circular area, almost as if someone had momentarily switched on a giant aerial torch. Alexander is positive the light burst occurred directly above East Field, possibly even over the 'eye' formation. On this occasion the sky had been relatively clear and the air temperature had been fairly high, showing that predicting the best conditions for such luminosities is not as simple as it might at first seem. Once again, the meteorological office at nearby RAF Lyneham confirmed that no storm activity had either been reported or forecast for the night of 27/28 July 1994.

Nocturnal flashes continued to occur in the vicinity of East Field through into early August.(4) One localised flash was even seen during daylight hours. Andy Buckley from Cheshire was standing on the road overlooking East Field at around 17.30 on Saturday, 30 July when he witnessed a 'very bright flash' occur inside a single crop circle.(5) He described it as similar to that of a powerful camera flash, but emphasised that no one was actually in the circle at the time. It is perhaps important to remember that localised flashes have been reported in connection with crop circles since 1987(6) and that nocturnal crop artists have frequently reported seeing both airborne and close-proximity light bursts in the same area.

The Orange Streak

The mysteries for Tuesday, 26 July 1994 did not end with the big flash either, for the very last frame taken during the GWR presentation was still being exposed when the aerial flash took us by surprise at 22.58. Ironically, the camera was facing in the opposite

PLATE 40. The curious deep orange streak caught on a time exposure photograph at the same time that a low-level airborne flash occurred above the 'eye' crop formation in East Field, Alton Barnes, on 26 July 1994 - the anniversary of the big flash of 1993. This picture has been cropped left and top to leave 82% of the original frame (pic: Orgone 94).

direction at the time, but as I had witnessed the burst of light virtually overhead I hoped that at least something of its presence might have been recorded on the slide in question. When the roll of film was finally developed what was found baffled me completely, for on the final frame exposed between 22.52 and 22.59 there is an inexplicable orange streak in the open sky. It begins some two-thirds of the way across the picture at a point coincident to the southern horizon, somewhere in the vicinity of the Warminster/Westbury area. The orange line then climbs to the right-hand side of the picture, before arcing down slightly and then finally leaping out of shot almost half way up the side of the frame. It is a constant light source, as opposed to a pulsation, possessing a fairly low magnitude. There appears to be no indication of its origin and no darkened shadow suggesting the presence of someone in the frame when the picture was exposed.

As the rest of the frame shows distant lights as sharp pin-points, this orange streak is clearly a light source moving slowly across the exposed frame as the camera shutter remains open. Since the streak appears in the sky, it is not the result of a torch being carried past the camera lens during exposure. Moreover, torch trails are orange-white colour, not deep orange. The only possibility is that the streak records the passage of a cigarette fairly close to the lens, but this seems unlikely as we made sure no one walked in front of the camera and the movement of the streak is inconsistent with someone holding and smoking a cigarette.

There is no simple solution to this single anomaly - the only example achieved using time-exposure photography during the whole week of experimentation. The fact that it occurred coincident to the appearance of the aerial flash over East Field should not, I feel, be forgotten.

32

The Furious Host

As the Orgone 94 experimentation progressed it became clear that some members of the Earthquest group were feeling ill at ease with the style of Ed Sherwood's 'extra-terrestrial' meditations. This had come as no surprise as they had openly voiced their opinions on this matter even before the start of the project. In their minds it would have been preferable to have continued the 'ancestor spirit' theme used so successfully the previous year. These opinions I could understand, so by way of compromise we decided to conduct two 'terrestrial'-based meditations on the final day, Friday, 29 July 1994. It would also give us a chance to compare any results gained with those already achieved during the 'extra-terrestrial', open-communication meditations.

These re-scheduled meditations were to feature the Anglo-Saxon concept of the Furious Host, a form of the Wild Hunt of Norse tradition. This theme was chosen following the findings of an earlier meditation Polly Carson, Debbie Benstead and I had conducted in Tawsmead Copse on Monday, 4 April 1994. I wanted some clue as to why Tawsmead Copse produced so many sightings of orange balls of light and, finding no obvious answers, I had turned to intuitive means.

While in a light meditational trance at a chosen spot by an old oak tree deep within the woods, Debbie had begun receiving sequences of unsolicited 'clairvoyant' imagery which she had related to tape directly after the psychic session. She had spoken of seeing Tawsmead Copse from an aerial position and finding that it was three times larger than it is today with the immediate area devoid of any habitation. Realising that she was seeing the location in the past, Debbie made her way down into the centre of the great woods towards what appeared to be a secluded crossroads. Here she saw a torchlight procession of silhouetted figures approaching out of the darkness. On drawing closer she could see that the crowd, which consisted of both men and women, were carrying aloft a young man who they placed down at the centre of the crossroads. After some minutes of waiting, they walked away leaving the young man resigned to his fate. Debbie actually felt she wanted to go with the procession, but instead was forced to remain in position to witness something that was about to occur.

It was then that she began to hear coming from behind her the distant sound of horses' hooves, like the slowly rising peel of thunder. As the noise grew gradually louder and the ground began to vibrate, she had wanted desperately to turn around and confront whatever approached. Yet she found she was 'frozen' to the spot, able only to watch the crowd as they withdrew into the distance. The thundering sound still increased and when she was eventually able to turn around she could see orange balls of light rushing towards her over the tops of the trees. They remained as glowing spheres until they passed overhead, at which moment they became the flaming eyes and fiery breaths of black horses supporting silhouetted riders, like some kind of nightmarish 'dark hunt'. They had then whisked up the young man and carried him into the night. With this unexpected imagery she had asked in her mind: 'What are you?' to which she had gained the reply: 'The Hosts of Hela'.

The setting then changed to another group of people, this time all women, sitting with children at the same cross-roads. All bore blue body tattoos with dark areas around their eyes, making their faces look like skulls. As Debbie watched she saw the women making the children drink from cups containing a hot narcotic liquid drawn from a vessel placed over a fire. It induced ecstatic states among the children who were then left as the women gradually drew back into the undergrowth, leaving them to their own devices. Once again the 'Hosts of Hela' approached in the guise of fiery orange orbs. This time, however, the glowing spheres descended down into the clearing. On their departure,

Debbie saw that some of the children were no longer present, implying that they had been spirited away by the lights. Debbie believed this was a symbolic message showing that these 'wild women' had been shamanesses, devotees of the goddess Hela, who believed that children could be taken away by her as the consort of the 'dark hunt', which we assumed was akin to the Wild Hunt of European folklore tradition. Furthermore, she believed that the earlier scenario involving the torchlight procession had been part of a yearly ritual conducted in Saxon times by local villagers around 1 August each year. This, she felt, was done to appease the nightmarish hosts of the goddess Hela, whom they saw in terms of the mysterious orange spheres witnessed around this time above the great woods that included what we know today as Tawsmead Copse.

At the time I knew very little about Hela and the hosts of the night, although I took Debbie's inspiration seriously as I knew that nearby Woodborough Hill almost certainly gained its place-name from its former connections with Woden, the Germanic underworld god-king who was patron of the Wild Hunt. I also knew that Adam's Grave is equated by historians with the *Wodnes beorh* (Woden's barrow) of the *Anglo-Saxon Chronicle* where battles were allegedly fought in AD 592 and in AD 715, and that the fifth-century Wansdyke derived its name from Woden's Dyke. All this strongly connected Woden with the Vale of Pewsey.

I was, however, unprepared for what I was to eventually discover concerning Debbie's vivid psychic imagery. After conducting extensive research into European Teutonic mythology with my colleague Richard Ward, I learnt that balls of light *seen over woods at night* were once regarded as the fiery tongues and exhalations of the Furious Host, a form of Wild Hunt presided over by Woden and his consort Holda.(1). Holda, or Holle, is the Germanic form of Hela, a dark goddess presiding over the souls of the dead in Norse underworld tradition. Like her classical counterpart Hekate, Holda (and Odin) is known to have been worshipped at crossroads and, furthermore, her female devotees were mythologised as 'das wilde frouwelin' or the 'wood-wives', who were said to have inhabited the great woods of Europe.(2) Lastly, as with *Ignis Fatui*, the Furious Host were said to steal away the souls of unbaptised children.(3)

None of this information can tell us whether or not fiery orbs of orange light *were* seen in Saxon times above Tawsmead Copse, or whether local Saxon communities ever viewed such mysterious lights as visible manifestations of the Furious Host. Nevertheless, it was stunning verification of Debbie's psychic imagery and impressions, and was undoubtedly food for thought.

Putting aside this psychic exploration in favour of arranging the Orgone 94 project, I thought no more of the matter. Yet having now decided to conduct two final 'terrestrial' meditations on our last day, it seemed only reasonable to utilise this Furious Host imagery in the visualisations. Although the Earthquest team were unaware of the Furious Host material, it would undoubtedly appeal more to their earth mysteries/psychic questing background than the quite different 'extra-terrestrial' communications we had conducted so far.

With these thoughts in mind, Karl and Lisa Dawkins, Jason Digby, Fiona Johnson, Ed Sherwood, Debbie and I visited Tawsmead Copse during the afternoon of Thursday, 28 July and conducted a brief meditation to attune our minds with the environment in preparation for the following day. Interestingly enough, the remote spot Sherwood had led us to as the place he had seen lights and experienced other psychic events, was just 10 m from where Debbie, Polly and I had conducted the 'Hosts of Hela' meditation by the old oak tree in April that year. Sherwood pointed out that this location was the wettest point in the woods and, as a consequence, probably marked the position of underground springs. This fitted in well with Debbie's own views on why there was such a proliferance of lights over Tawsmead Copse. Following the 'Hosts of Hela' meditation she had become convinced that this activity was due to the woods' low-lying position in the Vale of Pewsey and the presence of underground water deposits. The possible connections between the Alton Barnes phenomenon and the geology and hydrology of the Pewsey Vale is discussed in Chapter 13.

A Glistening Ball

Having completed our trial meditation in Tawsmead Copse, we returned along the track to Woodborough Hill and departed the area. No one, other than ourselves, were aware that we had conducted this meditation or that we intended conducting two further meditations involving the Furious Host the following day. The only person we spoke to was Paul Hailey who was stationed at the base of Woodborough Hill overlooking the tree-tops of Tawsmead Copse. Revealing our interest in the woods, we asked him to keep a watch out for any possible unusual phenomena over the next 48 hours or so.

This turned out to be sound advice, for after monitoring our own control experiment on Woodborough Hill that night, Hailey switched off the last of his equipment in the half-light and almost immediately noticed a bright light directly overhead Tawsmead Copse. On closer scrutiny, he saw it was, in his words, 'a glistening, golden ball of light' stationary above the tree-tops. Mesmerised by this breathtaking sight, he gazed in awe for some several seconds before the sparkling ball winked out of view, having remained in one position for the entire sighting. The time he recorded for this event was 22.11.

The size of the object was said to have been that of a football and, despite trying, Hailey could find no logical explanation to explain what he saw. He did, however, comment on the curious fact that the golden ball became visible to him the minute he had switched off the last of his equipment which might well have registered some kind of instrumental response. What's more, this was also the first recorded observation of a mysterious light over Tawsmead Copse since Malcolm Emery's second sighting of an orange ball five months beforehand. The fact that we had earlier conducted a meditation in the woods was yet another curious synchronicity. If nothing else it made us confident that we might achieve further results during the actual experimentation.

Call of the Shaman

I have described the events leading up to the Furious Host meditations in the light of what was to transpire when they actually took place. Some of what follows may seem a little hard to swallow and perhaps out of character with the rest of this book; however, I feel it is worth citing in its entirety.

Six people took part in the Friday lunchtime meditation on Woodborough Hill which was conducted by Debbie. The visualisation featured her recall of the 'wild women' ceremony conducted in the presence of children at the crossroads in the great woods she first saw in her mind during the initial meditation in April. The whole experiment was monitored using the usual equipment and a steady increase in the background radiation count was, once again, registered during the meditational period. Aside from this result, however, no further anomalies were reported.

The Orgone 94 team returned to the hill shortly after nine o'clock that evening to set up the equipment for the final experiment. For this we were joined by a whole host of visitors including German journalist Jurgen Kronig, farmer Polly Carson, Austrian crop circle researchers Oliver Stummer and Daniela Schroter, as well as John and Julie Wakefield.

The pre-control period began at 21.27 and following the call for meditation nine people took their places in the circle - Polly Carson, Jurgen Kronig, John Wakefield, Earthquest members Duncan Bittle and Grace Carey, Sue and Andy Batey from West Overton, and, of course, Debbie who once again conducted the session. Oliver Stummer monitored the Jupiter radiation counter, Rodney Hale tended the electromagnetic instrumentation, while Karl Dawkins and myself operated the camera and video equipment, which was directed north-east, through the group of meditators, towards Tawsmead Copse. Standing with us were Julie Wakefield and her friend, Kevin Muttett.

The sky was perfectly clear, the air was warm and there was a very slight southerly wind (at 7 knots, according to the meteorological office at RAF Lyneham). By the time the meditation got under way at 21.42, the sun had vanished and the light was fading fast. The wind began gusting some one minute into the session and continued to do so periodically for the next several minutes. Photographs were taken at 21.42 and 21.47 without incident and then, at exactly 21.51, the tenth minute into the meditation, those gathered around the camera bank heard the sound of voices approaching from the direction of the trees, just beyond the southern extremes of the hill-top. All could plainly hear what appeared to be several people talking all at once, in between the clear sound of children laughing and yelling.

My first reaction was one of mild frustration. Quite obviously a group of people with children was ascending the only path onto the hill and very soon they would appear over the ridge and make their way over to our position; this was all we needed to spoil the meditation. Unexpectedly, we each then heard a distinct sound identified as a long horn blast - one single note lasting for approximately two and a half seconds. The video recording of the experiment records that this noise took place nine minutes and 17 seconds into the meditation. It happened again inside a minute (although on this and on all subsequent occasions it was not picked up by the audio mic) as the cacophony of voices grew steadily louder, leading us to jokingly suggest that the commotion heralded the approach of the Wild Hunt.

Seeing my frustration, Julie Wakefield finally said: 'I'll go and talk to them,' assuming that she could persuade the visitors to either keep the noise down or leave the hill completely.

At this moment Paul Hailey, who had been approaching the group by making a long perambulation around the outside of the 'background' EM coil, arrived at the camera bank. He revealed that as he had approached the southern edge of the hill he had distinctly heard the sound of low chanting of the sort that an Amerindian medicine man might make when in a trance. It had appeared to be close and had continued until he was within sight of the meditational group, a time period of perhaps two to three minutes. He assumed it had originated from the group of meditators and so wondered what they were doing as chanting was not normally used in such sessions.

On the other side of the hill Julie now approached the copse of trees with the sound of the male voices and children laughing and yelling directly in front of her. She continued down-hill towards the wooden stile, over which anyone must pass if approaching from the Woodborough barns. Half way between the edge of the trees and the wooden stile, she became aware that the aural commotion seemed to be right upon her. It was coming from all sides - voices, some of adults, some of children, laughing, talking, yelling - and yet despite all this *she could see no one at all.* Deeply perplexed, she continued on, assuming she would be able to see more from the stile. The voices then ceased, but still she could periodically discern the peculiar horn-like noise as well as a strange, low chant which, like Paul Hailey, she later compared to the sound an Amerindian shaman might make when in a trance. It seemed to be coming from just metres away, and on reaching the stile she climbed onto its wooden step hoping to trace the source of the voices. In silence, she gazed around her and realised that she was *completely* alone. No one was hiding in the thickets, or concealing themselves in the ripened wheat fields below. Yet still the clear sound of the low shamanic chant continued unabated. Most eerie of all, the only signs of life she *did* notice as this vocal cacophony came to an end were small animals, rabbits most probably, scurrying wildly about in the nearby undergrowth as if greatly disturbed by something; never before had she noticed this type of uncharacteristic behaviour in local fauna.

Julie waited and listened for another couple of minutes before returning to the camera bank and revealing what had occurred. I cannot doubt her word in this matter. At the time she was highly mystified and unnerved by the whole experience, but later, once she had begun to unwind at The Barge Inn, Honey Street, she became quite overwhelmed by what had happened. She later admitted that the event had so profoundly affected her that she had been unable to get it out of her mind for over a week.

The rest of the meditation had gone without incident. However, on analysing the results it was found that Rodney Hale's triple-tubed Geiger counter had registered a dramatic increase in the background count rate during the meditation. This was confirmed on the Jupiter counter which also measured a similar rise. Furthermore, the 'local' EM channel had recorded a whole sequence of low frequency oscillations, the most in any one experiment for the entire week. These had begun during the first minute of meditation and had petered out one minute into the post-control period at a point when those taking part had still been seated in a circle. Even without any knowledge of what had happened, some of the meditators later revealed that they had come out of the visualisation so 'spaced out', they had still felt like they were in an altered state of consciousness some hours later.

Screaming Goats or Rutting Deer?

Peculiarly enough, none of the meditational group, or those monitoring the equipment, heard *any* voices whatsoever. Most did, however, hear one or more of the strange sounds identified by those positioned at the camera bank as long horn blasts. Some, however, interpreted them in a different way. Polly Carson initially identified the sounds as one of her goats screaming in agony - a noise she had heard before. So much had she believed this that she nearly broke the circle, feeling that she should return to the farm and deal with the problem. It was not until after the meditation that she had begun questioning this explanation. Although she still describes the sound as like a goat in pain, she realised that the farm's own two goats could *not* have been responsible for the noise as at the time they were located 1.3 km north-west of Woodborough Hill. Since there was a gusting southerly wind during the period of the meditation it would have meant that any animal noises would have originated from this direction. In addition to this, no one heard anything at the Old Manor and the goats were found to be in perfect health upon Polly's return around 23.30 that evening.

This left the possibility that the strange sounds were in fact made by some other animal, a rutting deer perhaps. Although most types of deer rut in October, roe deer rut between mid July and mid August. The sounds they make might be described as sounding like horns or the cries of a goat, so could they have been to blame for the curious sounds? Roe deer are known to inhabit the area and have been seen on the Alton Barnes estate, especially around Tawsmead Copse, so there is always a possibility that this was the case. This solution does, however, pose a few fundamental problems. Firstly, the sounds were coming from the south where only corn fields, the Woodborough barns and the Kennet and Avon Canal are to be found, and these are not normally the habitat for rutting deer. Secondly, Julie failed to see any sign of deer when she had stood on the stile and stared out across the open fields towards Woodborough Barns in the half light, even though the horn blasts had seemed to be coming from just metres away.

In addition to this, John and Julie Wakefield lived in a caravan at the base of Woodborough Hill for over a year and say they never once heard the sound of rutting deer. Polly Carson confirmed this fact, adding that she is familiar with the noises deer make and feels that what she and others heard that night is incompatible with this sound. What's more, those who did hear the strange sounds all agree that they sounded as if they were relatively close, possibly only 100 m or so away. This is borne out by the fact that the video equipment has preserved this sound on tape and yet it failed to record any of the phantom voices. Those who have listening to this recording confirm that the noise is that of a horn, not an animal of some kind.

Appeasing Hela

There was obvious excitement among the assembled party after the realisation of what had just occurred. Yet more important was to establish from Debbie the exact contents of the meditation, bearing in mind that only Polly had known the full details of the original Hosts of Hela material. As those taking part will confirm, following some simple breathing exercises and the raising of the cone of power, Debbie had asked everyone to visualise the torch-lit procession approaching the crossroads in the darkness carrying aloft a young man. Before the silhouetted crowd walked a wild shaman, covered in animal skins, tattoos and dried blood. On reaching the central clearing the young man is made to sit down and face north. The crowd then move slowly around the crouched figure and begin to chant and bang drums and bells. They gradually increase in speed and fervour until he is writhing around in a trance and small globes of orange light are moving towards him through the trees. They then stop abruptly as the shaman raises his arms and starts chanting an invocation. Once this has been completed they leave behind the seated figure and depart the area. As the silhouetted crowd disappear in the distance, the entranced man discerns, coming from the south, a low vibration in the ground, a distant rumble that gradually increases in strength until it becomes a constant drone of thunder and horses' hooves.

Neither the meditators or the man are permitted to look around at what approaches, even as the dreadful din grows steadily louder. Not until the very last moment, when the sounds are right upon them, were those taking part allowed to turn around and witness, all at once, the dark silhouetted riders racing through the air upon black horses with eyes of burning light, fiery exhalations spurting from their gaping jaws and glowing balls of fire keeping pace with the hunt. The victim is then yanked upwards by the clutches of unseen hands and carried high over Tawsmead Copse until the whole nightmare slowly fades into the darkness. With the yearly offering of a human soul made in the name of Hela, the crops could now be harvested without fear of storms or blight. The meditators were then asked to return in mind to Woodborough Hill and see the cone of power being slowly dismantled.

FIG 32. The Furious Host or Wild Hunt of Teutonic and Norse mythology. Did the Anglo-Saxon inhabitants of the Pewsey Vale see the appearance of orange orbs over woodland as the fiery exhalations and glowing eyes of its black steeds and spectral night-riders? Was the ghostly cacophony of voices and horns heard by members of the Orgone 94 team on Woodborough Hill during the evening of 29 July 1994 confirmation of the Furious Host's past significance to the location? (pic: Mary Evans Pictury Library)

These were the essential elements of the 29-minute meditation, and this is all it was - a meditation featuring creative visualisation. So could there have been a direct link between its vivid imagery, played out in the mindscape of those involved, and the very real sound effects heard by Karl Dawkins, Paul Hailey, Kevin Muttett, Julie Wakefield and myself? The answer is quite clearly yes. None of us were aware of exactly what visualisation Debbie was going to use. Yet despite this there are clear elements of what she had asked the group to visualise in what occurred that night. For instance, there was the approach of mature voices from the south, the direction from which the Furious Host was seen to come. There was the repeated sound of horn blasts, like those that accompanied the Wild Hunt seen at night in the deer park and woods around Peterborough in Northants and Stamford in Lincolnshire, according to the entry in the Anglo-Saxon Chronicle for AD 1127. On this occasion of its appearance it was said that 'a pack of huntsmen in full cry' rode spectral black horses alongside 'black bucks' and 'pitch black' hounds 'with staring hideous eyes'. There was also the shamanic chanting heard at two different locations at least 200 m apart - this matched the chanting of the shaman invoking the Furious Host (no meditator actually chanted aloud). Lastly, there was the clear sound of children approaching - the souls of unbaptised children were taken by the night riders of the Furious Host.

I re-emphasise that no one, not even myself, was aware of *exactly* what Debbie intended using in the two meditations on Friday, 29 July 1994. I had some idea, of course, but these thoughts would have been lost in the constant co-ordination of the Orgone 94 monitoring programme. If this can be accepted then the most bizarre aspect of this affair is that the aural commotion, including the shamanic chanting, occurred between the tenth and fourteenth minute of the 29-minute meditation. Knowing that the preliminary breathing exercises and raising of the cone of power takes around seven to eight minutes to complete, then the Furious Host visualisation would hardly have begun when the strange events occurred; this is confirmed by those meditators who actually heard the horn blasts soon after the raising of the cone of power. In other words, the audible sounds, especially the shamanic chanting, appeared to *pre-empt* the sequence of imaginary events created by Debbie during her meditation.

'Supernatural Thing'

If the sound of the voices and the horn blasts were paranormal effects, then what on earth was happening on Woodborough Hill that night? Firstly, it is important to remember that this particular experiment also produced noticeable radiation increases and more low frequency oscillations than at any other time that week. All this strongly hints at the fact that the meditation was having its desired effect - modifying instrumental and environmental conditions through unconscious non-local interaction or psychokinesis. Indeed, I have to admit that in this capacity the Furious Host meditation worked better than any of the extra-terrestrial meditations we had conducted on previous days. With this in mind, it is therefore not outside the realms of possibility that the human mind had also catalysed the manifestation of sound effects impregnated into the fabric of the localised energy matrix through past human interaction with the site, whether in Saxon or more recent times. Again, this may seem as if we are going outside the parameters set during the earlier phases of this book, but read on.

There are already precedents for paranormal sounds of precisely this nature occurring in Wiltshire. For example, Kathleen Wiltshire recorded that the 'sounds of horses galloping, chains rattling and horns blowing' were associated with a round barrow named Gun's Church in the parish of High Deverill, near Warminster. This spectral activity was seen as evidence of a 'phantom hunt' that, although linked with the ghost of an eighteenth-century lord of the manor, almost certainly has Norse origins.(4)

Kathleen Wiltshire also recorded details of a 'haunted field' bordering Berricot Lane, Badbury, near Chiseldon. A Mrs Trixie Selman of Berricot Lane was out walking her dog when it suddenly froze to the spot and displayed 'signs of terror'. The animal was trembling all over and refused to budge. Puzzled, Mrs Selman and her two children then clearly heard the sound of 'many children's voices and laughter, which went on and on.' Moving on with a very reluctant dog, the three searched the field for the source of this joviality but found nothing. Returning to the same spot, situated next to a gate, they again heard the children's voices. Passing back through the gate into the adjoining field they could hear nothing, but on returning once more to the original spot the same sounds were discerned. The party repeated the process several times, always receiving the same result. Eventually they concluded that it must be some kind of 'supernatural thing' and thereafter spoke of the location as the 'haunted field'. These events took place in 1961. Eight years later when the field made way for the M4, 'the remains of a Roman villa' were apparently unearthed.(5)

If we can accept these accounts at face value, and also accept that the unaccountable vocal cacophony heard on Woodborough Hill was indeed a 'supernatural thing', then it is possible that if Saxon processions and dark goddess rites did ever take place in Tawsmead Copse around the beginning of August, then conducting the meditation at the correct time of year increased our chances of success. Of course, this knowledge could simply have induced the right psychological state of mind in those taking part, or perhaps the human mind is naturally more receptive at certain times of the year. It could also be possible that the annual solar cycle temporarily recreates an energy-related environment receptive to the sort of activities once conducted in the same area - in this case rites to appease Hela, the Norse goddess of the underworld.

We had hoped and expected that the Furious Host meditations would catalyse the appearance of mysterious light phenomena over Tawsmead Copse. And yet other than the glistening, golden light witnessed by Paul Hailey on Thursday, 28 July, this was not to be the case. Instead, something quite unexpected had occurred - an unaccountable vocal commotion of no apparent human origin. This I must accept until such time as I know otherwise.

The Last Laugh

In the wake of the excitement surrounding Orgone 94's final 'terrestrial'-based experiment, the rest of the group departed Woodborough Hill leaving Paul Hailey and myself to quietly reflect on the week's activities. We remained on the hill until two o'clock the next morning and in this time, despite constantly scanning the skies, we saw nothing out of the ordinary.

On the other side of East Field, however, it was quite another story. Tom and Kerry Blower from Cardiff were sky-watching from their vehicle in Knap Hill car-park when around midnight they noticed something highly unusual above Woodborough Hill. Looking closer they could see three *square* lights - one white, one orange and the other red - stacked one above the other at a slight angle as if mounted vertically on the underside of an invisible object shaped like a spinning-top. In sequence, these lights continually blinked out to be immediately replaced by an identical set on their right-hand side. In turn these would then blink out and be replaced by a similar set, and so on and so forth until after a fifth line of lights had blinked out the invisible object would be left momentarily in darkness as the lights on its reverse side presumably continued the sequence. The first set of lights would then re-appear and the whole sequence would start again. This light spectacular continued for some 60 seconds before the couple made a grab for their video recorder. Holding it in position they pressed the operate button, only to find that the battery was flat. Replacing it quickly, they were frustrated to find that this battery was also flat even though both had been fully charged only a few hours beforehand.

FIG 33. Sketch by Tom and Kerry Blower explaining the mysterious sequences of *square* coloured lights they witnessed directly over Woodborough Hill during the late evening of 29 July 1994. At the time Paul Hailey and the author were relaxing on the summit of the hill, but saw nothing. Why?

All they could do was continue to watch the revolving light display from their elevated position for an estimated three to four minutes. During this time they became certain that it was positioned *directly over* Woodborough Hill at a height of no more than 30 m above the copse of trees crowning the summit. So clear were these strange lights that when they did finally extinguish, Tom and Kerry Blower concluded that they must have been connected with the Orgone 94 experimentation - some sort of aerial balloon perhaps. Furthermore, shortly after this event they also saw bursts of light, like 'fireworks fanning out', that appeared to come from the side of the hill. Others apparently joined them by their vehicle who had also seen this 'firework' display. They too concluded that this activity must have been connected with the Orgone 94 experiments.

Well, I can safely assure Tom and Kerry Blower that none of this was connected with Orgone 94 in any way, shape or form. Furthermore, neither Paul Hailey or myself saw any rotating lights above Woodborough Hill. I have often been accused of being 'blind', but I fail to see how either of us could have missed such blatant aerial activity, whatever its origin. It was for this reason that I later asked Tom and Kerry Blower if they were *sure* the lights had been positioned above Woodborough Hill. There response was emphatic - yes, they had been positioned *directly* over the copse of trees!

The weather that night had been fine and clear so there is very little chance that what the Blowers saw was some kind of laser light show bouncing off low cloud, so how might we explain what they quite clearly witnessed that night? Perhaps there is a logical explanation for what they saw, but if so, then why did neither Paul Hailey nor I see anything of what was going on? There are too many cases in ufological history where one set of witnesses see inexplicable aerial phenomena, while another group of people down the road see nothing, so the Blower's sighting cannot be dismissed lightly. In the light of the results obtained during the Furious Host meditation only an hour or so beforehand, the likelihood of aerial light phenomena occurring in the vicinity was, I believe, extremely high.

The fact that the stacked sequences of *square* lights were seen directly over both Woodborough Hill, and our own heads, shortly after the completion of the final Orgone 94 experiment, seemed like the cosmic joker's last laugh, particularly in view of our opinions regarding structured spacecraft, and perhaps there really *is* a message in here somewhere.

33

Thoughtography

Following our departure from Wiltshire on Friday, 30 July 1994, the long, arduous job of analysing and assessing the final results began. The first major let down came in respect to the use of an orgone accumulator to measure the energy-related tension in the environment. This had been placed inside a white-painted Stevenson Screen alongside an equal-sized dummy accumulator. The internal temperature of both boxes were constantly compared with the ambient air temperature using three separate sensors. This operation was placed in the hands of Earthquest member Jason Digby who diligently kept a log of all temperatures throughout the entire project.

The results of this work, which was infinitely more objective and methodic than our earlier efforts during Orgone 93, were subsequently deemed unusable on the grounds that the Stevenson Screen was causing erratic temperature readings.(1) This knowledge greatly frustrated the Orgone 94 team, but could not detract from the significance of the instrumental results already recorded on other equipment used during the project.

'Poks' and Whistlers

In respect to the use of a WR-3 receiver to monitor VLF radio waves, I can reveal that, as with Orgone 93, curious sounds were recorded during the week-long period. These included something I might describe as a small 'pok' (the noise one might expect to make when flicking an index finger from the side of the mouth) which occurred on three occasions between 14.14 and 14.22 on Sunday, 24 July. At 14.20 there was also a strange metallic 'clang', while at 13.46 on Monday, 25 July there were two very slow 'dump' noises like those heard on Thursday, 22 July 1993. None of these strange sounds recurred during the rest of the week; however, similar sounds were recorded during the preliminary experiments on Woodborough Hill during the afternoon of Sunday, 26 June. Although I am no nearer to determining the source of these peculiar noises, the fact that they have occurred on a Sunday afternoon in June tends to dispel the possibility that they are in some way connected with military activity on Salisbury Plain, since the armed forces very rarely train on a Sunday (certainly no big guns were heard or parachute flares seen).

In addition to the anomalous sounds, there were two nights when lightning whistlers were recorded in great abundance. These were Saturday, 23 July, when 24 were heard, and Wednesday, 27 July, when 30 or more were recorded. Yet, other than on these two occasions, only one other whistler was heard during the whole week - at 14.56 on Saturday, 23 July. If we ignore this final date, then can we find any correlations between the two nights when whistlers occurred in abundance and the instrumental and visual results obtained during Orgone 94? Certainly, low frequency activity was recorded on the 'local' EM channel during the evening experiments on both these dates, but these were also recorded on four other evenings as well, including Friday, 29 July when the greatest number of cycles for any experiment were registered. No whistlers were heard on these nights.

There were also aerial light manifestations reported on both occasions that whistlers were recorded in abundance, *i.e.* Tom and Kerry Blower Avebury Avenue sighting at 02.30 on Sunday, 24 July and Stephen Alexander's aerial flash at 02.45 on Thursday, 28 July (CSETI apparently witnessed lights over Avebury that night as well). There were, on the other hand, unidentified aerial lights seen in the area on almost every night that week, ruling out any obvious relationship to the proliferance of whistlers on the two dates in question.

Another area of study that revealed no positive results was the electro-static air potential. Throughout the week it rose and fell, rose and fell, and rose and fell, either between the lunchtime session and the evening session, or from one day to the next. No links could be found between these readings and any paranormal activity occurring during this same period. The only point worth mentioning is the exceedingly high air potential registered at lunchtime on Friday, 29 July. Here the readings rose from 500 V/m to a massive 1200 V/m at one stage. However, that evening the air potential had reduced enormously with the electro-static volt meter giving readings of between 20 and 50 V/metre. It was, of course, during this experiment that the greatest amount of low frequency activity was recorded on the EM instrumentation and the Furious Host incidents occurred, while on Knap Hill Tom and Kerry Blower witnessed the inexplicable sequences of coloured lights over Woodborough Hill. Interestingly enough, a high air potential was *not* recorded in the experiments prior to the mysterious aerial flashes witnessed during both the evening of Tuesday, 26 and the early hours of Thursday, 28 July, leading us to question the connection between electro-static activity and the big flash of 26 July 1993. Only further work in this area will determine whether such links are real or not.

On a geological note, the only time that the British Geological Survey's magnetic observatory at Hartland, Devon, (the nearest one to Wiltshire) measured a noticeable disturbance in the earth's magnetic field between 23 and 30 July, was from 04.00 onwards on Wednesday, 27 July. This resulted in a day of highly unsettled activity, the most recorded during the whole week. Whether or not this had any bearing on the two aerial flashes seen above East Field around this time is difficult to say.(2)

No tremors or earthquakes were recorded at all in Wiltshire for the whole of July, virtually ruling out a link between such geophysical events and the inexplicable aerial anomalies taking place in and around Alton Barnes during the summer of 1994.(3) Furthermore, this knowledge hints strongly at the fact that, in the case of the Pewsey Vale, local faulting and, when they occur, tremors have *not* been to blame for the increase in UFO sightings within the region since the summer of 1990. Underground water deposits held in the porous chalk and greensand, as well as increased human activity in the area, will I feel eventually provide more realistic answers to this curious enigma.

PLATE 41. Karl Dawkins (standing) and the author tend the cameras during the Orgone 94 experiments in July 1994 (pic: Johnny Merron).

The Imagemakers

This brings us to the results of Orgone 94's black and white, infrared photography. Once again we used HIE high speed film throughout the entire duration of the 14 experiments with shots being taken at five minute intervals. This resulted in five exposed rolls of film which were handed to professional photographer Ian James of Westcliff-on-Sea for development. He is one of the few people who still use black and white photography in the Southend area and, although he had never dealt with infrared film before, he prided himself on 25 years' experience during which time he had never once suffered either from 'air-bells' or any of the processing 'problems' we were suffering at a regular rate.

With these thoughts in mind, in total darkness James took the first roll and pre-washed it in a developing tank. Tap water was used and the tank was knocked, inverted and agitated to free the film of any trapped air bubbles. It was then left to stand for two minutes before the water was removed and replaced with a solution of Kodak D-76 developer, recommended for IR processing work. The tank was again agitated, inverted and knocked constantly for a full minute and a half. The process was then repeated three times every minute for the prescribed processing period, after which the film was fixed, washed and hung up to dry. The remaining four rolls were then placed inside a much larger tank and developed in exactly the same way.

Ian James and myself spent some time studying the resulting 180 negatives and found no less than 73 circular marks of different sizes and consistencies. Many appeared to be randomly spaced, while others were grouped together on single or double frames. They appeared to constitute two slightly different types of artefact - the first being the traditional 'air-bell', *i.e.* transparent circular areas of varying sizes, many of which bore striking similarities to the 'anomalies' achieved during Orgone 93. The second type were opaque circular or near-circular marks that, at a glance, looked like tiny splashes of chemical, even though this was clearly not the case. Many of these strange marks, which appeared grey when printed, possessed character, depth and, as you will see, some kind of pseudo-relationship to the rest of the imagery on the frames in question. As well as the 73 circular blobs, the unexposed regions of the film contained a number of tiny black marks surrounded by transparent circular coronas. These were probably caused by undissolved chemical.

With one possible exception, not one of the circular blobs were found to have reproduced in stereo; in other words, none matched a similar anomaly on the corresponding half-frame. This was a great disappointment, for it meant that Orgone 94 had failed to confirm the existence of unseen energy forms through the use of IR photography. It also cast grave doubts on the authenticity of the photographic achievements, not only of Orgone 93, but also those of Boccone, Constable, Cox and Reich.

To the sceptics and the outside world the casebook on black and white, IR anomaly photography should perhaps be closed. But is it as easy as that? Has everyone been totally wrong in their interpretation of unaccountable photographic imagery for the last 50 years? Has all supernormal photography simply been the result of either misinterpreted photographic artefacts or blatant hoaxes of one kind or another?

Let me return to the 73 circular blobs discovered on the five rolls of film exposed during Orgone 94. Ian James is completely baffled by the sheer existence of these circular marks and is at a loss to explain how they might have been achieved. Even though he had never developed IR film before, he had never seen anything like this in all the years of his professional career; if a problem such as this had occurred on one of his assignments it would have been considered a personal catastrophe.

In addition to this, if one looks more closely at the resulting negatives definite patterns begin to emerge that defy the logic of reason. For instance, of the 73 circular marks, Roll One (developed individually) produced just two 'air-bells', Roll Three produced nine, Roll Four produced 13, Roll Five produced two, while Roll Two produced *47*. Furthermore, of the 47 blobs found on Roll Two, 36 occurred during one experiment alone. Indeed, they appeared on just eight frames taken between 13.40 and 14.25 on Tuesday, 26 July 1994 - that familiar date which in 1994 also produced the visual sighting of the aerial flash at 22.58, as well as the orange streak on a time exposure photograph.

Even closer scrutiny of the 'air-bells' on Roll Two reveals that no less than 27 blobs occurred on just four shots - four at 13.45, six at 13.50, nine at 13.55 and eight at 14.00. The last two frames show the meditational group with the copse of trees to their left and in

PLATE 42. Frame 27 taken at 13.45 on 26 July 1994 using black and white, infrared-sensitive film and showing four anomalies. Compare the large blobs seen here in the right-hand half-frame with the main pair in Frame 29 taken at 13.55 the same day (pic: Orgone 94).

the air between the two are distinctive blobs that give the impression of having some relationship to what's going on. Some of these 'air-bells' are opaque and shaped like a three quarters moon. There are other peculiarities as well. The right-hand picture on Frame 27 shows two blobs over the place of the meditation, while the right-hand picture on Frame 29 shows two slightly larger blobs over the same position, their distance apart being exactly the same. These same pair are again above the meditational group in the left-hand picture on Frame 30, one of them remaining in the corresponding right-hand frame. To add insult to injury, in Frame 29, taken at 13.55, there is even a fairly large circular 'air-bell' in exactly the same position as the one caught on film above the western-most tree of the copse crowning the heights of Woodborough Hill at 13.29 exactly one year beforehand!

Roll	Frame	Left HF	Right HF	Experiment		Date	Time	Total/Roll	Total/Exp
1	13		01	02		23.7.94	21.55		2 = 1
1	28	01		03		24.7.94	14.45	1 = 2	3 = 1
2	0				1				ex = 1
2	7		01	05		25.7.94	13.55		
2	8	01		05		25.7.94	14.00		
2	12	02		05		25.7.94	14.10		
2	13	01		05		25.7.94	14.11		5 = 5
2	15	01G		06		25.7.94	21.20		
2	16	01H		06		25.7.94	21.25		
2	18	01H		06		25.7.94	21.35		
2	20		01H	06		25.7.94	21.45		6 = 4
2	26		01G	07		26.7.94	13.40		
2	27		04G	07		26.7.94	13.45		
2	28	01	05	07		26.7.94	13.50		
2	29	02 (1H/1G)	07G	07		26.7.94	13.55		
2	30	04 (2H/2G)	04G	07		26.7.94	14.00		
2	33	02G	02G	07		26.7.94	14.15		
2	34	01H	01G	07		26.7.94	14.20		
2	35	01H	01H	07		26.7.94	14.25		7 = 36
2	37				1			2 = 47	ex = 1
3	14	01H		08		26.7.94	21.55		8 = 1
3	31		01G	010		27.7.94	21.25		
3	32		01H + 3E/M	010		27.7.94	21.30		
3	36	01	02	010		27.7.94	21.50		
3	37	03		010		27.7.94	21.55	3 = 9	10 = 8
4	6	01		011		28.7.94	13.35		
4	7	03	01	011		28.7.94	13.40		
4	8	01	01 (B/C)	011		28.7.94	13.45		11 = 7
4	13	01G		012		28.7.94	21.35		
4	14	01G		012		28.7.94	21.40		12 = 2
4	19	01	01	013		29.7.94	14.40		
4	33				1				
4	34				1			4 = 13	ex = 2
5	7	01		013		29.7.94	14.55		
5	8	01		013		29.7.94	15.00		13 = 4
Totals -		L/F = 34	R/F = 35	Ex = 4				73	73

G = Grey H = Pinhole Ex = extra pic.

FIG 34. Summary of the photographic anomalies achieved during the Orgone 94 experimentation of July 1994.

As previously stated not one of these circular blobs appears in stereo, even though many show similar objects in both half-frames. One double-frame, taken at 14.15 on 26 July 1994, shows a small example in the left-hand frame that matches almost precisely an example seen in the corresponding right-hand frame, although this is more likely to be a sheer fluke than a stereo image.

If we look again at the distribution of the blobs we find further anomalies - four of the 14 experiments produced none at all, three produced single examples, one produced two, while another five produced anything between four and eight examples. If we then compare these results against the 36 examples produced during the lunchtime experiment on 26 July 1994, then it becomes clear that this disproportionately high amount should not have occurred by chance alone. If we then study the distribution of the anomalies in respect to the timing of the pre-control, meditational and post-control periods we find another curious pattern. There is a clear and quite steady rise in the number of blobs appearing during the pre-control period. This trend reaches its peak at

PLATE 43. Frame 28 taken at 13.50 on 26 July 1994. Six anomalies may be seen in this picture, timed at five minutes before the start of the meditation. What do they represent - anomaly or artefact? (pic: Orgone 94)

the start of the meditation before gradually tailing off during the next two five-minute periods. It then stabilises out to a new low level and finally fades away after the twentieth minute of the meditation (the average meditational period was 24 minutes). The post-control periods produced a mere five circular anomalies during the entire 14 experiments.

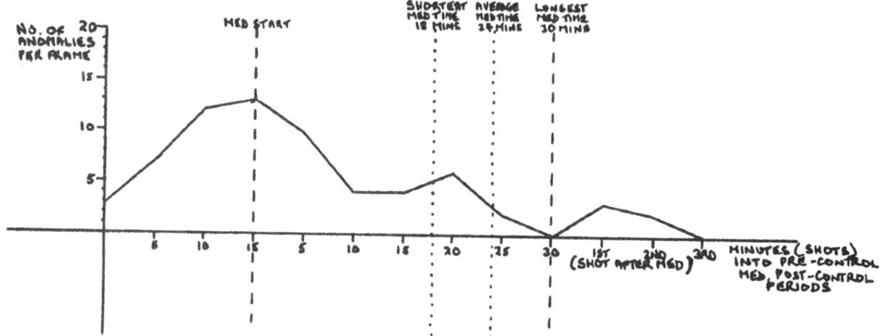

FIG 35. Graph showing the relationship of the 73 photographic anomalies produced during the Orgone 94 experimentation against the time-frame of the pre-control, meditation and post-control periods (includes those taken during the control tests of Thursday, 28 July 1994).

These patterns are quite striking, so what could have caused them? Was it simply random clustering of photographic artefacts, or are there any other possible answers? Ian James could not explain why Roll Two should have produced such a high 'air-bell' count. Was this film therefore more defective than the other four, or was it because it was loaded at the bottom of the spool, leaving it more vulnerable to undissolved chemicals sinking to the bottom of the developing tank? Although this last suggestion remains a remote possibility, it is unlikely that these 'air-bells' were caused by chemicals and it does not explain why there is a clustering of circular blobs on the frames exposed during Experiment Seven on Tuesday, 26 July. The two other experiments recorded on the same roll produced a relatively low 'air-bell' count - five during Experiment Five and four during Experiment Six. Moreover, when in September 1994 James deliberately exposed a roll of Kodak HIE high speed black and white, IR-sensitive film and developed it in exactly the same way, using exactly the same chemicals, the resulting negatives revealed just four tiny pin-hole marks that bore little resemblance to the majority of the 'air-bells' produced either during Orgone 93 or Orgone 94.

Is this all just a series of interesting coincidences? It is feasible; however, there *are* other possible solutions, and one of these I am beginning to favour more than any other. The radiation tests have clearly shown the way in which the human mind is seemingly able to modify the count rate produced by a Geiger-Muller tube time and time again. What's more, it is becoming clear that the pure intention to begin a meditation can affect the count rate up to seven or eight minutes beforehand. The work on focused human attention by William A. Tiller at Stanford University's Department of Materials Science and Engineering between 1977 and 1979 has also shown that subjects and technicians alike have inadvertently modified the count rate of gas discharge tubes either by talking about the project or by entering the room where the apparatus is in use.

Orgone 94 has also tentatively demonstrated that, not only can meditational practices modify EM field strengths to produce extremely low frequency oscillations, but that these same effects, as with the radiation increases, may well be catalysed by the intention to conduct a meditation.

Should this psycho-interactive communion with both instrumentation and the environment prove to be correct, then I see no reason why unconscious thoughts should not be able to influence the light-sensitive silver halides used in the production of photographic imagery on the emulsion surface of panchromatic films. If so, then it is very

PLATE 44. Frame 29 taken at 13.55 on 26 July 1994 at the start of the meditational period. A total of nine anomalies may be seen - two in the right-hand half-frame even appear to be poised overhead the meditators. A similar pair appear in the right-hand half-frame of Frame 27. Note too the black object over the western-most tree on Woodborough Hill, the same spot a black blob appeared in a picture taken during Orgone 93 exactly one year beforehand (pic: Orgone 94).

likely that at least some of what we have seen as 'air-bells' are in fact blacked out areas on the developed film caused by psychokinetic processes.

There *are* precedents for this extraordinary explanation for photographic anomalies, the most well-known being the extraordinary thought images or 'thoughtographs' produced in the 1960s and 1970s by Chicago psychic Ted Serios. Using mostly a Polaroid Land camera, Serios produced literally hundreds of anomalies on prints. Some showed completely black prints, as if all light had been prevented from affecting the emulsion, others showed totally white prints, while the majority showed supernormal imagery that had either been projected from Serios's own memory or had been obtained without any conscious knowledge of the subject.(4) No parapsychologist has ever been able to adequately explain Serios's remarkable photographs without concluding that some kind of psychokinetic effect must have been involved.(5)

Ted Serios used a camera to obtain his thoughtographs, but many other psychics have simply used unexposed photographic plates or film to achieve similar results, demonstrating that the created imagery is almost certainly some kind of mind effect. The late Cyril Permutt outlined the history of thoughtography in his essential 1983 book *Beyond the Spectrum, a Survey of Supernormal Photography* and summed up its feasibility in the following, quite pertinent words:

> Recent experiments in psychokinesis have shown that many people have the ability to move and manipulate small objects by an effort of will without touching them physically. The mental force that they exert in experiments when they move a box of matches or a table tennis ball or something of this nature is immeasurably greater than that necessary to cause the movement of individual electrons in a delicately balanced photographic emulsion, so people with this ability should have little difficulty in at least affecting the condition of photographic materials and, with practice and training, many could probably produce recognisable thoughtographs.(6)

So is this what Orgone 93 and Orgone 94's black and white, IR photographs actually show - images created by the human mind? It is a distinct possibility, and it was this very conclusion that Graham Phillips and I had come to with respect to the two Prestatyn shots, taken using Ilford HP5 film and showing amorphous black blobs, as early as September 1979. Yet if thoughtography is the answer, then are the 'air-bells' produced by Orgone 93/94 simply the result of the group's desire to want photographic results, or could they be something more?

The cluster of 36 black blobs on the frames recording Experiment Seven on 26 July 1994 might well exemplify the group's collective optimism drawn from the knowledge that, because this date had produced alleged paranormal events in previous years, it would surely produce further anomalies in 1994. The circular black blob to be seen above the most westerly tree of Woodborough Hill in the picture taken at 13.55 that day bears out this notion almost too well. Yet this same enthusiasm and desire for results could well have worked in quite another manner as well. What if such states of mind can actually act as very real, non-local beacons to unseen bioforms which then approach the group on some intangible level before eventually achieving manifestation in one of an assortment of different ways. The appearance of the flash with a ball-like core at 22.58 that night is evidence of this possibility, as is the CSETI sighting of 26 July 1992.

Following Experiment Seven on 26 July 1994, Ed Sherwood came up to me and said that before and during the meditation he had been seeing 'etheric lights', both above the circle of meditators and over by the trees. He said he had heard the camera shutters click just as one 'etheric light' had been in view and was positive that we would obtain good results that day. I noted down his comments on a report form. This was the only time he came up to me and made such a claim, despite him seeing the occasional 'etheric light' throughout the entire week. When I told him about the 36 photographic anomalies produced during this experiment he was over the moon, suggesting that this was excellent confirmation of his predictions and too much of a coincidence to be wrong.

And Sherwood is right, this *was* too much of a coincidence. Even though, like everyone that day, he had displayed a noticeable optimism which might well have induced such subjective imagery, it *is* possible that, despite the fact that the photographic anomalies may well have been influenced or even created by thought alone, they do

PLATE 45. Frame 30 taken at 14.00 on 26 July 1994, five minutes into the meditational period. Eight anomalies are visible, including two on the left-hand half-frame similar to the pairs seen in the left-hand half-frames of Frame 27 and 29 (pic: Orgone 94).

actually represent unseen bioforms. Not directly, but indirectly through the unwitting involvement of the human mind recognising their presence and registering this fact as a representational image on film emulsion. In other words, our minds could well act as the channel or medium by which such energy forms can register their very real existence as photographic anomalies. If so, then it would mean that, without our involvement in this paranormal process, there would be no such thing as photographic anomalies, only mundane photographic artefacts which we know from experts such as Ian James are usually pretty rare.

Spirit Photography

Tentative evidence of this hypothesis is, I believe, the alleged spirit photography of the early 1900s. Here a spirit photographer would attempt to capture psychic imagery around the sitter in question. On development, the picture might be found to contain fluffy white areas or hazy veils containing the clear faces of deceased persons, usually departed loved ones, overlaid onto the original backdrop. These faces would almost always look as if they had been taken straight from an existing photograph of the deceased, leading sceptics to accuse the photographer of breaking into the sitter's home, stealing the picture concerned, copying it, replacing it unnoticed and then fabricating the resulting spirit photograph. Perhaps this *was* the case in some instances, although in my opinion the most intriguing aspect of these spirit images is the fact that the deceased appears in the likeness of existing photographs. Was it possible therefore that for the spirit to appear on film it necessitated the combined effort of the photographer's psychokinetic abilities and the sitter's cherished memory to re-create its earthly image from photographs depicting them when they were still alive?

Taking this matter one step further, I find that in the 1920s stereoscopic cameras were frequently used to capture supernormal imagery on film. The spirit faces and whispy forms continued to appear, although usually only in mono - in other words the anomalies

PLATE 46. A perfect example from 1905 of how spirit photographs often reproduced the facial image of a deceased person from an existing photograph - in this case the sitter's late sister. Do energy forms need to use both the memory of the sitter and the psychokinetic abilities of the photographer to reproduce their image on film? If so, then does this have any bearing on photographic anomalies of the sort produced by the likes of Constable and ourselves?

PLATE 47. Frame 33 taken at 14.15 on 26 July 1994, 20 minutes into the meditational period. Four anomalies are visible, including two small examples that almost appear to be in the same position in each half-frame. This, however, is more likely to be a fluke than an actual stereo image of a real object (pic: Orgone 94).

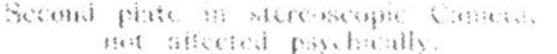

Psychic effect in stereoscopic Camera
on one plate only

PLATE 48. Stereoscopic photograph taken in 1922/3 by renowned spirit photographer William Hope and showing alleged ectoplasmic energy around the shoulders of the sitter, Charles Lyle of the British College of Psychic Science, in the right-hand frame only. This mono imagery was seen by him as 'absolute proof' of the reality of these energy forms.

would appear on one frame and not the other. However, unlike us, who see such results as evidence of the anomaly being a photographic artefact, the parapsychologists of the day saw mono imagery as good evidence of the picture's abnormal nature!(7)

The principal difference between these controversial spirit photographs and modern-day circular blobs is that the former relies on superimposing light-related imagery on the photographic emulsion surface, while the latter appears to prevent light from reaching the emulsion to create grey or black objects. Sceptics might suggest that the two processes are so different that they cannot possibly be linked; however, we do know that thoughtographers such as Ted Serios were able to create either all white or all black Polaroid pictures, thus demonstrating that the human mind *can*, not only create light-related imagery, but can also prevent light from reaching the film emulsion during exposure. Furthermore, there *are* in existence photographs that show silhouetted spirit forms.

The Brinklow Picture

One example of a shadow-like form appearing on a photograph when nothing was seen by those present features the earthwork known as Brinklow Castle in Warwickshire. On 16 September 1982 Jean Smith (pseudonym at her request - name on file) of Coventry visited this probable Iron Age encampment with a party of friends, including Graham Phillips. She wanted to photograph the trunks of three huge trees that had recently been pulled down, and since she did not know how to use the camera properly, Phillips offered to take them for her. Several shots later, Phillips handed the camera back and the group departed. The film was then processed by a local chemist and on studying the resulting prints, Jean found that on one of the frames showing the summit of Brinklow there was an eerie silhouette of what can only be described as a Victorian gentleman wearing a heavy overcoat and a top hat. The figure stands with his back to the camera and his left arm slightly raised behind him. Both hands appear to be in his pockets while his legs and feet are hidden behind the curve of the hill. At the time the photograph was taken two of the party were standing just to the right of the camera's field of vision, and yet neither saw anything at the time, ruling out the likelihood of a hoax.

Psychic questing enthusiasts will recognise this photograph from Graham Phillips and Martin Keatman's 1985 book *The Eye of Fire*. It was taken just three days before the dramatic appearance of the eponymously-named carnelian stone which featured alleged psychic confrontations with a Victorian spirit entity that had appeared in dreams and visions dressed in dark clothes and a top hat. This character therefore bore an uncanny resemblance to the silhouetted Victorian gentleman seen in the picture. What's more, one of the party, Sheila Bavington, had dreamt of this man only the night before and had felt this man's sinister presence on the hill when the pictures were being taken. Yet if this presence had been some kind of tangible apparition, then why did it appear in one picture alone? Others were taken of the same location and no strange anomalies appeared on any of these. Why?

PLATE 49. Above, the eerie image of a Victorian gentleman caught on film at Brinklow castle mound, Warwickshire, on 16 September 1982, even though nothing was seen at the time. Is this picture evidence to suggest that unseen energy forms can only create their image on film by utilising the photographer's psychokinetic abilities? Right, blow up of the same picture (pic: Jean Smith).

Could it be possible that the Brinklow party's fervent belief and fear in the existence of this spirit entity had allowed the creation of this chilling image on film - one that bears striking similarities to the shadow archetype used so often to portray Victorian London's most notorious villain Jack the Ripper? Did it impose itself on the developing emulsion by utilising the psychokinetic faculties of those present, in particular Sheila Bavington and the photographer Graham Phillips? If so, then this is important evidence in support of the idea that the circular black blobs obtained during our own projects might well be the result of very real energy forms utilising non-local processes to manifest as photographic anomalies. It might also help us to understand why some unseen UFOs may not appear as stereo imagery, just amorphous black blobs like those captured on film by the likes of Boccone, Constable, Cox, Reich and ourselves.

As Graham Phillips has rightly pointed out, the comparisons between the Brinklow picture and the ones taken at Prestatyn, North Wales, in September 1979 are remarkable. On both occasions a 'presence' had been felt quite independent to the appearance of the photographic anomaly, and in both cases the resulting imagery supported the belief-orientated views held by those present - a sinister Victorian gentleman in the first instance and a disc-shaped UFO in the second.

At the moment these are simply speculations, for such a hypothesis is still beset with many unsolved problems. However, it does create exciting new avenues for future research programmes that will hopefully continue where Orgone 93 and Orgone 94 left off. Yet having already taken up the gauntlet by pledging to scientifically investigate the inter-relationship between UFOs, ritual landscapes and the human mind, we may now find ourselves exploring even stranger regions of parapsychology in the hope that one day we shall fully comprehend the ultimate capabilities of the multi-dimensional energy continuum.

34

Flashes of Inspiration

> After some 14 years of extensive research, it is my conclusion that the so-called unidentified flying objects that have been seen in our atmosphere are not space ships from another planet at all, but are groups and masses of living organisms that are as much a part of our atmosphere and space as the life we find in the oceans. The only major difference in the space and atmospheric organisms is that they have the natural ability to change their densities at will.(1)

These are the words of Kenneth Arnold as quoted in a 1962 issue of Ray Palmer's *Flying Saucers* magazine. Arnold was the commercial pilot who inadvertently began the 'flying saucer' era by describing the movement of each of the nine glowing objects he witnessed above the Cascade Mountains of Washington State on Tuesday, 24 June 1947 as 'like a saucer if you skip it across water'.(2) This statement was conveyed to Bill Becquette, a reporter on the *East Oregonian* at Pendleton where Arnold later landed after his fateful journey. In his subsequent news-story on the affair, Becquette misquoted Arnold by describing not the movements, but the *objects themselves* as 'saucer-like' in appearance, and there began the popular misconception that Kenneth Arnold was the first person to see a 'flying saucer'.

In many ways Arnold really *was* the first person to witness UFOs in the way we perceive them today, for on 24 June 1947 sightings of unusual aerial phenomenon, which had been witnessed in many different guises and forms since time immemorial, suddenly acquired a new role-model. No longer were their mostly nocturnal visitations viewed as fiery dragons, the Furious Host, mystery rockets, phantom airships, portents of change, signs from the gods or the lanterns of elemental beings. Now they were examples of alien technology of the sort that had filled Marvel comics since the 1930s. Even Arnold had no choice but to conclude that the strange, flat disc-like objects he had observed were some form of unknown aircraft, for he admitted: 'I just couldn't discern any tails on them, and I had never seen an aircraft without a tail!'(3)

Curiously enough, it had been 'a tremendously bright flash' illuminating his whole aircraft, that had begun Arnold's classic sighting. A second, similar flash had then drawn his eyes to the group of bright glowing objects flying in an echelon formation between Mount Rainier and Mount Baker. As they drew nearer and nearer, Arnold said the 'craft... fluttered and sailed, tipping their wings alternately and emitting those very bright blue-white flashes from their surfaces... At the time I did not get the impression that these flashes were emitted by them, but rather it was the sun's reflection from the extremely highly polished surface of their wings.'(4) Arnold's preconceptions led him to assume that the bright flashes he had witnessed were not light sources in themselves, simply reflections from the discs' highly polished surfaces - the same highly polished surfaces to be found on almost all commercial and military aircraft in America during the 1940s.

Just 15 years later this experienced pilot had changed his opinions completely. Despite all the media attention and pulp paperbacks concerning UFOs during the 1950s, including claims that some people had actually ridden inside the saucers, Arnold came to the bold conclusion that what he had seen flying in formation above Mount Baker in 1947 were in fact living organisms - lifeforms existing in our atmosphere. So what made him change his mind? Was it the years of exhaustive research he had conducted into the UFO enigma? Had it been some kind of spiritual revelation?

Perhaps we shall never know.

Between 1976 and 1982 I interviewed literally hundreds of alleged witnesses to reported UFO sightings. At the time I whole-heartedly believed that these aerial objects were inter-planetary craft visiting earth from distant galaxies, having digested literally dozens of mostly American pulp paperbacks on UFOs and alleged alien encounters. Yet seven years of intensive research convinced me that there was very little evidence to indicate that UFOs were anything other than unknown aerial phenomena that appeared out of nowhere, showed themselves to isolated witnesses before vanishing into oblivion. In addition to this, hardly ever did the appearance of UFOs and, when seen, their occupants ever correspond with existing cases. What's more, very rarely did the alleged alien entities from these craft ever act like sane and sober visitors from another planet, like ET and his famous plant collecting episode in the film of the same name.

Armed Entities in Brighton

One case I investigated in 1978 typifies this madness. It occurred in Brighton, East Sussex, during the month of September 1951, just four years after Arnold's classic sighting. The single witness to this incident was a woman in her late teens named Sheila Burton who was staying at the home of her parents in the district of Withdean, just days before her wedding.(5) She awoke early one morning and glanced out of the window at the late summer flowers in the back garden. No one was up, and no sound could be heard. Then, suddenly, her eyes caught sight of a large disc with red flashing lights descending at an incredible speed. It came to rest on the lawn just as three large, evenly-spaced panels began to open. An alien entity then emerged simultaneously from each door and proceeded to walk in a straight line away from the vertical central axis of the craft. They were between 1.5 and 1.8 m tall with egg-shaped heads and Mr Spock ears. Each wore a one-piece silver space suit, complete with a black diagonal sash and a thick belt, while held up against their hips was a science-fiction style ray-gun.

After some 20 or so paces, the three identical-looking entities suddenly stopped and began to walk backwards in a synchronised manner until they simultaneously re-entered the landed object. The large, square panels then closed, red lights started flashing again and almost instantly the silvery disc shot vertically upwards and was lost from view. The whole event had lasted no more than 40 to 50 seconds at the most. It was as if someone had hit the rewind button on a video machine, making the tape run backwards at an exaggerated speed until the gradually unfolding scenario had totally reversed itself. Such absurd actions are not what one might expect of highly advanced, extra-terrestrial visitors who would presumably have crossed galaxies to be here, and yet Sheila Burton, who is a mature and sensible woman, appeared to be sincere and I found no good reason to doubt her testimony. Furthermore, the descriptions of the entities might also be described as a perfect cross between an astronaut and an elf.

Cases such as this, and many more like it, convinced me that, although the witnesses might be truthfully relating very real experiences, physical spacecraft from another planet was simply not the answer.

The Light of Consciousness

The idea, presented by Paul Devereux and others, that UFOs are exotic energy created by the earth is attractive and appears to confirm many of my own findings in this respect. Despite this, the earth lights hypothesis in no way accounts for the assortment of high strangeness cases involving close proximity entity encounters and abduction experiences.

The concept of light consciousness brings us closer to understanding how balls of light, and similar such phenomena, might achieve some form of basic or natural consciousness and intelligence through non-local interaction with not only the human mind but, presumably, the earth itself.

Yet, as I have tried to demonstrate, the inexplicable luminosities appearing in the skies above Alton Barnes can and frequently do respond to the witness or witnesses on the ground in a way that suggests the involvement of some form of omnipotent communion. The best examples of this are undoubtedly the Steven Greer/CSETI sighting of the light cluster at Woodborough during July 1992 and John and Julie Wakefield's sighting of the orange ball above trees at nearby Wilcot just two days later. However, sightings such as that experienced by Tom Trubridge and Julie Whitear on Woodborough Hill in 1994, even

Paul Hailey's observation of a glistening golden ball over Tawsmead Copse, also point towards this sense of the phenomena knowing your every thought.

The reality of non-local communion of this kind is, I believe, strengthened by the psycho-interactive effects repeatedly obtained using radiation and electromagnetic apparatus during 1993 and 1994. These results clearly show the apparent ability of the human mind to influence either scientific instrumentation and/or the environment through the employment of meditational practices. Such beliefs have long been understood by shamans, priests and mystics of faiths and cultures across the world. In addition to this, it seems that emotionally-charged belief is responsible, as in the cases of Steven Greer, Mary Jones, Graham Phillips, Ed Sherwood and many more for creating the temporal conditions necessary to affect and manipulate the outside environment.

Whether such interactions take the form of 'vectoring' 'structured spacecraft' into appearance, employing the use of the Star Exercise or contacting *genius loci* at prehistoric sites, they can all equally result in psychic communication with individualised products of the energy continuum. Bioforms, 'critters', ether ships, plasmas, site guardians, thought constructs, or even the tulpas of Tibetan Buddhist tradition, are just some of the titles given to these unseen energy forms. Whatever the description, there is overwhelming evidence to suggest that they exist independently of the human mind and can, and frequently do, respond to mental empathy either as electromagnetic anomalies or as light manifestations. It is when this process occurs that the best examples of non-local interaction, or light consciousness, appear to take place - leading the witness or witnesses involved to assume some form of intelligent, non-human agency behind such sightings. There is, however, one final example of light consciousness I would like to cite which, I feel, exemplifies not only non-local communication with UFO-related energy forms, but its continued occurrence in the Alton Barnes area.

The event in question once again features John and Julie Wakefield, and their friend Nick Riley - three people who as permanent residents of Alton Barnes are now very much accustomed to the man-made and natural phenomena to be seen in the night sky.(6)

The date was Monday, 15 March 1993 and visiting them at their caravans parked up next to the Woodborough barns (SU11596106) was Rob Baker, a UFO enthusiast in his late forties from Bristol, Avon. The group was watching television when at around 20.00 Baker decided to conduct an impromptu skywatch in the uninterrupted darkness outside the caravans. Almost immediately he spotted a slow moving light and became excited. Hearing his calls, John Wakefield stepped outside and quickly realised that Baker was in fact watching a satellite and so told him so, adding that if it was a *real* UFO then it would probably respond to flashes from a torch-beam (after the style of the CSETI operations at Gulf Breeze, Mexico and elsewhere, and the Hessdalen project in Norway). As an example of how a torch could be used in this manner, Wakefield grabbed a flashlight and marked out the three corners of an invisible triangle in the north-eastern sky. In immediate response to this act, all present saw a bright light of immense magnitude flash three times from a position central to the unseen triangle, some 85 degrees up from the northern horizon.

Everyone was dumb-struck. Wishing to confirm the reality of this totally unexpected response, Wakefield raised the torch and pointed it to where the light source had appeared to emanate. He flashed up two further triangles and as soon as he had finished defining their corners he was answered with two clear flashes from the same aerial light source.

Without further word, Wakefield flashed the corners of three more triangles, only to be answered with three distinct 'explosions of light' which allowed him to estimate the relative size of the light source as 'a one pence piece at arm's length'.

Wondering whether the light had some mundane explanation, Wakefield and the others now watched and waited for around 30 seconds, but no flashes came out of the sky. He then signalled one further triangle and, he says, 'the second' he completed his invisible design, one single flash occurred.

More signals were tried, but there were no further responses, despite flashing various shapes into the open sky. With the episode over, everyone was left in utter astonishment. The only additional information Wakefield could offer was that each flash appeared to be in a slightly different position as if the source was moving slowly away from them. On one occasion, however, a flash occurred adjacent to its previous position, implying that it had shifted backwards before quickly resuming its original course. The incident left the group totally perplexed and insistent that what they had seen was not the navigation lights of an aircraft or a tumbling satellite reflecting sunlight.

What baffled John Wakefield more than anything else was that they had sky-watched hundreds of times before without anything like this ever occurring, and yet on this occasion he had simply stepped outside his mobile home in response to Rob Baker's cries of excitement on mistaking an obvious satellite for a UFO.

Many readers will find the above episode difficult to accept and, of course, it is presented here simply to demonstrate the very real possibilities of psychic communication with unknown energy forms if, and only if, we permit ourselves to cross the psychological barriers preventing us from trying similar experiments with the same conviction of mind.

Yet I believe we need to go much further than this to truly express the nature of the phenomenon under review here. The idea popularised by Constable, and suggested many years beforehand by Kenneth Arnold, that the majority of UFOs are living creatures existing in a sea of atmosphere is stunning in its simplicity. Even though Constable saw these etheric entities as composed of a semi-solid, plasmatic state, I feel it is more likely that they are indigenous life-forms existing in an energetic state spanning the entire extent of the multi-dimensional energy continuum. They appear to us as aerial flashes, balls of light, daylight discs, or light clusters only when their oscillations shift into the visible spectrum. On other occasions they can simply create radar reflections or produce electromagnetic effects and so remain undetected by the naked eye.

Abduction Scenarios

In so many cases of UFO close encounters the percipient or percipients at first sees only a ball of light or a light mass of some sort; this was something that UFO researcher and author Jenny Randles noted on numerous occasions during the wave of sightings of all descriptions that occurred in the Pennines of north England during the late 1970s, an orange ball in particular.(7) Then, as the object draws nearer, it will transform into a more structured craft with obvious features of an inter-planetary vehicle, such as doors, headlights, landing gear, port-holes, windows, etc. Even closer and the witnesses may see the object's apparent occupants, who will either just appear or emerge from its interior.

So if this phenomenon really is manifesting as electromagnetic energy, then how is it able to transmogrify into such obvious features? The answer probably lies in the fact that just preceding these more stranger aspects of a UFO encounter the witness often reports a sudden shift in consciousness. Busy roads will become devoid of life, the whole setting will appear to slow down or speed up, or they will experience a sense of overwhelming warmth and well-being. Jenny Randles aptly refers to these shifts in consciousness as the Oz factor, and so frequent is this state of mind reported that it must play a key role in the mechanics of such encounters. The cessation of such effects generally marks the end of the sighting, usually with the object or any other sign of the experience having already disappeared from view. The sheer number of high strangeness cases where these shifts of perspective occur would tend to indicate that they are not simply the result of a fantasy-prone mind or some psycho-somatic effect induced by the witness, but a physically real effect. So what is their possible cause? Could it be due to the presence of some kind of energy field emitted by the object?

We shall return to this matter later.

Time Lapses

After the initial close encounter, the percipient might well suffer from a series of adverse physiological effects, such as intense dehydration, nausea, severe headaches, maybe even welts or burns. Most peculiar of all is the time distortions so often reported in the wake of such experiences. These can vary from a few minutes to a few hours, or even a few days, during which time the percipient simply goes missing and has no real memory recall of what took place. Quite obviously if the time lapse is relatively short the witness will either not realise it is missing, or they will probably put it down to bad time keeping.

When so-called time-lapse or missing time events present themselves to ufological circles the natural assumption is to presume that the witness has been subjected to some kind of on-board UFO experience, and indeed, this is quite often what the brain will suggest has occurred during this loss of time. Recurring themes such as medical examinations, video-like screens projecting the future of the planet and white light pouring from cornerless walls and ceilings crop up again and again. Hypnosis, particularly in the United States, is frequently used to retrieve lost memories associated with UFO encounters. These too appear to support the notion that many of the witnesses involved have been abducted, generally against their will by alien entities. Yet these visual representations of the lost time, although consistent in some respects, are often nonsensical in content and disproportionate to the unaccounted time. For instance, wood-cutter Travis Walton from Snowflake, Arizona, was abducted in 1975 after rushing towards a glowing disc-like object seen near ground level and subsequently went missing for five whole days. His eventual recall of the experience under hypnosis only ever accounted for a time period of just two hours.(8) To this day he has no real idea of where he was or what he was doing for the rest of the missing time. Travis Walton's story subsequently became the subject of a 1992 feature film entitled *Fire in the Sky*.

Quite obviously those involved in abduction cases are not usually aware of the time distortion until after they return to a conscious, waking state. To them it has passed by in an instant of time, and this is a very significant observation for there is some evidence to suggest that these time jumps could occur outside of linear time. In other words, the missing time experienced by UFO abductees is not spent somewhere else and then blanked out of the conscious mind, it is lost *instantaneously*.

The Aveley Abduction

In my previous work *The Circlemakers* I cited the case of the Avis family (pseudonym at their own request - name on file) of Aveley in Essex who experienced just such a missing time episode in the deserted lanes of west Essex during the evening of Sunday, 27 October 1974.(9) This case was Britain's first recorded UFO abduction, and it is of such paramount importance to our understanding of time-lapse phenomena and abductions in general, that I feel compelled to re-examine it once again.

Around 22.00 on the evening in question the family's Vauxhall Victor left the town of Hornchurch and turned east onto the secluded country lanes of Rainham and Aveley, most of which are bordered by fenced off gravel pits. In the driving seat was 29-year-old John Avis, a carpenter by trade and a warm and friendly character of East London descent. Next to him was his wife, Susan, and in the back seat were the couple's three young children, two of whom were asleep. The normal 20-minute journey from Sue's parents in Harold Hill to their home in nearby Aveley was being paced as there was a play on television Avis wanted to see, and they did not have videos in those days.

The quiet country lane was bordered either side by intermittent hedgerow, broken only by a few more welcoming features, such as a public house and the odd terraced cottage. Quite unexpectedly Kevin, the eldest son, caught sight of a roughly oval mass of electric-blue light moving across their line of vision at some height in front of the car. It passed overhead at an angle that necessitated Avis craning his head to see the light pass out of view through the windscreen. Kevin watched it disappear out of the rear window, before he rose excitedly to a standing position behind the two front seats. Either side, his younger brother and sister still slept, oblivious to the commotion going on in their midst.

The fateful journey continued for another mile before the vehicle turned a right-hand corner, marked by a group of four terraced houses. Suddenly the car began to act oddly as they saw in front of them a thick wall of luminous green mist stretching across the entire width of the empty road. A sense of non-reality overwhelmed the interior of their vehicle as simultaneously the engine noise died, the lights failed and the car radio crackled, smoked and faded, just as Avis wrenched out its wires to prevent a fire. A dreamy silence followed (Jenny Randles' Oz factor), without even the sound of the tyres rolling over the road, as they glided helplessly into the dense bank of *glowing* green fog.

The family's recollection of what happened next is a little vague. Whether still moving or not, both John and Sue Avis experienced a tingling sensation as if their hair was standing on end, and then they can remember no more. The very next thing Avis recalled was the car juddering, as if the engine had restarted, and then finding that they were driving past White Post Wood, some 800 m on from where they had encountered the inexplicable green mist. Sue, on the other hand, could only recall the journey as they crossed a small hump-back bridge over a stream by Running Water Wood, 400 m further on from where Avis first picked up the journey again. For some reason, the interior light was on and Kevin still stood with his hands gripping the front two seats. Both John and Sue Avis recall feeling distinctly nauseous, weak and decidedly tired.

'Is everybody here?' Sue remembers asking, but no more was said until after they had reached their home at Aveley, several minutes later.

Switching on the television to watch the play, Avis found the channel lifeless. A little confused, he turned the tuner but found there were no programmes on at all. A clock in the kitchen showed the time was well past one o'clock, which just had to be wrong. However, a telephone call to the Speaking Clock confirmed the time was accurate. Suddenly a disconcerting realisation befell the couple as they stood there in their lounge - *three hours* were missing from their lives.

The encounter was shut out of their minds; no one talked about it at all. Okay, so there had to be a direct link between their encounter with the green bank of mist and the lost hours, but no one felt they should discuss the matter. Its implications were too unnerving, so it was best the subject was dropped from conversation.

Yet in the months and then years that followed the whole family began to change their lifestyles. All but the youngest son gave up eating meat. Indeed, the two young children became vegetarians *before* their parents. Avis, a smoker of 60 to 70 cigarettes a day, screwed up his last cigarette packet and gave up completely. The same happened with alcoholic drinks. Avis, who had previously 'liked a good drink,' found he could no longer enjoy the taste of beer or any other sort of alcoholic beverage.

The two adults also began changing in themselves. From a happy-go-lucky lad of East London origin, Avis became environmentally conscious, went to college to learn art and sculpture, and suddenly found he possessed an unshakable affinity with the hidden mysteries of the landscape. Stone circles, ancient places of power and the subject of ley lines and earth energies dominated his personal beliefs and interests. He even took part in the early stages of the Dragon Project.

Sue changed in slightly different ways. She found an affinity with the ancient magic and wisdom of our past heritage, and as soon as the children were old enough she became first a nurse, and then a mid-wife. Both John and Sue Avis also developed marked psychic abilities, which although present before the encounter, seemed greatly enhanced afterwards.

Many strange events plagued their Aveley home. These included poltergeist activity, spectral figures seen in the half-light of rooms, and bursts of light that were occasionally caught flitting across open spaces before vanishing from view.

Most curious of all were the incomprehensible nightmares that recurred without explanation from 1974 onwards. They involved memories of tall figures in grey-white one-piece suits, visions of bright rooms like operating theatres and laying on tables like those in a morgue.

By now they had realised that only outside help might begin to explain what was happening to them. So in August 1977, after reading a feature in a local newspaper on my work as a UFO investigator, John Avis introduced himself.

Investigations got under way and even though Spielberg's *Close Encounters of the Third Kind* was still a year away, I immediately concluded that these sincere, credible people may have been abducted aboard an alien spacecraft. There was no other answer in those days. Hypnotic regression sessions with distinguished London psychologist Leonard Wilder took place and Avis revealed a fantastic account of the car being lifted upwards. The rest of the story concerned a full-blown abduction event on board an extra-terrestrial vehicle manned by tall alien figures wearing skin-like suits with skull-caps and face masks. Also present were smaller, uglier characters with bat-like heads and medical gowns. These were examiners of some sort.

Both John and Sue Avis gradually pieced together their own separate accounts of what had happened, and much of it tallied with the other's recall. Avis would not allow his son to be regressed due to his tender age, although he later vindicated much of his parents' own accounts.

As a young and sometimes naive UFO researcher who had read volumes of books on the UFO phenomenon, I openly accepted the alien abduction solution to the Avis family's paranormal experiences. Not just because the family seemed sincere and genuine, but because I desperately wanted to believe in extra-terrestrial intelligences visiting our planet. Despite this, neither one of the couple could actually recall seeing anything more than a bank of green-glowing mist, and readily pointed this out to investigators. What's more, John Avis retained a contradictory memory of looking down upon himself and his family slumped unconscious inside their own vehicle after entering the mist. Admittedly he saw this in association with the interior of a 'spacecraft', but even Avis realised that the whole event might well have been an out-of-the-body experience; for which reason he readily questioned the actual tangibility of the craft's interior details. Despite this he became convinced of the absolute reality of the alien intelligence encountered during the abduction. He referred to the abductors as the Watchers, and believed they could mentally communicate with him on occasions. More curious still was Avis's statement, under hypnosis on Sunday, 2 October, 1977, that the Watchers 'need us... as hosts, and they know how, and they... and they are us.' What exactly was this supposed to mean?

In the years that followed I became good friends with John and Sue Avis, witnessing strange phenomena in their home on several occasions. This included further poltergeist activity and the appearance of a tall, silhouetted figure around dawn one Saturday morning in late 1977. Both adults continued to feel they were in touch with the Watchers, either by telepathy or night-time out-of-the-body experiences where they would join with the collective mind of the Watchers. I even found I could speak to this extra-terrestrial intelligence through the vocal chords of both John *and* Sue Avis, using direct voice communications, or trance mediumship as it is known in Spiritualism.

As completely absurd as this situation may now seem to the outsider, the Aveley couple were sensible and sober people who possessed great wisdom and a profound understanding of life. And yet they were quite obviously linked through mental processes with some sort of exterior force for, like other UFO contactees, they were able to predict UFO events; not to order, but with an uncanny accuracy on occasions. For instance, one night in 1978 Avis felt that the intelligence would make a further appearance at the same location as their original encounter in 1974. Sure enough, driving along that very same stretch of road a few nights later, both he and Sue witnessed a dense mass of blue-white light on the ground, close to a small reservoir encircled by trees. There was at least one independent witness to this event.

In spite of this confirmatory evidence of his contactee claims, Avis remained happy to accept that he had never actually boarded a physical spacecraft, but instead had undergone a subjective, though truly alien contact played out in some form of astral domain. This is a very bold statement, coming, as it does, from someone whose memory still holds the vivid recall of a full-blown abduction experience. However, although Avis openly accepts that the memory of the abduction he and his family underwent in 1974 was simply a means of conveying knowledge of higher realms and intelligences in a manner acceptable to their own minds, even to this day he holds a firm belief in the reality of the Watchers, an alien race of great stature who inhabited the earth long ago and live on in our dreams and desires. I therefore find it intriguing that in European occultism the term *eggregori*, Greek for Watchers, was the name given to balls of etheric light that watched over the affairs of mankind. Perhaps John Avis might have been closer to the truth than he could ever have imagined.

35

Lifeforms

So what really did happen to the Avis family out on the secluded country lanes of west Essex in 1974? I do not believe for one moment that they brought the car to a halt without crashing, before losing consciousness and remaining slumped in their seats for three hours. The Aveley road may be quiet, but someone driving past would have seen the parked car and stopped to find out whether they were alright or not.

To add to the mystery, the very first thing the family recalled after the encounter was the vehicle juddering back to life. They then became aware of driving along the same stretch of road, yet a full 800 m on from their original position (1.2 km in Sue's case). Their eldest son, Kevin, was still standing up in front of the rear seat and the two smaller children were still asleep. It was as if the time had passed instantaneously, without any break between entering the mist and coming out again further along the same stretch of road. If we are to accept the family's word as genuine, then this is the only logical solution available - the time jump was instantaneous, which therefore implies that they were removed from linear time for three whole hours.

Gerry Armstrong

There are other examples of this time-jump phenomenon as well, such as the case of Gerry Armstrong (pseudonym), a UFO 'repeater' witness featured in a book entitled *The Missing Seven Hours*, written by UFO researcher David Haisell and published in 1978. Armstrong had emigrated from England to Jackson's Point, Toronto, in 1967 where he had settled down with his wife Susan. Here he had frequently reported UFO sightings, prompting Haisell to approach him in 1973 - a meeting that eventually led to the publication of the above mentioned book.

It is, however, Armstrong's first ever UFO-related event that is of importance to us here. At the time he was just 12 years' old and lived with his parents at Sydenham in south-east London. According to Armstrong's story, in July 1953 he attended a summer camp with teachers and other school-children at an undisclosed location in the county of Kent. Whilst there, Armstrong went on a field trip with a teacher and around 30 to 40 other children. They crossed hills and valleys, passed through woods and forests, and finally ended up in a disused quarry sometime before one o'clock. After a suitable rest the school party took part in a game of hide and seek with the teacher, leaving Armstrong to wander off and sit beneath a nearby tree to have a sneaky cigarette, a Players Weight he recalls.

Taking out a brand new pack of five, he lifted one out, lit it with a match and then something peculiar occurred. As he put it himself: 'And then nothing. Blackness. Dark. Very very dark. Voices. "Over here," was the first thing I heard. "Over here, Mr Rice. Found him, sir. Put that cigarette out, Gerry. Rice is coming." And this is the crazy thing. I had my cigarette and it was still burning, and I still had four left in the pack.'(1)

On arrival, the teacher and the other school children questioned Armstrong, for it seemed he had been missing for *seven* hours. The time was now nine o'clock and it was virtually dark. He had no recollection at all of the lost time and as far as he was concerned he had been beneath the tree for only a few minutes. This baffled the others as they had apparently checked the location when it had become apparent that he was missing and, despite passing the spot on more than one occasion, they had seen nothing.

Armstrong was carried back to the camp by two teachers and later examined by a doctor who found him to be suffering from dilated eyes and an unaccountable red sore on his neck. These symptoms were, however, dismissed as the result of sunstroke. At the time Armstrong was in such a dream-like state that he did not question the decision of his superiors. He was eventually allowed to return to the dormitory where he quickly fell into a deep sleep. The next day he shrugged off the experience by telling the other children he had simply fallen asleep.

After this date Armstrong experienced a number of UFO sightings as well as a recurring dream implying that his missing seven hours had involved an abduction scenario. He also repeatedly received glimpses of a UFO-related entity approaching him as he had sat beneath the tree smoking his cigarette.

To me the most important element of this whole story was the cigarette. Armstrong appeared *sure* that he was smoking the same cigarette both before and after the black out in which the missing time occurred. So, if we can accept his testimony at face value, then it seems clear that the time passed instantaneously, *i.e.* he did not spend the seven hours somewhere else, either beneath the tree or aboard an alien spacecraft (unless the aliens removed and extinguished his cigarette, and then allowed him to light up again just before his departure from the vessel!). This conclusion is tentatively substantiated by the fact that the location Armstrong had sat down to have his sneaky cigarette was thoroughly searched in between the time of his disappearance and his later rediscovery. One is also reminded of the folk story quoted in this book's Introduction of the couple out riding in a horse and trap who went missing on the banks of Loch Ness only to re-appear again one hundred years later in a dazed and confused state. Might some time-jump experiences last much longer than a few hours or a few days? It is a mind-bending concept if nothing else.

So, if abduction encounters are induced experiences occurring in an instant of time, then how can we explain such phenomena in scientific terms?

Electromagnetic Effects

Canadians Michael Persinger and Gyslaine Lafreniere have put forward a solution to the abduction scenario. They suggest that during close-proximity UFO encounters the enormous electromagnetic currents pulsing from the phenomenon would stimulate body organisms and affect electrically-sensitive regions of the brain, in particular the temporal lobe cortex. Apparently, two areas of the temporal cortex, the hippocampus and the amygdala, are so sensitive that electrically-stimulated malfunctions over short or long periods of time can induce changed or modified memory, as well as visionary states similar to drug-influenced hallucinatory experiences. Persinger and Lafreniere believe this would include altered states of consciousness, distortions of time and space, supernatural visitations, meaningful messages and a drastic updating of post-memory recall to accommodate the dramatic effects produced by such altered states. It might also result in out-of-the-body experiences. Similar effects have been produced under laboratory conditions by artificially stimulating the hippocampus and amygdala. They also mirror the sequence of events that befell the Essex psychic Bernard when he approached the tumulus in Cambridgeshire during 1981, and bear striking similarities to the effects reported in association with crop circles and orgone accumulators. Near death experiences are likewise considered by Persinger and Lafreniere to trigger such responses, and it seems realistic to suppose that those persons of a psychically-sensitive disposition are effected far sooner than non-psychics.

Even accepting the temporal cortex hypothesis, these ideas do not explain the time jumps experienced by percipients in such close encounters, or why the UFOs and their occupants appear to be physically real. So how can we explain these more baffling aspects in the light of Persinger and Lafreniere's appraisal of the subject?

Earthly Reflections

There exist many cases where light phenomena has mimicked human thought by appearing to observers as obvious earthly symbols. Shape-shifting abilities were always accredited to Will-o'-the-Wisps which were said to have been able to transform themselves into the desires and wishes of the lone traveller, whether it be a beautiful young girl or a crock of gold, in an attempt to lure them into the marshes and swamps.

I have already suggested that earth light consciousness might well have some association with the quantum process of non-locality, linking our own minds with that of the object being observed. Could it be possible therefore that lifeforms of pure energy can reflect the subconscious thoughts of the human mind, both individually and through the collective unconscious?

FIG 36. Will-o'-the-Wisp, the supernatural figure believed in English folklore to be behind the appearance of mysterious lights seen over marshy areas. He was said to have been able to change his form into anything from a crock of gold to a beautiful woman in an attempt to lure the lone traveller into the quagmire. Does this recollect the shape-shifting characteristics of the UFO phenomenon?

An excellent example of this apparent non-local interaction between witnesses on the ground and the phenomenon observed may be found in a case that occurred close to the Cornwall/Devon border in 1971. At around 18.15 on the night of Saturday, 23 October, Mrs Marilyn Preston and her friend Michael Mansergh were driving through Ellbridge, just outside Saltash, Cornwall, when they witnessed a 'large pink and golden ball of light' hanging in the sky. In an attempt to gain a closer look, the witnesses turned off the main road, only to see the aerial lightform disappear from view. Somewhat disappointed, they returned to the position they had first seen the ball of light, hoping that it might return. Sure enough, after just a few minutes of waiting the object reappeared at exactly the same spot in the open sky. Although it still retained the same golden-pink hue, it had now taken on the shape of a cigar.

The witnesses watched in awe at the stationary object, and it is what happened during this phase of the sighting that is of utmost importance to our own debate, for Mrs Preston observed that: 'Whilst we watched, it changed shape six times in about 30 minutes, in accord with our conversations as to what experts might say it was. Slowly, we realized the space ship was attuned to our thought-waves, and when it finally went we contacted the press and television studios'.(2)

And they were not the only ones to do so, for according to Cornish writer Michael Williams in his book *Supernatural in Cornwall* over 30 people contacted the local radio and television stations to report UFO sightings in Cornwall that evening. In addition to this, local radio and television transmissions were also affected throughout this same period by a mysterious bout of blackouts and interference, with TV viewers reporting that the picture was either fading in and out or being superimposed by other channels.

Mrs Preston and her friend appear to have been blatantly aware of the object's ability to transmogrify into whatever image they were inadvertently placing upon it. This is a unique realisation, and one that clearly demonstrates that the UFO experience almost certainly reflects whatever thoughts and emotions are impressed upon it by the observers on the ground, even up to distances of many hundreds of yards - something that Carl Jung came very close to realising in his 1959 book *Flying Saucers A Modern Myth of Things Seen in the Sky*.

Such earthly forms will undoubtedly be based on both our collective and individual interpretations of the UFO enigma. In turn this will formulate very real archetypes in the human psyche, such as the idea that most UFOs are saucer-shaped discs, a popular misconception begun when Bill Becquette, the reporter on the *East Oregonian*, misquoted Kenneth Arnold's statement concerning the 'saucer-like' movements of the nine glowing objects seen above the Cascade Mountains in 1947. Such ideas were quickly transferred to the collective consciousness by the power of the international media and, as a consequence, this archetype has been unshakable ever since. As I mentioned earlier in this book, the bizarre photographs of the saucer-like UFOs produced during the late 1970s by Swiss contactee Billy Meier exemplify the view that the 1950s-style flying saucer archetype is here to stay.

Such archetypes are, I believe, conveyed by the unconscious mind to manifested lightforms which can then re-mould themselves to express some semblance of this original thought. In Mrs Preston's case, the idea that some UFOs are cigar-shaped was first made popular by 1950s contactee George Adamski who claimed that the flying saucers were simply scout ships attached to much larger cigar-shaped mother ships orbiting the earth.

Archetypes and symbols also appear to act as acceptance levels of communication between the human mind and the extra-terrestrial intelligences believed to be behind the UFO phenomenon. Certain archetypes feature again and again in UFO lore, each being slightly updated on a collective level from one decade to the next as our own earthly technology steadily advances. These include the tall, blonde-haired Caucasian types dressed in long, flowing robes and the shorter, black-eyed entities with spindly bodies commonly referred to as 'Greys'. These are our most modern views of higher intelligences.

Multi-dimensional States

With all this in mind it seems likely that the closer a percipient comes to a manifested lightform, the more an interaction takes place between the human mind and the phenomenon observed through the intervention of non-local processes. This, I propose, enables the object to transmogrify its energy matrix to reflect the deep and hidden desires, fears, hopes and/or wishes within the psyche of the witnesses concerned. This living energy can therefore re-form itself into anything from a Christmas tree to an alien spaceship, a crock of gold, a little green man, a pretty girl or a vision of the Virgin Mary, in fact whatever the unconscious human mind expects to see and experience under such strange circumstances. These encounters will have an objective and often physical reality that will last only for the duration of the encounter and be experienced only by the percipients involved. The objects will then evaporate like camphor, back into the intangible realms of the energy continuum, the only visible evidence of their temporary existence being either physical traces left on the ground and/or the subsequent physiological effects so often reported by close encounter witnesses.

In our technological age these tangible visions have generally taken the form of encounters with alien technology. However, the unconscious mind of an individual will reflect differing archetypes depending on its own religious and social upbringing. Often these visitations will be accompanied by warnings of doom and destruction if mankind does not mend his wicked ways.

Taking the matter one step further, I now feel that if a percipient encounters a fully-manifested lightform - as the Avis family appear to have done in 1974 - he or she will, through the altered states induced by temporal cortex stimulation, take an active part in this temporarily real, multi-dimensional event. In doing so, the percipient enters into their own, personally-induced mystical experience, something that allows them to momentarily break free from the space-time continuum. This may all sound a little fantastic, but I believe that it is only in the presence of such concentrated levels of manifested electromagnetic energy that we can truly experience altered or shifted realities that pass beyond our perceptions of space-time. If we also accept that these energy forms are composed of complex primary matrixes that span all dimensions, then it may mean that they actually act as doorways or gates into trans-dimensional realms.

Unfortunately, however, I am convinced that this state only occurs beyond the normal parameters of our own four-dimensional, space-time continuum. Yet when it does happen it can and frequently does result in time-jump experiences. Afterwards, the brain will supplant the true memory of the incident with a more accessible version that is enhanced as and when necessary by the use of dreams, flash-backs and, if employed, hypnotic regression.

A good example of religious archetypes appearing in recalls of on-board abduction experiences is the case of police officer Anthony Dodd, who suffered a time-lapse experience during an encounter with an object likened to 'a child's spinning top' seen hanging above a road at Todmorden in West Yorkshire during the early hours of Friday, 28 November 1980.(3) Dodd underwent hypnotic regression in an attempt to reveal details of the missing time. The results of the four sessions conducted with two separate hypnotists produced a stereotypical abduction scenario in which the witness found himself on a table undergoing a medical examination in a futuristic room with glowing, cornerless walls. However, on the point of occupants, Dodd described seeing a tall man with a beard and a long thin nose, wearing a white garment and a skull-cap. He smiled at Dodd and gave his name as 'Yosef', or Joseph. With him were around eight, small ugly-looking creatures around 3ft to 3ft 6in in height.(4)

As Jenny Randles rightly points out in her 1983 book *The Pennine UFO Mystery*, Joseph is a popular biblical name. It was also the first-name of Dr Yosef Jaffe, the doctor conducting the session, a fact Anthony Dodd was unaware of when placed under hypnosis. Was this name picked from the mind of the hypnotist and grafted onto the image of the benign, biblical-like character viewed by Dodd's mind as the entity responsible for his UFO encounter? I feel the answer is firmly yes.

Fairy Abductions

The concept of multi-dimensional experiences, or MDEs, also provides us with answers for other baffling enigmas as well, such as encounters with the fairy folk. Archaic folklore records several stories where a person comes across either a bright light or an illuminated door in a grassy knoll that has never been noticed before. Inside they find the elven folk in revelry, with singing, dancing, and food and drink galore. When, after what seems like only a few hours, they leave the mound and return home, many days, weeks, even years are found to have mysteriously gone by. Respected French UFO author Jacques Vallee was the first to note the obvious comparisons between fairy encounters and UFO occupant cases in his 1970 classic *Passport to Magonia - From Folklore to Flying Saucers*. Furthermore, it is difficult to deny the similarities between UFO entities, such as the 'Greys', and the hobgoblins or Jack-o-Lanterns of the past.

One has only to search the pages of fairy literature to find representations of the Hidden People, as they were known, that match almost exactly the present-day image of the 'Grey'. For example, in the 1978 book *Faeries* by Brian Froud and Alan Lee there is a representation of a winged fairy whose face is more or less identical to that of a 'Grey'. Its triangular jaw, tiny nose, smooth grey skin and large, elliptical black eyes make the two faces almost interchangeable, their only differences being the elfin ears, long straggly hair

FIG 37. Fairy abductions and enchantments, like the one depicted in this line drawing, may well represent pre-flying saucer era multi-dimensional states induced by the presence of unmanifest bioforms or aerial lightforms. Are alien abductions simply the modern-day equivalent of such encounters?

and gossamer wings of the fairy and the astronaut's suit of the 'Grey'. Brian Froud, who also created the elfin characters in the fantasy film classic 'The Dark Crystal', tells me that the illustrations for *Faeries* were done in 1976, two years before 'Close Encounters of the Third Kind' first popularised the image of the 'Grey'-like alien. The fairy picture in question was, he says, painted intuitively based on how he felt a fairy should look, as opposed to the quaint romantic image of the Hidden People portrayed by many artists in the past; he had not thought of it in terms of an alien entity. He was therefore intrigued when an elderly psychic woman, who lived near his home in Devon and claimed to be able to 'see' elemental spirits, told him the picture conveyed a true likeness of a fairy and that he too must be gifted with the power of 'second sight'.

Modern-day UFO occupants are hybrid developments of the elvish characters of yester-year. Moreover, both alien entities and elemental beings have been repeatedly accredited with causing the very same type of supernatural phenomena, including abductions, kidnappings, time lapses, and the appearance of floating balls of light, localised aerial flashes and unexplained ground markings. Only our interpretation of those responsible for such occurrences has changed. It is time to accept that the 'Greys' come, not from outer space, but from inner space - the deep, dark astral worlds, delineated by the multi-dimensional energy continuum and accessed by the subtle mechanics of the human mind.

Heaven and Hell

Should MDEs be based solely on our preconceptions of manifested bioforms, then what happens when the percipient or percipients possess a devout religious background? They will quite probably interpret the appearance of such lights as either signs or portents of God or the devil, depending on the circumstances of the sighting. All too often visions of the Blessed Virgin Mary, Jesus Christ, angels and saints have been accompanied by the appearance of mysterious lights; and sometimes this has even resulted in some quite remarkable photographs.

Among the isolated monasteries and eyries on the promontory of Mount Athos in Greece there exists, even to this day, a form of age-old mysticism known as *hesychasm* or omphaloscopy ('navel gazing'). It teaches that divine illumination and one-ness with God can be achieved through deep meditational practices (indeed, this is where the term 'contemplating your navel' comes from). The goal of the holy mystic, or *hesychast*, is to

PLATE 50. The similarity between the face of this 1976 fairy illustration by Brian Froud and the modern-day concept of a Grey is striking. Are alien entities simply hybrid forms of the same basic archetype that has haunted the human mind since the dawn of time? (pic: Brian Froud)

witness what they see as the Light of God, which is not a spiritual concept but a form of light manifestation occasionally witnessed on the peninsula. Some monks even retire to remote caves and become ascetics for years on end in the hope of attaining this physical enlightenment.

Sometimes these illumination experiences are accompanied by visions of Christian divinities, such as the Blessed Virgin Mary, Jesus Christ, or one or more of the saints. Divine light is itself an important symbol in the beliefs of Mount Athos's insular monastic communities and the appearance of quite clear light manifestations feature in the foundation of no less than three of its monasteries.(5) It seems certain that *hesychast* mysticism reflects an idealised Christian view of aerial light phenomena and light consciousness.

When, however, light manifestations appear to percipients holding more evangelical or fundamental beliefs, they are sometimes accompanied by the appearance of Satan in the form of a man-in-black and/or a black dog, as we have seen in the case of the Welsh Religious Revival of 1904-5.(6) This puritanical attitude towards unexplained light phenomena probably only existed from the 17th century onwards, and yet it may well account for the hell-fire and devil place-names occasionally found at locations where repeated earth light occurrences are frequently reported.(7)

Paradise Regained

Yet what might a devout Christian expect to experience if they come too close to a manifested lightform and enter into MDEs of their own creation? A trip to paradise in the company of Jesus Christ, perhaps? Well, believe it or not, this is exactly what happened on one, possibly two, occasions during the Welsh Religious Revival.

The following account, featured in the *Proceedings of the Society for Psychical Research* for December 1905, begins with a classic example of the phenomena moulding itself into precisely what the unnamed witness truly expected to see - Jesus Christ. The

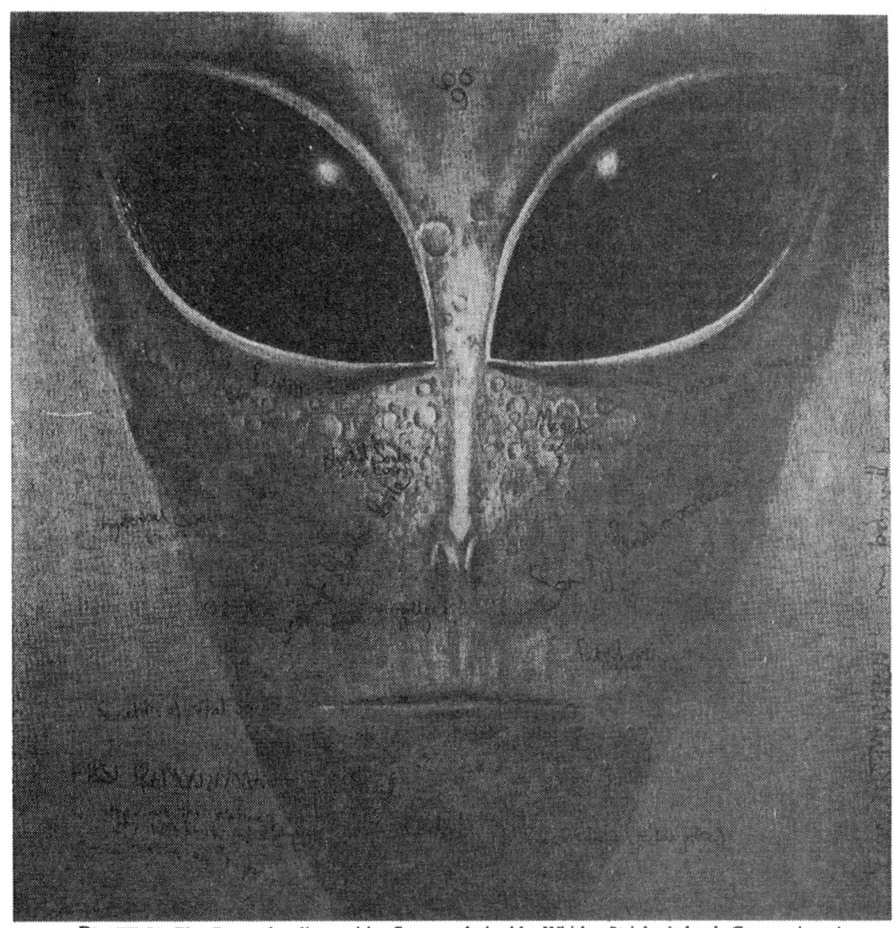

PLATE 51. The Greys, the alien entities first popularised by Whitley Strieber's book *Communion*. Are they not hybrid forms of the hobgoblins of yester-year and the more conventional space beings reported in connection with 'flying saucers' during the 1950s? (pic: Rod Dickinson)

scenario then gradually transforms into an idealistic vision of paradise. The incident in question was translated from a letter in Welsh dated 26 August 1905:

> In the month of November (1904) missioners in connection with the revival came to the neighbourhood... I understood that Jesus of Nazareth was walking through our country, but I was unable to feel him, nor see him to myself, and that was my anxiety for many days... But on the 12th of December, on a Monday night, I had this heavenly vision which the tongue of man cannot relate or describe appropriately... On the night stated, I was travelling by myself on the high road on a work night which was very dark, but in the darkness overhead I beheld a faint light playing over my head and approaching earth, and as it came nearer it increased and strengthened; and lest I was being deceived by my own eyes, I determined to close them, but I was seeing it [the light] in the same way.

> Then I opened my eyes to behold the vision, and then it came downwards and stood before me, about the size of a man's body, and in the bright and glorious light I beheld there the face of a man, and by looking for the body in the light a shining white robe was covering it to its feet and it was not touching the earth, and behind its arms there were wings appearing, and I was seeing every feather in the wings, but they were not natural or material feathers, but the whole was heavenly beyond description. And then the palms of the hands were appearing, and on each hand there were brown spots as they appeared at first. But after I had noticed more minutely, I beheld that they were the marks of the nails, and then I recognised Him as Jesus and I went forward shouting, 'O my blessed Jesus!', and then He ascended on his wing without noise, moving a little further ahead, and appearing much more bright and clear, so that the marks of the nails were so fiery and plain that I can say they were square nails of the cruellest description, and by the work of Joseph of Arimathea and Nicodemus pulling him down from the Cross, the sores of his dear flesh had come out to the palms of His hands; and this appearance gave such peace to my breast, so that it filled it through with love...
>
> And in the light of this presence, the old, ugly world came before me in its entirety, so that I saw its mountains, its rocks, its moors, its reshes, its thorns, its entangled growths, its stones, and all hindrances on my way, so that I was retreating, lest its stones should throw me over, lest its thorns and its entangled growths should rend me. Which journey I would think every true Christian must go through. And after He had led me through this journey in that way, and I beseeching him to come with me, and when he had stayed the third time, behold he ascended up and out of my sight... The appearance of the world I saw by means of the light was one vision - not a light showing the earth around, because I am well acquainted with the place - but the surface of the whole world losing itself in the distance... Not a word was uttered by Jesus, but the movements went on silently and noiselessly...(8)

If we strip away the layers of religious indoctrination placed on the episode by this Welshman, it seems clear that what he saw as 'one vision' of Christ leading him down the road to paradise, was in fact the consequences of him encountering a descending lightform at close quarters. I see no other way to interpret this visionary incident, other than to suggest that Jesus Christ really did appear to this man in the guise of his most cliched Christian archetype.

It is almost certain that in the past those who, like the Welshman, underwent MDEs after encountering close-proximity lightforms, generally entered utopic domains conforming largely to their own preconceptions of higher intelligences and spiritual realms beyond the earthly plane. This I firmly believe to have been so.

Why nothing happened to Eugenio de la Terra, the Philippino UFO witness featured in the Preface who attempted to light his cigarette on a one-metre diameter purple sphere he encountered, is a complete mystery. Perhaps it had something to do with the way he himself perceived the object, for if he did not connect its presence with any deeply-held spiritual beliefs concerning higher intelligences, then maybe it had no way to affect his brain. On the other hand, perhaps the spherical lightform, which was said to have been cold to the touch, was within a frequency range that does not cause noticeable physiological and psychological effects in the percipients involved.

Guiding Lights

Even if the appearance of close proximity light phenomena can induce mysterious experiences, create time lapses and transmogrify itself into more acceptable forms reflecting the personal beliefs of the percipients involved, this is not evidence of intelligent behaviour in its own right. The sometimes playful or purposeful responses of lightforms to human beings *is* evidence of intelligence, yet still only on a most basic level. UFO believers would cite the many encounters with alien entities as real examples of extra-terrestrial intelligence, although, as we have seen, these should not be taken at face value and may well be the result of a mind-created scenario with quite physically real overtones.

If we were to find clear indications of the lightforms displaying acts of conscious decision-making and purposeful action before they were seriously influenced by the proximity of the witnesses, then this might well constitute independent intelligence. Such examples can, I believe, be found among what are probably one of the most fascinating aspects of light interaction, and these are cases of alleged guiding lights - lights that guide lost travellers back to safety. In past ages supernatural rescues of this sort were always seen as acts of God, but when the cases are studied in detail it appears that this is simply the opinion of those involved in the story; infernal spirits were, in contrast, blamed on ghost lights that led lone travellers *into* the quagmire.

In Britain guiding light stories are almost exclusively recorded in remote moorland areas such as Dartmoor and the Yorkshire Moors, regions noted for archaic and more recent cases of mysterious light phenomena. S. Baring-Gould gave a perfect example of this tradition in his work *A Book of Dartmoor* first published in 1900. He tells the story of a Devonian miner who crossed the moors one Sunday night having visited his sick brother in Cornwood. He was heading back to the mine at Whiteworks and in time night overtook him and he became lost and entangled in the bogs. Unable to go forward or return from whence he came, he became distressed and began to pray to God.

It was then that 'all at once' a light came into view and moved towards the miner. He recognised it as a Will-o'-the-Wisp, which were considered to lead men into dangerous places. Yet being a strong Christian, he was sure that the light had been sent in answer to his prayer so he placed his trust in its presence and followed it. 'He was conducted over ground fairly firm, though miry, till he reached heather and a sound footing, whereupon the flame vanished. Thanking God, he pursued his way, taking his direction by the stars, and reached his destination in safety'.(9)

Baring-Gould admitted that this account was third hand, so its authenticity could not be guaranteed, although he goes on to quote an old folk song given to him by a Cornishman concerning another example of this guiding light phenomena, this time from Yorkshire, which includes the following lines:

As I trudged on at ten at night
  My way to fair York city,
I saw before a lantern light
  Borne by a damsel pretty.
I her accos't, 'My way I've lost,
  Your lantern let me carry!
Then through the land, both hand in hand,
  We'll travel. Prithee tarry.'

She trippd along, so nimble she,
  The lantern still a-swinging,
And 'Follow, follow, follow me!'
  ...She sped along, I in the lurch,
A lost and panting stranger,
  Till, lo! I found me at the Church,
She's led me out of danger.(10)

We must also not forget the folklore account of a guiding light preserved by Kathleen Wiltshire in her 1985 book *Ghosts and Legends of the Wiltshire Countryside*. Here a man, on his way home from work one night, becomes inexplicably lost in the darkness of a dense wood at West Kennett. Almost at his wit's end, a mysterious light then suddenly appears before him and guides the poor fellow to safety.(11)

One might question the reliability of such quaint folk stories remembered by remote rural communities who were want to blame any ill-omen or misfortune on supernatural deeds. However, Yorkshire UFO researcher Nigel Mortimer has recently uncovered a modern-day example of a guiding light that led three lost mountaineers to safety from a location near White Wells on Ilkley Moor.

If these guiding light stories *are* evidence of a real phenomena that has not been grossly misinterpreted, then I feel they are the only evidence to demonstrate that manifested lightforms may well possess an independent consciousness, intelligence, and possibly even memory. If we are to accept these clearly animistic characteristics, then we must also accept that they might also possess other, almost human qualities, such as self-motivation, reason and will-power.

Universal Intelligence

If these theories are correct, then it means that many, if not all true, UFOs, are sentient lifeforms that, although possessing a universal intelligence beyond our current understanding, manifest to us through the interjection of hybrid archetypes, personalities and symbols drawn both from our individual psyche and the Jungian collective unconscious. This is why individuals from out of the way communities in Puerto Rico can encounter alien entities that are similar, but are not necessarily the same, as those repeatedly seen by UFO percipients in the western world, for these space-age archetypes are now present within the fabric of the collective mind. We use these self-same archetypes to continue our communion with these intelligences through an assortment of psychic processes, such as channelling, clairvoyance, dreaming, meditation, out-of-the-body experiences, precognition and telepathy. Whether it be 'Greys', creator gods, mother earth, ancestor spirits or some other belief system, if the faith is strong enough they can all act as an effective means of either drawing this phenomenon into visible manifestation or predicting the moment of its appearance.

Despite this continued contact, it is unlikely that we have *ever* really seen or understood the true nature of this phenomenon. If only we could strip away these layers of perception and deal directly with whatever lies behind the mask. What would we find? What would happen if we ran towards a manifesting bioform, having accepted this new knowledge? What kind of 'one vision' should we expect then? Perhaps the human mind is just not ready to accept the idea of sentient lifeforms manifesting as pure light.

UFO contactees and some psychics tell us that the relatively small earth lights are terrestrial entities, such as ancestor spirits or elemental beings, while the much larger atmospheric vehicles of light are alien spacecraft containing highly-advanced entities of extra-terrestrial origin. Perhaps they are correct and different types of lightform do represent an assortment of otherworldly intelligences programmed by archetypes from our own past contact with their collective nature. Strip away the layers and you would be confronted with a universal intelligence completely beyond our comprehension - one which I feel it would be quite appropriate to refer to as extra-terrestrial in origin. Yet these higher intelligences are not physical entities travelling inside nuts and bolts hardware - the balls of light, the daylight discs and the light clusters we see as UFOs *are themselves* sentient lifeforms.

If the abduction scenario really does reflect encounters with alien races on board intergalactic spacecraft, then it would have to mean that there are literally hundreds of individual races visiting this planet, which is simply absurd. Astronomers say that even if there *is* life on other worlds, the chances of coming across upright bipeds like ourselves is millions to one against, owing to the vast differences in planetary climates that would necessitate entirely different evolutionary processes to those found on earth. This does not necessarily mean that extra-terrestrial civilisations do not exist out in the universe somewhere, simply that the vast majority of modern-day UFO sightings and close encounter cases do not appear to constitute evidence of flesh and blood aliens visiting this planet. As for claims that the US Government has retrieved crashed saucers complete with dead occupants, well, I shall reserve judgement on this matter until one of these alleged space vehicles is wheeled out for public display.

Constable came to the conclusion that UFOs were living entities - sky creatures existing unseen in the atmosphere - and, as we have already seen, even the man who initiated the flying saucer craze back in 1947 came to this same extraordinary conclusion. I think we owe it to them to continue to pursue this concept, for it has much more far reaching implications than the more popular idea of physical aliens abducting a few unwilling individuals and waiting to zoom in and save us from self-destruction when the time is right. The concept that we could well be sharing our atmosphere with intelligent, trans-dimensional lifeforms that have probably existed since before the birth of man is simply awesome.

Reich's theories of orgone energy are just the start. If the concept of a multi-dimensional energy continuum, with all its individual components, could be wholly accepted and understood, the answers needed to deal with this planet's ever increasing destruction would almost certainly be revealed and messiahs from heaven or outer space would not be necessary.

My mind keeps harking back to the oh so poignant words of Trevor James Constable who predicted that: 'By the year 2000 - if there is one for our species - hosts of young investigators in exobiology will be in full pursuit of the critters of our atmosphere. They will undoubtedly marvel at our stupidity in not tumbling to such presences far earlier.'(12)

The year 2000 is fast approaching and unless we adopt a whole new attitude towards the UFO phenomenon then it will only ever reflect the spirit of the age. So, if like the Avis family, Eugenio de la Terra and Anthony Dodd, you ever encounter a manifestation of alien energy at close quarters, what will you do? Would you run towards it and suffer the unknown consequences? or would you simply back away and miss the chance of a lifetime? The choice is yours...

Appendix I

Orgone 93 and 94 Anomaly Charts

The accompanying charts show the breakdown of anomalies recorded by Orgone 93 between Sunday, 18 July and Friday, 30 July 1993. Those registered both by Paul Hailey and by the Relate equipment are also included on this list, as are the various other inexplicable incidents reported in and around Alton Barnes during the period in question. These have been added to the grand total at the end of each day but do not appear in the anomaly count for the individual Orgone 93 experiments.

All photographic anomalies produced by Orgone 93 are included in the listing, with each frame's *total number* of objects and the time it was taken, cited in the column provided. Where two or more times appear together in one column, each entry signifies an individual photograph. For the moment I have deliberately ignored the possible explanations for many of these photographic anomalies to allow their study in respect to the overall events that occurred during the experiments in question.

I have also included the off-scale ultrasound readings recorded mainly at dawn during the first week of experimentation. These ceased completely after Rodney Hale re-set his detector on Friday, 23 July. The presence of crop circles in this chart is for reference purposes only; they are not included in the total.

The times given for each experiment denote the start of the first control period, which was usually 10 minutes in duration; the exception being Experiment 22, where the first and second control periods were 20 minutes each.

Studying this chart several points of interest emerge for the first time, throwing new light on the activities of the Orgone 93 team in the following manner:-

Meditational Work

The significance of meditational work, and in particular the potential of individual archetypes and symbols, was of paramount importance to the idea of interacting with the environment using non-local processes. Both visually, and in respect to the many radiation rises registered during the Orgone 93 experimentation, it seemed clear from the early results that the use of ancestor spirits as a selected archetype in meditations was achieving the most successful results.

This assumption is borne out by the fact that on the four occasions that ancestor spirits were used during a meditation, there was a high average of 3.8 anomalies per experiment. However, due mainly to the success of Experiment 16 on Monday, 26 July, the four meditations featuring no archetype also scored an above average of 3.8 anomalies per experiment. On the four occasions when aliens and nuts and bolts spacecraft were used as the selected archetype an average of 2.8 anomalies was achieved, while in the two experiments where the Gaia/Goddess archetype was employed an average of three anomalies was achieved. By comparison, the two OED experiments gained an average of just 2.9 anomalies per experiment, while the seven control tests only managed to produce an average of 1.7 anomalies per experiment, supporting the contention that the experiments were actually achieving their goals.

Location Count

So much for the use of individual archetypes during meditational experiments, but what about the sites themselves - how did they fair in the anomaly count? Woodborough Hill produced an average of 3.5 anomalies per experiment, while Church Meadow produced 3 per experiment, Adam's Grave produced 2.5, the control site produced 1.5 and the crop circle and Avebury both scored a total of one anomaly each. The last two sites were not used enough for any real assessment to be made in this respect; however,

Woodborough Hill's above average anomaly count is quite significant. Exactly why this should have been so is still a matter of speculation. Three of the experiments took place there at dawn while five took place at midday, and since the greater proportion of anomalies occurred at lunchtime then this obviously had some bearing on the final anomaly count.

Is it possible that Woodborough Hill, a site almost certainly sacred to Woden in Saxon times (see Chapter 32), causes more energy excitation in the localised energy matrix than, say, Adam's Grave or the Water Site? If so, then perhaps this is due to its conical shape or the tall copse of trees that crown its summit and dominate the local skyline. It is also just a few hundred metres from Tawsmead Copse where mysterious lights have been seen with frequency since the summer of 1992. We should not, however, dismiss the apparent potential of Adam's Grave. Even though all four of the experiments conducted here took place at dawn, its average of 2.5 anomalies per session is also curiously high.

Church Meadow proved to be the most conducive site for our purposes. It was sheltered from the elements and was just five minutes' walk from the cottage. The eight experiments conducted here produced a relatively high anomaly count, although this did include most of the early ultrasound anomalies obtained during the first week. The presence of the slightly radio-active glauconite in the Upper Greensand found at this location did not appear to have any real effect on the radiation results one way or another.

Even though the average anomaly counts were not drastically different from site to site, they were all considerably higher than the results obtained at the control site, *i.e.* the back garden of Brown's Cottage. In retrospect, I realise that more experiments should have been conducted here to gain a more balanced picture of the anomaly count per site. As it stands, little else can be said about the effectiveness of individual sites until we are more certain on the origin of the anomalies achieved.

Black and White Photography

Out of a total of 26 photographic anomalies achieved in 18 separate pictures, six were produced during the seven control tests; three occurred coincident to the six meditational experiments, a further two appeared coincident to the two OED experiments (where meditations were not used), two resulted from the only occasion we used the Star Exercise, while a total of 13 anomalies resulted from the eight experiments where we combined the use of both the OED with meditations. Presupposing that the photographic anomalies produced during the single use of the Star Exercise was a freak result, then this meant that only the experiments incorporating the use of both the OED and a meditation produced an above average count per experiment, *i.e.* 1.6 anomalies per experiment against 1.0 with the OED, 0.9 with the control tests and a measly 0.5 using meditations alone.

Colour Photography

The trend found in the black and white anomaly pictures is replicated in respect to the visible light, colour anomalies achieved during the same experiments, with the combination of OED and meditation coming out tops with an average of 0.9 anomalies per experiment as opposed to 0.5 for OED experiments and 0.2 for meditations alone. There were no colour anomalies produced during any control test or during the employment of the Star Exercise.

Radiation Increases

When we come to the increases recorded in the background radiation count during the various experiments, another pattern seems to emerge. Only one rise was recorded during the seven control tests, whereas five similar increases were recorded during the use of meditations, and another four instances were reported when meditations were combined with the use of the OED. This gives an average result of 0.8 per meditation alone, with 0.5 when combined with the use of the OED and 0.1 for the control tests. In addition to this, statistics show that in respect to the recorded radiation rises, there was a 50% success rate using four or five people, and a 100% success rate on the five occasions we used between six and 11 persons. The one time the meditation featured just three people, no notable results were obtained and, likewise, when 70 or so people took part nothing occurred. No radiation anomalies were recorded during either the use of the Star Exercise or when the OED was employed on its own. These figures suggest that, not only are the meditations linked to the radiation rises, but that the probability of their occurrence is increased in accordance with the number of people taking part in the meditation.

Time of Day

12 experiments were conducted at dawn and 12 at midday GMT, suggesting that by chance alone a roughly equal amount of anomalies should have occurred at either time. We chose dawn because it is considered to be the point in the day when the environmental excitation is at its most potent. Similar conclusions can be drawn from the findings of the Dragon Project which registered more anomalies over the period of dawn than at any other time of the day.

With this information in mind it was therefore intriguing to see that of the 68 anomalies recorded by Orgone 93, 25 or 37% occurred during dawn experiments whilst 42 or 63% occurred during the lunchtime sessions. These contradictory results had, however, been expected as I had realised at an early stage that the lunchtime sessions were consistently producing better results than their dawn counterparts, regardless of the site being used. This probably had something to do with the fact that those involved were more awake at lunchtimes, and there were more variables around that might have caused false readings and results, such as human activity, the presence of insects and the weather.

Orgone 94 Results

The Orgone 93 anomaly charts should now be compared against the Orgone 94 charts for the period between Saturday, 23 July and Friday, 29 July 1994. Since the style of the experiments was focused more on using just one type of experiment, the extra-terrestrial based 'open-communication' meditation at one just one site, Woodborough Hill, the same statistical analyses as those conducted for Orgone 93 have not been done. However, the results should be viewed against the control tests of Thursday, 28 July and the Furious Host meditations of Friday, 29 July. These last two mentioned experiments were the most successful in terms of instrumental responses, proving once again the potency of terrestrial-based meditation sessions. Yet in respect to photographic results it was the extra-terrestrial based experiment conducted at lunchtime on Tuesday, 26 July that was by far the most productive. In future years combinations of each of these types of meditation will be used to further compare their success rate in the Alton Barnes landscape.

Orgone 93:	Dawn Sun. 18 July	Midday Sun. 18 July	Dawn Mon. 19 July	Midday Mon. 19 July
Experiment No.	01	02	03	04
Type of Experiment	OED/Med. no arch.	Control tests	Star Exercise	Med. arch iii
Location	WS	WS	AS	WS
Experiment Start Time	04.52	12.46	04.50	12.48
Number in Meditation	04		03	07
Orgone 93 Results:				
IR Black and White	01 04.55		02 04.55 & 05.20	01 12.48
Visible Light colour				
Radiation Anomalies	Result			Result Abnormal NTD
Orgone Temperature Differential				
Air Potential				
Ultrasound	100+ at 26kHz		100+ at 26kHz	
VLF Anomalies				
Electrical Anomalies				
Visual Sightings				
Project Relate:				
Earth Currents				Bursts 01.50 20.7.93
Magnetic Anomalies				
Microwave Anomalies				
Underground Sounds				
Paul Hailey:				
Tape Anomalies				Whistle 23.59
Seisic Pulses				Signal 00.00 20.7.93
Visual Sightings				Knap 00.02 20.7.93
Other:				
Visual Sightings				
Electrical Power Failure				
Crop Circles	5sc W Kennet			
Total Number of Anomalies per Orgone 93 Experiment =	03	Nil	03	03
Total Anomalies per Day =		03		10

Orgone 93:	Dawn Tues. 20 July	Midday Tues. 20 July	Dawn Wed. 21 July	Midday Wed. 21 July
Experiment No.	05	06	07	08
Type of Experiment	Control tests	Med. arch i	Control tests	Control tests
Location	HS	HS	WS	HS
Experiment Start Time	04.50	13.00	04.50	12.50
Number in Meditation		04		
Orgone 93 Results:				
IR Black and White	02 04.52			
Visible Light colour				
Radiation Anomalies		Result Abnormal NTD		
Orgone Temperature Differential				
Air Potential				
Ultrasound	100+ at 26kHz	100+ at 26kHz	100+ at 26kHz	100+ at 26kHz
VLF Anomalies				
Electrical Anomalies				
Visual Sightings				
Project Relate:				
Earth Currents				
Magnetic Anomalies				
Microwave Anomalies				
Underground Sounds				
Paul Hailey:				
Tape Anomalies				
Seisic Pulses				
Visual Sightings				
Other:				
Visual Sightings				
Electrical Power Failure				
Crop Circles	7cs Etchilhampton			
Total Number of Anomalies per Orgone 93 Experiment =	03	03	01	01
Total Anomalies per Day =		06		02

Orgone 93:				
Experiment No.	Dawn Thurs. 22 July 09	Midday Thurs. 22 July 010	Dawn Fri. 23 July 011	Midday Fri. 23 J 012
Type of Experiment	OED	Med. arch ii	Control tests	OED/Med. arch ii
Location	WS	HS	AS	WS
Experiment Start Time	05.00	12.55	05.05	12.50
Number in Meditation		06		06
Orgone 93 Results:				
IR Black and White	01 05.35		02 05.25	05 13.15
Visible Light colour		01 13.05		01 13.05
Radiation Anomalies				
Orgone Temperature Differential		Result Abnormal NTD	Natural rise	Result Abnormal NTD
Air Potential				
Ultrasound			100+ at 26kHz	
VLF Anomalies				02 whistlers
Electrical Anomalies				
Visual Sightings				
Project Relate:				
Earth Currents				
Magnetic Anomalies				
Microwave Anomalies				
Underground Sounds				
Paul Hailey:				
Tape Anomalies				
Seisic Pulses				
Visual Sightings				
Other:				
Visual Sightings				
Electrical Power Failure				
Crop Circles				
Total Number of Anomalies per Orgone 93 Experiment =	01	03	04	08
Total Anomalies per Day =		04		11

Orgone 93:				
Experiment No.	Dawn Sat. 24 July. 013	Midday Sat. 24 July 014	Dawn Mon. 26 July 015	Midday Mon. 26 Jul 016
Type of Experiment	OED/Med. arch i	Control tests	OED	OED/Med. no arch
Location	HS	CS	HS	HS
Experiment Start Time	05.23	12.55	05.10	13.15
Number in Meditation	04			08
Orgone 93 Results:				
IR Black and White		02 13.00	01 05.45	02 13.29 & 14.01
Visible Light colour			01 05.21	02 13.43
Radiation Anomalies				
Orgone Temperature Differential				Result Abnormal NTD
Air Potential				V high 400 v/metre
Ultrasound				
VLF Anomalies			02 whistlers	
Electrical Anomalies				02 13.20 & 13.25
Visual Sightings			AC W'Boro hill 05.35	OS W'boro Hill 13.1
Project Relate:				
Earth Currents				Sounds 23.00-24.00
Magnetic Anomalies				
Microwave Anomalies				
Underground Sounds				'Doomph' 23.00-24.0
Paul Hailey:				
Tape Anomalies				
Seisic Pulses				
Visual Sightings				
Other:				
Visual Sightings				Flash 01.20 27.7.93
Electrical Power Failure				A/Barnes am 27.7.93
Crop Circles	1cf E Kennet			
Total Number of Anomalies per Orgone 93 Experiment =	00	02	03	10
Total Anomalies per Day =		02		17

Orgone 93:	Dawn Tues. 27 July	Midday Tues. 27 July	Dawn Wed. 28 July	Midday Wed. 28 July	
Experiment No.	017	018	019	020	
Type of Experiment	Med. arch ii	OED/Med arch iii	Control tests	OED/Med arch i	
Location	AS	HS	CS	WS	
Experiment Start Time	05.10	13.00	05.13	12.50	
Number in Meditation	05	05		11	
Orgone 93 Results:					
IR Black and White		01 13.40		02 13.05	
Visible Light colour		01 13.16		03 13.02, 14 & 16	
Radiation Anomalies	Result			Result	
Orgone Temperature Differential		Abnormal NTD			
Air Potential		V high 400 v/metre			
Ultrasound					
VLF Anomalies			01 05.30		
Electrical Anomalies					
Visual Sightings					
Project Relate:					
Earth Currents					
Magnetic Anomalies					
Microwave Anomalies					
Underground Sounds					
Paul Hailey:					
Tape Anomalies					
Seisic Pulses					
Visual Sightings					
Other:					
Visual Sightings		Manton 00.00 28.7		Trench E/Field 22.30	
Electrical Power Failure					
Crop Circles					
Total Number of Anomalies per Orgone 93 Experiment =	01	04	01	06	02
Total Anomalies per Day =		06		08	

Orgone 93:	Dawn Thur. 29 July	Midday Thur. 29 July	Dawn Fri. 30 July	Midday Fri. 30 July
Experiment No.	021	022	023	024
Type of Experiment	OED/Med. arch i	Med no archetype	Med. arch ii	OED/Med. no arch
Location	AS	CC	WS	AS (Avebury)
Experiment Start Time	05.20	13.00	05.25	13.30
Number in Meditation	04	05	05	70+
Orgone 93 Results:				
IR Black and White	02 05.50 & 05.55	01 13.11	01 05.35?	
Visible Light colour				
Radiation Anomalies			Result	
Orgone Temperature Differential				Abnormal NTD
Air Potential			down to -200 v/m	
Ultrasound				
VLF Anomalies				
Electrical Anomalies				
Visual Sightings				
Project Relate:				
Earth Currents		Spikes 23.00-00.00		
Magnetic Anomalies		Spikes 23.00-00.00		
Microwave Anomalies		Spikes 23.00-00.00		
Underground Sounds				
Paul Hailey:				
Tape Anomalies				
Seisic Pulses				
Visual Sightings				
Other:				
Visual Sightings		E/field 01.50 30.7		
Electrical Power Failure				
Crop Circles				
Total Number of Anomalies per Orgone 93 Experiment =		01	03	01
Total Anomalies per Day =		07		04

Orgone 94 - Details and Known Results

Orgone 94:							
Experiment No.	Midday Sat 23 July 01	Dusk Sat 23 July 02	Midday Sun 24 July 03	Dusk Sun 24 July 04	Midday Mon 25 July 05	Dusk Mon 25 July 06	Midday Tues 26 July 07
Type of Experiment	Med ET	Med ET	Med ET	Med ET	Med ET	Med ET	Med ET
Location	Woodborough Hill	W/Hill	W/Hill	W/Hill	W/Hill	W/Hill	W/Hill
Pre-control Start Time	14.20	21.44	13.55	21.10	13.25	21.20	13.40
Pre-control End/Experiment Start	14.35	22.00	14.10	21.25	13.40	21.35	13.55
Experiment End/Post-Control Start	14.53	22.21	14.32	21.48	14.04	22.00	14.20
Post Control End	15.05	22.30	14.45	22.00	14.15	22.10	14.30
Number in Meditation	06	08	11	13	11	13	09
Orgone 94 Results:							
IR Black and White 'Airbells' 01	Nil	01 21.55	01 14.45	Nil	01 13.55 01 14.00	01 21.20 01 21.25	01 13.40 04 13.45 06 13.50
IR Black and White 'Airbells' 02					02 14.10 01 14.11	01 21.35 01 21.45	09 13.55 08 14.00 04 14.15
IR Black and White 'Airbells' 03					Total of 5	Total of 4	02 14.20 02 14.25 = 36
Visible Light Colour Anomalies 1							
Visible Light Colour Anomalies 2			01 14.05 confirmed fly				
Radiation Counts	Fall	Increase	Large increase	Flat	Increase	Large increase	Data Unusable
Background EMS	Nil	Nil	HF 20 sec burst 14.29	HF 21.39	No data recorded	No data recorded	Nil
Local EMS 01	Nil	LF 21.56-22.00, 22.16	Nil	LF 21.32	Nil	LF 21.40-3, 21.47-8	Nil
Local EMS 02							
Air Potential	80-90 V/m	100-70 V/m	500-400 V/m	10-25 V/m	400-50 V/m	40 V/m	10-40 V/m
VLF Anomalies 01	01 whistler 14.56	24 whistlers	03 'pok' 14.14,20,22				odd swishing/radar?
VLF Anomalies 02			01 'clang' 14.20				
Electrical Anomalies	DB w/stop 16.20					GC w/stops 20.55	
Visual Sightings		RH or LITS 23.30				DB & Fi or LITS 22.45	
Audible Effects							
Psycho/Physiological Effects 1			GC metallic taste		Dun B metallic taste		DB & Su m/taste
Psycho/Physiological Effects 2					Deb B nausea		TB flu symptoms
Other:							
Visual Sightings 01		T & KP BOL Ave 02.30					
Visual Sightings 02							
Crop Circles		Avebury Avenue					

Orgone 94:							
Experiment No.	Dusk Tues 26 July 08	Midday Wed 27 July 09	Dusk Wed 27 July 10	Midday Thur 28 July 11	Dusk Thur 28 July 12	Midday Fri 29 July 13	Dusk Fri 29 July 14
Type of Experiment	Med ET	Med ET	Med ET	Controls	Controls	Med Ter 'Wild Hunt'	Med Ter 'Wild Hunt'
Location	W/Hill	W/Hill	W/Hill	W/Hill	W/Hill	W/Hill	W/Hill
Pre-control Start Time	21.09	14.00	21.25	13.30	21.25	14.15	21.27
Pre-control End/Experiment Start	21.24	14.15	21.40	13.45	21.40	14.35	21.42
Experiment End/Post-Control Start	21.49	14.38	22.10	14.05	22.00	14.57	22.11
Post Control End	21.59	14.50	22.20	14.15	22.10	15.10	22.21
Number in Meditation	10?	07	11	N/A	N/A	06	09
Orgone 93 Results:							
IR Black and White Anomalies 01	01 21.54	Nil	01 21.25 01 21.30	01 13.35 04 13.40	01 21.35 01 21.40	02 14.40 01 14.55	Nil
IR Black and White Anomalies 02			03 21.50 03 21.55	02 13.45		01 15.00	
IR Black and White Anomalies 03			Total of 8	Total of 7	Total of 2	Total of 4	
Visible Light Colour Anomalies 1	or. streak 22.52-59	01 14.05 01 14.20					
Visible Light Colour Anomalies 2		01 14.25 prob flies					
Radiation Counts	Data unusable	Data unusable	Increase	Fall	Flat	Increase	Increase X 2
Background EMS	Nil	Nil	Poss local related	Nil	Nil	Nil	Nil
Local EMS 01	HF burst 21.24	Nil	LF 21.41-2, 43, 44,	Nil	slight LF 21.48-50	Nil	LF 21.42-4, 47-8, 55, 57
Local EMS 02			21.28-9, 50-1, 52-3				22.09-10, 13
Air Potential	5-40 V/m	200-100 V/m	200-100 V/m	200-160 V/m	90-45 V/m	500-1200 V/m	50-20 V/m
VLF Anomalies 01			30 plus whistlers			'chuk' 14.18	
VLF Anomalies 02							
Electrical Anomalies	GWR link fault 22.55						
Visual Sightings	BOL flash 22.58				PH gold BOL 22.11		
Audible Sounds							Voices/horn/etc 21.51-5
Psycho/Physiological Effects 1	KD w/stops 03.25						
Psycho/Physiological Effects 2							
Other:							
Visual Sightings	ZM LITS S/Tump 22.28		SA BOL flash 02.45 CSETI LITS Ave				T & K B LITS 24.00 ES & JM gr LITS W/O
Crop Circles			W/Overton figure 8				

Appendix II

The Air-bell Experiments

In the wake of the various black and white photographic anomalies produced during the Orgone 93 experimentation of July 1993, Roger Wilkins conducted a series of experiments during August and September that year in an attempt to evaluate the possibility that so-called air-bells were the cause of these curious visual effects. He used the same type of IR film, the same camera (my Nikon FG20 with 50 mm lens) and the same developing solution made up in the cottage at Alton Barnes during the experimentation. In the first instance three films were exposed against a blank surface and then developed in a slightly different manner.

The first film was placed in the developing tank and, as recommended by the manufacturers, the spool was agitated every 30 seconds. The resulting negatives displayed eight tiny pin-holes set against a blank background. These were randomly scattered throughout the film and matched the smallest anomalies produced during the July experiments. None, however, came near to the size of the larger examples achieved, such as the circular anomaly produced at Woodborough Hill on Monday, 26 July.

For the next experiment, Wilkins shook the developer before placing the second exposed film in the developing tank. In theory this should have increased the likelihood of air pockets being trapped in the developing solution. As before, the spool was turned once every 30 seconds. The resulting negatives showed 17 tiny pin-holes, each randomly spaced, with one comparable in size to the large circular anomaly produced during Experiment 16 on 26 July.

In the next experiment, the third and final film was placed in the same previously shaken solution of liquid developer, although this time the spool was agitated only once every minute. In theory this should have dramatically increased the likelihood of air-bells, but instead only seven tiny pin-holes were produced - a result not anticipated by Wilkins.

At a slightly later date Wilkins tried a similar experiment using his partner Judi's Canon A35F camera, instead of my Nikon. He exposed two 36-frame, black and white, IR-sensitive films and, as before, exposed each frame against a blank surface. Using the last of the developer made up at Alton Barnes in mid July, the first film produced five tiny pin-holes. For the second film Wilkins shook up the solution before placing it in the developing tank. This produced a total of 25 small blobs and one fairly large example.

Rodney Hale was still unconvinced by the air-bell solution. Over the years he had taken and developed thousands of black and white photographs for historical archiving without suffering from air-bells. Curious as to what results he could achieve using the same IR-sensitive film, as well as the same recommended developing solution, he repeated Wilkins's experimentation. To his complete surprise he produced three tiny pin-holes for the first time ever. Despite these results he remains unconvinced that the circular marks actually represent air-bells. Instead, he proposes that these minuscule specks are, in fact, film faults.

Roger Wilkins responded by conducting further experiments using standard Ilford black and white HP5 film to see if this too could produce similar photographic artefacts. The results were completely negative - no air-bells or emulsion stains were produced in any way, shape or form. This added weight to Rodney Hale's suggestion that the root of the problem was the Kodak HIE high speed film, not the developer or the developing process being used. We have tried to inform Kodak of this possible fault, but they say they no longer have a department dealing with photographic artefacts, suggesting instead that we take the matter up with the supplier who would, if necessary, make an official complaint to themselves. The company's clearly dismissive attitude made us reluctant to pursue this line of enquiry any further.

Fade to Grey

I spoke about the air-bell problem to Terry Cox, who over the years had produced a number of similar IR photographs in his home county of Cornwall. He accepted the findings, but said that air-bells possess entirely different characteristics to true anomalies. He pointed out that if known air-bells are printed on very so-called 00 paper they will appear a light grey like the rest of the frame's imagery. If, however, the same process is applied to a true anomaly, then it will remain a solid black, while the rest of the picture will fade to a faint grey.

This information did not make any photographic sense; however, I conveyed these facts to Roger Wilkins who subsequently used Pegasus Photographic Laboratory's darkrooms to put the theory to the test. He took the largest air-bell produced so far and printed it on OO paper. As predicted, it faded to grey. He then took the negative of the large black ball captured above Woodborough Hill at 13.29 on Monday, 26 July and printed this using the same type of paper. Sure enough, just as Cox had suggested, it remained a solid black while the rest of the picture, which shows the trees capping the summit of the hill, faded to a pale grey.

Quite obviously this simple test was not going to convince the outside world of the authenticity of any photographic anomaly when a perfectly logical explanation had already presented itself. Despite this, it did give us further grounds to question the air-bell solution to many of the strange images we had captured on IR-sensitive, black and white film during the summer of 1993.

The contents of this appendix should be reviewed in the context of the Orgone 94 photographic experimentation outlined in Chapter 33.

Notes and References

Preface - The Tale of Eugenio de la Terra
1. Bach, E., *Philippine UFOs (St Elmos) of the Volcanoes*, 1994, p. 24. Paper presented at the first international workshop on the unidentified atmospheric light phenomena at Hessdalen, Norway, on Friday, 25 March 1994.
2. Ibid., p. 17, 20-1.
3. Ibid., pp. 1-2.

Introduction
1. Collins, A., 'UFOs and Psychic Abilities - What is the Link?', *Strange Phenomena*, Vol 1 No 1, pp. 8-10.
2. Phillips, G., 'Psygenics', *Strange Phenomena*, Vol 1 No 2, pp. 9-11.
3. Collins, A., *The Circlemakers*, pp. 51-2.
4. Phillips, G., and A. Collins, 'The Deeper Mysteries of Loch Ness', *Why? A Television Documentary Series*, privately published, 1980.
5. Ibid.
6. Ibid.
7. Phillips, G., 'The Stones', *Strange Phenomena*, Vol 1 No 2, pp. 17-22.

Chapter 1 - Reich's Legacy
1. Sharaf, M., *Fury on Earth, A Biography of Wilhelm Reich*, p. 224. See also W. Reich, *Ether, God and Devil*, pp. 151-2.
2. Kelley, C.R., 'What is Orgone Energy?', *The Creative Process*, Vol II No 1. Quoted in W. E. Mann and E. Hoffman's *Wilhelm Reich - The Man who Dreamed of Tomorrow*, p. 259.
3. Reich, W., *Contact with Space: ORANUR Second Report 1951-1956*, p. 37.
4. Constable, T.J., *The Cosmic Pulse of Life*, p. 321.
5. Reich, W., *The Orgone Accumulator*, pp. 16-20.
6. Constable, T. J., *The Cosmic Pulse of Life*, p. 318, and W. Reich, *Ether, God and Devil*, pp. 151-2.
7. Baker, Dr E. F., *The Journal of Orgonomy*, Vol 1 Nos 1-2, November 1967.
8. Constable, T.J., *The Cosmic Pulse of Life*, p. 336.
9. Ibid., p. 342.
10. Ibid., p. 340.
11. Reich, W., *Contact with Space: ORANUR Second Report 1951-1956*, p. 23.
12. Ibid., p. xxiii.
13. Ibid., p. 22.
14. Ibid., pp. 67-77.
15. Ibid., pp. 55-65.
16. Ibid., p. 61.
17. Ibid., p. 7.
18. Ibid., p. 3.
19. Ibid., pp. 23-30.
20. Ibid., p. 26.
21. Ibid., pp. 90-1, 132.
22. Ibid., pp. 34-5.
23. Ibid., p. 35.
24. Ibid., p. 36.
25. Ibid., p. 36.
26. Ibid., p. 44-5.
27. Constable, T. J., *The Cosmic Pulse of Life*, p. 347.
28. Reich, W., *Contact with Space: ORANUR Second Report 1951-1956*, pp. 208-11.
29. Ibid., pp. 162, 165-9, 258.
30. Ibid., p. 95.

Chapter 2 - The Constable Controversy
1. Constable, T.J., *The Cosmic Pulse of Life*, p. 47.
2. Reich, W., *Contact with Space, ORANUR Second Report 1951-1956*, pp. 37-9.
3. Constable, T.J., *The Cosmic Pulse of Life*, pp. 97-8.
4. Constable, T.J., *Sky Creatures: Living UFOs*, p.12.
5. Eden, J., Review of *The Cosmic Pulse of Life*, *Journal of Orgonomy*, Vol 11 No 1, pp. 121-31.
6. Ibid.
7. Constable, T.J., *The Cosmic Pulse of Life*, p. 130.

8. Ibid., p. 297.
9. Lagarde, F., *Flying Saucer Review*, Vol 14 No 4, 1968.
10. Michell, J., *The View Over Atlantis*, p. 188-9.
11. Bach, E., *Philippine UFOs (St Elmos) of the Volcanoes*, 1994, p. 6-7, 13-4.
12. Devereux, P., and P. McCartney, *Earth Lights*, pp. 188-9.
13. Devereux, P., *Earth Lights Revelation*, pp. 197-8.
14. Devereux, P., and P. McCartney, *Earth Lights*, p. 60.
15. Persinger, M., and G. Lafreniere, *Space-Time Transients and Unusual Events*.
16. Meaden, T., 'Crop Circles and the Plasma Vortex', *The Crop Circle Enigma*, p. 77.

Chapter 3 - The Bioform Connection

1. See J. Randles and P. Whetnall's *Alien Contact - Window on Another World*.
2. Andrews, C., and P. Delgado, *Circular Evidence*, p. 50.
3. Kronig, J., ed., *Spuren Im Korn*, p. 168.
4. Ibid., p. 169.
5. Constable, T.J., *The Cosmic Pulse of Life*, p. 364.
6. '1966, Tully...', *Australian Flying Saucer Review*, Sydney edition, No 9, November 1966.
7. Ibid. Other later sources spoke of an anti-clockwise rotation.
8. Basterfield, K., *Circles Down Under*, UFO Research Australia, January 1992. Five new circular areas were found in a lagoon area at Euramo, Tully. They formed an arc and ranged from three to nearly five metres in diameter.
9. Henry, G., *Girroo Gurrll: The First Surveyor and Other Aboriginal Legends*, p. 55.
10. Devereux, P., *Earth Lights Revelation*, pp. 153-9.
11. Personal communication with Paul Fuller and supplemented with lists published in various issues of *The Crop Watcher*.
12. Basterfield, K., 'Circles Down Under', private paper published in 1992 and updated in 1993.
13. Rutkowski, C., 'Combined and Sorted List of North American UGMs', privately published 1993 and combining Ted Phillips' *Physical Trace Catalogue* published by the Center for UFO Studies in the 1970s.

Chapter 4 - Curse of the Fairies

1. Randles, J., and P. Fuller, *Crop Circles A Mystery Solved*, p. 150.
2. Devereux, P., *Earth Lights Revelation*, p. 82.
3. Wingfield, G., 'The English Crop Circles in 1988', *The UFO Report 1990*, ed. T. Good, p. 57.
4. In early 1994 a copy of the 1678 mowing devil pamphlet came up for auction in Salisbury. Previous to this only three original copies were known to exist, two in the United States, at Princeton and Yale Universities, and one in the British Museum. However, shortly before the sale the auctioneers realised that the example in their possession was in fact a facsimile printed in London between 1810-20. Further enquiries revealed that only a small number had been reprinted, begging the question why an obscure tale about the plight of a Hertfordshire farmer should have warranted republication 140 years later. Could it be possible that an incident of a similar nature had triggered a fresh demand for this pamphlet somewhere between 1810 and 1820? I dug around and found that in 1811 an account of an apparent Will-o'-the-Wisp occurrence in Lincolnshire is preserved in a woodcut that occasionally features in UFO-related books including David Clarke and Granville Oldroyd's *Spooklights, A British Survey*. Whether publicity surrounding this incident had any bearing on the republication of the Mowing Devil account is a matter of speculation. See also *The Crop Watcher*, Issue 22, Summer 1994, pp. 15-6.
5. Westwood, J., *Albion: A Guide to Legendary Britain*, p. 66.
6. Lucas, E.V., *Highways & Byways of Sussex*, pp. 426-8.
7. Ibid., pp. 425-6.

Chapter 5 - The Plughole Effect

1. Clift, D., and L. Pringle, 'Human Effects of Crop Circles - The Story So Far', *The Circular*, Vol 3 No 3, October 1992, pp. 12-4. Also L. Pringle 'Reactions to Crop Circle Visits An Analysis of 187 Experiences', 1994.
2. Kronig, J., from a paper given at the Cornference, Dorchester, Dorset, Sunday, 10 October 1993.
3. From a letter dated 16 September 1994 as well as subsequent telephone calls with the circlemaker in question.
4. Sharaf, M., *Fury on Earth, A Biography of Wilhelm Reich*, p. 281.
5. Reich, W., *The Orgone Accumulator*, pp. 16-20, and personal communication with orgone specialist Joel Carlinsky in August 1993.
6. Reich, W., *Contact with Space: ORANUR Second Report 1951-1956*, pp. 45, 232.
7. Constable, T.J., *The Cosmic Pulse of Life*, p. 318.
8. Devereux, P., *Places of Power*, pp. 154-5.
9. Ibid., p. 155.
10. Ibid., p. 155.
11. Bach, E., *Philippine UFOs (St Elmos) of the Volcanoes*, 1994, p. 16.

Chapter 6 - In the Eye of the Dragon

1. Michell, J., *The View Over Atlantis*, p. 77.
2. De Meo, J., *The Orgone Accumulator Handbook*, p. 43.

3. Robins, D., 'The Dragon Project and the Talking Stones', *New Scientist,* Vol 96 No 1328, 21 October 1982, pp. 166-71.
4. Sullivan, D.P., 'Chasing the Dragon', *The Ley Hunter,* No 120, Midwinter 1993/4, p. 13.
5. Seto, A., *et al,* 'Detection of Extraordinary Large Bio-magnetic Field Strength from Human Hand during External Qi Emission', *Acupuncture & Electro-therapeutics Res. Int. Journal,* Vol 17, 1992, pp. 75-94.
6. Reich, W., *Contact with Space: ORANUR Second Report 1951-1956,* p. 37.
7. Gribbin, J., *In Search of the Big Bang,* pp. 326-31.
8. O'Brien, J., with Kwok Man Ho, *The Elements of Feng Shui,* p. 37.

Chapter 7 - A Guiding Light
1. Bach, E., *Philippine UFOs (St Elmos) of the Volcanoes,* 1994, pp. 6, 17, 21-2, 24-5.
2. Ibid., p. 28.
3. Kaarbo, M., 'Observations in 1991', *UFO-Norway News,* No 1/2, 1991, pp. 29-31.
4. Ibid., p. 29.
5. Strand, E., 'Project Hessdalen, Instrumentation of Possible Ball Lightning', preliminary paper prepared for Vizotum '93, Montafon, Austria, 20-3.9.1993.
6. Strand, E., *Project Hessdalen 1984 Final Technical Report Part 1,* p. 16.
7. Ibid., pp. 20-1.
8. Ibid., p. 26.
9. Ibid., p. 22.
10. Devereux, P., *Earth Lights Revelation,* p. 143.
11. Gribbin, J., 'Atomic Telepathy is Faster than Light', *New Scientist,* Vol 141 No 1914, 26 February 1994, p. 16.
12. Gribbin, J., *In Search of Schrodinger's Cat,* p. 261.

Chapter 8 - The Wiltshire Mystery
1. Shuttlewood, A., *The Flying Saucerers,* p. 39.
2. Clarke, D., and G. Oldroyd, *Spooklights, A British Survey,* pp. 19, 21-2, 30, 32.
3. Shuttlewood, A., *Warnings from Flying Friends,* pp. 265-6.
4. Wingfield, G., 'The English Crop Circles in 1988', *The UFO Report 1990,* ed. T. Good, pp. 84.
5. Wiltshire, K., *Ghosts and Legends of the Wiltshire Countryside,* p. 19.
6. Ibid., p. 18.
7. Ibid., p. 31.
8. Ibid., p. 12.
9. Ibid., p. 35.
10. Ibid., p. 12.
11. The allegations made against the United Bureau of Investigation, alias the United Believers in Intelligence or UBI, were based solely on the fact that its group members, Wiltshire youths Paul Randall and Matthew Watkins, were found to have constructed a formation for communication purposes in oil seed rape at Urchfont, Wiltshire, during May 1992. Previous to this they had admitted making a small grass circle near Warminster in 1991 and adding extra features to a dumb-bell formation that had appeared at Avebury Trusloe that same summer. In this knowledge, the group came under deep suspicion at a time when, in the wake of recent hoaxing revelations from Southampton sexagenarians Doug Bower and Dave Chorley, the race was on among the crop circle sceptics to unmask the identities of those responsible for the many formations discovered in Wiltshire during the summer of 1990 and 1991. Unfortunately these youths were subsequently seen in the proximity of certain 1992 formations by those out to catch them in the act, and this led to accusations made against them in one national newspaper and in a crop circle book published in 1993.

Since then no primary researcher in the crop circle subject has bothered to ask them their side of the story, which was why they were more than happy to open their hearts in a taped conversation with the author recorded during the evening of Thursday, 28 July 1994. They seemed most anxious to clear their names in the light of their sudden elevation to the rank of master hoaxers in many people's eyes. Paul Randall and Matthew Watkins both deny having constructed any formation as the UBI subsequent to the Urchfont design of 1992. However, individually Watkins admits to having made one small formation, just prior to meeting Randall for the first time on Colin Andrew's Operation Blackbird staged at Bratton Castle in late July 1990. He says it was a small 'stick man' placed in the corner of a field at Bishops Canning, near Devizes, in May that year.

The UBI group was originally formed to investigate not only crop circles, but also the possibilities of extra-terrestrial contact with the earth. One of its main aims was to see whether alleged ET intelligences, believed by them to be behind the construction of 'genuine' crop circle events, would respond if they were to either make their own formation or add features on to an existing example. It was for these reasons alone that the early experiments at Avebury Trusloe in 1991 and Urchfont in 1992 were undertaken.

Since 1993 Paul Randall and Matthew Watkin's activities have centred around furthering the idea of meditational contact with ET intelligences using crystal-linked devices constructed from ideas gleamed from alleged psychic communications. Randall believes whole-heartedly in the reality of such intelligences and has himself experienced various UFO-related events since early childhood.

Having spoken at great length with both members of the UBI, and having monitored one of their crystal-linked meditational experiments at Alton Barnes in July 1994, I see no good reason to doubt their word in this matter. I found them to be open-minded individuals with a flare and enthusiasm for the crop circle debate. I do not believe they constructed the Alton Barnes pictogram of July 1990 and I do not believe they are the enigmatic A-team. So if not them, then who?

Another name linked with the UBI was geometrist and crop circle researcher John Martineau, whose wife experienced the strange light phenomenon in the 1990 Alton Barnes formation. He has been accused of masterminding the A-team and constructing some of the major Wiltshire formations of 1990 and 1991 - the sceptics claiming that he was the only one with any knowledge of the complex geometry encoded in these landscape designs.

In a taped interview with the author on Saturday, 30 July 1994, Martineau openly admitted his friendship with Randall and Watkins, adding that it was he who tipped off the CCCS concerning their construction of the Urchfront oil seed rape formation in 1992. When Randall and Watkins discovered Martineau's betrayal, they were naturally quite annoyed, so severed their links with him. That summer Martineau spent much of his time surveying crop formations in Hampshire and Wiltshire. This included a large pictogram that appeared beneath the Old Sarum Iron Age camp in July.

A few days after Martineau had entered the formation, an American female psychic visited the huge pictogram and pronounced it to be of man-made construction, adding that she could clairvoyantly see individuals with poles moving about in the darkness. Shortly afterwards this American psychic pointed out Martineau at a CCCS conference, claiming that he was one of the 'hoaxers' she had 'seen' in the Old Sarum formation. Quite obviously, Martineau denied these bizarre allegations, pointing out that the woman had probably glimpsed some place memory of him surveying the formation after its discovery; indeed, the rest of her psychic imagery appeared to match the description of a person who had erected a tent inside one of the circles that same night.

In the wake of this extraordinary incident, Martineau was seen by some as the leading contender for the mastermind behind the A-team's clandestine activities. To make matters worse, Martineau failed to adequately respond to these accusations and simply made light of the matter in the crop circle press. However, no real evidence has ever been forthcoming to implicate Martineau in crop circle hoaxing, and since 1993 he has dedicated his time to the geometry of prehistoric sites and the solar system. I can therefore see no further point in linking either his name, of that of Paul Randall and his colleagues, with the existence of any hypothetical A-team unless evidence surfaces to indicate the contrary.

This does not now preclude the probability of these formations being of man-made construction, only that in their haste to identify the Wiltshire hoaxers the crop circle sceptics pointed accusing fingers without sufficient evidence to back-up their claims. Unfortunately, since other primary researchers accepted their informed positions in this affair (most of them are circlemakers themselves), these vague claims were hastily, and quite blindly, accepted by many, allowing the casebook on this matter to be conveniently closed. Now, I'm afraid, it will have to be re-opened again.

Chapter 9 - Euphoria

1. From a telephone interview with Gary Williamson on Tuesday, 12 April 1994.
2. Letter from A. N. Gibson, Business Manager (UK MOD) of Pains-Wessex Schermuly of Salisbury to Ralph Noyes of the CCCS, reference ANG/ajh/CROP, dated 1 August 1991.
3. Westwood, J., *Albion: A Guide to Legendary Britain*, p. 65.
4. Some months after the appearance of the famous Barbury Castle formation a rumour surfaced suggesting that military police from nearby RAF Wroughton had seen empty vehicles close to where the pictogram appeared just a few hours later. Intrigued by this story, I made enquiries at the base and discovered that no such report appears in the military police's occurrence log for the night in question. A spokesman (name on file) informed me that he was completely baffled by this claim. The military police do not venture beyond the limits of the perimeter fence and any vehicle noted just outside the base is unlikely to have been linked with nefarious activities at Barbury Castle, which lies one mile south of Wroughton. He did, however, reveal that in 1991 there was also a Royal Naval Air Yard on the base who came under direct MOD control, and although he has been unable to trace their occurrence log for the date in question, he stresses that the same argument applies in that any suspect vehicle noted beyond the perimeter fence is unlikely to have been linked with Barbury Castle.

Chapter 10 - Nocturnal Lightshows

1. Greer, S., *Close Encounters of the 5th Kind: Contact in Southern England, July 1992*, p. 10.
2. From an interview with Chris Mansell on Sunday, 1 August 1993 and supplemented by the account given on pp. 7-9 of *The Circular*, Vol 3 No 3, October 1992.
3. Greer, S., *Close Encounters of the 5th Kind: Contact in Southern England, July 1992*, p. 18.
4. From an interview with Chris Mansell on Saturday, 1 August 1993 and supplemented by the account given on pp. 7-9 of *The Circular*, Vol 3 No 3, October 1992.
5. Strand, E., 'Project Hessdalen, Instrumentation of Possible Ball Lightning', preliminary paper prepared for Vizotum '93, Montafon, Austria, 20-3.9.1993.
6. Devereux, P., *Earth Lights Revelation*, p. 220.
7. In the wake of the extraordinary Woodborough sighting of 26/27 July 1992 rumours began to circulate suggesting that what Greer, Mansell *et al* had actually seen that night was a bank of disco lights positioned on nearby Urchfont Hill. Urchfont Hill is 8.8 km south-west of Woodborough Hill. It rises to a height of 215 m and forms part of the downland marking the northern-most limits of Salisbury Plain - so could a bank of disco lights really be to blame?

Chris Mansell said he had seen a small orange light depart from the main object and enter the fog, before re-appearing and returning to its original position. This prompted me to check the weather conditions that night with the Meteorological Office at nearby RAF Lyneham. According to a spokesman (name on file), at midnight BST on the 26th slight rain and drizzle had reduced the visibility to just 3 km. Then, as the rain had gradually receded, the visibility had slowly increased to 6 km by 01.00 local time. Although this report applies to the weather above Lyneham, which lies some 17.6 km north-north-west of Alton Barnes, the same conditions almost certainly prevailed in the nearby Pewsey Vale.

If this is correct, then one does not need to be a mathematician to work out that between midnight and 01.00 on 26/27 July any disco lights positioned on Urchfont Hill *would not have been visible* from Woodborough Hill owing to poor visibility and rising fog. In addition to this, Lyneham recorded a 5/8th cloud-cover at 120 m and a 8/8th cover at 180 m. This is so low that it virtually rules out the possibility that the lights belonged to either a low-flying aircraft or a helicopter. Moreover, even if the weather *had* permitted the viewing of disco lights positioned on a hill 8.8 km away, then they would have appeared to anyone at Woodborough as tiny pin-points of flashing light positioned on the very edge of Salisbury Plain - something that any reasonable observer would have instantly dismissed as unidentified military activity.

Other crop circle sceptics have suggested that what Greer, Mansell *et al* witnessed was a cluster of illuminated balloons. Certainly, experiments with balloons were conducted in the Alton Barnes area during the second half of 1992, although these only occurred in response to the publicity surrounding the CSETI sightings of late July that year. Since the same individuals responsible for the illuminated balloons were also responsible for spreading the rumour about disco lights being to blame for the sighting of 26/27 July, then it hardly seems likely that they should have concocted such a story if they *knew* balloons to be the true answer. Indeed, the main perpetrator of the disco lights story has admitted to me that he believes Greer to have been 'set up' by someone in his own camp, a completely unsubstantiated claim that clearly shows that he has no real explanation for what occurred that night. Many people would not believe Greer no matter what he claimed to have seen. Mansell, however, is a level-headed character who just happened to be at the right place at the right time. Having spoken to him on more than one occasion concerning this affair, I am satisfied that whatever he saw that night was aerial, moving and at least 10 times nearer to them than Urchfont Hill.

Chapter 11 - Tawsmead Stirs

1. From an interview with Julie Wakefield on Saturday, 2 January 1993 and supplemented by the account that appears on p. 6 of *The Circular*, Vol 3 No 3, October 1992.
2. From an interview with John and Julie Wakefield on Tuesday, 4 January 1994. This information was not given earlier as the Wakefields felt it was a personal experience to be conveyed to close friends only.
3. Crop circle sceptics were to later claim that what people witnessed during the late evening of Tuesday, 28 July 1992 was probably an orange balloon containing a battery-operated light bulb, or a tray of ignited sodium, deliberately brought into the area to fool the gullible. Such a suggestion is highly improbable as I know from personal communications with the individuals involved that these mischievous antics were not initiated until after news of Greer's sighting became publicly known at the very end of July 1992. Indeed, some reports would tend to suggest that these nocturnal exploits did not begin until November that year.
4. From a written report by Steve Trench dated 28 April 1994.
5. The Trench family's approach to John Wakefield, Nick Riley *et al* was confirmed to me on Tuesday, 4 January 1994. The couple recall them turning up at East Field and giving a preview of their new video evidence.

Chapter 12 - Bouncing Balls

1. From an interview with Paul Vigay on Sunday, 10 October 1993 and supplemented by his own written account.
2. From a telephone interview with Judith Daw in September 1993.
3. Clarke, D., and G. Oldroyd, *Spooklights, A British Survey*, p. 2.

Chapter 13 - A Geological Perspective

1. Devereux, P., *Earth Lights*, p. 195.
2. Barron, R.S., *The Geology of Wiltshire: A Field Guide*, J. Chandler, *The Vale of Pewsey*, and H. J. Osborne White, *The Geology of the Country Around Marlborough.*
3. Devereux, P., *Earth Lights Revelation*, p. 83.
4. Osborne White., H. J., *The Geology of the Country Around Marlborough*, p. 57.
5. Ibid., p. 65.
6. Devereux, P., *Earth Lights Revelation*, p. 164.
7. Constable, T.J., *The Cosmic Pulse of Life*, pp. 369-70.
8. Grist, B., 'The Aquifer Attractor', *The Cerealogist*, No 5, Winter, 1991/2, pp. 18-9.

Chapter 14 - A Psychic Interface

1. Devereux, P., *Earth Lights Revelation*, p. 154.
2. see K. and S. McClure, *Stars, and Rumours of Stars* for a full account of Mary Jones' connection with the Egryn lights of 1904-5.
3. Evans, Beriah, article on Mary Jones and the Egryn lights in March 1905 issue of *Occult Review*, and quoted in *Stars, and Rumours of Stars* by K. and S. McClure, p. 9.
4. McClure, K., and S. McClure, *Stars, and Rumours of Stars*, pp. 26-7.
5. Ibid., pp. 25-6.
6. Devereux, P. *Earth Lights Revelation*, pp. 171-4.

7. McClure, K., and S. McClure, *Stars, and Rumours of Stars*, p. 36.
8. Devereux, P., *Places of Power*, p. 45.
9. Schwarz, B. E., 'SORRAT Report', *Anomaly*, No 3, March 1987, pp. 32-6. See also *SORRAT: A History of the Neihardt Psychokinesis Experiments, 1961-1981* by J. T. Richards.
10. Andrews, G., Report on SORRAT project in *Anomaly*, No 3, March 1987, pp. 37-40.

Chapter 15 - Pointing at the Sky
1. Reich, W., *Contact with Space: ORANUR Second Report 1951-1956*, pp. 179-80
2. Constable, T.J., *The Cosmic Pulse of Life*, p. 346.
3. Ibid., pp. 346-7.
4. see J. Eden's *Scavengers From Space.*

Chapter 16 - Monitoring the Unseen
1. Details originally given by Hessdalen project director Leif Havik at the BUFORA International UFO Congress 1983 and confirmed by telephone with Norwegian researcher Ole Jonny Braenne on Sunday, 20 February 1994.
2. Devereux, P. *Places of Power*, p. 51.
3. Collins, *The Circlemakers*, pp. 85-6.
4. Graves, T., *Needles of Stone*, pp. 103-11.
5. Conversion Research, PO Box 535, Descanso, CA 91916, USA. WR-3 VLF radio receivers are available postage paid at $66 overseas and $58 interstate (7.5% sales tax for California).
6. Hendricks, E. C., 'Marfa Lights Seen, Whistlers Heard', *Crop Circle Secrets Part Two, America's First Crop Circle*, pp. 85-9.

Chapter 17 - The Eye of the Camera
1. Constable, T.J., *Sky Creatures: Living UFOs*, pp. 176-84.

Chapter 18 - Choosing the Sites
1. *Victoria History of Wiltshire*, x. pp. 8.
2. Personal communication with David Carson of the Old Rectory, Alton Barnes.
3. From a conversation with John Wakefield who saw a bright flash of light with a ball-like centre at this position around midnight on Sunday, 26 December 1993. Without any knowledge of this occurrence, his colleagues Nick Riley and Chris Hitchen saw a similar localised flash at the same spot approximately one hour later (see also Chapter 26).
4. Wiltshire, K., *Ghosts and Legends of the Wiltshire Countryside*, p. 21-2.

Chapter 21 - Does the Camera Never Lie?
1. *i.e.* the examples taken during Experiment 10 at 13.05, during Experiment 12 at 13.05, during Experiment 15 at 05.21 and during Experiment 20 at 13.14 and 13.16.

Chapter 22 - Ultrasound
1. Devereux, P., *Places of Power*, pp. 76-7.
2. Hale, R. B., 'A Report on Two Anomalous Signals Recorded from a VLF Electrostatic Receiver', Orgone 93. July 1993. Plus a second, follow-up report dated August 1993.

Chapter 23 - Raising the Radiation
1. Beddoe, T., 'Orgone 93 ORTEC Project Report', 1993.
2. Hale, R. B., Report on Experiment 12 conducted at the Water Site on Friday, 23 July 1993.
3. Hale, R. B., 'Report on Meditation Meeting and Gamma Count at... Leigh-on-Sea. 28 November 1993'.
4. Ibid.
5. Hale, R. B., 'Technical report on Meditational exercise of 27th March 1994'.
6. Hale, R. B., 'Notes on data accumulated for Radioactivity on seven occasions of Meditational exercise. 15.4.94.'
7. Tiller, W. A., 'A Gas Discharge Device for Investigating Focused Human Attention', *Journal of Scientific Exploration*, Vol 4 No 2, 1990, pp. 255-71. I am indebted to Dr Roger Taylor for bringing this work to my attention in May 1994.
8. Ibid., p. 267.
9. Ibid., p. 268-9.

Chapter 24 - The ORANUR Effect
1. Beddoe, T., 'Orgone 93 ORTEC Project Report', prepared for Orgone 93.

Chapter 25 - The Monitoring Game
1. Personal communication with John and Julie Wakefield on Tuesday, 4 January 1994. I suggest the leaving of badger's fur was simply to arouse the undue interests of the crop circle community and did not have any sinister motives.
2. Hale, R.B., 'Report on Computerised Monitoring for Project Relate July 11 to August 5 1993', 19 September 1993.
3. Hailey, P., extract of report summary of 1993 monitoring operation at Alton Barnes.

4. Hale, R.B., 'Report on Computerised Monitoring for Project Relate July 11 to August 5 1993', 19 September 1993.

Chapter 26 - The Big Flash
1. From a telephone interview with Reg Presley in November 1993.
2. From an interview with Sven Reuss on Saturday, 31 July 1993.
3. From an interview with Nick Riley on Sunday, 10 October 1993.
4. From a telephone interview with Mr Kevin Small of Southern Electricity in November 1993.
5. From a telephone interview with a spokesman (name on file) for the meteorological station at RAF Lyneham in November 1993.
6. Randles, J., *The Pennine UFO Mystery,* p. 195.
7. Ibid., p. 195-9.
8. Collins, A., 'The Great Totham Mystery - An Earth Light, Crop Circle, Mystery Photograph and Folklore Continuity in Deepest Essex', *Earthquest News,* Vol 2 No 2, Winter 1992, pp. 7-20.
9. Halliwell, J.O., *Rambles in Western Cornwall by the Footsteps of the Giants, etc.*, p. 204.
10. Strand, E., *Project Hessdalen 1984 Final Technical Report Part One,* p. 44.
11. Kaarbo, M., *Nordic UFO Newsletter,* No 1, 1988, p. 28-9.
12. McClure, K., and S. McClure, *Stars, and Rumours of Stars,* p. 22.
13. Hale, R.B., *Project Relate 1993 - Further Report on the 'Black Box' Tapes,* 1.10.93.
14. Constable, T.J., *Sky Creatures: Living UFOs,* p. 13.
15. Petit, C., 'Videotaped Proof of Heavenly Lights', *San Francisco Chronicle,* 25 September 1993.
16. Watts, S., 'Scientists mystified by "red jellyfish" in the sky', *The Independent,* 11 August 1994, p. 3.
17. From an article in *The Times* of 19 January 1994, summarised by J. Randles in *Northern UFO News,* No 164, New Year 1994, p.4.

Chapter 27 - The Cosmic Joker
1. From an interview with Mike Saunders in November 1993.
2. From a telephone conversation with Gillian Trench on Monday, 25 April 1994.
3. Hale, R.B., 'Report on Computerised Monitoring for Project Relate July 11 to August 5 1993', 19 September 1993.
4. From a telephone interview with Leonie Starr in November 1993.
5. From a report prepared by Andrew Buckley in March 1994.
6. Hale, R.B., 'Report on Computerised Monitoring for Project Relate July 11 to August 5 1993', 19 September 1993.
7. See F. W. Holiday's *The Dragon and the Disc.*

Chapter 29 - Orgone 94
1. From a telephone interview with Malcolm Emery at 22.00 on the night of his first sighting.
2. Personal communication with the witness who is a woman of local standing who does not wish to be named.
3. From a telephone interview with Malcolm Emery in February 1994.
4. From an interview with John Martineau on Saturday, 30 July 1994.
5. Bach, E., *Philippine UFOs (St Elmos) of the Volcanoes,* 1994, pp. 6, 11.
6. Ibid., p. 2.
7. Wiltshire, K., *Ghosts and Legends of the Wiltshire Countryside,* p. 22, 27.
8. Personal communication with Paul Damon Parsons and Paul Vigay on Sunday, 26 June 1994.
9. From written accounts prepared by Tom Trubridge and Julie Whitear in August 1994 and supplemented with further information taken from an initial interview on Saturday, 23 July 1994.

Chapter 30 - Mind Effects
1. Usually these above and below average trend graphs are based on the average count rate registered during the entire time period the equipment is in use. For the Orgone 94 results, however, Rodney Hale decided to base his assessments on the pre-control period.
2. Hale, R.B., 'Notes on the graphs of Geiger data for the period 23-29 July 1994, Woodborough Hill', 18.9.94: 'It is becoming apparent that the increases in the count rate associated with a meditational period start to occur some time before the actual start of the meditation. This gives a problem determining the period of time to be used for calculating the "average". Obviously, if the act of meditating increases the count rate, then these readings can no longer be regarded as average. What I have chosen to do is to use the period of time from the start of recording up to a point where, in all cases, it can be judged that no major increase has occurred which could be attributed to arising from the meditation. This method of choosing can be criticized, but with a growing number of records available from which a pattern of events may be discerned, does give a certain consistency to results.

'The Woodborough Hill results allow the first 15 minutes to be used for calculating an average value for each of eight records, ending 10 minutes before the start of meditation. The ninth record, for 24th July, dusk session, was unfortunately started late and could not meet this criterion.'
3. Seto, A., *et al*, 'Detection of Extraordinary Large Bio-magnetic Field Strength from Human Hand during External Qi Emission', *Acupuncture & Electro-therapeutics Res. Int. Journal,* Vol 17, 1992, pp. 75-94.
4. Outside interference from an unknown source - perhaps the military on Salisbury Plain - seemed the obvious solution to this enigma; however, if this was so then the 100-Henry coil measuring changes in the

background EM field strength should also have picked up such bold signals. On one occasion alone, during the dusk experiment on Wednesday, 27 July, there seemed a possibility that the background coil had indeed picked up some trace of these local-related signals, yet on closer scrutiny they were not only much smaller, the timing of individual groups of waveforms did not correspond with each other. Moreover, on every other occasion that the low frequency wave oscillations occurred, the resulting graphs for the background coil were completely 'flat', showing no adverse or unexplainable activity whatsoever.
5. For instance, on Wednesday, 27 July the slow pulses began one minute into the session and continued periodically until the thirteenth minute; none occurred during either control period. On Friday, 29 July they again appeared during the first minute of the meditation and continued sporadically throughout the rest of the 30-minute session, with one final burst being recorded during the first minute of the post-control period when the meditators were still in position.
6. The first control test was conducted in Rodney Hale's back garden at Bricket Wood, St Albans, during the evening of 3 August 1994. It produced bursts of low frequency activity between 21.38 and 21.40, and again between 21.44-45. The following night Hale tried another 50-minute experiment. This time he removed the coils completely and replaced them with a resistor positioned at the end of the 10 m length of cable. If these low frequency oscillations were a genuine mind effect, then in theory nothing would be registered by the equipment. Yet on analysing the finished tape he was perplexed to find a slight burst of low frequency activity during the very last minutes of the experiment. On 5 August Hale conducted yet another experiment in which he kept the resistor but removed the 10 m length of cable. This time there were no unusual signals at all. When he replaced the cable for still another experiment on 9 August, a short 3-cycle burst of low frequency activity was again recorded during a 50-minute session. He was therefore led to conclude that it had been the cable and not the coils that had been acting as an amplifier to record the low frequency changes in the electromagnetic field.

Further tests conducted with the apparatus during the evening of Thursday, 29 September 1994, using the cable and resistor alone, failed to produce any low frequency activity whatsoever.
7. During the first control test at Rodney Hale's home on 3 August 1994 the equipment was left running outdoors from 21.07 onwards. Some 40 minutes later Hale walked into the back garden and saw that the tape recording the signals was still running. He then remembered that this was a C-100, not a C-90, meaning that it had an extra 5 minutes to run. I mention this as on analysing the resulting tape he found that bursts of low frequency activity had occurred between 21.38 and 21.40, and again around 21.44-45 - some 37 to 38 minutes into the experiment. This last burst of activity, he is sure, occurred at a time coincident to his entry into the garden before the tape had finished. Was there some kind of connection here? Could his mind have triggered this second sequence of wave oscillations? Even if this was the case, then what about the first sequence, how might they be explained?
8. Collins, A., *The Seventh Sword*, pp. 28-9.

Chapter 31 - The Templemakers
1. From an interview with Tom and Kerry Blower on 24 July 1994.
2. Some might doubt the integrity of Cornelius Crowley and Andrew Potter due to their loose affiliation to the United Bureau of Investigation, or UBI group, falsely accused of constructing many of the major crop pictograms during 1990 and 1991 (see Chapter 8, Note 11). However, it must be pointed out that they have never themselves been involved in circlemaking and having spoken at length to both men over a two-day period neither myself, or any of my colleagues, found any grounds to suggest they fabricated either their testimonies or the event itself.
3. From an interview with Stephen Alexander on Saturday, 6 August 1994.
4. A blue-white flash was seen illuminating East Field by a friend staying with John and Julie Wakefield, who now live on the southern edge of East Field, around 01.00 on Sunday, 7 August 1994. In addition to this, various circlemakers constructing circles and formations in the same area also reported similar airborne and close-proximity flashes during the same period (see Chapter 5).
5. From an interview with Andy Buckley on Saturday, 6 August 1994.
6. Delgado, P., and C. Andrews. *Circular Evidence*, p. 95.

Chapter 32 - The Furious Host
1. Grimm, J., *Teutonic Mythology*, pp. 918-9, 922, 937, 943.
2. Ibid., pp. 430-3.
3. Ibid., pp. 269, 918.
4. Wiltshire, K., *Ghosts and Legends of the Wiltshire Countryside*, p. 25-26.
5. Ibid., p. 40.

Chapter 33 - Thoughtography
1. i) The dummy box did not act as a true control since it was made of celotex soundboard alone. Interior layers of rock wool would have allowed it to gain and lose heat at the same rate as the accumulator;
ii) If Reich's understanding of orgone is justified, then the Stevenson Screen acted as an outer 'skin' to both the accumulator and the dummy box it contained. Since wood is not considered a good conductor of orgone, then incoming energy 'particles' would either be halted or slowed down as they tried to pass through the structure giving a false assessment of the orgonomic tension;
iii) The temperature sensor positioned between the two boxes would have been affected by the wind as it passed through the Stevenson Screen. As the screen remained in one of either two positions for the entire duration of the experiments then the changing wind would have increased or decreased the temperature

registered by the sensor, depending on whether or not it blew between or around the two boxes. This therefore resulted in an unfair comparison with the temperatures being recorded inside the boxes.

These points might seem trivial, possibly even a little pedantic, but Earthquest member and orgone researcher Jason Digby emphasised that as our equipment failed to take these considerations into account, then any results obtained using this method would be deemed invalid by conventional orgonomy.
2. At 04.00 on Wednesday, 27 July 1994 there was a major swing of declination of 1/5th of a degree off true north. This shift heralded a day of disturbed activity in which the horizontal field strength varied by 80 nanoTeslas. Thursday, 28 July was also unsettled, although the rest of the week was fairly normal for July, according to the British Geological Survey at Edinbrugh.
3. Information supplied by the British Geological Survey at Edinburgh.
4. Permutt, C., *Beyond the Spectrum, a Survey of Supernormal Photography*, pp. 100-7. See also J. Eisenbud, *The World of Ted Serios*.
5. Giles, R., 'A physical analysis of the psychic photography of Ted Serios', *Journal of Research into Psi Phenomena*, Vol 1 No 2, Ontario, 1976
6. Permutt, C., *Beyond the Spectrum, a Survey of Supernormal Photography*, p. 110.
7. 'To me it is absolute proof (although I had it before) that these markings are abnormal.' Charles Lyle of the British College of Psychic Science on mono imagery achieved with a stereoscopic camera when working with noted spirit photographer William Hope and his medium partner Mrs Buxton in 1923. Quoted in *Psychic Science*, ed. F. Bligh Bond, Vol 2 No 1, April 1923, pp. 82-83.

Chapter 34 - Flashes of Inspiration
1. Constable, T.J., *Sky Creatures: Living UFOs*, p. 119.
2. Devereux, P., *Earth Lights Revelation*, p. 29.
3. Arnold, K., 'How it All Began', *Proceedings of the First International UFO Congress*, 1977, Warner Bros, 1980.
4. Devereux, P., *Earth Lights Revelation*, p. 28.
5. Collins, A., 'Entities with "Kojak" Shaped Heads in a Brighton Garden', September 1978, Report prepared for BUFORA/UFOIN.
6. From an interview with John and Julie Wakefield on Tuesday, 4 January 1994.
7. Randles, J., *The Pennine UFO Mystery*, pp. 73-4.
8. Walton, T., *The Walton Experience*, pp. 179-80.
9. Collins, A., 'The Aveley Abduction, Part One', *Flying Saucer Review*, Vol 23, No 6, pp. 13-25, and A. Collins, 'The Aveley Abduction, Part Two', *Flying Saucer Review*, Vol 24, No 1, pp. 5-15.

Chapter 35 - Lifeforms
1. Haisell, D., *The Missing Seven Hours*, p. 29.
2. Williams, M., *Supernatural in Cornwall*, pp. 58-9.
3. Randles, J., *The Pennine UFO Mystery*, pp. 122-31.
4. Ibid., pp. 156-7.
5. Collins, A., 'Mount Athos', *The Ley Hunter*, No 104, Autumn/Winter 1987/8, pp. 15-23.
6. McClure, K. & S., *Stars, and Rumours of Stars*, pp. 25-7.
7. Randles, J., *The Pennine UFO Mystery*, p. 199.
8. *Proceedings of the Society for Psychical Research*, December 1905, and quoted in *Stars, and Rumours of Stars* by K. and S. McClure, p. 27-8.
9. Baring-Gould, S., *A Book of Dartmoor*, pp. 245-6.
10. Ibid., p. 248.
11. Wiltshire, K., *Ghosts and Legends of the Wiltshire Countryside*, p. 19.
12. Constable, T.J., *The Cosmic Pulse of Life*, p. 130.

Bibliography

Books and Publications
Bach, Egon, *Philippine UFOs (St Elmos) of the Volcanoes*, 4712 Oakdale Rd., Modesto, CA 95351, 1994
Bach, Egon, *UFOs from the Volcanoes*, Hermitage Publishers, PO Box 410, Tenafly, NJ 07670, 1993
Baring-Gould, S., *A Book of Dartmoor*, Methuen & Co, London, 1916 (1st 1900)
Barron, R.S., *The Geology of Wiltshire: A Field Guide*, Moonraker Press, Bradford-on-Avon, Wilts, 1976
Chandler, John, *The Vale of Pewsey*, Ex Libris Press, Bradford-on-Avon, Wilts, 1991
Clarke, David, and Granville Oldroyd, *Spooklights A British Survey*, privately published, 1985
Collins, Andrew, *The Circlemakers*, ABC Books, Leigh-on-Sea, Essex, 1992
Constable, Trevor James, *The Cosmic Pulse of Life*, Neville Spearman, Sudbury, Suffolk, 1977 (1st 1976, USA only)
Constable, Trevor James (as Trevor James), *They Live in the Sky*, Saucerian Books, Clarksburg, WV, 1958
Constable, Trevor James, *Sky Creatures*, Pocket Books, New York, NY, 1978
Cyr, Donald L., ed., *America's First Crop Circle, Crop Circle Secrets - Part Two*, Stonehenge Viewpoint, Santa Barbara, CA, 1992
Dames, Michael, *The Silbury Treasure, the Great Goddess Rediscovered*, Thames & Hudson, London, 1992 (1st 1976)
DeMeo, James, *The Orgone Accumulator Handbook*, Natural Energy Works, El Cerrito, CA, USA, 1989
Delgado, Pat, and Colin Andrews, *Circular Evidence*, Bloomsbury, London, 1989
Devereux, Paul, *et al*, *Earth Lights Revelation*, Blandford, London, 1989
Devereux, Paul, and Paul McCartney, *Earth Lights: Towards an Understanding of the UFO Enigma*, Turnstone Press, Wellingborough, Northants, 1982
Devereux, Paul, *Places of Power: Secret Energies at Ancient Sites*, Blandford, London, 1990
Eden, Jerome, *Scavengers From Space*, Eden Press
Field, John, *English Field Names*, Alan Sutton, Gloucester, 1989 (1st 1921)
Good, Timothy, ed., *The UFO Report 1990*, Sidgwick & Jackson, London, 1990
Graves, Tom, *Needles of Stone*, Granada, London, 1980
Gribbin, John, *In Search of the Big Bang*, Corgi Books, London, 1986
Gribbin, John, *In Search of Schrodinger's Cat*, Black Swan, London, 1993
Grimm, Jacob, *Teutonic Mythology* 4 vols, *1880-8*
Haisell, David, *The Missing Seven Hours*, PaperJacks Ltd., Ontario, 1978
Halliwell, J.O., *Rambles in Western Cornwall by the Footsteps of the Giants, etc.*, John Russell Smith, London, 1861
Henry, Gladys J., *'Girroo Gurrll' The First Surveyor*, W. R. Smith & Paterson Pty., Brisbane, Australia, 1967
Holiday, F.W., *The Dragon and the Disc*, Futura, London, 1973
Jung, Carl, *Flying Saucers A Modern Myth of Things Seen in the Sky*, Ark Paperbacks, London, 1987 (1st 1959)
Kronig, Jurgen, *Spuren Im Korn*, Zweitausendeins, Frankfurt, Germany, 1992
Lucas, E.V., *Highways & Byways of Sussex*, Macmillan, London, 1924
Mann, W. Edward, and Edward Hoffman, *Wilhelm Reich: the Man who Dreamed of Tomorrow*, Crucible, Wellingborough, Northants, 1990
McClure, Kevin and Sue, *Stars, and Rumours of Stars*, privately published, Market Harborough, Leics, 1980
Meaden, Terence, *The Circles Effect and its Mysteries*, Artetech, Bradford-on-Avon, Wilts, 1990
Michell, John, *The Flying Saucer Vision*, Abacus, London, 1974
Michell, John, *The View Over Atlantis*, Garnstone Press, London, 1975 (1st 1969)
O'Brien, Joanne, and Kwok Man Ho, *The Elements of Feng Shui*, Element Books, Shaftesbury, Dorset, 1991
Osborne White, H. J., *The Geology of the Country Around Marlborough*, HMSO, London, 1975
Permutt, Cyril, *Beyond the Spectrum, a Survey of Supernormal Photography*, Patrick Stephens, Cambridge, 1983
Persinger, Michael, and Gyslaine Lafreniere, *Space-Time Transients and Unusual Events*, Nelson-Hall, 1977
Randles, Jenny, *The Pennine UFO Mystery*, Granada, St Albans, Herts, 1983
Randles, Jenny, and Paul Fuller, *Crop Circles A Mystery Solved*, Robert Hale, London, 1990
Randles, Jenny, and Paul Whetnall, *Alien Contact - Window on Another World*, Neville Spearman, Suffolk, 1981
Reich, Peter, *A Book of Dreams*, Barrie & Jenkins, London, 1974
Reich, Wilhelm, *Contact with Space: ORANUR Second Report 1951-1956*, Core Pilot Press, New York, 1957
Reich, Wilhelm, *The Discovery of the Orgone, Volume Two: The Cancer Biopathy*, Orgone Institute Press, New York, NY, 1948
Reich, Wilhelm, *The Function of the Orgasm*, Condor, London, 1973
Reich, Wilhelm, *Ether, God and Devil*, Farrar, Straus and Giroux, New York, NY, 1979 (1st 1949)

Reich, Wilhelm, *The Orgone Accumulator, its Medical and Scientific Use,* Orgone Institute Press, Rangeley, Maine, 1951
Reich, Wilhelm, *Selected Writings, an Introduction to Orgonomy,* Vision, London, 1961
Robins, Don, *Circles of Silence,* Souvenir Press, London, 1985
Robins, Don, *The Secret Language of Stone,* Rider, London, 1988
Sharaf, Myron, *Fury on Earth, a Biography of Wilhelm Reich,* Hutchinson, London, 1984
Shuttlewood, Arthur, *The Flying Saucerers,* Sphere Books, London, 1976
Shuttlewood, Arthur, *The Warminster Mystery,* Neville Spearman, London, 1967
Shuttlewood, Arthur, *UFOs - Key to the New Age,* Regency Press, London, 1971
Shuttlewood, Arthur, *Warnings From Flying Friends,* Portway Press, Warminster, Wilts, 1968
Thomas, Nicholas, *A Guide to Prehistoric England,* B. T. Batsford, London, 1960
Vallee, Jacques, *Passport to Magonia from Folklore to Flying Saucers,* Tandem, London, 1975 (1st 1970)
Walton, Travis, *The Walton Experience,* Berkley Medallion Books, New York, NY, 1978
Westwood, Jennifer, *Albion, A Guide to Legendary Britain,* Paladin, Grafton Books, London, 1985
Williams, Michael, *Supernatural in Cornwall,* Bossiney Books, Bodmin, Cornwall, 1974
Wiltshire, Kathleen, *Ghosts and Legends of the Wiltshire Countryside,* Colin Venten, Melksham, Wilts., 1985

Articles and Papers

Andrews, George, Report on SORRAT project in *Anomaly,* No 3, March 1987, pp. 37-40
Arnold, Kenneth, 'How it All Began', *Proceedings of the First International UFO Congress,* 1977, Warner Bros, 1980
Beddoe, Tony, 'Orgone 93 ORTEC Project Report', prepared for Orgone 93
Burton, Simon, 'Organic Energy, A Theoretical Energy Model for Cereology', *The Circular,* Vol 2 No 1, 1991
Burton, Simon, 'Orgone and Spirit Traps?', *The Ley Hunter,* No 119, 1993, pp. 18-9
Clarkson, D., 'Coping with Radiation', *Electronics Today International,* October 1992, pp. 24-8
Clift, Diana, and Lucy Pringle, 'Human Effects of Crop Circles - the story so far', *The Circular,* Vol 3 No 3, October 1992, pp. 12-4
Collins, Andrew, 'The Aveley Abduction, Part One', *Flying Saucer Review,* Vol 23, No 6, pp. 13-25
Collins, Andrew, 'The Aveley Abduction, Part Two', *Flying Saucer Review,* Vol 24, No 1, pp. 5-15
Collins, Andrew, 'Entities with "Kojak" Shaped Heads in a Brighton Garden', September 1978, report prepared for BUFORA/UFOIN
Collins, Andrew., 'Mount Athos', *The Ley Hunter,* No 104, Autumn/Winter 1987/8, pp. 15-23
Collins, Andrew, 'UFOs and Psychic Abilities - What is the Link?', *Strange Phenomena,* Vol 1 No 1, Wolverhampton, 1979, pp. 8-10
Collins, Andrew, 'Does the Camera Never Lie? or the Return of the Blob, An Investigation into the History and Nature of Photographic Anomalies', *Earthquest News,* Vol 2 No 2, Winter 1992, pp. 30-46
Collins, Andrew, 'The Great Totham Mystery - An Earth Light, Crop Circle, Mystery Photograph and Folklore Continuity in Deepest Essex', *Earthquest News,* Vol 2 No 2, Winter 1992, pp. 7-20
Collins, Andrew, 'The Tully Reeds Mystery: Aboriginal Lights, a Sacred Mountain and Mysterious Ground Markings...', *Earthquest News,* Vol 2 No 2, Winter 1992, pp. 24-30
Collins, Andrew, *Orgone 93 Update,* Nos 1-3, 1993-4
Davidson, Alison, '*Contact with Space* by Wilhelm Reich, a Review', JBR, September-October 1988, pp. 1-6
Devereux, Paul, Paul McCartney and Don Robins, 'Bringing UFOs down to Earth', *New Scientist,* Vol 99 No 1371, 1 September 1983, pp. 627-30
Diedrich, Hans, 'Summary of FGK Monitoring, Wiltshire, 1993'
Giles, R., 'A physical analysis of the psychic photography of Ted Serios', *Journal of Research into Psi Phenomena,* Vol 1 No 2, Ontario, 1976
Greer, Steven, 'Close Encounters of the 5th Kind: Contact in Southern England, July 1992, An Interpretive Report', CSETI, November 1992
Gribbin, John, 'Atomic Telepathy is Faster than Light', *New Scientist,* Vol 141 No 1914, 26 February 1994, p. 16
Grist, Brian, 'The Aquifer Attractor', *The Cerealogist,* No 5, Winter, 1991/2, pp. 18-9
Hale, Rodney B., 'Orgone 93 - Analyses of Two More Anomalous Sounds', August 1993
Hale, Rodney B., 'Report on Computerised Monitoring for Project Relate, July 11 to August 5 1993', prepared for CCCS, 19 September 1993
Hale, Rodney B., 'Project Relate 1993, Further Report on "Black Box" Tapes', prepared for CCCS, 1 October 1993
Hale, Rodney B., 'Technical Report on the Meditational exercise of 27th March 1994'
Hale, Rodney B., 'Report on Meditation Meeting and Gamma Count at... Leigh-on-Sea. 28 November 1993'
Hale, Rodney B., 'Notes on data accumulated for radioactivity on seven occasions of meditational exercise. 15.4.94'
Hale, Rodney B., 'Notes on the graphs of Geiger data for the period 23-29 July 1994, Woodborough Hill', 18.9.94
Hendricks, Edson C., 'Marfa Lights Seen, Whistlers Heard', *Crop Circle Secrets Part Two, America's First Crop Circle,* 1992, pp. 85-9
Krogh, Jan S., *The Hessdalen Report,* NIVFO, Trondheim, Norway, 1990
Mansell, Chris, 'Dramatic UFO Sighting at Woodborough Hill, 26th/27th July 1992', *The Circular,* Vol 3 No 3, October 1992, pp. 7-9

Meaden, Terence, 'Crop Circles and the Plasma Vortex', *The Crop Circle Enigma*, ed. Ralph Noyes, Gateway Books, Bath, Avon, 1990, pp. 76-98
Petit, Charles, 'Videotaped Proof of Heavenly Lights', *San Francisco Chronicle*, 25 September 1993
Phillips, Graham, 'Psygenics', *Strange Phenomena*, Vol 1 No 2, Wolverhampton, 1979, pp. 9-11
Phillips, Graham, 'The Stones', *Strange Phenomena*, Vol 1 No 2, Wolverhampton, 1979, pp. 17-22
Phillips, Graham, and Andrew Collins, 'The Deeper Mysteries of Loch Ness', *Why? A Television Documentary Series*, privately published, 1980
Phillips, Ted, *Physical Trace Catalogue*, CUFOS, 1970s
Pringle, Lucy, 'Reactions to Crop Circle Visits An Analysis of 187 Experiences', 1994
Richards, John Thomas, *SORRAT: A History of the Neihardt Psychokinesis Experiments, 1961-1981*
Robbins, Don, 'The Dragon Project and the Talking Stones', *New Scientist*, Vol 96 No 1328, 21 October 1982, pp. 166-71
Robbins, Peter, 'Wilhelm Reich and UFOs', *Journal of Orgonomy*, Vol 24 No 2, pp. 166-80
Robbins, Peter, 'Wilhelm Reich and UFOs, Part II: Examining Evidence and Allegations', *Journal of Orgonomy*, Vol 25 No 1, pp. 107-28
Rutkowski, C., 'Combined and Sorted List of North American UGMs', privately published, 1993
Schwarz, Berthold E., 'SORRAT Report', *Anomaly*, No 3, March 1987, pp. 32-6
Seto, Akira, *et al*, 'Detection of Extraordinary Large Bio-magnetic Field Strength from Human Hand during External Qi Emission', *Acupuncture & Electro-therapeutics Res. Int. Journal*, Vol 17, 1992, pp. 75-94
Strand, Erling P., *Project Hessdalen 1984 Final Technical Report Part One*, Project Hessdalen, 1984
Strand, Erling P., 'Project Hessdalen, Instrumentation of Possible Ball Lightning,' prepared for Vizotum '93, Montafon, Austria, 20-23 September 1993
Sullivan, Danny P., 'Chasing the Dragon', a Report on Orgone 93, *The Ley Hunter*, No 120, Midwinter 1993, pp. 8-13
Taylor, Dr Roger, 'RELATE a Report on Research into Electromagnetic and Other Terrestrial Effects', CCCS, January 1994
Tiller, William A., 'A Gas Discharge Device for Investigating Focussed Human Attention', *Journal of Scientific Exploration*, Vol 4 No 2, 1990, pp. 255-71
Watts, Susan, 'Scientists mystified by "red jellyfish" in the sky', *The Independent*, 11 August 1994, p. 3
Wingfield, George, 'The UFO Connection', *The Circular*, Vol 3 No 3, October 1992, pp. 4-6

Relevant Periodicals

The Cerealogist, George Wingfield, Hearne House, North Wootton, Shepton Mallet, Somerset BA4 4HW
The Circular, Barbara Davies, Old Stables, Lescrow, Cornwall PL23 1JS
The Crop Watcher, Paul Fuller, 3 Selborne Court, Tavistock Close, Romsey, Hampshire SO51 7TY
Enigmas, Malcolm Robinson, 41 The Braes, Tullibody, Clackmannanshire FK10 2TT
Gloucester Earth Mysteries, D. P. Sullivan and Jo Anne Wilder, PO Box 258, Cheltenham, Glos GL53 0HR
The Ley Hunter, Paul Devereux and D. P. Sullivan, PO Box 92, Penzance, Cornwall TR18 2XL
Magonia, John Rimmer, John Dee Cottage, 5 James Terrace, Mortlake Churchyard, London SW14 8HB
Mercian Mysteries, Bob Trubshaw, 12 Cromer Road, St Annes, Notts NG3 3LF
New Ufologist, 71 Knight Avenue, Canterbury, Kent CT2 8PY
Northern Earth, John Billingsley, 10 Jubilee St., Mytholmroyd, Hebden Bridge, W Yorks HX7 5NP
Northern UFO News, Jenny Randles, 37 Heathbank Road, Stockport, Cheshire SK3 0UP
UFO Norway, Mentz Kaarbo, Strandgaten 221, N-5004 Bergen, Norway

Selected Organisations

The American College of Orgonomy, PO Box 490, Princeton, NJ 08542, USA, publishes *Journal of Orgonomy*
ASSAP (Association for the Scientific Study of Anomalous Phenomena), 31 Goodhew Road, Croydon, Surrey, publishes *Anomaly*
BUFORA (British UFO Research Association), Ken Phillips, The Leys, 2c Leyton Rd., Harpenden Herts AL5 2TL, publishes *UFO Times*
CCCS (Centre for Crop Circle Studies), SKS, 20 Paul St., Frome, Somerset BA11 1DX, publishes *The Circular*
CERES (Circles Effect Research) and TORRO (Tornado and Storm Research Organisation), 54 Frome Road, Bradford-on-Avon, Wiltshire BA15 1LD, publishes *Journal of Meteorology*
Earthquest, Andrew Collins, PO Box 189, Leigh-on-Sea, Essex, SS9 1NF, publishes *Earthquest News*
London Earth Mysteries Circle, Rob Stephenson, PO Box 1035, London W2 6ZX
Orgone Biophysical Research Laboratory, James DeMeo Ph.d., PO Box 1395, El Cerrito, CA 94530, USA, publishes *Pulse of the Planet*
Project Earth Link, Oliver Stummer & Daniela Schroter, Komodiengasse 3/24, fl-1020 Vienna, Austria
Wilhelm Reich Museum, PO Box 687, Rangeley, Maine 04970, USA

Index

UFO

57 Un seen
58 playful
59 info exchange

Dimensional

59 Force

Energys

3) manifests
+ forms
Jung
4) BRAIN

11) BIONS (particle
energy)

18-19 Upper Air Bodys
55 unmanifested

Colors

purple - 14

Years

12-13) 1950 +

53-54 Dragon

SPace / Time

53) 5th Element